NORTH CAROLINA CARROLLS

1600s–1850

Elizabeth Carroll Foster

HERITAGE BOOKS
2010

HERITAGE BOOKS
AN IMPRINT OF HERITAGE BOOKS, INC.

Books, CDs, and more—Worldwide

For our listing of thousands of titles see our website at
www.HeritageBooks.com

Published 2010 by
HERITAGE BOOKS, INC.
Publishing Division
100 Railroad Ave. #104
Westminster, Maryland 21157

Copyright © 2010 Elizabeth Carroll Foster

The author's website: www.elizabethcfoster.blogspot.com
and email: hteb963@suddenlink.com

Other Heritage Books by the author:
Virginia Carrolls and Their Neighbors, 1618–1800s

All rights reserved. No part of this book may be reproduced or transmitted in any form or by any means, electronic or mechanical, including photocopying, recording or by any information storage and retrieval system without written permission from the author, except for the inclusion of brief quotations in a review.

International Standard Book Numbers
Paperbound: 978-0-7884-5199-7
Clothbound: 978-0-7884-8583-1

Information in this book is recorded as found on records in National and State Archives, Library of Congress and nearly every courthouse in North Carolina. Addresses for Items 7-12, below, may have changed since information was gathered.

MISCELLANEOUS FACTS

1. Marriage bonds were issued from **1741-1868**. After, **1868** marriage licenses became the official documents.
2. **North Carolina and South Carolina** were made separate colonies in **1710**.
3. **1790** Census: 236 **Carrols** listed, spelled 22 ways; among "most common surnames in the U.S. (The North Carolinian Quarterly, Mar. 1959, p. 520).
4. 1890 Census records: lost to fire in Commerce Dept. Bldg. in Jan. 1921. Few records that survived consists of approximately 6,000 individuals in some 1200 households. Available at the Washington D.C. National Archives, Roll #1 - Washington, DC; Roll #2 - Perry Co., AL; Roll #3 is the remainder. Following regarding: Mary Elizabeth Carroll, age 23 or 34, born in MD, black, female, domestic, 1, Washington, DC, p. 756.
5. Some old marriage records contain letters "HF" next to bride and groom's names. **HF indicates "handfasting,"** a legal type of marriage. Such occurred when a minister could not be found for various reasons – remoteness, weather, ... A couple was considered legally married when their hands were raised before witnesses. Most chose a minister to marry them in the traditional manner at a later date. This may account for different marriage dates recorded in Family Bibles and legal records. (Carroll Cables, Apr. 1997)
6. L. Polk Denmark's map: "Mil. Dists. in N. C., Rev. War, 1780," shows Guilford, Surry, Wilkes, Rowan, Burke, Montgomery, Richmond, Anson, Mecklenburg, Lincoln and Rutherford counties were in Salisbury Military District.
7. North Carolina Dept. of Cultural Resources, Raleigh, NC 27611
8. North Carolina Division of Archives and History, 109 East Jones St., Raleigh, NC 27611
9. The North Carolina Genealogical Society Journal, P. O. Box 1492, Raleigh, NC 27602
10. North Carolina State Library, 109 E. Jones St., Raleigh, NC 27611
11. Southern Historical Collection, Univ. of NC Library, Drawer 870, Chapel Hill, NC 27514
12. The NC Historical Review, 109 E. Jones St., Raleigh 27611

Virginia Tax Payers 1782-1787

King & Queen Co.: **Berry Carrol**, 1, 0 sl.
Augusta Co.: **Peter Carrell**, 1 polled, 9 sl.
Fauquier Co.: **Elizabeth Carrell**, 1, 3 sls.
Bedford Co.: **Jesse Carriel**, 0 polled,0 sl.
Southampton Co.: **Jesse Carrell**, 1, 7 sls.
Loudoun Co.: **Dempsey Carroll**, 1, 2 sl., **Rebecca Carroll**, 1, 4sl., **William Carroll**, 1, 1 sl., **Priscilla Carrell**, 0, 0 sl.

Henry Co.: **Cornelius Carroll**, 1, 0 sl.
Goochland Co.: **Booker Carrel**, 1, 0 sls.
John Carrel, 1, 1 sl.; **Roger Carrel**, 1, 0 sl.
William Carrel, 1, 0 sl.
Westmoreland Co.: **John Carrol**, 1, 0 sl.

Carrolls and their Connections in North Carolina Counties

William F. Currell; May/Maye Carroll; Thomas Carrell/Carroll; James Carrol; Martha Carril; Elizabeth Carrill; Charles Carroll; Britton Caroll, Jno. Caroll, Hardy Carrell, Benj. Carroll/Carrell; Butler Carroll, Douglass Carroll; William Carroll (Hathaway Indx., vs. 1-3, pp. 2, 4, 17, 108, 188, 198, 199, 241, 367, 388, 389, 559, 560, 578)

Irish Roots

Carroll surnames: O'Carroll and Mac Carroll (variations: MacCarroll, MacCarrill, Carroll. Some 16,00 are in Ireland today (1974), most are O'Carrolls.

Before the Anglo-Norman invasion, there were six distinct septs of O'Carrolls. Most important were the O'Carrolls of Ely O'Carroll (Tipperary and Offaly counties) and those of Oriel (Monaghan and Louth counties). O'Carrolls of Ely derive the name from Cearbhal, Lord of Ely, one of the leaders of an army that defeated the Danes at Clontarf in 1014. Ancestry can be traced to a third century king of Munster, Oilioll Olum.

Maolsuthain O'Carroll (d. 1031) of Kerry sept was confessor of Brian Boru whom he accompanied on his circuit in Ireland in 1004. He is mentioned in the priest's short passage written in Latin in *The Book of Armagh*.

Today, most O'Carrolls in Ireland are found in counties Kilkenny, Louth and Offaly. One each of the MacCarroll septs are in south Leinster and Ulster. In Ulster, the Irish MacCearbhaill is usually anglicized to MacCarvill. The sept is situated at Ballymaccarroll and noted for musicians.

Margaret O'Carroll (d. 1451) was referred to by Four Masters as "the best woman of her time in Ireland." She contributed to building churches, roads and bridges, was hospitable and encouraged learning. (Black, *Your Irish Ancestors*)

Knight. Sir James Carroll, Kt. Bach (1903), chairman Queenstown, Urban District Council during the visit of Her Majesty to Ireland, served in Royal Navy in Ashanti and China: born 1846, married 1880 Ellen, daughter of Timothy Coleman, Esq., Res. 21 East Beach, Queenstown.

Knight's widow, Lady C. (Margaret Elizabeth, daughter of the late Jno. Pearson, Esq.) married in 1844 Sir William Carroll, MD, twice Lord Mayor of Dublin (d. 1890). (*Whitaker's Peerage*, 1905 - National Archives, Wash., DC)

Surnames in Ireland: surnames with varieties and synonyms, #238 - Cardwell; #210 - Cardle & Carroll, Caddow, Caddoo, Cadoo, Kaddow (McCaddo), Caroll, Carrolly, (M'Carroll); #250 - Carroll (Cardwell). #1244 - M'Carroll (Carroll), Mackarel, Mackerel, MacKrell, M'Carrell, M'Garrell, M'Harroll, M'Kerel, M'Kerrall, Mekerrel (Matheson, pp. 34, 35, 50)

British surnames: Carroll. From the Irish O'Cearbhoil, M'Carroll, personal name. **Carrell.** From **Caril**; a local name, near Lisieux, Normandy (Barber, p. 111)

Carrolls Come to New World

Immigrants left Europe in search of something different and better. Their aspirations were not unlike those that caused them to cross the Appalachian Mountains in the early 19th century."
Jonathan Yardley
The Washington Post Book World. "On the Trail of Pioneers and Ancestors." Sept. 22, 1985

Passengers to New World; Emigrant Lists & Land Patents:
1623 - **John Kerrill** dead at Martin's Hundred (VA). On 1624 Feb. 16 list of those living in Virginia and of those who have died since **April 1623** (Nugent, v. 1, p. 42)
1634 - **Christopher Carroll**, St. Mary's Co., MD (O'Brien, An Alleged First Census ..., p. 49)
1635 July 31 - Persons to be transported [from London] to Virginia by Merchant's Hope, Mr. Hugh Weston, after examination by the Minister of Gravesend, Port of London: **Henry Carrell 16**, (Public Records Office, England: E157/20; v. 1, p. 159; Hotten, p. 117); **1638 -Benjamin Carril** ... 700 acs., James City Co., VA, 16 May 1638 for transporting **wife Elizabeth** and 12 persons including **Henry Carrill** (Nugent, Land Patents 1623-1800); **1638** - 163 acs (Indx. of Patents, 1623-1774); **1638** - **Elizabeth Carrill**, early immigrant to Virginia (M. Tepper, Passengers to New World, p. 72; Passgr. Indx.); **1663** - **Benjamin Carroll** died, escheat (no heirs, property returned to the Crown) (Foster, Virginia Carrolls and Their Neighbors, p. 45)
1638 - **Christopher Carroll**, Protestant, among those trying to proselytize, Maryland (trial of Wm. Lewis, overseer for Father Copley, a Catholic) (Matthews, p. 158; St. Mary's Co., MD Wills); **1646** - **?Christopher Carnoll**, immigrated (Bk. ABH, p. 27; 2 folio, 528; Skordas, p. 80)
c1640 - Some **Carroll families** emigrated from Ireland and first settled in Virginia; came to Maryland (Jones, Hist. of Dorchester County, p. 276)
1653 - **David Carrell**, early immigrant to Northumberland Co.,VA; Nov. 28, Christopher Boyce granted 62½ acs. for transporting 12 persons, including **David Carroll** (Tepper, p. 72; Passgr. Indx.; Greer; Nugent, v. 1, p. 220)
1654/1655 June 22 - **Myles, son of John Carrill** of Waterford, Ireland, labourer, bound to Hugh Jones of Bristol, mariner, to serve 5 years in Barbadoes (British Record Office, City of Bristol, The Council House, College Green, Bristol BS15TR, England; Rcds. to America from Bristol, Eng.,p.163; References to manscript volumes titled "Servants to Foreign Plantations, p. 291 & v. 11, "Middle Sex 1617-1775")
1661 - **John Caril** transported (Bk. 5, p. 181; Skordas, The Early Settlers of Maryland, p. 79)
1664 - **John Carroll**, Isle of Wight Co., VA, **wife Elizabeth, Richard Carroll, John Carroll, Mary Carroll** among 24 persons transported by Robert Pitt & Wm. Burgh who received 1200 acs. (Nugent; Indx. of Patents 1679-1774, VA ST. Lib.)
1666 - **John Carroll**, Topsfield, MA (O'Brien, p. 49)
1667 - **William Carrell** transported (Bk. 12, p. 205; Skordas, Early Settlers of Maryland, p. 81)
1668 - **Anthony Carroll**, Topsfield, MA (O'Brien, p. 49)
1670 - **Thomas Carrell Sr.** of Somerset Co., MD immigrated from **Accomac** in VA; **1670** - **Mary Carrell** transported, wife of **Thomas Carrell Sr.**; **1670** - **son Thomas Carrell Jr.** (Bk. 13. p.119; Skordas, Early Settlers of Maryland, p.81); **1670** - John Hilliard owned "Seaman's

Choice," 150 acs. which he sold to **Thomas Carroll** of Somerset Co., MD (Torrence, Old Somerset..., p. 446); **1681**, Oct. 19 - **Thomas Carroll Jr.**, Somerset Maryland, md. **Rebecca Walton (widow)** (Clements, American Marriages Before 1699, p. ?); **1686** - **Thomas Carroll**, Somerset Co., MD (O'Brien, p. 49)

1672 - **George Carroll**, transported to Maryland, service (Bk. 17, p. 454; Skordas, p. 81; Filby's 1982 Supplement)

1673 - **Daniel Carroll**, ? MD; **1675** - **Daniel Carroll** AT Feb.; **1678** - **Daniel Carnell** immigrated to MD (Bk. 15, p. 22; Skordas, p. 80) (v. 11, "Middle Sex 1617-1775; O'Brien, p. 49)

1674 - **? Carroll**, Boston MA (O'Brien, p. 49)

1677 - **Will Carell** transported (Bk. 15, p. 446; Skordas, Early Settlers of Maryland, p. 79)

1678 - **Abigail Carroll**, Ipswich, MA (O'Brien, p. 49)

1678 - **James Caoll?** transported (Bk. 15, p. 553; Skordas, Early Settlers of Maryland, p. 79)

1678 - **Teig Carrell**, ? MD, transported (Bk. 15, p. 527; Skordas, Early Settlers of Maryland, p. 81; O'Brien, p. 49)

1679 - **Philip Carol** transported to MD (Bk. WC2, p. 128; Skordas, Early Settlers..., p. 80)

1679 - **George Carroll**, Talbot Co., MD (O'Brien, p. 49)

1679/1689 - **Thomas and Elizabeth Carroll**, 720 acs.; **1679/1689** - **Thomas Carrill** and John Wright, 102 acs. (Pat. Indx. 1623-1774, 1679-1774)

1683 Feb 1-Mar 5 - on *Society* bound from **London** to **New England**, **Robert Carroll** (PRO: E 190/115/1; Coldham, ... Emgs., p. 407)

1683 - **Tim Carrall**, St. Mary's Co., MD (O'Brien, p. 49; Orton Family, A 12 A 128, p. 9, Mormon Temple Library, Kenningston MD: **Timothy Carroll**, b. c1686, Lewes, Sussex, England; **wife: Elizabeth Orton**, dau. of John Orton, b. 1690, Leichester Co., England)

1687 - **Joseph Carroll**, Hartford, CT (O'Brien, p. 49)

1688 - **Thomas Carroll**, Salem MA (O'Brien, p. 49)

1688 - **Charles Carroll**, the Immigrant and grandfather of **Charles Carroll of Carrollton**, arrived in Maryland; **his sons: Henry (1697-1719) no issue; Charles of Annapolis (1702-1782), one son, Charles of Carrollton; Daniel (1707-1734), one son, Charles of Carrolburg (1729-1773) and daus.** (Carroll books in my library); **1689**, May 3 - "Carroll's Forest" to **Charles Carroll (1660-1720)**, 500 acs., Charles Co., MD, "the Immigrant" (MD Ld. Grts, v. 23)

1692 - **Dennis Carroll**, Talbot Co., MD; **Dennis Carroll**, Talbot Co., MD, witness to will of Alice Rich (O'Brien, p.49; MD Calendar of Wills, 1685-1702, v. 2)

1693 - **John Carroll**, Virginia, 75 acs (Indx. of Patents 1679-1774)

1694 - **Thomas Carroll**, New York, NY (O'Brien, p. 49)

1695 - **Charles Carroll**, Charles Co., MD (O'Brien, p. 49)

1695 - **John Carroll**, Virginia, 102 acs. (Indx. of Patents 1679-1774)

1695 - **John Carroll, wife Ann with child, dau. Mary** (Lancaster Co., VA Wills)

1698 - **Richard Carroll**, St. Mary's Co.; William Lowery will: To John Hall, . . . Robt. Ridgley, **Richard Carroll**. Test: Robt. Ridgley, **Richard Carroll** (md. **Rachel Croxall, dau. of Richard and Joanna [Carroll] Croxall, sis. of James, Daniel & Michael Carroll** mentioned in (Charles the) Immigrant's will (O'Brien, p. 49; MD Cal. Of Wills, 1685-1702, v. 2)

1702 - James Cock, 570 acs. on so. Side of James River (VA) for transporting 12 persons including **Roger Carrell and Hannah Carrell** (Foley, p. 42)

1714 - **Charles Carroll** to Maryland; **1715** - **Dr. Charles Carroll (1691-1755)**, Anne Arundel Co., MD, father of **Charles Carroll**, the Barrister (1724-1783), came to county from Ireland (Filby's 1982 Supplement)
1718 - **John Carroll/Carrill** S 1718 MD/VA; **1730/1731** - **John Carrill/Carroll**, 40, S Feb. T Mar 1731 *Patapscoe* (ship) LC to Annapolis, MD June M, Capt. Darby Lux, 102 persons boarded 9 Mar.; **John Carrill**, from Newgate bound for Maryland (PRO, #T53/35, pp. 496, 497) (1217.3, 1222, 1223, Coldham List, pp. 28, 48; Filby's List, p. 300; PRO #T53/35, pp. 496, 497; Kaminkows) [Newgate, London prison, plus Murshalsea Prison in Surrey, England] (See Daniel)
1720 - **John Carrell**, Baltimore (#6223, Nugent; Coldham's List, p. 223)
1725/1730 - **John Carril**, 140 acs.; **1728/1732** - 300 acs. (Pat. Indx. 1623-1774)
1725 Oct. 26 - Mary Blair, 1600 acs., transport of 10 persons including **Margaret Carrol** (Foley, p. 42; ?, p. 65)
1727 - **William Carrell**, 32 E from Surry, destination Virginia on *Susanna*, Capt. John Vickers, 11 persons on board 27 June (PRO #T53/33, p. 365; J.&M. Kaminkow, Original Lists of Emigts.)
1736 - **Capt. John Carrell**, "Meeting Sept. 22, 1736 . . . persons were reported as having been brought from Ireland by Capt. John Carrell . . . The Selectmen admitted all as inhabitants" (Boyer, Journal, p. 188; Tepper, p. 464)
1736 - **John Carroll** #462 Christ Church Parish, Spittlefields Co., occupation weaver, to serve 3 years Carolina or West Indies, 21 plus, made his mark, date of indenture 10 Aug. (Kaminkows, List of Emigrants . . . 1718-1759, p. 52)
1738 - **Patrick Carroll** #463 Dublin, Ireland, clerk, 4 years in Jamiaca, 18, signed his name, indenture began 2 Oct. (Kaminkows, p. 53)
1742/1743 - **William Carrill** and others, 187 acs; **1746/1749** - 325 acs.; **1750/1751** - 180 acs.; **1751/1755** - 265 acs.; **1756/1761** - 158 acs.; **1768/1770** - **William Carrill** and James Moore, 37 acs. (Pat. Indx. 1623-1774, VA ST Lib.)
1746 - **Jacob Carroll** to Philadelphia (Filby's 1982 Supplement)
1746 - **Anne Carroll** to Philadelphia (Filby's 1982 Supplement)
1750 - **John Carroll** R Sept T For life Oct. 1750 *Rachael* (Filby's 1982 Supplement)
1751 - **John Carroll** S Jan (Filby's 1982 Supplement)
1752 - **Ann Carroll** S Feb-Apr T May *Litchfield* (Filby's 1982 Supplement)
1752 - **Andrew Carroll** (alias Dutton) S Sept-Oct T Dec. *Greyhound* (Filby's 1982 Sup.)
1753 - **Thomas Carroll** S May-June T July *Tryal* (Filby's 1982 Sup.)
1754 - **Timothy Carroll** S Apr-May (Filby's 1982 Sup.)
1760 - **Ann Carroll** S July (Filby's 1982 Sup.)
1763 - **Patrick Carroll** S Feb T Mar *Neptune* (Filby's 1982 Sup.)
1763 - **James Carrol**, Boston (Tepper, p. 467)
1764 - **Eleanor Carroll wife of Owen** S Oct, Sir Thomas Newcombe T Jan 1765 *Tryal* (Filby's 1982 Sup.)
1765 - **John Carroll** (alias Carlow) S Feb **wife: Mary** acquitted (Mary Carrol-alias Macgee) [qv] convicted (Filby's 1982 Sup.)
1765 - **Robert Carrel** from County Cork to Boston Dec. 27 on *Freemason* (Tepper, p. 468)
1766 - **Michael Carrell** from Cork to Boston on *Willmott* Nov. 15 (Tepper, p. 470)
1766 - **Catherine Carrill** on *Willmott* from Cork to Boston Nov. 15 (Tepper, p. 469)

1767 - **John Carroll** S Apr T May *Thornton* (Filby's 1982 Sup.)
1769 - **Joseph Carell**, Brig. *Ann & Margaret* from Ireland Oct. 14 (Tepper, p. 471)
1769 - **Winnifred Carry (Carryl)** S May T Aug *Douglas* (Filby's 1982 Sup.)
1769 - **John Carroll** S Dec (Filby's 1982 Sup.)
1770 - **Hugh Carroll** S Feb T Apr *Thornton* (Filby's 1982 Sup.)
1771 - **Jane Carroll, wife of Peter** S Dec T Dec *Justitia* (Filby's 1982 Sup.)
1772 - **John Carryl** SW 7 T July *Taylor* (Source Coldham, ?)
1773 - **Thomas Carroll (Thom)**, 10 Shoemaker, Ireland, *Etty*, Maryland, Indentured for 4 years service, Port of London, 25 Dec. to 2 Jan. 1774 (Tepper, Passgrs. . . ., p. 229)
1774 - **John Carroll**, 22 Husbandman, Dublin, *Neptune*, Maryland, indentured servant, Port of London, Sept. 5 to 12th (Tepper, p. 320)
1775 - **William Carroll**, 29, Laborer from Bath, *Ann*, Philadelphia (port of entry), Indentured servant from Port of Bristol (pt. of departure), February 27th to March 6th (Tepper, p. 437)
1804 - **Peter Carroll**, of Mogherow, Laborer, Bound for New York on *Charles & Harriott*, sworn at Sligo, 29 March (Tepper, p. 437)
1804 - **Eliza Carrol**, age 22, height 5'4", spinstress, Randalstown, MD, brown, servant to Jenny Carrothers, the American Brig *Atlantic* from Boston, Robt. Askins, Master, burden 196 tons, Sworn at Dublin 19 June (Tepper, p. 458)
1806 - **Edward Carroll** to America (Filby's1982 Supplement)
1807 - **Samuel Carroll**, b. c1807, of Dublin, Ireland, md. **Elizaeth M. Gaven**, b. c1811 in Dublin (F Ire.Dub. D lb. James Hudson. Carrell. Olive O. Curfew, 120 No. Main St., Salt Lake City, UT)
1808 - **Robert Carrol** to America (Filby's1982 Supplement)
? - **Dennis Carrall**, Belfast, County Tyrone, Ireland, Port of NY, *Maria Duplex*, 54 days, 15 passengers (Tepper, New World Immigrants, p. 333)
? - **John Carroll**, Tipperary, Dublin, NY on *Shamrock*, 60 passengers, *Nativity* (Tepper, Passgrs. . . ., p. 333)
1810 - **James Carroll** to America (Filby's 1982 Supplement)
1812 - **Charles Carroll**, 20, to NY (Filby's 1982 Supplement)
1812 - **Christopher Carroll**, 38, to NY (Filby's 1982 Supplement)
1812 - **Daniel Carroll**, 27, to Maryland (Filby's 1982 Supplement)
1812 - **Dennis Carroll**, 25, to NY (Filby's 1982 Supplement)
1812 - **Edward Carroll**, 24, to NY (Filby's 1982 Supplement)
1812 - **John Carroll**, 20, to NY (Filby's 1982 Supplement)
1812 - **John Carroll**, 25, to NY (Filby's 1982 Supplement)
1812 - **John S. Carroll**, 31, to NY (Filby's1982 Supplement)
1812 - **Lawrence Carroll**, 33, to NY (Filby's 1982 Supplement)
1812 - **Matthew Carroll**, 28, to NY (Filby's 1982 Supplement)
1812 - **Owen Carrol**, 22, to New Jersey (Filby's1982 Supplement)
1812 - **Patrick Carrol**, 26, to NY (Filby's 1982 Supplement)
1812 - **Patrick Carrol**, 34, to Maryland (Filby's 1982 Supplement)
1812 - **Peter Carrol**, 35, to NY (Filby's 1982 Supplement)
1812 - **Thomas Carrol**, 26, to NY (Filby's 1982 Supplement)
1812 - **Thomas Carrol**, 29, to NY (Filby's 1982 Supplement)

1812 - **William Carrol**, 43, to Maryland (Filby's 1982 Supplement)
1813 - **Dennis Carroll**, 48, to Maryland (Filby's 1982 Supplement)
1813 - **John Carroll**, 40, to Maryland (Filby's 1982 Supplement)
1813 - **Patrick Carrol**, 35, to Maryland (Filby's 1982 Supplement)
1813 - **Rose Carrol**, 26, to Massachusetts (Filby's 1982 Supplement)
1815 - **Michael Carrol** to NY (Filby's 1982 Supplement)
1816 - **Mary Carrol** to NY (Filby's 1982 Supplement)
1816 - **Patrick Carrol** to NY (Filby's 1982 Supplement)
1816 - **Terence Carrol** to NY (Filby's 1982 Supplement)
1816 - **William Carrol** to Philadelphia (Filby's 1982 Supplement)
1817 - **Michael Carrol** to NY (Filby's 1982 Supplement)
1819 - **Daniel Carroll**, 38 in 1821, *Nativity*, County of Tipperary from London to NY, 21 June, naturalized 8 May 1826 (Tepper, New World Passgrs., p. 252)
1819/20 - **Letitia H. Carroll**, Immigrants arriving 1 Oct./Sept.1820, Custom House 199, 201
1819/20 - **P. Carroll**, Custom House 191 (Immigrants arriving . . .)
1822 - **Joseph Carroll**, 50, to America with 2 children (Filby's 1982 Supplement)
1825 - **John Carroll**, 30 in 1836, Tipperary, from Waterford to Baltimore, 28 June 1825, naturalized 27 Nov. 1839 (Tepper, N W Passgrs., p. 268)
1829 - **John Carroll** to Texas (Filby's 1982 Supplement)
1834 - **Michael Carrol**, 25 to Baltimore, MD (Filby's 1982 Sup.)
1835 - **Philip Carrol** to Texas (Filby's 1982 Sup.)
1848 - **John Carroll** to Buffalo, NY (Filby's 1982 Supplement)
1849 - **Thomas Carrol**, 31, to Quebec, wife: **Bridget**, 23; brother: **John**, 22; brother: **Micheal**, 24; sister: **Bridget**, 15; sister: **Mary and Ann**, 18; **1894 - Thomas Carroll**, 31, 17 Aug. 1894, of Irvilloughter, **son of Patrick & Bridget**, from Galway, Northumberland, 2 Oct. 1849, **wife Bridget**, 23; **brother John**, 22; **brother Michael**, 24; **sister Bridget**, 15; **sister Mary Ann**, 18; **Ann Rafferty**, 20, (relationship unspecified); **Mary**, ½ (6 mos.) (Filby's 1982 Supplement; Tepper, N W Passgrs . . ., p. ?); **1849 - Ann Rafferty Carroll**, 20, Quebec (Filby's 1982 Sup.)
1849 - **Mary Carroll**, 6 mos., to Quebec (Filby's 1982 Supplement)
1851 - **J. Carroll**, to San Francisco (Filby's 1982 Supplement)
1851 - **Thomas W. Carrol** to San Francisco (Filby's 1982 Supplement)
1853 - **Andrew Carroll**, 42 (Filby's 1982 Supplement)
1853 - **Thomas Carrol** to NY (Filby's 1982 Supplement)
1855 - **James Carroll** to San Francisco (Filby's 1982 Supplement)
1855 - **Maurice Carrol** to NY (Filby's 1982 Supplement)
1858 - **James Carroll** to St. Clair Co., IL (Filby's 1982 Supplement)
1860 - **Michael Carrol** to St. Clair Co., IL (Filby's 1982 Supplement)
1862 - **William Carrol** to Victoria, British Columbia (Filby's 1982 Supplement)
1865 - **Thomas Carrol** to Minnesota (Filby's 1982 Supplement)
1869 - **Lewis Carrol** to Washington Co.,PA (Filby's 1982 Supplement)
1872 - **Dennis Carroll** (Filby's 1982 Supplement)
1872 - **Kate Carroll**, 20, to NY (Filby's 1982 Supplement)
1880 - **John A. Carroll** to Washington Co., PA (Filby's 1982 Sup.)

Revolutionary War Pensioners of US for 1776 and 1813/14
Applicants & Prisoners, and Military Land Grants & Warrants [Not a complete list.]

State unknown:
Charles Carrol, 4 Reg., Lt. Dragoons, CA
George Carroll, Naval
Henry Carroll, Patton's Reg., Continental Army, CA
Hugh Carroll, pvt., b. c1760, md. Marcial Willis, d. 1815
Jackson Carroll, alleged Capt. James L. Henderson's Co., 21st US Troops, SO 34166 (Indx. War of 1812 Pens. Appl. Files, MF #313, Roll 16)
Jacob Carroll, pvt., b. 27 Apr. 1735, md. Elizabeth Jamison, d. 3 July 1817
James Carroll, Hazen's Reg., CA
James Carroll, pvt., b. 26 Mar. 1730, md. Sarah ?, d. 18 Mar. 1804
James Carroll, John Carroll, Michael Carroll, Perance Carroll, prisoners (Brit. War Dept; Dandridge, Amer. Prisrs. of the Rev.)
Jeremiah Carrol, Forman's Reg., CA
John Carroll, 6034, pvt., Keene's Co. of Foots, John Patton's Regt., Continental Troops, Apr. 1777, Sept. 1777, CA (Rev. War Gen. Indx.)
John Carroll, Count Pulaski's Legion Regt., Continental Troops, CA (Rev. War Gen. Indx.)
John Carroll, 6035, 1st & 2nd Reg., Light Dragoons, Continental Army, CA
John Carroll, 1 Artillery Regt., Continental Troops, fifer, CA (Rev. War Gen. Indx.)
John Carroll, 4 Reg., Lt. Dragoons, CA
John Carroll, 8 Reg., CA
John Carroll, pvt., b. 7 Mar. 1756, md. Maria Van Alstyne, d. 15 Sept. 1855
John Carrell, Continental Army (3 Johns)
Joseph Carrell, German Battalion, CA
Mark Carrol, Hazen's Reg., CA
Michael Carrol, Hazen's Reg., CA
Stephen Carrol, 23 Reg., CA
Thomas Carrell/Carroll, Continental Troops
Thomas Carrick (Carroll), sgt., b. c1762, md. Mary Montgomery, d. 1823
Thomas Carrill, 6135, Gist's Reg., CA
Thomas Carroll, Grayson's Reg., CA
William Carroll, S44227, pvt., b. 22 Aug. 1755, md. Phoebe Wortman, d. 21 Jan. 1824

Alabama
William W. Carroll, Capt. John Winston Co., AL Militia, widow Sarah Carroll, WO 39243

Connecticut
Amos Carroll, Lt., Conn., b. 23 Jan. 1728, d. 28 Jan. 1792, md. 1st Mary Smith, 2nd Mrs. Lucy Hosmer Barrett (Rev. War Pens. Appls. Indx.; Gwathney, p. 62; DAR Patriot Indx.)
Elisha Carrel, 6032, Conn.
John Carrel, S12416, Conn., 6036
William Carroll, 4 Conn. Reg.

William Carroll, drummer, Capt. Robert Colfax Co., CT, 8 Nov. 1814-9 Dec. 1814, Wid. Orig. 13242, Wid. Ctf. 10720; md. **Harriett A. Darrow** 11 Sept. **1825 in Montville, New London Co., CT**; **1855** in New London Co., CT, d. 18 Mar. **1877** in New London Co.; **1878, 1887** widow in New London Co., CT; she d. 16 Apr. **1889** in New London Co. (Indx. War of 1812 Pens. Appl. Files, MF #313, Roll 16)

Delaware

Isaac Carroll, 3 Continental Line; Sussex, DL, pvt., 96 annual, 199.76, 14th Regt. U.S. Inf., Marshall's Delaware Vols., 15 Aug. 1816, 6 Aug. 1814 (Clark, M. J., Pens. Roll 1835, v. 4, p. 3); **Isaac Carroll**, 3 CL (Gwathney; Virginians in the Revolution)
Peter Carrell, DE
William Carrol, DE

Georgia

John Carroll, pvt., #38, Muster Roll, Capt. Paul Demere's Co., Independent Foot Co., SC & Georgia, 25 Aug. 1756-24 Oct. 1756, Georgia Militia; Highland Independent Co., on list of Georgia Militia, Oglethorpe's Soldiers & Settlers, #112, Darien, **1749-1764** (Clark, Col. Sldrs., pp. 981, 993) [See SC]
John Carroll, b. **1798** in NC, d. **c1875** in GA, md. **c1825** in GA to **Cynthia ?** in GA (Indx. NC Ancestors, v. 1, p. 32, Mary B. McBride, #60082)
Thomas W. Carroll, pvt., Capts. Butts, Boons, & L. Worthy's cos., GA Militia 23 Aug. 1813-7 Feb. 1815 as substitute (unnamed), **wounded** in Battle with Indians at Caleba, GA Jan. **1814**, OW Inv. Ctf. 3745, OW File 12685, SO 26400, SC 21116, WO 17209, WC 24299; **1st wife ?**; md. **Frances A. Sears** (1st husband John **Campbell**) 21 Apr. **1840 in Daviston, Talbot Co., GA**; in **1846, 1851, 1853, 1866, 1867 in Tazewell, Marion Co., GA**; **1872 in Americus, Sumter Co., GA**, d. 26 Sept. **1874** in Tazewell Co., GA; in 1878 widow resided in Americus, Sumter Co.; in 1879 she resided in Ellaville, Schley Co., GA (Indx. War of 1812 Pens. Appl. Files, MF #313, Roll 16)

Kentucky

Daniel Carroll, Duddington, KY., 12/1/1831, 7,200 acs., Russell, Garve & Rough Creek (Bk. 2, p. 235; ?, p. 477)
John H. Carroll, pvt., Capt John Hornbeck's Co., KY Militia from 18 Sept. 1812-30 Oct. 1812, Thames River Battle 5 Oct. 1813, Capt. Brown's Co. from 24 Aug. 1813-9 Nov. 1813, SO 4892, SC 6221; **1851, 1855, 1871 Taylor Co., Campbellsville, KY**; wife **Lucinda Musgrove**, md. 11 Aug. **1818** in **Washington Co., KY** (Indx. War of 1812 Pen. Appl. Files, MF #313, Roll 16)

Louisiana

John Carroll, pvt., Capt. R. J. Sackett's Co., LA Militia from 6 Oct. 1814-20 Apr. 1815, SO 19689, SC12739, WO 30121, WC 26768; 1st wife **Susannah ?**, 2nd **Jane ?**, 3rd **Elizabeth J. (Hamilton) Webb** md. 16 Jan **1868** in **Caldwell Parish, LA**; 1853 in Caldwell Parish; in **1855 in Jackson Parish, 1871 P.O. Vernon, LA**, d. 1 Nov. **1873** in **Jackson Parish, LA**; **1878** widow in **Caldwell Parish, P.O. Carter, LA** (Indx. War of 1812 Pens. Appl. Files, MF #313, Roll 16)

Maryland

Bryon Carril, 6131, 2nd Maryland Regt.
Charles Carroll, Esq., #92, on list of accts. for quartering; MD, patriotic service, b. **1751**, d. 9 Oct. **1836**, md. **Elizabeth Warfield** (Clark, Col. Sldrs. . . ., p. 93; Rev. War Pens. Appl. Indx.; DAR Patriot Indx.)
Charles Carroll Jr., #91, soldiers in Annapolis; widow orig. 40775, **Rachel Ann Carroll**, MD Militia (Clark, Col. Sldrs . . ., p. 93; Indx.,War of 1812, Pens. Appl. Files, MF #313, Roll 16)
Charles Carroll, pvt., Capt. James Veitche's Co., MD Inf., served 6 mos. from 1813-1814; BLW 27, 544-40-50; BLW 92. 544-120-55; SP 3298; SC 5070; WO14472; WC12598; widow: **Ann (Follin) Carroll** (Ann md. 1st ? **Pearson**); 1st wife: **Susan Vermillion**; **1850, 1855, 1856, 1871, 1878** in Fairfax Co., VA (P.O. Springvale), md. Ann Follin 25 Nov. **1856** in Vienna, VA; d. 18 Jan. **1874** in Springvale, VA; Ann d. 5 May **1886** in Gt. Falls, VA (Indx., War of 1812, Pens. Appl. Files, MF #313, Roll 16)
Daniel Carroll letter to **Col. George Washington**, Rock Creek, 1 Sept. 1773 (Clark, Col. Sldrs . . ., p. 625)
Dennis Carroll, 4 MD Reg.
George Carrel, 7 MD Reg., S42138 (Rev. War Pens. Appl. Rcds.)
Henry Carroll, MD Artillery, Gate's Co.
Jeremiah Carroll, 2 MD Reg.
John Carroll, MD, pvt., enlisted for 3 yrs. in **1778**, md. **Isabella** in Apr. **1789**, W6118, d. in Annapolis Dec. **1789**; Isabella married to **Samuel Smith** May 1795 who d. 1843; in 1844, age 76, **Isabella Smith**, a widow, was in Halifax Co., VA, she d. 6 Nov. **1844**; ch.: Nancy Younger, Thomas Smith & Martha Sneed (Rev. War Pens. Appl. Indx.)
John Carrol, MD, pvt., BLWt 11091 issued 2/1/**1790** to ? (Rev. War Pens. Appl. Indx)
John Carrol, MD, S30913 (Rev. War Pens. Appl. Indx.)
[one MD John, sol., b. c1754, d. p1840, md. **Frances Hamilton**, one in 2 MD Reg., one in 3 & 5 MD Regs., one in 6 MD Reg.; both **John Sr. & John Jr.** were in 1 MD Reg. (DAR Patriot Indx.; Rev, War Gen. Indx.]
Joseph Carroll, 4 MD Reg.
Joshua Carroll, MD
Patrick Carroll, MD, pvt., b. c1760, d. p14 May **1819**, md. **Jemima Hayes** (Rev. War Pens. Appl. Indx.; DAR Patriot Indx.)
Thomas Carroll, 5 MD Reg.
William Carrol/Carrell, 3 MD Reg., pvt., S2107, b. 10 Apr. **1755**, d. 16 Mar. **1845**, md. **Elizabeth Fee** (Rev. War Pens. Appl. Indx.; DAR Patriot Indx.) [one Wm. in 7 MD Reg.]

Massachusetts

Aaron Carrel, MA, **Sally**, W18858 (Rev. War Pens. Appl. Rcds.)
Benjamin Carrell, Continental Line., MA, md. **Eleanor**, W25387, Bounty Land Warrant 12839-160-55 (Rev. War Pens. Appl. Rcds.)
Ebenezer Carrol, sol., MA (Rev. War Pens. Appl. Rcds.; Gwathney, p. 62)
Hot Carril, 6132, Mass.
Jesse Carrell, S39268, MA (Rev. War Pens. Appl. Indx.; Gwathney, p.64; DAR Patriot Indx.)
John Carrol, pvt., MA, b. 13 Apr. **1736**, d. ?, md. **Tamer King**; **John Carrol**, sol., MA, b. 17

Mar. **1728/1756**, d. 19 Jan. **1781**, md. **Mary King**, died 19 Jan. 1781 (Rev. War Pens. Appl. Indx.; Gwathney, p. 64; DAR Patriot Indx.)
John Carrell, 6133, Mass.
    [one **John** in 3 MA Regt., one in 5 MA Regt., one in 6 MA Regt., one in 15 MA Regt., one in 17 MA Regt.; one in Gerrah's MA Regt.]
Jonathan Caryl, b.**1730**, d. **1806**, pvt. Capt. Bartholomew Woodbury's Co., Col. Jonathan Holman's Reg., MA troops, b. in Hopkinton, MA, d. Chester, VT, md. **1702** to **Anne Clark**, b. **1734**, d. **1816**; son: **Jonathan Caryl Jr.**, b. **1760**, d. **1832**, Jonathan Jr.'s son: **Harvey Caryl**, b. **1790**, d. **1859**, Harvey's son: **Jonathan Harvey Caryl**, b. **1819**, d. **1906**, Jon. Harvey's son: **Clark H. Caryl**, b. **1842** (Source ?)
Joseph Carroll Jr., MA, pvt., b. 26 Aug. **1755**, d. 8 Aug. **1785**, md. **Esther Pond** (Rev. War Pens. Appl. Indx.; Gwathney, p.64; DAR Patriot Indx.); **Joseph Carroll**, 4 MD Reg. (?)
Joshua Carroll, MD
Lawrence Carrol, 9 MA Reg.
Patrick Carroll, MD, pvt., b. c**1760**, d. p14 May **1819**, md. **Jemima Hayes** (Rev. War Pens. Appl. Indx.; DAR Patriot Indx.); **Patrick Carrill/Carroll**, MA
Samuel Carroll/Carll, 12 MA Reg.
Thomas Carrell, MA; **Thomas Carroll**, 5 MD Reg.
William Carrol/Carrell, 3 MD Reg., pvt., **S2107**, b. 10 Apr. **1755**, d. 16 Mar. **1845**, md. **Elizabeth Fee** (Rev. War Pens. Appl. Indx.; DAR Patriot Indx.) [one Wm. in 7 MD Reg.]
William Carroll, MA, sol., **Hannah** W14440 (Rev. War Pens. Appls. Indx.; Gwathney, p. 65)

Missouri
Elijah Carroll, lived in **MO**, d. 21 Dec. **1875** in Montank, Dent Co., MO,; 1st wife **Elizabeth Poindexter**; 2nd wife **Nancy ?**, md. 21 Oct **1849** in Cole Co., **MO**; she later md. **? Bryan**, d. 1 Nov. **1903** (Indx. War of 1812 Pens. Appl. Files, MF #313, Roll 16)

New Jersey
Abra'm Carrel, 6030, NJ
David Carrol, NJ, **R1732**, pvt., Bounty Land Warrant (BLWt) #8213 issued 8 Sept. 1789 to Samuel Rutan, assignee, rejected (Rev. War Pens. Appl. Indx.; Gwathney, Patriots & Veterans, p. 61)
Ephriam Carle/Carrol, NJ
James Carrol/Carrell/Carroll, 4 NJ Reg.
Jeremiah Carroll, 2 NJ Regt.
John Carrel, 6033
John Carrill, 6134 (Coryell), NJ
William Carroll, b. 22 Aug. **1755**, pvt., NJ, **S44227**, Alleghany Co., NY, pvt., 96, 575.27, New Jersey Line, 5 Oct. 1821, 24 June 1818, d. 21 Jan. **1824**, md. **Phoebe Wortman** (Rev. War Pens. Appl. Rcds.; Clark, v. 4, p. 206; Gwathney, Pats. & Vets., p. 65; DAR Patriot Indx.)
William Carrel, 6042, NJ

New York
David Carrell, 6044, NY

George Carrell, NY
John Carroll, NY, pvt., b. 17 Mar. **1756**, d. 15 Sept. **1855**, md. **Maria Van Alstyne** (Rev. War Pens. Appl. Indx.; Gwathney, p. 64; DAR Patriot Indx.)
Jury Carrel, 6039
Martin Carroll, NY Co., NY, pvt., 48,00 annual, 208.27, 4th Reg., U.S. Inf. Rifles, 21 Oct. 1816, 21 May 1815, d. 26 Feb. **1831**, raised rate (disability) 23 Sept. **1819**, 96 annual, total 1,096.80 (Clark, Pens. Roll 1835, v. 4, p. 132)
Stephen Carroll, pvt. Capt. Martin Barber's Co., NY Militia, 27 Aug. 1812-27 Oct. 1812, SO 17605, SC 11794; wife: **Olive Burgess**, md. 11 oct. **1818 in Sempronius, NY; 1850, 1871 in Cayuga Co., NY** (Indx. War of 1812 Pens. Appl. Files, MF #313, Roll 16)
William Carrel, NY, War of 1812, W25395, md. **Naoma ?**, Washington Co., NY, pvt., 48.00, 495.00, 4th Reg. U.S. Inf., 8 Feb. 1817, 22 Nov. 1814, d. 15 Mar. **1825**; BLWt 33559-160-55 (Rev. War Pens. Appl. Indx.; Clark, v. 4, p. 175)
William Carrel, pvt., NY, 2nd Battalion, pvt., b. **1755**, d. 8 Dec. **1815**, md. **Elizabeth Hicks** (Rev. War Pens. Appl. Indx.; Gwathney, p. 65; DAR Patriot Indx.)

North Carolina
Abso. (Absolum) Carroll, militia, #475, Newbern Dist. (NC DAR Roster, p. 347)
Benjamin Carroll/Carrell, W10587, muster roll of militia regt., command of Col. Wm. Eaton, Oct. 8, **1754**, Capt. Osborn Jefrey's Co.; **1771**, NC sol. in Capt. William Bufford's Co.; 25 May **1781**, pvt., Hall's Co., 10th Regt., Col. Abram Shepard, NC Continental Line, Rev. War, 12 mos., out 10 Nov. 1782; #2435, 32p,10s, received by Philip Fishburn; **Benjamin Carroll**, NC, pvt., 10th Regt., Hall's Co., 10 May 1833, 80 yrs. old, resident of Orange Co., militia, volunteer, Col. Lock, Capt. Whitedall, entered 1780, served into 1782, b. in Orange Co. Date unknown, always lived in Orange Co. md. **1786** (to **Nancy Peeler** not Peter), d. 31 Jan. **1846**, **Nancy** in Orange Co. home of Christian Peeler in July 1846, appeared to petition 7 Aug. 1847 (Rev. War Pen Appl. Rcds.) wife **Nancy**, md. **1783/84**, lived in **Orange Co., NC** in May **1833**, **80 yrs. old**; Benj. served from 1780-82; **believed he was b. in Orange Co.** but date unknown; d. 31 Jan. **1846**; **Nancy, c80 yrs. old**, was in Orange Co. home of **Christian Peeler** in July **1846**; **Nancy Carroll** petitioned in Orange Co. 7 Aug. **1847**; **Benjamin Carroll**, #2435, 32p10s, recd. by Philip Fishburn; **Benjamin Carroll**, #1091, 27p16s1d, recd. by B. McCulloch; **Benjamin Carrol**, Pierce's Register, #90569 (Worth,...and Its People, List of Early Inhabs. of Granville Co., NC, p. 292; Clark, v. 2, pp. 370-380; v. 16, p. 1037; v. 17, pp. 199, 201; v. 22, pp. 61, 164; House List of Private Claims, v. 1; Surnames w/Col.& Rev. Pedigrees, v. 17, p. 199; NC DAR Roster, pp. 6, 116, 205, 515, 517, 574; Gwathney, p. 62)
Benjamin Carroll, Continental, #807, Halifax Dist (under Harvey family name (NC DAR Roster, p. 366)
Benjamin Carrell, pvt., Coleman's Co., 14 May **1777**, 5th Reg., Col. Edward Buncombe, 2½ yrs., NC Continental Line, d. Aug. **1777** (Hathaway, NC Hist. & Gen. Reg., v. 2; NC DAR Roster, p. 79)
Britton Caroll, pvt., Hogg's Co., 20 July **1778**, 9 mos., 10th Regt., Col. Abram Shepard, dischd. 2 Nov. 1778; NC Line, #1088, 27p16s1d, B. McCullock, Warrenton; **Britian Carol**, militia, #629, Newbern Dist. under Harvey Family; **Brittor Carroll**, Continental, #804, Halifax Dist., Harvey Family (Clark, v. 17; Hathaway, NC Hist. & Gen. Reg., v. 2; NC DAR Roster, pp. 114, 366, 515)

Butler Carroll, esn., 10th NC, 1777, officers of Continental (NC DAR Roster, p. 30)
Daniel/Laniel Carrell/Carril/Carriel, b. 17 Oct. **1748**, pvt. in Capt. Benjamin Simm's Militia Co. [same list as **Benjamin**]; **R1726**,, NC Line, living in Bute Co., NC when enlisted; 12 Mar. 1785, discharged in Halifax, NC; 1787 - **Daniel Carroll**, 640 acs., #488, #460 issued 15 Sept. 1787, entry #1605, Bk. 63, p. 167, gt. assigned to John Marshall (NC Mil. Ld. Gts., TN) #229 assigned NC land grant #1134 issued 26 Nov. **1789**, entry #1601 21 Sept. 1787 in Sumner Co., TN, 228 acs. "on Manskers trace creek" mil. gt. assigned to John Marshall, #229, #1134 issued 26 Nov. 1789, entry #1601, 21 Sept. 1787, (Bk. 74, p. 14, 146; NC Ld. Gts. TN 1778-1791) R1726, wife: Hannah; md.11 Nov. **c1793** in **Union Dist., SC**, wife **Hannah** (dau. of Edward & Esther Insco), d. 12 Apr. **1840** w/o having a child; brother **Grief Carrell** in Limestone Co., AL; **has brother in GA**, letter written from Lauderdale Co., AL July **1820**, had wife age 42 and girl age 15; **182?** in Athens, Limestone Co., AL; in **1832** in Lincoln City, TN; d. 20 Apr. **1837** in Lincoln City, TN; **Daniel Carroll** named as **Harwell Carroll's heir**, June 1785; **Laniel Carroll**, Continental, #1338, Halifax Dist. Under Cooper Family name; **Daniel Carroll**, #762, 49p5s3d, recd. by H. Montfort for **Daniel Carroll**; **Danil Carroll**, Continental, #506, Halifax Dist., under Harvey Family name; **Daniel Carroll**, #886, 40p10s4d, received by William Sanders (NC DAR Roster, pp. 266, 329; Ray,... and Its People, p. 292; Clark, v. 2, pp. 370-380, v. 17, p. 199; Pens. Appl. Rcds., p. 553; House List of Private Claims, v. 1; CumberlandRiver Settlers; (See Bertie Co.); Surnames with Col. and Rev. Pedigrees, #762, #886; NC DAR Roster, pp. 329, 368, 514) [**Daniel Carroll**, pvt., assigned his NC land grant in Sec. III, Sumner Co., TN on Maney Fork Creek, #1132, 228 acs, **1789**, to John Marshall (NC Ld. Gts. in TN 1778-1791, pp. 104, 142); Two **Daniels????** Which **Daniel Carroll** was appointed by the U.S. Congress as a commissioner along with Col. Benjamin Hawkins and William Perry to treat with the Cherokee Indians? Worth, ... and Its People, p. 287]
[Family Records: Jonathan Parker md. Esther Collier 2 Aug. 1748; dau. Mary Parker, b. 3 June 1749, md. 3 Jan. 1771; dau. Esther Parker, b. 4 July 1754, md. 12 June 1776; dau. of Wm. & Mary Scott, b. Aug. 1805; Timothy Parker b. 8 Oct. 1751; Jerimiah Parker, b. 24 Apt. 1757; **Jesey or Georg Carrell, b. 16 Feb. 1780; Daniel Carrell, b. 8 Nov. 1819**]
Dempsey Carrol, S32161, NC, in **Wilcox Co., AL** on 9 Jan. **1833** when sworn testimony for pens. appl. given: b. 22 Dec. **1762**, entered service age 16, on muster roll; age 17 volunteered in Capt. Michael Kinian's Co. ... commanders: Gen. James Kinian & Col. Richard Clinton, 6 mos. duration, citizen of **Duplin Co., NC** (now Sampson Co.); in 2-hr. skirmish between Duplin Co. & Wilmington, marched to Wilmington, to Fayetteville, to Bluford Bridge (near Wilmington) to guard against British expected to invade the co.; claimed age was recorded in family Bible in SC if not destroyed, resided in Duplin Co. (in area now in Sampson Co.), moved to SC, then to Wilcox Co. AL, minister of the Gospel, believed he was 71 yrs. old, wits. to test.: **Elias & Demcy Carroll**, 28 Jan. 1833, D. C. Smith, CC; an invalid, **Dempsey** received $20, 7 June 1832, pd. again from 4 Mar. 1837-4 Mar 1838 and 4 Mar. 1838-4 Sept. **1838**; **Dempsey Carol**, Continental, #1677, Wilmington Dist. (Rev. War Pens. Appl. Indx.; NC DAR Roster, pp. 327)
Dennis Carroll, sol. NC unit, **R1724**, age **72, Shelly Co., AL**, Oct. **1834**, md. ?, submitted, rejected (Rev. War Pens. Appl. Indx.; House List of Private Claims, v. 1; Gwathney, p. 63)
Douglas Carroll, pvt., enlisted 1 June 1776, 3 yrs., NC Continental Line, 18 July 1777, Cap*t*. Clement Hall's Co., 2nd Battalion, Col John Patten, White Plains, mustered out June 1778, 36 mos., 10th Reg., Col. Abram Shepard, Rev. War 6045; md. ?; #1614, 22 Oct. 1783, 428 acs. in

13

Davidson Co., TN "on N. Cross Creek, a mil. ld. gt. #1342 issued 10 Dec. **1790**, entry #136, Col. Murfee, assigned to Bennett Hill (Hathaway, NC Hist. & Gen. Reg., v.2; Pens. Appl. Rcds.; Bk. 74, p. 379; NC Ld. Gts./TN 1778-1791; DAR Patriot Indx.,1776; NC DAR Roster, pp. 114, 184, 235, 607)

Elisha Carroll, militia, #s1192, 3356, Wilmington Dist. under Harvey Family name (NC DAR Roster, pp. 368, 369)

George W. Carroll, WO42429, WC32765, pvt., Capt. John L. Langton's Co., NC Militia, served as substitute (name not given) from 24 Sept. 1814-5 Feb. 1815; BLW 361-80-50, BLW 21 328-80-55; **1850-1855 in Wilson Co., TN**, d. 1 Mar. **1865** in Wilson Co., **TN**; 1882, widow at Oak Point, Wilson Co., TN; 1st wife: **Elizabeth Tucker**; widow **Susan** md. 1st ? **Blankenship** 27 Jan. **1835** in Wilson Co., TN; she d. p30 June **1899** (Indx. War of 1812 Pens. Appl. Files, MF #313, Roll 16)

Hardy Carrell, S41469, pvt., NC, Duplin Co., Capt. Joseph I. Rhode's Co., 1 Aug. 1782, 1st or 10th Regt., NC Line, 1 Dec. **1782**, 18 mos., discharged 1 Mar. 1783, Col. Abram Shepard, NC Continental Line; **1819 Willis Carrol and Hardy Carrell**, James Moore all sworn for him, Daniel Merrit; "On the 17th day of Oct. **1820**, he was 60 years old." b. **c1760**; Hardy Carrel, Pierce's Register, #91099 (Hathaway, NC Hist. & Gen. Reg., v. 2; Rev. War Pens. App. Indx. & Recds.; House List of Private Claims, v. 1; Clark, v. 16, p. 1038; NC DAR Roster, pp. 6, 118; Gwathney, p. 62) [See Duplin Co.]

Harwell Carroll, pvt., deceased, **#488 NC ld.** grant #460 issued 15 Sept. 1787, entry #1605 in Sec. III, Davidson Co. "on Maney Fork Creek," Stone River, #462, 640 acs., assigned **1787** to John Marshall; **Harvel Carroll**, #1604, the **heirs: Daniel Carroll**, 640 acs., 12 Mar. 1784, J. Marshall; "on Stone River," a military grant assigned to John Marshall, 1787, **Daniel heir of Harwell Carroll**, 1785 (Cumberland River Settlers); **1787 - Harwell Caroll**, decd., mil. ld. gt. in Davidson Co., TN "on Maney fork creek," (another source says "on Stone River", heir: **James Carrol**, pvt., #25, Muster Roll Capt. Isaiah Hogan's Co., NC Militia, **19 Sept. 1772**; 4 Mar 1831, 69 yrs. old, pd. $99.99

James Carrell, W6899, pvt., NC, b. **1765**, d. 16 May **1834 in Johnston Co.**, md. **Rhoda Stevenson/Stevens** 1 Feb. **1792**, mar. bd. recorded in Smithfield; [1 Feb. 1792, **John Carroll** of Johnston Co. swore to James & Rhoda marriage in Johnston Co., by Rev. William Taylor; **W6899**, BLWt. 86103-160-55; volunteered in Cumberland Co., Fayetteville, NC where he lived until near 40 yrs. old; Col. Raiford; discharged in Charleston, SC; moved to Johnston Co., NC in 1792 where resided when placed on pension roll; **brothers James, & William Carrell lived in Johnston Co., NC 7 June 1832**; Rhoda moved to **AL** with sons: **James, Lazarus & Mathew** in 1836; she wrote "all the **Carrells from Maryland** within from one to 3 miles from me." Signed A. Coates, J. P.]; **children** mentioned: **Margaret** b. spring **1793**, d. c1836, md. **Briton Langdon**; **John**, eldest son, age **64 in 1858**, **James**; **David** moved to Dale Co., AL in 1835; 31 Aug. **1855**, **Rhoda** in Dale Co, AL was 78 yrs. old; **David Carroll & James Carroll** were wits. for **Rhoda** in Dale Co. in **1858**; **C(ader). Carrell** was a wit. in **1859** (Rev. War Pens. Appl. Indx.; DAR Patriot Indx., 1776; House List of Private Claims, v. 1; NC DAR Roster, pp. 266, 439, 573; NC Ld. Gts. in TN, 1778-1791, pp .91, 141; Bk. 63, p. 167; (Clark, Col. Soldrs . . ., p. 817)

Jesse Carroll, sol., NC, b. **c1750**, d. 10 Mar. **1802**, md. **Mary Rachel Gavin** (Rev. War Pens. Appl. Rcds.; DAR Patriot Indx., 1776)

John Caroll/Curl, pvt., Baker's Co./Ballard's Co., 20 July **1778**, 9 mos. 10th Regt., Col. Abram Shepard, dis'd 23 July **1778** (Hathaway, NC Hist. & Gen. Reg., v. 2; Clark, Col. & St. Rcds., v. 16, p. 1034; NC DAR Roster, pp. 114)
John Carrol, Army accts. pd. by John Armstrong (NC DAR Roster, p. 191)
John Carrell, militia, #1188, Newbern Dist, under Cooper Family name (NC DAR Roster, p. 330)
John Carroll, sol., Continental, #1018, Halifax Dist., under Harvey Family name (NC DAR Roster, p. 366)
John Carrell, pvt., Raiford's Co., 11 June **1781**, 12 mos., ?time out 11 June **1782**, 10th Reg., Col. Abram Shepard, NC Continental Line (Hathaway, NC Hist. & Gen. Reg., v.2; NC DAR Roster, pp. 115)
John Carroll Sr., b. **1761**, Clinton, Sampson Co., NC
John W. Carrell, 400 acs., **1782**, Washington Co., TN on Sinking Creek and waters of Nolochucky River (NC Ld. Grts./TN 1778-1791, Roll M68, #130; Surnames w/Col. & Rev. Pedigrees)
John Carroll Esq., testimony in Alston case: Col. Philip Alston commanding corps of militia, on death of Thomas Taylor, begged issue of pardon for Col. Alston in suppressing the Tories (Gen. Greene) retreating before British Army; John Kendrick also testified (Clark, v. 17, pp. 397-399; Surnames w/Col. & Rev. Pedigrees) [See Moore Co., NC]
John Carroll, pvt., #11091, army ld. Warrant, 100 acs., 1 Feb. **1790**, registered by James Williams for himself, 4000 acs., Mil- 12-5-3, 19/calendar, 11 Feb. **1800**, A/1/209 (Smith, Fed. LD. Sers., p.5 8)
Jonathan Carrell, #3121, NC Line, 97p4s, received by Timothy McCarthy, Warrenton (Clark, v. 17, p. 203; Surnames w/Col.& Rev. Pedigrees, p. 201; NC DAR Roster, p. 518)
Peter Carrell, militia, #2423, Salisbury Dist., under Cooper Family name (NC DAR Roster, p. 329)
Thomas Carrel, militia, #1290, Salisbury Dist. (NC DAR Roster, p. 329)
William Carroll/Carrell, pvt., Doherty's Co., 24 May 1776, W, omitted Jan. 1778, Col. Edward Buncombe, 6th Reg., NC Continental Line, Col. Gideon Lamb; deceased, a 1783, 640 acs., NC ld. gt. in Davidson Co., TN, #2044 "on the second creek that the boundry line crosses," #2044, #2064 issued 2 May **1793**, entry #1754 (Bk.1, p.140), "on waters of the west fork of Mill Creek," **heir: John**, military grant assigned to **Nancy Sheppard** on 23 April **1785**, Col. Martin Armstrong, NC, was required to lay out and survey for heirs of **William Carroll** _____ in the line of this state 640 acs. within the limits of the lands reserved by law for the officers and soldiers of the continental line of this state, Col. Martin Armstrong's; **heirs: John Carroll, Charles Carroll, Nancy Carroll md. John Sheppard; William Carrell**, #2202, 19p7s1d recd. by John Sheppard in Warrenton, NC; NC Line, #136, 77p11s3d recd. by Jos. Hadly (Hathaway, NC Hist. & Gen. Reg., v. 2; Bk. 81, p. 140; NC Ld.Gts./TN, 1778-1791, p. 85, v. 2, p. 180; Clark, v. 16, p. 1030, v. 17, pp. 198, 201; v. 22, p. 60; Surnames w/Col. & Rev. Pedigrees; Mil. Ld. Gts. of NC in TN)
1831 Mar. 4 - **William Carroll**, rank do, NC Line, **Keziah, W6640, Roane Co., TN**, commencement of pension 4 Mar. **1831**, ?placed on pension 15 Feb. 1833; **William Carrol**, Pierce's Register, #89624 **William Carroll**, NC, **1781**, pvt., Hall's Co., 10th Reg., Col. Abram Shepard, Continental Line, 12 mos., out 10 Nov. 1782, Rev. War, S____; **Lincoln Co., NC**,

pvt. 40, 120.00, NC militia, 10 Apr. 1833, 4 Mar. 1831, age 82; Roane Co., TN, 20, 60,00, NC Line; **W6640**, testimony given 2 Oct. 1832: b. ? in **Fairfax (or Halifax) Co.**, VA, moved to **Granville Co.**, NC on Tar River, enlisted in **Granville Co.**, NC near the Tar River, b. in pvt., served 3 mos., substituted for his **brother Jesse**, discharged **1781**, lost discharge, returned to **Warren Co.**, NC, md. **Keziah (last name unknown)** Sept. **1777** in Granville Co; removed to **Caswell Co.**, NC; drafted and attached to Capt. Dickson's Co. in NC regt. commanded by Col. Moore, marched to Charleston 1782, returned to **Caswell Co.**, NC, lived in **Lincoln Co.**, NC, moved to **Hawkins, TN** for 10-12 yrs., to **Roane Co.**, TN where resided 2 Oct. **1832**, age 77; pensioned 15 Feb. 1833 commencing 4 Mar. 1831, d. 28 Dec. **1835**, age 83; **Kesiah** lived in **White Co.**, TN from 1835-1845, d. 9 Feb. **1845**, age 83; **ch.: Jesse, b. 19 Nov. 1778; John, b. 3 Aug. 1779; Betty Dover, b. 12 Dec. 1780; Elijah, b. 7 Apr. 1781; Henry, b. 26 Feb. 1783; and Nancy Dover, b. 21 Sept. 1785.** [In testimony given in Roane Co., TN ?**2 Oct. 1832, William was age 77, said he substituted for his brother George.**] Record states he left service 10 Nov. 1782 after 12 mos., rank pvt., 10th Regiment, Hall's Co. under Capt. Burfet in ? Regt. of NC militia from Warren Co., had marched to Charleston, joined Gen. Lincoln; [#W6640, enlisted in Granville Co., NC, **b. in Fairfax Co., VA**, moved to Grnville Co. on Tar River, pvt., served 3 mos., out in 1781, **substituted for bro. Jesse**, returned home to Warren Co., md. Keziah ? Sept. 1777 in Granville Co., removed to Caswell Co., NC, drafted & attached to Capt. Dickson's Co. In NC Line, Col. Moore's Regt., marched to Charleston 1782, returned to Caswell Co., lived in Lincoln Co., NC, moved to Hawkins, TN for 10-12 yrs.; to Roane Co., TN where he resided 2 Oct. 1832, age 77, **substituted for bro. George**, Capt. Hall's Co. under Capt. Burfet, regt. of NC militia from Warren Co., marched to Charleston, joined Gen. Lincoln, **Thomas Carroll,** wit.; pensioned 15 Jeb. 1833 commencing 4 Mar. 1831, d. 28 Dec. 1835; Kesiah lived in White Co., TN from 1835-45, d. 9 Feb. 1845, age 83; ch.: Jesse, b. 19 Nov. 1778; John, b. 3 Aug. 1779; Betty, b. 12 Dec. 1780; Elijah, b. 7 Apr. 1781; Henry, b. 26 Feb. 1783; Nancy, b. 21 Sept. 1785 (Rev. War Pens. Appl. submitted by widow)]; **Thomas Carroll** witnessed **testimony of William's dau. Nancy in White Co.**, TN, also witnessed by her brother **Elijah** and a **Joseph Carroll Jr.**, magistrate. **Both Nancy and Betty md. Dovers**; oldest child was Jesse not James (Nancy Dover made correction 19 Nov. 1845); Keziah Carroll lived in Sparta, White Co., TN 28 Dec. 1835, she d. 9 Feb. 1845; she had applied for pension under Act of July 4, 1836, (suspended by resolution of US Senate 16 Sept. 1850) her application was rejected, reason: for (lack) of proof of marriage and of service from the South Carolina records (should have been NC) (Indx. Rev. War Pens. Appl.; Clark, v. 12, p. 60, v. 16, p. 1037, v. 22, p.60; Gwathney, pp. 62, 65; Rejected or Suspended Appls. For Rev. War Pens.,p.394; Rev. War Pens. Appl. Rcds.; House List of Private Claims, v.1; NC St. Rcds.; NC DAR Roster, pp. 6, 116, 197, 226, 269, 328, 330, 441, 479, 513, 517, 573; Pens. Roll/1835, v.3; Surnames w/Col. & Rev. Pedigrees; DAR Patriot Indx., 1776) [Testimony for William is confusing. Did records get mixed together? **William who md. Kesiah** did not have a brother **George**. He did have a brother **Jesse** according to father's will of 1781 in Granville Co.,NC. Info above is redundant because apparently testimony was given by Kesiah and her daughter Nancy.]

Index to 1812 North Carolina Soldiers (MF #250, Roll 1)
George Carroll, Militia, 1 NC Reg., McDonald's Reg.
Henry Carrow?, Militia, Major Tisdale's command

Henry Carrow?, 2 Reg., Bruton's
James Careel, Militia, Capt. Wiley's
Joab Carrel/Carrol, Militia, Brunswick Reg., Moore's
John Carrow?, Militia, Gibbs', Middle Creek Co.
Jonathan Caral/Carroll, Militia, 3 Reg., Moore's
Jordon Carrow?, Watson's Reg., Hyde Co.
Joseph Carrol, Militia, Tisdale's 2 Reg.
Lemuel Carroll, Atkinson's 5 Reg.
Owen Carroll, Militia, Major Lillington's Det.
William Carrel/Carrol, Militia, Pearson's 7 Reg.

Ohio
Philip Carroll, Jefferson Co., OH, pvt. 2nd Reg., 10 Dec. 1813, heirs: **John, Mary, Margaret, Joseph, Armstrong, Catharine, Henry, Jane & Philip Carroll**, 16 Feb. 1819, 17 Feb. 1815, end of pens. 17 Feb. 1820 (Clark, v. 4, p. 163)
Stephen Carroll/Carle, pvt., Capt. Ephraim Brown's Co., Ohio Militia from 25 Apr. 1812-24 Apr. 1813, SO 22493, SC 18075; wife: **Sarah French**, md. 3 Mar. **1814/1815** in **Hamilton Co., OH**; **1853-1858** in **Linn Co., OR**, **1871** Linn Co., Lebanon, OR (Indx. War of 1812 Pens. Appl. Files, MF #313, Roll 16)

Pennsylvania
Alexander Carroll, PA
Benjamin Carroll, pvt., PA, b. 25 Aug. **1755**, d. **p1793**, md. **Permelia Proctor** (Rev. War Pens. Appl. Rcds.; DAR Patriot Indx.)
Dennis Carrol, PA, **S2117**
Edmond Carrol, PA
Henry Carroll, 1 PA Reg., 1779-1780
Hugh Carroll, pvt., PA, b. c1760, d. **1815**, md. **Marcial Willis** (Rev. War Pens. Appl. Indx.; DAR Patriot Indx.) [**Hugh Carrin?**, Granville Co., NC (Bentley Cens. Indx., p. 41)
Jacob Carroll, pvt., PA, b. 27 Apr. **1735**, d. 3 July **1817**, md. **Elizabeth Jamison** (Rev. War Pens. Appl. Indx.; DAR Patriot Indx.)
James Carle/Carroll, pvt., PA, b. 26 Mar. **1730**, d. 18 Mar. **1804**, md. **Sarah** (Rev. War Pens. Appl. Rcds.; DAR Patriot Indx.)
James Carroll, WO 39738, WC 30426; widow **Juliana (Kepler) Carroll**, md. Feb. **1814/1816** in **Erie Co., PA**; in **1852, 1855 in Erie Co, PA**, d.2 Apr. **1846 in Erie Co., PA**; in **1880** widow in **Bremer Co., Iowa** (Indx. War of 1812 Pens. Appl. Files, MF #313, Roll 16)
John Carroll, pvt., 2 PA Reg., 5th Battalion, b. c1745, d. p13 Aug. **1825**, md. **Rhoda Niblak** (Rev. War Pens. Appl. Indx.; DAR Patriot Indx.)
John (Jno.) Carrell, Philadelphia, 1/8/1807, 15, 196 acs., Tygerts Creek & Forks of Sandy (Bk. L, p. 284; ?, p.403)
Joseph Carroll/Carrell,Carle, 3 PA Reg., 7 PA Reg., 1776
Patrick Carrill/Carrol, 5 PA Reg.
Thomas Carrel, 6041, PA,
Thomas Carroll, sgt., b. c1762, d. **1823**, 3 PA Reg., 4 PA Reg., 5 PA Reg., md. **Mary**

Montgomery (Rev. War Pens. Appl. Indx.; DAR Patriot Indx.) [Two Thomases in 4th Reg.]
Thomas Carroll, pvt., Capt. Armand Martin's Co., PA Militia, 3 Jan. **1814**-5 Feb. **1814**, WO 14478, WC 7920; md. **Elizabeth Mulvin** 16 Mar. **1818 in Waterford, Erie Co., PA**; **1852**, **1855** in Erie Co., PA, d. 15 Apr. **1857** in Labeuff, PA (Indx. War of 1812 Pens. Appl. Files, MF #313, Roll 16)
William Carroll, PA, pvt., Capt. Askey PA Troops, #128673 b. **1745**, d. p13 June **1830**, md. **Joanna Wakefield**, dau. **Elizabeth Carroll**, b. **1780**, d. **1854**, md. **John Hoge (Houge)**, b. **1777**, d. **1845**; son **David Carroll**, b. **1796**, d. **1869**, md. **Elizabeth Alcorn**, b. **1800**-85, d. **1817** (Rev. War Pens. Appl. Indx.; DAR Honor Roll Indx.; DAR Patriot Indx.)

South Carolina
Benjamin Carroll, BLW 30, 523-40-50; BLW 80, 304-120-55, widow: **Elizabeth S.**, maiden name: **Eliz. S. Evans**, md. 20 Apr. **1833** in **Abbeville, Hall Co., GA**; pvt., Capt. P. B. Roger's Co., SC Militia; enlisted 10 Dec, 1813; disch'd: 15 Mar 1814; in **1850-1855 in Anderson & Pickens Cos.**, SC; in **1883**, **1887**, widow in Hall Co. (P. O.: Flowery Br.), GA; death of sol.: 9 May **1864**, Abbeville Co., SC – fraudulent claim, name dropped from rolls (Indx.,War of 1813 Pens. Appl. Files, MF #313, Roll 16)
Daniel Carroll, widow orig #43818, widow **Peggy Carroll**, Capt. P. B. Rogers Co., SC Militia (Indx.,War of 1812, Pens. Appl. Files, MF #313, Roll 16)
Daniel Carroll, BLW 30151-40-50, BLW 44536-120-55; SO26718; SC17455; pvt., Capt. Samuel Perrin's Co., SC Militia from 10 Dec. 1813 to 15 Mar. 1814; **1850** in **Benton Co., AL**; **1870** Peck's Hill, **Calhoun Co., AL**; **1872**, Calhoun Co., Jacksonville P.O., AL; 1st wife: **Margaret Mann**; 2nd wife: **Sarah Phillips**, Apr. **1811, Greenville Co., SC** (Indx., War of 1812, Pens. Appl. Files, MF #313, Roll 16)
Daniel Carroll, widow orig. #2053, **Charlotte Carroll**, US Navy
Jacob Carroll, pvt., SC, b. **1748**, d. June **1815**, md. **Elizabeth Fair** (Rev. War Pens. Appl. Rcds.; DAR Patriot Indx.)
James Carol/Carrell, SC, 1 SC Reg.
James Carroll, pvt, Capt. P. G. Roger's Co., SC Militia from 10 Dec. 1813-15 Mar. 1814 as a substitute (unnamed); SO 22492, SC 14475. WO 39152. WC 30222; md. **Cynthia Copeland** 28 Aug. **1828 in Putnam Co., GA**; in **1850**, **1855**, **1871**, **1875**, **1877 in Coosa Co., P. O. Rockford, AL**, d. 17 Oct. **1879** in Coosa Co; **1880** widow in Rockford, AL, d. 31 Jan. **1897** in Coosa Co., AL (Indx. War of 1812 Pens. Appl. Files, MF #313, Roll 16)
?John Carrol (page torn; indx. states **John**), pvt., #38, Muster Roll, Capt. Paul Demere's Co. Independent Foot, SC & Georgia, **25 Aug. 1756-24 Oct. 1756**, Georgia Militia; #54, on Muster Roll of SC Militia, Capt. James Leslie's Co., Col. Richard Richardson Regt., **8 Oct. 1759-8 Jan. 1760** (Clark, Col. Soldrs ..., pp. 888, 993) [See Georgia]
John Carroll, pvt., Capt. Jonathan Beatty's Co., SC Militia from 1 Oct. 1814-7 Mar 1815, SO 27365, SC 19508, WO 27828, WC 18893, **1850**, **1855**, **1872 in Tuscaloosa Co., P. O. Woodstock, AL**, d. 16 Mar. **1873**; widow Catherine (Johnson) Carroll, md. 27 Oct. **1819** in Jonesboro, **AL**, lived in **1878** in Tuscaloosa Co, P.O. Green Pond, **AL** (Indx. War of 1812 Pens. Appl. Files, MF #313, Roll 16)
John Carroll, SC, R1733, sol., pens. rejected (Rev. War Pens. Appl. Rcds.)
John Carroll, Lt., Rev. War, 4 yrs., 7th Regt., Continental Line, signed by Herod Gibbs, Lt.,

Union Dist., SC; **Lt. John Carroll**, 11 Dec. **1800** received land bounty for services in Rev. War, 500 acs. each for heirs, #5956, #5959, #5960 for self, 666 2/3 acs. in **Elbert Co., GA**, Nov. 10, assigned his claim to "Hobson's (claims agents of Bty.Ld.) who we shrewd at a Bargain." **John Carroll** tried to reclaim this land, but was rejected by Congress of Virginia 4 June **1834** (Claims of Bounty Land; Burgess, Virginia Soldiers of 1776, v. 3, 263, V8 B9, copy 2)
John Carroll, pvt., Capt. Twigg's Co., 8 US Inf. From 20 June, 1812-29 Dec. 1813, WO 32648, WC 26519; md. **Frances Franklin** 8 Jan. **1814** in SC; **1853** in Larne Co., **KY**, d. 28 Aug. **1866** in Edmondson Co., **KY**; **1878, 1879** widow in Edmondson Co., **P. O. Dog Creek, Hart Co., KY** (Indx. War of 1812 Pens. Appl. Files, MF #313, Roll 16)
Joseph M. Carroll, W9778, SC, Quartermaster Sgt., enlisted **1775**, b. **1746**, son of **Joseph Carroll** of York Dist., SC, md. **Martha Swansey/Swancy** 28 Feb. **1771**; d. 17 Feb. **1803**, brothers **Thomas & John Carroll**; **Martha** resided in **York Dist.** in Jan. **1846**, age 92; ch.: **Samuel**, b. Jan. **1772**; **Elizabeth**, b. 4 Oct. **1774**; **Je**(paper torn), b. 6 Nov. **1776**; **Sarah**, b. 20 Mar. **1778**; **Joseph**, b. 25 Sept. **1781**; **John**, b. 2 Feb. **1784**; **Henry**, b. 19 June **1789**; **Isabell**, b. ? (Rev. War Pens. Appl. Indx.; DAR Patriot Indx.)
Michael Carrol, 1 SC Reg.
Mordeca/Mordica Carrol, pvt., #31, Muster Roll, Capt. Thomas Fletcher's Co. under Ensign Wells, Col. R. Richardson's Regt., SC Militia, **8 Oct. 1759-8 Jan. 1760** (Clark, Col. Soldrs ..., pp. 883, 900)
Richard Carrol, pvt., Capt. James Leslie's Co. Pay List, Col. Richard Richardson's Regt., SC Militia, **8 Oct. 1759-8 Jan. 1760** (Clark, Col. Soldrs ..., p. 904)
Samuel Carroll Sr., b. Ireland a1740, d. SC p1790, md. **Margaret Leslie**, pvt. under Capts. Thomas & John Henderson, Lt. Creswirth, list of Rev. War Sldrs; during war a resident of York Dist., SC, ch.: **Joseph R.**, b. **1778**, md. **Martha Love**; **Elizabeth**, b. ?, md. **John Davy**; **Samuel Jr.**, b. **1788**, md. **Hilda (Elizabeth) Davy**; **Mary**, b. **1774**, md. **James Allison** ((DAR Mag. 1912; DAR Patriot Indx.; Whitley, Edythe Rucker. DAR Membership Roster and Soldiers, The Tennessee Society of the Daughters of the American Revolution 1894-1960. DAR, 1961, p. 413.]
Silas Carrol, pvt., Capt. Edward Musgrove's Co., Col. John Chevillette Battalion, **6 June 1760**, Cherokee Expedition, SC Militia (Clark, Col. Soldrs ..., p. 911)
Thomas Carroll, pvt., Capt. John Key's Co., SC Militia, served from 4 Feb. 1815-16 Mar. 1815 as substitute for John Deason, SO 29899 rejected, WO 381777, WC 28001; 1st wife: **Charity Mitchell, 1850** in Franklin Co., **GA, 1855** in Gilmer Co., **GA**; md. **Lucinda Caroline Morehead**, Sept **1856**; **1874** in Franklin Co., P. O. **Carnesville, GA**, d. Oct. **1875** in Franklin Co., **GA**; **1879 & 1887**, widow in Franklin Co., **Martin, GA** (Indx.War of 1812 Pens. Appl. Files, MF #313, Roll 16; v. 19, p. 428)

<u>Tennessee</u>
John Carrol/Carroll, BLW 35279-160-50, SO19685, SC12532, pvt., Capt. James Cuming's Co., TN Militia, enl'd.: 17 Oct, **1813**; disch'd.: 17 Jan. **1814**,; **1850 in Clay Co., MO; 1855 & 1871 DeKalb Co., MO** (P.O. Stewardville); wife nee: **Elizabeth Stubblefield**, md. July in Hawkins Co., TN **1812** - son, **Nathaniel Carroll**, b. 1 Jan. **1812** in TN, md. **Mahala Mar** 23 Feb. **1832** in Clay Co., **MO** (Indx., War of 1812 Pens. Appl. Files, MF #313, Roll 16; Carroll Cables, Oct. 1966)
John Carroll, pvt., Capt. Peter Searcy's Co., TN Militia from 20 June 1814-2 Feb. 1815, S

12740, SC 18844, WO 12442, WC 27293, widow **Rebecca Baker** md. 7 Apr. **1833** in **Wilson O Co., TN; 1851, 1855, 1871** in **Crawford Co., P. O. Cherryville, MO**, d. 10 Aug. **1871** in Crawford Co., **MO**, she d. c**1893** (Indx. War of 1812 Pens. Appl. Files, MF #313, Roll 16) **John Carroll**, Capt. Samuel Tunnell's Co., TN Militia, orig. **30474** (Indx. War 1812 Pens. Appl. Files, MF #313, Roll 16)

Virginia
Bartholomew Carrol, E, VA, S35827, pvt., b. **1722**, d. 7 Dec. **1827**, md. **Catherine** (Rev. War Pens. Appl. Indx.; Gwathney, Virginians in the Revolution; DAR Patriot Indx.)
Batt Carrell, 6043, Va
Berry Carroll/Carrel, VA, S39270, 6031, entered **1777**, in **Essex** Co., 2nd VA St. Reg.; in **Essex Co., VA** in **1818**, **77 yrs. old**; 100 acs., Warrant #1728, 3 yrs. Sol. VA Line, enlisted Sept. 8, **1783** (Rev War Pens. Appl. Indx.; Military Warrants 1781-1793, p.322; Gwathney)
Daniel Carroll, S3132, pvt., #52, HMShip Lyon, Muster, Gooch's American Regt. **20 Jan 1740-Jan/Feb. 1742**, Jamaica, borne for victuals, dated 6 Feb. **1741**, Port Royal VA, entered May **1781** in Albemarle Co., VA (Charlottesville); in **Warren Co., TN** in **1834**, **79 yrs. old on 1 Jan. 1834** (Clark, Col. Sldrs ... p. 175; Rev. War Pens. Appl. Rcds.)
David Carroll, VA, S9144, drafted Apr. **1777**, b. in Corry Co., Ireland 22 May **1761**; lived in Washington Co., VA & PA where testimony was given (Rev. War Pens. Appl. Indx.)
Dempsey Carrol on Maj. Laurence Washington's copy of Fairfax Co. Polls, 13 June **1748**, VA Militia; Freeholders names polled by Mr. Wm. Elzey for Col. G. W. Fairfax, VA Militia, 11 Dec. **1755**, Fairfax Co. (Clark, Colonial Soldiers ..., pp. 278, 280, 335, 337)
Dempsey Carroll, Capt. Darlington, VA Militia, WT 40431-40-50; WT 97912-40-50; WT 687-80-55, no pension claim (Indx. War of **1812**, Pens. Appl. Files, MF#313, Roll 16)
Dennis Carrol, #29, HMShip Russell, Muster Bk., Col. Gooch's Reg., 16 Feb. 1740/41-Gooch's American Regt. **1739-1741**, date 3 June **1741** (Clark, Col. Sldrs ..., p. 204)
Edward Carroll, #55, pvt. HMShip Chichester, Muster Roll Bk., soldiers borne on bound for victuals, Gooch's American Regt., Capt. Prescott's Co., **20 May 1741** 400 acs., Bounty Warrant #353, Sgt., VA Line, duration of war, enlisted Apr. 17, **1783** (Clark, Col. Sldrs ... p.144; Military Warrants 1781-1793,p. 322; Gwathney)
George Carroll, 6 VA Reg., Continental Line (Gwathney, Virginians in the Rev.)
Henry N. Carroll, pvt., Capt. Merriweather Taliaferro's Co., 35 US Inf from 26 Feb. 1814-15 Mar. 1815, SO 19686, SC 17438; BLW 14265-160-12; **1871** in **Bedford County, P.O. Big Island, VA**, d. p19 Apr. **1883**; wife **Martha**, md. 7 Sept. **1818** (Indx. War of 1812 Pens. Appl. Files, MF #313, Roll 16)
Isaac Carroll, 3 VA Reg., Continental Line (Gwathney)
James Carroll, E, sol., VA, 12th VA Reg., b. **1756**, d. **1829**, md. **Delphia Gualtney**; **James Carroll**, E (Rev. War Pens. Appl. Indx.; DAR Patriot Indx.; Gwathney, Vas. in Rev.)
James Carrell, 14 Regt., VA
John Carroll, R1731, b. 20 Mar. **1754**, on roll of offrs. & soldrs. Who engaged in Battle of the Meadows **3 July 1754** in Stobo's Co.; "report of various companies of VA regiment under **Col. Washington** made the 9th **of July 1754** at Will's Creek, just after the battle of the Great Meadows." Return of Capt. Stobo's Co., 9 July **1754**; **1754**, **John Carrol**, #32, pvt., Capt. Robert Stobo's Co. received bounty money, VA Militia. Men fit for duty: **John Carroll**, ... #9

Pay Roll of Capt. Robert Stobo's Co.; on list of Recruitment by Maj. John Willoughby of men out of Norfolk Co., enlisted 19 May 1756, 5 ft. 6 in., age 25, Irish, waterman (trade). **1756 - John Carrell**, pvt., #5 & 8 on payrolls of Capt. Robt. McKenzie's Co. & Capt. Robt. Stewart's Troop of Light Horse **16 Jan. 1756**, VA militia; **13 July 1756, John Carrol**, #35, Size Roll, Capt. Robert McKenzie's Co., VA Militia, 24 age, 5 1/4', VA, Sailor, Spotsylvania. Following named privates each received 2.08 pounds: **John Carroll**, ... Members of the VA regiment who have received bounty money. The following lists are preserved in the "Force Manuscript" in Library of Congress; on the back of each of the 5 rolls is the indorsement of **Washington**. A list of Capt. Stobo's Co. who have received ..., **Jno. Carroll; Prisoner John Carroll**, Col. Washington's Co., mentioned by Board in Minutes of a Court of Inquiry held at Ft. Loudon 30 Mar. 1757, **John Carroll**, VA, wife **Ann**, Capt., **son of John Carroll**, enlisted in **1776** in Edgefield Dist., SC, served until 1782, **d. in Warren Co.**, NC **13 Oct. 1832; Ann d. 25 Dec. 1844 in Warren Co., NC**; dau. **Nancy** md. **John Paterson**, was **70 yrs. old** in 1852 and lived in **Chatham Co.**, NC, swore her father was a resident of **Mecklenburg Co., VA** & moved to Warren Co., NC; Nancy claimed to be only heir of **John and Ann**; son **John** (only heir?) lived in **Lincoln Co., GA** in **1855** (Clark, Col. Sldrs., pp. 287, 303, 344, 366, 375, 393, 435, 590, 597; Virginia Colonia Militia 1651-1776, pp. 111, 115,118; Rev. War Pens. Appl. Indx.)
John Carroll, Lt., Rev. War, 4 yrs in 7th Reg., Continental Line, signed by Herod Gibbs, Lt., Union Dist., SC; **1800** - Bounty Warrant, **Lt. John Carroll**, 11 Dec. 1800, for services in Rev. War, 500 acs each for heirs (Warrants 5956-5959 & 5960 for self for 666 2/3 acs. in Elbert Co., GA); 10 Nov. **1809** - **John Carroll** assigned his claim to "Hobson's (Bounty Ld. Claims agents) who we shrewd at a Bargain;" 4 June **1834** - **John Carroll** tried to reclaim this land but was rejected by Congress of Virginia (Claims of Bty. Ld.; Burgess, Va, Soldiers ..., v. 3; Gwathney)
John Carroll, pvt., 2 VA Regt. (Rev. War Gen. Indx.)
John Carroll, pvt., 1 & 4 Regt. Lt. Dragoons, Continental Troops (Rev. War Gen. Indx.)
John Carroll, pvt., 6 VA Regt. (Rev. War Gen. Indx.)
John Carroll, 8 VA Regt. (Rev. War Gen. Indx.)
John Carrole/Carroll, 1741 June/Dec. 1742 - **John Carrole**, pvt., #25, Col. Gooch's Regt. of Foot,; 2 VA Reg., 6 VA Reg., CL, nbll (Clark, Col. Sldrs ..., p. 161; Gwathney) [May be two John's, one in 2nd and one in 6th Reg.]
John Carroll, 200 acs., Warrant #1840, 3 yrs., Sgt., VA Line, enlisted Oct. 9, 1783 (Military Warrants 1782-1793, p. 322); 3 VA Reg., 7 VA Reg., 5 VA Reg., CL (Rev. War Gen. Indx.) [More than one John?]
John Carroll, 200 acs., Warrant #434, duration of war, sol., VA Line, enlisted Apr. 26, **1783** (Military Warrants 1782-1791, p. 322)
John Carroll, pvt., #11091, army land warrant, 100 acs., 1 Feb. 1790, registered by James Williams for himself, 4000 acs. [St not given] (Mil - 12 5 3, 19/calendar, 11 Feb. 1800, A/1/209, p. 58;Smith, Fed. Ld. Series, 1799-1835)
John Carroll, seaman, Navy; #8 on His Majesty's Ship Oxford Muster Book 25 Jan. **1740**, Colonel Gooch's American Regiment; **July 1740-Sept. 1742**, , HMShip Grafton, Muster Bk., Col Gouch's (sic) Reg.; 26 Nov. **1741, Hospital**; **1756** - **John Carrell**, pvt., #62, 25, 5'7", **Ireland**, Seaman, enlisted May 1756 at Norfolk, Roll of Capt. Mercer's Co. 2 Aug. 1756; **John Carrol**, #63, Size Roll, Col. Washington's Co., 28 Aug. **1757**, 24 age, 5'7", **Ireland**, Sailor, Apr. 1756, Norfolk, VA Militia (Clark, Col. Sldrs., pp. 158, 192, 405, 461; Gwathney, Vas. in Rev.)

John Carrel, 6037, VA
Joseph Carroll & Col. John Carlyle mentioned by Charles Smith to George Washington, Ft. Loudoun, **26 July 1758** (Clark,Col. Soldrs. ... p. 521); 1st VA St. Reg., 100 acs., Warrant #1216, 3 yrs., sol., VA Line, enlisted June 26, **1783**; 100 acs., Warrant #1492, 3 yrs., sol., enlisted Aug. 8, 1783 (Military Warrants 1782-1793, p. 322).
Joseph Carrel, 6038, VA
[One **Joseph** was in in 4th VA Reg., Continental Line] (Gwathney)
Joshua Carroll, Widow Orig. #44316, **Catharine H. Carrol**; Capt. Harris' Co., VA Militia; Capt. Morgan's Co., VA Militia (Indx. of War of 1813 Pens. Appl. Files, MF #313, Roll 16)
Juliet Carrol, VA State Troops (Gwathney)
Luke Carroll/Carwell, MD origin, 43871, Capt. Kiles Co., VA Militia, **Elizabeth Carroll**, 4 CL, 8 CL, 12 CL; sol. in Capt. William Bufford's Co., 1771; patent of 400 acs., 1749-1751 (Gwathney; Pat. Indx. 1623-1774, VA ST Lib.; Clark, v. 22, p. 164)
Malachi/Malachia Carroll, S8180, pvt., E, VA, served 2 yrs., marched to Charleston, SC; lived in **Princess Anne Co., VA, 78 yrs. old in Nov. 1832** (Rev War Pens. Appl. Indx.; Gwathney)
Mathew Carrill/Carrol, pvt., #8, Woodward's VA Mil. Co. Aug. **1756**; Woodward's Necessary Roll at Ft. Lyttleton, 22 Aug. **1757**; #18, Virginia Militia Roll of Capt. Henry Woodward's Co., 24 Sept. **1757**, 26 age, 5'8", Ireland, planter, Spotsilvania (sic) (Clark,Col.Sldrs, pp.416,458, 469)
Nicholas Carrell, VA (Rev. War Pens. Appl. Indx.; Clark, v. 16, p. 973)
Patrick Carrick?, VA, S35825 (Rev. War Pens. Appl. Indx.)
Pleasant P. Carroll, pvt., Capt. Isaac T. Preston's Co., 35 US Inf. From 3 Sept. 1814-20 Mar. 1815, Sur. Orig. 10486, Sur. Cf. 13092, Wid. Orig. 27829, Widow Cf. 21991; md. **Lydia Nighten 1854** in **Rockingham Co., VA**; **1852** in **Orange Co., VA**; **1871 Rockingham Co.**, P. O. Rawley Springs, VA, d. 14 Jan. **1878** in Rockingham Co., VA where widow was in 1878 (Indx. War of 1812 Pens. Appl. Files, MF #313, Roll 16)
Samuel Carroll, 6040, VA St. Troops, Clark's Ill. Reg. (Gwathney)
Samuel Carroll, Capt. Christopher Brown's Co., VA Militia, widow **Juliet Carrol**, WO 9999 (Indx. War of 1812 Pens. Appl. Files, MD #313, Roll 16)
Thomas Carroll/Carrill, 6136, Capt., 1 VA St. Reg., Cleon Moore's Co., Grayson's Regt.; 200 acs., Warrant #1796, duration of war, sol., VA Line, enlisted Sept. 26, **1783** (Clark, v. 19, p. 428); Gwathney; Military Warrants 1782-1793, p. 322)
Thomas R. Carroll, pvt., Capt. George Judkin's Co., VA Militia, 24 July 1814-8 Aug. 1814, sur. Orig. 5120, sur. Cf. 25201; md. **Nancy Stacy** 28 Dec. **1820 in Isle of Wight Co., VA**; **1855** in Mahoning Co., **OH**, 1871, **1878** in Mahoning Co., P. O. Canfield, **OH**, d. 17 Aug. **1888** (Indx. War of 1812 Pens. Appl. Files, MF #313, Roll 16)
William Carrel, Jan. **1740/Feb.1741**, pvt., #17, HMShip Torrington, Muster Bk, Gooch's American Regt.; Soldier **Wm. Carrol**, #8 on HMShip Norfolk, Muster Roll, Gooch's American Regt. **14 Mar. 1740**, dated 5 May **1741**, Carthagena Harb (?harbor); **Wm. Carroll**, pvt., #96, HMShip Lyon, Muster, Jamacia, **31 May 1741**, Port Royal, Gooch's American Regt.; Frederick Co., VA Militia, 24 July **1758** (Clark, Col. Sldrs ..., pp. 176, 180, 236, 513)
William Carroll/Carrill, 6137, 6 VA Reg., CL, Capt. Hanby's Co. (Gwathney)
[Source: Index of Revolutionary War Pension Application, Bicenntennial Ed., National Genealogy Society, Washington, DC, 1976.]

Civil War Soldiers

Barnard A Carroll, Major., 2 MO Inf.
Chandler W. Carroll, Lt. Col, 184 Ohio Inf.
Edward Carroll, Lt. Col, 95 PA Inf.
Howard Carroll, Col., 105 NY Inf.
James Carroll, G?, 7 MS Inf.
James Carroll, MO Cav., AR Cav., 988864 or 988364 MO
James S. Carroll, KY Inf., **Elizabeth Carroll**, AR
John S. P. Carroll, Lt. Col., 1 W. VA Vet. Inf.
Madison Carroll, F US U?, SC Inf., A U U? SC Inf., AR
Samuel S. Carroll, Col., 8 Ohio Inf.
William B. Carroll, Col., 10 ID Inf.
William C. Carroll, Maj., 13 IL Cav.
William Carroll, K? TN Inf.
William Carroll, K U TN Inf.
William Carroll, KY, ??? TN ?, **Sarah C. or E.**
William Carroll, AR
(Rebellion 1861-1865)

War with Spain and Philippine Insurrection
Benajah H. Carroll, Chaplain, 1 TX Cav.
Edward Carroll, 2 Lt., 1 PA Inf.
Frank W. Carroll, Capt., 1 Colo. Inf.
Garrett J. Carroll, Maj., 7 IL Inf.
Henry Carroll, Capt., 9 Cav., 7 Apr. 1880, San Andries Mountains, New Mexico, wounded, Lt. Col, 6 Cav., 1 July 1898, San Juan, Cuba, wounded
John C. Carroll, 1 Lt., 32 Inf., 5 Nov. 1867, near Camp Bowie, Arizona, killed
James M. Carroll, 1 Lt., 4 KY Inf.
John F. Carroll, Capt., 14 NY Inf.
John S. Carroll, 1 Lt., 1 AL Inf.
Joseph H. Carroll, 1 Lt., asst. Surg., 49 US Inf.
Richard Carroll, Chaplain, 10 US Inf.
William J. Carroll, Capt., 7 IL Inf.
(Historical Register and Dictionary of U.S. Army 1789-1903,v.2,War with Spain and Insurrection in Philippines, Apr. 21, 1898, printed 1903)

1790 Taxpayers in North Carolina Dists.

Demcy Carrol, Fayette Dist.	James Carrol, Fayette Dist.	Thomas Carrol Fayette Dist.
Demey Carrol, " "	John Carrol Esq. " "	John Carrol, WilmingtonDist
Elizabeth Carrol, " "	John Carrol Sr. " "	John Carrol, " "
Elisha Carrol, " "	John Carrol " "	Joseph Carrol, " "
James Carrol, " "	John Carrol " "	Thomas Carrol, " "
Jesse Carrol,	Stephen Carrol " "	Thomas Carrol Jr. " "

John Carroll, Halifax Dist.
Thomas Carrol, " "
Benjamin Carroll, Hillsborough Dist.
Henry Carroll, " "
Michael Carroll " "
Robert Carroll " "
Stephen Carroll " "
John Carrol, Morgan Dist.

William Carrol, Morgan Dist.
James Carrol, Newbern Dist.
John Carrol, " "
William Carrol, " "
William Carrol, " "
Benjamin Carroll, Salisbury Dist.
James Carroll, " "
William Carrol, " "

Marriages of Unknown Origin

1806 - Sarah Carah, b. 1806 in NC, d. 1864 in TN, md. C1821 in TN Philip Low (Indx. NC Ancestors, p.32 ,#60390)

1811- Mary Carroll, b. 1811 in NC, d. in ?MS, md. c1825 in TN Zachariah Pinkston (Indx. NC Ancestors, p.25, #28042)

1839 - Sarah P. Carroll, dau. of John Carroll, md. Joel W. Smith, Elder T. B. Humphreys, Dec. 12, 1839

1866 - Miss Clarence E. Carroll md. Samuel H. Parsons by Rev. W. G. Turner, Dec. 6, 1866

1885 - Laban T. (Rev.) Carroll md. Annie L., dau. of C. H. DeLorne by Rev. Robert W. Lide, Jan. 15, 1885

1888 - William Carroll md. Almeida Barnes by Rev. F. C. Clark Sept. 6 1888
 (Inventory of Church Archives ..., 1941, p. 97)

Index to Welborn's North Carolina Tombstone Records, vs.1,2,3

John Carrell, p. 9
Adeline Green Carroll, p. 229
John Martin, pp. 137, 279
Samuel Carroll, p. 229
Charles L. Carroll, p. 265
[See Moore County for Wades and Martins]

Jane Wade, p. 68
James Carroll, p. 235
John W. Carroll, p. 70
John P. Martin, p. 154
Margaret E. Carroll, p. 265

E. J. Wade, p. 98
John Carroll, p. 104
John B. Martin, p.137
C. W. Carroll, p. 126
S. L. Carroll, p. 263

A Brief History of North Carolina

North Carolina has between 400 and 500 years of history. It includes three distinct historical periods: 1. Exploration from 1500s; 2. colonization beginning with Raleigh's colonies in 1580s and 1584 territory above Spanish Florida known as Virginia; and 3. settlement from Raleigh's colonies to the end of the Revolution, some 200 years.

On 13 July 1584, English explorers claimed for Queen Elizabeth I what is now eastern North Carolina. A year later, 108 men sponsored by Sir Walter Raleigh, arrived on the outer banks. After ten months, the men disbanded and returned to England. In 1587, Raleigh sent a second party of 115 which came to be known as the "lost colony." Neither of the colonies was permanent, but they were the beginnings of England in America.

In 1629, England's King Charles I granted New World territory from 31 to 36 degrees north latitude to Sir Robert Heath. He called it Carolina, derived from the Latin form for Charles, Carolus.

King Charles II issued a Carolina Charter in 1663, granting full Palatine powers to eight "Lord Proprietors," and in 1665 to all land England claimed south of Virginia; thus, the Carolina Colony. The proprietors divided it into three parts: 1. the first permanent settlement made by a group of dissenters from Virginia north of Albemarle Sound a few years before 1663 – Albemarle County; 2. along the Cape Fear River to the ocean at Wilmington – Clarendon County; 3. the region now known as South Carolina – Craven County.

North Carolina grew at a rapid rate between 1663-1729. Capt. John Whittie was sent to establish a plantation in 1664, the first proprietary settlement in Carolina. Under the direction of Peter Carteret, it was abandoned after seven years.

In 1669, a grant to Roanoke Island was given to Gov. Samuel Stephens for the purpose of raising cattle. Roanoke Inlet, the main port of entry to Albemarle Sound and to northern Carolina, was narrow and hazardous for sea-going vessels. The Lord Proprietors ordered Carolina representatives to build the colony's "chiefe town" on nearby Roanoke Island in 1676, but orders seem not to have been carried out. The islands were homesteaded, and Roanoke Island was sold to a New England merchant, Joshua Lamb, by the Berkeleys (Sir Wm. Berkeley married the widow of Samuel Stephens). Lamb soon sold to Nicholas Paige of Boston, who later sold one fourth of the island to George Patridge.

The first permanent settlers occupied the Outer Banks well before 1700. Outer Banks settlers were livestock men, boatmen, or pilots who guided vessels through sounds and inlets. At this time, in the vicinity of Albemarle Sound, there were five counties in North Carolina: Currituck, Pasquotank, Perquimans, Chowan and Bath. In the 1730s, nature closed Roanoke Islet, leaving no direct reliable outlet through the banks from Roanoke Island and Roanoke Sound. [See map, Stick, *Dare County: A History*, p.33]

North Carolina settlements were administered under the governor at Charleston from 1691-1712, but the two Carolina territories (north and south) were divided in 1710 and each had its own governor and capital by 1712. In 1711, mainland Indians attacked settlers on Roanoke Island and across the sounds. Forty or more white people were killed or carried off in 1713.

With a fleet of four vessels in 1718, Capt. Drummond, or Edward Teach (or Thatch), came to Outer Banks as the infamous pirate, Blackbeard. Disclaiming all intent to pirate, he received a pardon from Gov. Charles Eden. When killed, his ship, *Adventure*, was destroyed.

In 1728, the proprietors sold colony shares to the Crown, but Lord John Carteret (later Earl Granville) refused to sell. He did give up governmental rights to obtain the "Granville Grant" – a long, most populated and wealthy strip in the northern part of the colony that hindered development and caused discontent until abolished by the patriot government during the Revolution.

From 1729-1775, the royal colony of North Carolina progressed with the population growing from 30,000 to 265,000. Settlers came from Virginia and South Carolina, and thousands of Scot Highlanders, Scots-Irish, Germans, Swiss and French entered the colony. The Scots-Irish, Scot Highlanders and English entered Cape Fear Valley around 1750.

In 1740, the 13 counties in North Carolina were: Currituck, Pasquotank, Perquimans, Chowan, Bertie, Tyrrell, Hyde, Beaufort, Craven, Carteret, Onslow, New Hanover and Bladen. A 1746 map of Old Granville County shows that the counties of Granville, Butte, Warren, Franklin and Vance were established from the Granville Grant. Granville County joined Edgecombe County by a line from the mouth of Stonehouse Creek on the Tar River, then across the river in a direct course to the middle grounds between the Tar and the Neuse rivers. The middle ground was the southern boundary. The western boundary was indefinite.

There were 25 counties in North Carolina in 1760: Currituck, Pasquotank, perquimans, Chowan, Hertford, Northampton, Tyrrell, Bertie, Halifax, Granville, Hyde, Beaufort, Pitt, Carteret, Craven, Onslow, New Hanover, Bladen, Duplin, Dobbs, Edgecombe, Johnston, Cumberland, Orange, Rowan and Anson. Butte County was formed in 1764 from Granville County by a direct line from where Jefferson Road crossed the Virginia line to where Morse Creek crossed the Johnston (now Wake) County Line.

In 1771, an abundance of ongoing problems concerned court over legal fees and land titles. North Carolina's colonial government prevailed over Orange County Regulators protesting against an administration dominated by coastal planter interests. Following several years of organized resistance, the colonial militia defeated the Regulators. Apparently a sizeable group (number unknown) of Regulators then moved into the Tennessee region. North Holston was the only one of four settlements located outside of Cherokee lands. Upon signing of the Lochaber Treaty, lines were surveyed in 1771, and the British ordered the other three settlements' inhabitants to evacuate their homes.

In the spring of 1772, the three settlements joined to form the Watauga Association and outlined a wilderness government in the Watauga Compact. The Watauga Association sent an emissary to Cherokee towns on the Little Tennessee River to arrange for white settlers to lease Indian lands. The treaty worked for three years with settlement populations increasing steadily. North Carolina Judge Richard Henderson met in March 1775 with the Cherokees at Sycamore Shoals (Elizabethton) and worked a treaty whereby his Transylvania Company purchased two huge tracts (all of Kentucky and most of middle Tennessee). Protest from the chief's son went unheeded.

In the same year, a provisional patriot government was established. From May 20-31, the Mecklenburg Declaration of Independence was signed. The first important battle on North Carolina soil was at Moore's Creek Bridge.

There were 35 counties in 1775 with settlements extending westward to the mountains. Currituck Co. included what is now Dare Co., the southern coast including Cape Hattera was part of Hyde Co., and the western part on the mainland was part of Tyrrell Co.

Witnessing Henderson's success, the Wataugans approached the Cherokees to buy the lands they had leased in East Tennessee. A bargain was struck. On April 12, 1776, the North Carolina delegation to the Continental Congress was instructed to vote for independence. In July 1776, the bargain with the Cherokees fell apart when militant Indians attacked white settlements. In September, Virginia and North Carolina troops with the Wataugans counter-attacked the Indians, burning Indian towns on the Little Tennessee River. Wataugan leaders decided they needed the protective wing of either Virginia or North Carolina.

The Revolutionary period of 1776 was a time of British forage raids through the colony for food. The American Revolution began when the 13 colonies declared their independence on July 4, 1776. On July 5, the Wataugans petitioned North Carolina for annexation. In September, Virginia and North Carolina troops along with the Wataugans counter-attacked the Indians, burning their towns on the Little Tennessee River. North Carolina's provisional government directed the Tennessee leaders to select representatives to send to the Constitutional Convention. Wataugan delegates signed the first state constitution on November 4.

North Carolina established Washington County (TN) which included most of the present state of Tennessee in 1777. The Watauga Association then dissolved.

In 1778, The *North Carolina Gazette* was established at New Bern.

Warren and Franklin counties were formed from Butte County in 1779 by a line from the Granville County line to Little Shocco Creek near Priscilla Nelms plantation, and the Little Shocco-Big Shocco Creeks to the Halifax-Nash line.

Three hundred pioneers migrated from 1779-1780 to the Cumberland River basin of Middle Tennessee, over 200 miles west by direct land route. Settlement was encouraged by Judge Richard Henderson, who hoped to gain from his 1775 purchase of the Middle Tennessee tract and stories of the fertile river basin. James Robertson, a leader of the Watauga settlements, directed and supervised this venture. John Donelson, of Southwestern Virginia, had charge of the group that traveled by water.

The Cumberland plateau stood between direct travel from east to middle Tennessee, so Robertson led an exploration party to the Cumberland Basin. He moved his scouts from upper East Tennessee into Kentucky, through the Cumberland Gap and along a path parallel with the Cumberland River to the vicinity of the old French Lick trading post (present Nashville).
The Robertson party returned to Watauga in the summer of 1779. On November 1, the first group of a hundred or so was ready to move on horse back or by boat. They traveled Robertson's earlier route and arrived on the Cumberland bank opposite French Lick in late December.

The 1780s began an uncertain period for the new American nation. Articles of Confederation linked the 13 states under a loosely federated governance. Each state retained its sovereignty, freedom and independence, and collectively took the document literally at the expense of the welfare of the nation. Under the Articles, an inclination to treat neighbor states as foreign powers erupted in economic rivalries.

James Madison felt the regulation of commerce was necessary to solve the problems between states. In a Virginia resolution, he called for the 13 states to meet and consider such regulations. Five states sent delegates to Annapolis, Maryland in September 1786. The delegates agreed to call a constitutional convention in Philadelphia in 1787 to craft a constitution. In Federalist Paper #51, Madison said: "But what is government itself but the greatest of all reflections on human nature? If men were angels, no government would be necessary." The

Constitution of the United States of America was ratified in 1788, and in 1789, Madison led the battle for the Bill of Rights.

In 1815, he became absorbed in the issue of slavery. Before death 28 June 1836, he saw the rising tensions between the North and South and advised the country to ensure that the Union be cherished and perpetuated. (The Wilson Quarterly, Summer 1985, v.9, no.3, p.80)

A new era began in the 1780s with land ownership a key element. Landholders were wealthy non-residents, and squatters lived on the islands. Independence changed this situation with the new government by and for the people. Land, previously owned by the British government or its agents, became state property and any citizen of North Carolina could apply for a land grant. Since squatters could establish title anyway, large property owners saw the ease of selling off small parcels to them at a profit. On Hatteras Island, the settlers were stockmen or mariners, and had by necessity to be carpenters, boat builders, fishermen and hunters to survive.

In the last year of the Revolutionary War, on March 15, 1781, fighting surrounded the Guilford Courthouse. North Carolina soldiers played important roles in the Cherokee Wars and in the Battle of King's Mountain.

By 1783, 25,000 people lived beyond the mountains. North Carolina ceded its western lands in 1784 to the United States but immediately rescinded the action after western settlers declared their independence and organized the new state of Franklin. North Carolina rejected the federal constitution in 1788. Western lands difficulties ended in 1789-90 when North Carolina finally ceded its western lands to the federal government. The state was admitted to the Union 21 November 1789, the 12th state with 136 years of territorial history. Raleigh was made the state capital in 1792.

The next three decades from 1790-1820, the state made little progress socially or economically with state government controlled by eastern planters unwilling to finance internal improvements and education. "Two story houses and comfortable living" impressed an 1806 visitor. The two-story houses were one-room deep with a breeze way (or dog run) between lower rooms and a detached kitchen in back. Corn, grown on the mainland, required windmills for grinding in every community. Lighthouses and light ships aided navigation. Oak and cedar forests provided material for the shipbuilding industry.

[Note: ". . . Perusal of county records, especially will books, makes it clear that movement of families occurred immediately after the death of the father or family patriarch . . . In such cases the patriarch was often unable or unwilling to leave the land he had acquired in America. Even though his sons may have desired to leave sooner, they postponed their departure until after his death. In some cases, this was evidence of filial affection; in others, it sprang from necessity, for the father customarily disposed of his lands among his faithful sons. Only by remaining until after probation of the will or other disposal of the estate could the sons obtain the shillings necessary for the acquisition of cheaper land to the south. There can be no doubt that the patriarchal position of the father in colonial America was a powerful controlling factor in the westward – and southward – movement of population. (Ramsey, pp. 21-22, see map on p. 33; David M. Maxfield, Smithsonian News Service, "Digging Up New Clues to an American Mystery, Oct. 1983-see photos of Roanoke Is.; Stick, p. ?; Lefler & Newsome., p. 211)

Carrolls in North Carolina Counties

Albemarle County, established in **1663**, was the first North Carolina county, but the first permanent settlement was made there a few years prior to 1663.
1687 - **Anthony Carrell**, juror, in case of slave sentenced to be hanged for killing his master (Haun, Old Albemarle ... pp.377-378); **1704** - **Anthony Carrell**, land rights, 159 acs. concerning William Vosse, Edmond Roe, Nightingale and his wife (Haun, Old Albemarle ... Misc.Recds., 1678-c1737, p. 29, item #97)
1715 - **Ed. Carrole**, 1p2s6p paid to him in claims (Haun, Old Albe ..., p. 88, #257)
1720 - **William Carroll**, 22, on roster given by Col. Robert Patterson's Co., a list of residents of upper parts of Chowan precinct lying W of Chowan River (Ray, Old Albemarle ..., p. 596)
1792 - **John Carroll**, grown, went across mountains for his grandfather Michael Thomas' marriage license in 1792 when he md. 2nd wife, Elizabeth Staton (Ray, Old Albemarle, p. 637)

Currituck County established in **1670** from **Albemarle County**. Denmark's map shows county in Edenton Military Dist. in 1780. The courthouse burned and there are no early records.
1755 - **Richard Cammil?**, taxable (Jones, p. 5)
1803 - **Milberry Carrell** and Mary Miller, daus of Dennis Capps (will dated 17 Jan./25 May 1803), son Caleb Capps, excr., wits: Ja's Phillips, Caleb Capps Sr. and Caleb Capps Jr. (Will Bk. 2; Jones, p. 72)
1810 - **Beny Carrell** (Cens. Indx., p. 42, Cens., p. 100)
c1815 - **Malachi Carral**, James Gornto and Edward Brown wit'd. George Chappel will of Princess Anne, VA, wife Mary; sons: George and Noah; daus: Lydia Chappel and Dorcas Chappel (Will Bk. 3; Jones, p. 74)
1820 - **Mary Carrel** (Cens. Indx., p. 75); **1830** - **Mary Carrel** (Cens. Indx.); **1831** - **Mary Carroll** will, 13 Jan./27 Jan. 1832: **son Joseph Grimstead**, excr.; **dau: Polly, wife of Caleb Borden with son Albert Borden; dau. Amy Ansell wife of ? Ansell with children Peggy, Betsy & Lydia Ansell, daus. Mary, Sarah & Amy Grimstead, gdch.: Holloway Robertson, Sally Carroll**; wits.: John B. Jones & Andrew Capps (Will Bk.3, p. 269; Jones, p. 73)

Pasquotank County, established in **1670** from **Albemarle County**, has no early records. It was in Edenton Military Dist. in 1780.

Perquimans County, established in **1670** from **Albemarle County**, has no early records. It was in Edenton Military Dist. in 1780

Chowan County was established in **1670/71** from **Albemarle County**. It was in Edenton Military Dist. #4 in 1780. (Carls, First NC Cos., p. 4)
1687 - **Anthony Carrell**, juror, case in which a slave was sentenced to be hanged for killing his master; **1704** - ld. rts., concerning William Vosse, 159-ac. rights; Edmd. Roe, Nightingale and wife, and **Anthony Carrell** (Col. Rcds. of NC, Higher Court Rcds., 1687, pp. 377-378; Haun, Misc. Rcds. 1678-c1737, #97, p. 29)
1715 - **Ed. Carrole**, 25s,6p paid to him in claims, Item #257 (Haun, p. 88, I. 257)
1720 - **William Carel** in Robert Patterson's Co. from Meherrin Creek to Meherrin River on both

sides, 11 Apr. (Misc. Items From Ct. Rcds, Chowan Precinct; Hathaway, NC Hist. & Gen. Reg., v. 1, no. 3, July 1900, p. 443)
1752 - **Thomas Carroll** will, June; **1767** - Thomas Bonner md. Margaret Jones 6 May, **Thomas Carroll**, sec. (Will Bk.; Clemens, p. ?; Hathaway, NC Hist. & Gen. Reg., v. 1, no. 2, Apr. 1900, p. 241)
1765 - **Miss Carroll** md. **John Black** 15 August (The North Carolinian Qrtly., Mar. 1957, p. 271; Cumb. Co. Marr. Bds.1808-1868; Clemens, p. 56)

Bath County was established in **1696** from **Albemarle**.

Archdale County was established in **1705** from **Bath County**.

Wickham County was established in **1705** from **Bath County**.

Pamplecough County, now non-existent, was established in **1705** from **Bath County**.

Beaufort County was established in **1712** from **Bath County** and was in Newbern Military Dist. #5 (Carls, First NC Cos., p. 4)
1746/1747 Jan.6/**1752** Apr. 7 - Andrew Simons, **John Carrol** wit. (Grimes, Absts. of NC Wills, p. 339)
1790 - **Three-William Carrolls**, Newbern Dist., 4 Free persons; Fayette Dist.; **1800/1810** - **William Carel**; **1820** - **Two William Carrolls** (Cens. Indx., pp. 29, 42, 51; Cens. Roll 2, pp. 126, 178; Hds./Fams., p. 122) [? - **William Carrel**, Beaufort Co., Rev. War Final Settlements]
1790 - **Alexander Carrol**, taxpayer, Fayette Dist.; **1820** - **Aley Carroll** (Cens. Indx.)
1790 - **Jesse Carol** (b. c1750), Newbern Dist., 3M16+, 1M16-, 4F, 5 sls (Hds./Fams., p. 126
1790 - **John Carrol**, Newbern Dist.; **1800** - **John Carroll**; **1810** - **John Carrel**, Buncombe Twp.; **1820** - **John Carroll** (Cens. Indx., p. 23; Cens., p. 78; Jackson Cens. Indx.) [See Buncombe Co.]
1790 - **James Carroll**; **1800** - **James Carroll**; **1810** - **Jha.? Carel**, Buncombe Twp.; **1820** - **James Carroll** (Cens. Indx.; Cens.; Cens. Indx., p. 29)
1800 - **Thomas Carroll** (Cens.)
1810 - **Dennis Carrel**, Buncombe Twp. (Cens. Indx., pp. 23, 42; Cens., p. 93; Jackson Cens. Indx.) [See Buncombe Co.]
1810 - **Nancy Carrel**, Buncombe Twp. (Cens. Indx., pp. 23, 42; Cens., p. 75; Jackson Cens. Indx.) [See Buncombe Co.]
1810 - **Willis Carrel**, Buncombe Tsp. (Cens.Indx., pp. 23, 42; Cens., p. 93; Jackson Cens. Indx.) [See Buncombe Co.]
1810 - **Mrs. Mary Carrett/Carrell?**, Bertie Twp. (Cens. Indx., p. 50)
1820 - **Benjamin Carroll** (Cens. Indx.)
1820 - **Dwany Carroll** (Cens. Indx.)
1820 - **Margaret Carroll** (Cens. Indx.)
1850 - **William Carroll**, b. 1808?, Mrs. **Arenda Carroll**, b. 1812; ch.: **John**, b. 1835; **Mary**, b. 1838; **James**, b. 1840 (The No. Carolinian Qtrly., Sept.1960, p. 754)
[**1879** - **John Carrow? Will** (Will Bk.1, p. 237; Mitchell Indx.) [See Hyde Co.]

Craven County was established in 1712 from **Bath and Archdale counties**, both non-existent today and originally Albemarle. It is in Newbern Military Dist. #5. (Carls, NC Cos., p. 9)
1744 - **John Carroll & Charles Carroll** witness will of William Prescott, 17 Mar./Sept. Ct.1745; Nov. 19 - To **John Carroll**, ld. gt., 200 acs., 19 Nov. 1744/5 Apr. 1750; - **John Carrol**, pvt., #48, Muster Roll, Capt. Solomon Rews' Co., New Bern, Craven Co., NC, **10 Oct. 1754**; **1756** - **John Carroll** (?); **1790** - **John Carrol**, Newbern Dist. (Grimes, Absts./NC Wills, p. 301; Hathaway, NC Hist. & Gen. Reg., v. 1, no. 3, July 1900, p. 367; NC Ld. Gt. Bk. 1, p. 411, #3724; Will Bk. 4, p. 947; Clark, Col. Sldrs., v. 4, pp. 704, 709; Radcliff, p. 40)
1790 - **James Carrol**, Newbern Dist. (Radcliff, p. 40)
1790 - **William Carroll**, Newbern Dist.; **1800** - **William Carroll**, 1F10-16, 1F26-45, 5sls (00000-01010-05) (Radcliff, p. 40; Cens. Roll 31, p. 247[290], l. 4)
1813 - **Henry Carroll** md. **Polly Jones** 19 Jan. (Burns, NC Gen. Rcds.)
1813 - **Nancy Carroll** md. **Richard Witherington** 1 June (Carroll Cables, July 1995)
1836 - **John B. Carroll** md. **Henrietta B. Smith** 2 Jan. (Carroll Cables, Apr. 1996)
1860 - **Joseph Carroll**, b. **1806** in NC, wife **Mittie**, b. **NC 1809; ch.:**
   1. **Mary F.**, b. **1839**
   2. **Sarah**, b. **1842**
   3. **Elizabeth**, b. **1844**
   4. **Josephine**, b. **1847**
   5. **George H.**, b. **1849** (Cens., FNC26, pt. 2, 4568, p. 71)

Hyde County was established in **1712** from **Bath and Wickham counties.**
1800 - **Henry Carrow; Henry Carrow Sr.; James Carrow; John Carrow Sr.; John Jr., Thomas Carrow (Carrolls?); 1820** - **Henry Carrow**, 102401-02201 (Cens. Indx. Roll 34, pp. 364, 365, 366)

Bertie County was established in **1722** from **Chowan County**. Edenton in1780 and Salisbury Military Dists. #4; County Seat: Windsor, NC. (Carls, First NC Cos., p .5)
1720 - **William Carroll**, 22, resident of Upper Chowan precincts lying west of Chowan River [Old Albemarle], Col. Robt. Patterson's List, 11 Apr.; **1750** - **William Carrell**, wit. ld. sale from Wm. Scott of Southampton Co., VA to Wm. Short of Northampton Co., NC, 21 Sept. 1750 (Ray, Old Albemarle, p. 596; Hofmann, Absts. Dds. Northampton Co., p. 72)
1728 - **John Carroll** of Barbie Precinct, sold to John Chapman, land adjoining George Walton, wits: John Walton, Geo. Walton & Richard Ledbetter; **1732** - Jurat with Alexr. Cotton when last will of **Wm. Martin** paid, Alr? Martin, qualified exr., 13 Feb.; - **John Carroll Jr. & Jno. Carroll** with Wm. Whitfield, Clemt. Hammond, **Wm. Martin**, Edwd. Outlaw, Wm. Whitfield Jr., Alex Cotton ... Thos. Jarnagan ... Henry Jarnagan ... two companies of militia ... **John Carroll** are overseers to clear and keep repair. Adjacent inhabitants of Jacks Swamp, 9 May; - John Jarnagan will proved ... by oaths of **John Carroll**, Berzilla Hewitt, Mr. Hill to pay fees; wit. w/Barzillas Hewitt, Benjn. Hill: Sons: Henry Jernagan, Thomas Jernagan, George Jernagan, David Jernagan, James Jernagan, (Ahosky?) Swamp. Wife: Temperance Jernagan, exrx. with Benj. Hill, 9 May 1732/**1733** Jan. 10; **1733** - **John Carrol** to Sam'l Sursum prod. jurat. Allex. Cotton, A. Cotton D(?) 4011, 15 Aug.; - **John Carrol**, overseers appointed 18 Nov.; **1735** - **John Carell Jr, John Carell Sr**, Alexr (A.) Cotton, wits. for Wm. Martin will, Aug. Ct. 1736, sons:

Richard Martin, Moses Martin, Thomas Martin, John Martin, dau. Mary Martin, wife: Else Martin, exrx., 8 Apr.1735 [**John Carrell Jr.'s dau. md. John Martin**, see Moore County, NC]; **?1736 - John Carroll**, inheritance of 100 acs. in Bertie; 1736 - John Jarnagan, Bertie Precinct, **John Carroll**, wit., 9 May 1736/Aug. Ct ; - Deed to **John Carrill** from Francis Benton, 340 p for 340 acs. on Elm Swamp "... mine by patent bearing date November the twelf (sic) one thousand seven hundred and twenty three...;" wits: William Whitfield, Elizabeth Whitfield, jurat, John Staple, Aug. Ct. 1737. John Wynns, D/C/ Clerk, 13 Nov. 1736; **1737 - John Carroll** of Brunswick Co., VA, from Francis Benton, of Bertie Co., NC, 340 acs. in Bertie Co.; **1738 - John Carroll**, grantor, absolute estate of inheritance, Goochland Co., VA to Samuel Sarsum, 100 acs., Bertie Co.; - **John Carrill** to Samuel Sarsums, 30p for 100 acs. adj. Jonathan Gilbert, **John Carrell**, Alexander Cotton; wits: Wm. Whitfield, Alex. Cottan, jurat, Ann Cottan, Feb. Ct./June 4; **1739 - John Carroll**, Bertie and Edgecomb Cos., on panel of jurymen 1740 Court, Feb. 23/25, 1739; **1739 - John Carol**, Wm. Whitfield Jr., overseer etc. in the room of **John Carol** etc., 13 Nov.; **1741**, 1 May - **John Carrell** from Thos. Linch, both of Bertie (Brunswick) Precinct, lease and release 400 acs, patent to Linch, divided for residue of patent line between VA and NC, 1 May; **1743 - John Carrell**, ld. gt., 300 acs., Northampton Co., NC 25 July; **1755**, 22 Apr. - **John Carroll**, wit. with Thos. Pugh, Geo. Harrell, for Jethro Butler of Barti County to George House, Sr., 4p,6s, 5 acs on Flagg Run adj. to John Warren(?), George House's Old field; Benj. Wynns C/C; **1745/1792 - John Carroll**, grown grandson of Michael Thomas (son of Joseph & Alice Thomas of Bertie Co., NC, brother of Joseph & James Thomas who md. Sarah Barnes) went across the mountains for his grandfather, Michael Thomas', marriage license in 1792 in Albemarle Co.,VA when M. Thomas md. 2nd wife, Elizabeth Staton; 1st wife unknown, but M. Thomas migrated to Albemarle Co., VA in 1745/1748, about the time the co. was carved from Goochland Co., VA and lived there in 1802. His father, Joseph Thomas, died in Bertie Co., NC in 1735. Michael Thomas was sheriff of Albemarle Co., VA. Edward Moore and Menan Mills were his deputies.
(Dds & W. Bk. 1, pp. 144-145; Haun,Ct.Mins., p. 47, item 101, p. 60,item 134, p. 85, item 181-91, p. 95,item 229, p. 100, item 240-123, p. 107,item 259; Feb. Ct.1733, No. 107; Gammon, pp. 30, 40; No. 144, Hathaway, v. 1, no. 3, p. 347, Grimes, pp. 186, 239; Goochland Co.,VA will; Bk. E, p. 144; Dunstan, s.3, p. 23; Bell, pp. 179, 198, 352; VA. Dd. Bk. E, p. 403; Clark, Col. & St. Recds., v. 4, pp. 521, 635; Dd. Bk. 2, p. 79; NC Gen. Soc. Journal, v. 3, 1977, p. 128; Bk. H,, p. 171; Ray, Old Albemarle, I. 331, p. 637) [Could William Standley be **John Carroll's** wife's father? **John Carroll**, b. c1720, d. **1761** in Johnston Co., **NC**, md. **c1740** to ? **Standley** - Indx. NC Ancestors, v. 1, p. 32, #60112; Francis R. Carroll] [The John Carroll above died in Northampton Co., NC in 1760. See his will in Northampton Co.]
1731 - Thomas Kerrall/Carrill accused by William Arrington of taking New Kerb bridle, ordered to pay 6s cash, 9 Nov.; **1732 - Thomas Carrell** to Lay out a road from Bonners Bridge to the Beaverdam Swamp ..., 9/12 May; **1733** May 8 - **Thomas Carrell**, Thos. Jarnagan, Jno. Brown to be added to the company belonging to Jeremiah Maglohon; - Read ... petition of Looseing Swamp Inhabitants praying ..., 8 May; ? on list of Militia company; - To **Thomas Carrell**, deed from John Jernigan of Nansemond Co, VA, 60p for 100 acs on So. side Loosing Swamp; wits: Thos. Jones, **William Standley** and Jacob Jernigan; "Present his Majesty's Justices." Oct. 7 1733/Ct. 1737; **1743 - Thomas Carril**, ld. patent requested, 160 acs., 21 Mar. 1; **1778 - Thos. Carrell** enters 640 acs. in Martin Company border, W corner of Ellis line and on

both sides of Cabbin Branch, 13 Mar.; **1779** - **Thomas Carral's** line ..., 12 July; **1784** - **Thomas Carnel's** corner pine ... Joshua Taylor enters 100 acs., 2 Apr.; **1787** - Joseph Redding enters between **T.(homas) Carnal** ..., 21 Aug.; **1789** - **Thos. Carnal** enters 9 acs. in Martin Co. ..., 16 Oct.; **1793** - John Taylor enters ... border Joshua Taylor's tract, **Ths. Carnal**, 15 Feb./Mar. 21 (Haun, Ct. Mins., p. 35, item 71-36, p. 55, I. 123-62, p. 83, I. 193-97, p. 85, I. 198; Dd. Bk. E, p. 184; Dunstan, s.3, p. 23; Bell, p. 182; Clark, Col./St. Rcds., v. 4, p. ?; Pruitt, p. 56, i. 602, p. 76, i. 825/274, p. 87, p. 92, I. 1013/88, p. 94, I. 1038/119, p. 101, I. 1109/211)
1733 - **Abm. (?Absalum/Absolum) Carnell**, Court Session, 8 May (Haun, p. 83); **?** - **Absolum Carroll**, from Cork, Ireland to Baltimore, MD, moved to Collington Dist., SC where he and wife died leaving five under-aged boys:

    1. **Absalom Carroll Jr.**, b. **1762** in Johnston Co., **NC**, d. **c1828** in Jones Co., **MS**, md. c1800 in SC to **Eleanor Robinson**; **Absolum Carroll Jr.** was given to a Collington Dist. family until age 21, served under George Washington in Rev. War, returned to Collington Dist., SC, md. 4 times, had ch. by 3rd wife: **Susannah Carroll**, b. **1795**, md. **Thomas Williams**;
        ch. by 4th wife, **Ellenor Robinson**:
          1. **Mary** md. **Edward Harper**
          2. **Benjamin** md. **Hulda Harper**
          3. **Harriett** md. **Daniel McDonald**
          4. **Sarah** md. **Samuel Clark**
          5. **John Edward** md. **Mary Strain**
          6. **Martha** md. **Allen Hargrove**
          7. **Moses** died young
          8. **James** md. **Mary Clark**
          9. **Absolum Carroll III**
    2. **Britten Carroll/Britton Carol**, pvt., 10th Regt., Hogg's Co., 20 July **1778** , 9 mos.; moved to **Georgia** after Rev. War, listed on Warren Co., GA censuses of 1820 and 1830
    3. **John Carroll**
    4. **James Carroll**
    5. **Moses Carroll**

(Carroll, *The Heritage of Our Children*; Clark, Col./St. Rcds., v. 16, p. 1034; contributor Francis R. Carroll, code #60112, Index/North Carolina Ancestors, v. 1. Raleigh: NC Gen. Soc., 1981.)
1733 - **Isaac Carill** signed petition of Bertie Precinct for altering seat of government.(Col. Rcds NC, Mins., p. 301)
1748 - **Daniel**, b. 17 Oct. **1748**, wife: **Hannah**, Rev. War Pens. **#R1726**; **1757** - **Daniel Carrol** on "List of Tithables taken by Heny. Hill;" **1784/87** - **Hannah Carroll**, Gloucester Dist., 2M21-, M60+, 4F (No. Carolinian Qtrly., Dec.1958, v. 4, no. 4,p. 501; Radcliff, pp. 3, 36; Rev. War Pen. Rcds.)
1753 - **Charity Carrell**, wit. w/Wm. Tayler, Aaron Ellis to John Cain/Cane and wife Sarah of Edgecombe Co. to Elias Hogges, 75p, 380 acs. on a branch of Rofuis adjacent to **Sam'l Carrin (Cerrin)** at Flagg Branch, 22 Dec./Aug. Ct. 1754, Samuel Ormes C/C (Bk. H, p.103; Bell, p.344)
1759, 25 Mar. - Francis Harrel will (A/25), wife: Mary Harrel; sons: Jacob, John, Francis, William, Shadrick, daus: Mary Averit, Sarah Saulsbury, **Eliz. Carril**; 25 Mar. 17/probate Nov. 1763 (Ct. Mins., I. 256; Gammon, p. 73)
1767 - **John Carroll** sold interest in father's estate along Six Runs to his **brother, Jesse**, and

moved to **Big Coharie** (now McDaniel's Twp., Sampson Co.) (Mary Shell MacArthur English)
1803 - Judeth Carol md. **David White**, 20 Feb., Jacob White, bdsm. (Fouts, p. 104; Carroll Cables, July 1995)
1829 - Mary E. Carrell to Mary F. Fuller (Dd. Bk. CC, p. 261)

<u>Carteret County</u> was established in **1722** from **Craven County.**
1926 - Charles Fisher Carroll md. **Agnes Estelle Robinson**; son **Dr. Charles Fisher Carroll Jr.**, b. 24 June **1926** in Carteret Co., md. 6 Sept **1952 Marilyn Patricia Wolf**; their sons are **Michael Wynne Carroll**, b. 8 Sept. **1953** in Baltimore, MD and **Daniel Charles Carroll**, b. 24 Sept. **1955** in Baltimore, MD (Southern Historical Families, v. 2, p. 274)

<u>Tyrrell County</u>, established in **1729** from **Bertie, Pasquotank, Currituck & Chowan counties**, was in Edenton Military Dist. #4. In 1784-87, the county was in Beaverdam Dist.
1755 - William Currell; **1761** Jan. 22 - John Davis, St. Andrews Parish..., wits:... **Wm. Currell**, examined by... Jos. Montfort; **1762** Dec. 17 - Robert Russell, chain carrier **William Currill**,...; **1784 - Elizabeth Carrel**, Beaverdam Dist., 3F [Wm.'s, d. 1781, **widow & daus. Mary and Jenny?**]; **1786 - Elizabeth Carrel**, 3F; **1789 /1791/1799 - Elizabeth Carrel** (Tax List; Ear. Amer. Series, v. 1, p. 30, v. 3, p. 53; Register, p. 159; Pat. Bk. 12,, pp. 72, 88, Is # 2335, 2413; Hofmann, The Granville Dist...., v. 2, pp. 108, 116), **?sons:**
    1. **1784 - William Carrel**, Beaverdam Dist., 1M21-60+, 3M21-1F [Wm. & Keziah?]; - **William Carrel (Jr.?)**, Beaverdam Dist., 1M21-60, 1M21-60+, 3F all ages; **1786** - William Carrel, Beaverdam Dist., 1M21-60+, 3M21-60+, 1F, John Pope count, pp. 1-2; **?1789/1791/1799** - William Carrel (Tax Lists; Register, p. 159)
    2. **1761 - Thomas Carroll**, exr. Samuel Gavin will, wit. Henry Hollingsworth; **1769 - Thomas Carroll** md. **Elizabeth Stubbs**, 17 Nov.; ?John Walker Jr.; **1784 - Thomas Carrell**, Tax list (Will Bk.; Hathaway, NC Hist. & Gen. Reg., v. 3, no. 1, Jan. 1900, p. 108; Clemens, p. 56; Tax List)
    3. **1784 - Jesse Carrel**, Beaverdam Dist., 1M21-60+; **1786 - Jesse Carrel**, 1M21-60+; **1789/1791/ 1799 - Jesse Carrel** (Tax List; Register, p. 159; Early Amer. Series, v. 1, p. 30)
    4. **1784 - Spencer Carrell** (Tax List)
    5. **1784 - John Carrell** (Tax List)
[Granville Co., NC where **William Carroll** d. in **1781**, was in Beaverdam Dist.; **Elizabeth was his widow and among his sons were: William Jr., Thomas, John, Spencer & Jesse**]
1762 - Mary Currell md. **George Walker** (The No. Carolinian Qtrly., Dec. 1959, p.630)
1763 - Margaret Carrell md. **Friley Jones** (The No.Carolinian Qtrly., Mar. 1958, p.408)
1766 - Sarah Currell, dau. of **Wm. Currell**, md. **John Spruill** (No. Carolinian Qtrly., Dec. 1959, p. 626)

<u>New Hanover County</u> was established in **1729** from **Craven County.**
1749, Apr. 6 - To **John Carroll**, 200 acs., 6 Apr.; **1790 - Two-John Carrolls**, one New Hanover, one in Wilmington (Col. Recds., Dd. Bk. 4, p. 947; Radcliff, p. 40)
1790 - Thomas Carrol, Thomas Carrol Jr., Wilmington; **Early 1800s - Thomas J. Carroll** md. **Isabella Cath. Lamb**, his cousin of New Hanover (Radcliff, p. 40;NCMarr.&Death Rcds.)
1800 - No Carrolls on census.

1803 - Charles Carroll md. Mrs. **Mary Blythe** (NC Marr. and Death Rcds., 1966)
1840 - Mary Quinlivan Carroll, b. 7 Mar. **1840**, d. 4 Dec. **1907** (Oakdale Cem., Wilmington)
1867 - Mary Carroll md. **Dery Greenwood** 28 Aug. (Carroll Cables, July 1995)
1905 - Kenyon Carroll, b. **1820?** in Bladen Co., NC, md. 1st **Mary Jane Blunt** in ?Bladen Co. c**1848**, 2nd **Lucenia Sutton c1885**, d. in New Hanover Co., **1905** (Indx. NC Ancs., p. 25)
1912 - Michael Carroll, b. ?, d. 11 May **1912** (Oakdale Cem., Wilmington, NC)

Bladen County was established in **1734** from **New Hanover County**, Precinct of Bath. In **1749** Bladen was divided with the western part to be Anson Co.
1760 - Joseph Carrel, inquest 18 Nov., d. with no estate, Wilmington, NC (Clark, v. 22, p. 825)
1790 - John Carrol, Wilmington Dist., 1M16+, 1F; **1800 - John Carroll**, Capt. Bryant's Dist., 2M10-, 1M26-45, 2F10-, 1F26-45; **1810 - John Carrol**; **1820 - John Carrol**, 020001-10001 (Hds./Fams., p. 188; Cens. Roll 31, p. 43/158; Cens. Indx., pp. 23, 42, 128; Cens., p. 201)
1790 - Thomas Carrol, Wilmington Dist., 1M16+, 2F; **1810 - Thomas Carroll** (Jackson Cens. Indx.; Cens., p. 163; Hds./Fams., p. 188) [See Sampson Co.]; Son:
    1790 - Thomas Carrol Jr., Wilmington Dist., 2M16+, 2M16-, 4F (Hds./Fams., p. 188)
1800 - Owen Carroll, Capt. Greene's Dist., 2M10-, 1M10-16, 1M26-45, 1F10-, 1F10-16, 1F26-45; (21010-110100-00); **1810 - Owen Carrol**; **1855 - Owen Carroll**, b. **1798**, d. 25 July **1855**, age 57 yrs., b. Allen Cemetery, northwestern Bladen Co.; wife, **Ruth Carroll**, b. 9 Sept. **1802**, d. 9 Sept. **1884**, age 82 yrs.; ch.:
    1. **Kenyon Carroll**, b. in Bladen Co. **c1820**, md. 1st **Mary Jane Blunt** in ?Bladen Co. c**1848**, 2nd **Lucenia Sutton** in Bladen Co. **c1885**, d. in New Hanover Co., NC in **1905**
    2. **Prudie V. Carroll**, dau. of **Owen & Ruth Carroll**, b. 23 Dec. **1834**, d. 11 July **1911**, b. Allen-Bethel Ch. Cem., Dublin, NC (Cens. Roll 31, p. 130; Cens. Indx., pp. 23, 42; Jackson Cens. Indx.; Cens., p. 197; Cems. Bladen Co., NC, v. 3, pp. 18, 19; Indx. NC Ancs., p. 25; WPA Indx., pre-1914)
Others b. in **Allen Cemetery**:
    Sarah J. Carroll, b. 26 Oct. **1843**, d. 16 Mar. **1927**
    Emma Odom Carroll, b. 14 June **1868**, d. 15 June **1883**
    Ethel Ann Carroll, b. 14 Jan. **1879**, d. 16 Apr. **1929**
    Owen Carroll, b. 8 June **1870**, 24 Jan. **1930**
1826 - Nathan(iel) Carroll, Co. K, 40th Reg. CSA, b. 10 Jan. **1826**, d. 18 Nov. **1892**, b. Allen-Bethel Ch. Cem., Dublin, NC (WPA Indx., pre-1914; Cems.Bladen Co., NC, v. 3, pp. 18-19)
    Nathan B. Carroll, b. 6 May **1875**, d. 16 July **1941**
    Vira King, wife of **Nathan B. Carroll**, b. 30 Oct. **1892**, d. 30 Apr. **1942**
    Elizabeth Carroll, b. 15 Oct. **1843**, d. 14 Feb. **1926**
    Sarah Carroll, b. 20 Jan. **1878**, d. 6 Aug. **1944**
    Infant dau. of Ballard & Pauline Carroll, b.&d. 16 Jan. **1950**
    Frank J. Carroll, b. 3 Aug. **1929**, d. 9 Feb. **1931**
    Coy Frank Carroll, b. 25 Feb. **1873**, d. 10 Nov. **1959**, wife, **Henrietta Bullard**, b. 5 July **1882**, d. 9 Jan. **1970**
    Wade S. Carroll, son of **C. F. and Etta Carroll**, b. **1922**, d. **1923**
    Margaret Carroll, wife of **Edward Thos. Garner**, b. **1919**-d.?

Charles F. Carroll, b. 12 Oct. **1889**, d. 13 Oct. **1889**, b. **W. D. King Cemetery**
1875 - **M. M. Carroll**, b. 25 Apr. **1875**, d. 14 Oct. **1902**, Allen-Bethel Ch. Cem., Dublin (Cems. of Bladen Co., NC, v. 3, p. 29)
Buried in **Carroll Cemetery** in Dublin area of Bethel community (Cems. Bladen Co., NC, v. 3, p. 29): **Joseph Washington Carroll**, b. 23 Jan. **1867**, d. 7 Aug. **1949**
    Ida A. Allen, wife of **Joseph W. Carroll**, b. 3 Dec. **1873**, d. 14 Oct. **1926**
    Infant of J. W. & Ida Carroll, no dates
    Infant of J. W. & Ida Carroll, no dates
    Hampton Carroll, son of **J. W. & Ida Carroll**, b. 31 Dec. **1905**, d. 24 Apr. **1906**
    Sam Wallace Carroll, son of **Sam & Cora L. Carroll**, b. 15 Mar. **1941**, d. 3 Mar. **1942**
    Betty Smith Carroll, wife of **Elijah Carroll**, b. **1854**, d. **1890**; **Pete Carroll**, b. **1873**, d. **1939**, b.Pinefield Family Cemetery, NW corner of Co.(Cems. Bladen Co., NC, v. 3, p. 50)
Buried in Bladen Union Baptist Ch. Cem., St. Pauls, NC, NW corner of Co. (Cems. Bladen Co., NC, v. 3, p. 53):
    Emma Carroll, wife of **C. L. Johnson**, b. 13 Dec. **1867**, d. 23 Aug. **1921**
    Albert W. Carroll, b. 21 Jan. **1864**, d. 23 Oct. **1920**; **Matilda Carroll**, b. **?**, d. 7 Feb. **1891**, wife of **A. W. Carroll**, b. in Carvers Creek Cem., Council, NC (WPA Indx., pre1914 graves)
    Robert N. Carroll, b. 11 Nov. **1874**, d. 27 May **1931**
    Julia Ann Carroll, wife of **Robert N. Carroll**, b. 15 Dec., **1877**, d. 18 Nov. **1959**
    Elizabeth Anne Carroll, wife of **John H. Carroll**, b. 12 May **1844**, d. 4 Oct. **1917**
    John H. Carroll, b. 17 Sept. **1834**, d. 17 Jan. **1901**
    Minnie H. Carroll, b. 17 Sept. **1879**, d. 22 July **1919**
    Daniel Curtis Carroll, b. 26 Aug. **1868**, d. 12 Nov. **1935**
    Mary C. Carroll, 23 Oct. **1862**, d. **1907**
Buried J.S. Melvin Cemetery, aka Robert Melvin Cem, 2.6 mi. W. of Ammon behind J. S. Melvin home:
"To the Memory of An Affectionate wife By a Devoted Husband, **Mrs. A. J. Carroll**, d. 1 Nov. **1869**, aged 63 yrs. 10 mos. 27 days;" **Mrs. A. J. Carroll**, b. 1 Nov. **1806**, d. 1 Nov. **1869**, buried in Edgar Melvin Cem., Roseboro, NC;(Cems. Bladen Co., NC, v. 3, p. 112; WPA Indx., Pre-1914 graves)
Buried in Shiloh Methodist Ch. Cem., Columbus Co. just below Bladen line 0.2 mi. W. intersect of Hwy 211 & SR 1704 (Cems. Bladen Co., NC, v. 3, p. 79):
    Arthur Haddock Carroll, b. 12 Sept. **1890**, d. 22 Jan. **1918**
    Margaret R. Carroll, wife of **A. W. Carroll**, b. 5 July **1865**, d. 7 Feb. **1924**
    Arthur Washington Carroll, b. 28 Jan. **1852**, d. 16 Mar. **1936**
    Major J. Carroll, b. 1 Dec. **1851**, d. 15 July **1932** (v. 3, p. 83)
Buried in Center Road Baptist Ch. Cemetery, SW Dublin between Hwy 131 & 410 on SR #1100 (Cems. Bladen Co., NC, v. 1, pp. 187):
    John D. T. Carroll, b. 4 July **1860**, d. 23 May **1938**
    Harriet L. Carroll, b. 28 Oct. **1858**, d. 15 Mar. **1925**
    Ruth Carroll, wife of **Lester Ward**, b. 14 May **1894**, d. 17 Dec. **1959**
    Margaret Jane Carroll, b. 12 Dec. **1883**, d. 21 May **1967**

Infant, son of O. J. & Atha Carroll, b.&d. 20 Sept. 1928
Ottie J. Carroll, b. 10 Apr. 1885, d. 23 Apr. 1980
Buried in Old Pait Cem., Center Roads Community (Cems. Bladen Co., NC, v. 1, p. 197):
William O. Carroll, b. 12 Jan. 1863, d. 29 June 1942
Minnie May Carroll, 20 Jan. 1878, d. 12 Mar 1954
Marshall Dudley Carroll, b. 9 Oct. 1898, d. 18 June 1972
C. H. Carroll, b. 9 May 1908, d. 1909
Dicie Kinlaw Carroll, b. 23 June 1904, d. 14 Jan. 1983
Infants, daus. of Dicie & M. D. Carroll, b.& d. 1920
1803 Apr. - **Charles Carroll**, Wilmington, md. **Mrs. Mary Blythe** (Marr. Notice)
1810 - **Manson Carrol** (Jackson Cens. Indx., Cens., p. 201) [See Rutherford Co.
1810 - **Rachel Carrole** (Cens. Indx., p. 23; Jackson Cens. Indx.; Cens., p. 202)
1810 - **Sarah Carroll** (Jackson Cens. Indx.; Cens., p. 156)
1834 - **John H. Carroll**, b. 17 Sept. 1834, d. 17 Jan. 1901, b. Bladen Union Cem., St. Pauls, NC
(1834 - **John H. Carroll** - 1891 - **Matilda Carroll**, WPA Indx., pre-1914)
1883 - **Walter Carroll**, b. 2 June 1883, d. 11 Apr. 1887, Carven Creek Cem., Council, NC
[Index of North Carolina Ancestors, v. 2, p. 25, gives same family Code **#28767** to **Andrew Albert Carroll/Carell/Carrel**, b. **1892** in Columbus Co., NC, d. **1943** in TX, md. **1911** in Colb. Co. to #1 **Della Register**, in **1919** #2 **Omer Gambill** in NY (#28767); and to **John Richard Carroll/Carell/Carrel**, b. **1854** in Bladen Co., d. **1938** in Colb. Co., md. **1881** in ?Columbus Co. #1 **Leanna Elizabeth Jones**, #2 **Senie R. Clewis** in **1915** in Columbus Co. (#28767)]

<u>Onslow County</u> was established in **1734** from **New Hanover County**.
1790 - **William Carroll**, Wilmington Dist., 4FP (Cens. Indx., p. 197)
1803 - **Mr. Charles Carral**, merchant, md. **Mrs. Mary Blythe**, Wilmington Dist., recorded Monday, 2 May; 1810 - **Charles Carral** (NC Marr. & Death Notices; Neal, p. 85; Indx., p. 42; Cens., p. 777; Jackson Cens. Indx.; Cens., p. 105) [John & Thomas Walton in this county.]

<u>Edgecombe County</u>, in Halifax Military Dist. in 1780, was established in **1741** from **Bertie County**. No **Carroll** wills prior to 1800 in this county (Courthouse Recds. Office)
1739 - **John Carroll** on jury list for 1740 court, 15 Feb.; **1748** Mar.25-16 Apr. - **William & John Carrol**, Granville Dist., chain carriers, surveyor James Alston, patent granted to James Cain, 260 acs on N. side of Tar River, joining mouth of a Great Branch and sd. river, 25 March 1749; wits.: W. Churton, Benj. Wynns (Pat. Bk 2, p.148, I. #630; Clark, Col. Recds., v.4, p. 521)
1742/43, Mar. 21 - **Thomas Carrell**, Edenton, 160-ac. Ld. Pat. Petition, on S. side of Conehoe, joining marsh and swamp; returned; **1750s** - **Thomas Carrell**, #10 on list of soldiers in Capt. Elisha Williams' Co., NC Militia ; **1755** - sold 160 acs; **1761** Feb. 28/3 Nov. - **Thomas Carrill**, Joseph Moore, 600 acs, joining John Norriss Jr., John Rial, Halifax Co. line, Col. James Conner, Michael Dorman, Deep Creek, **Thomas Carrill** & Thomas Norflitt; Or:/Signed: Joseph Moore; Wits: Edward Hall, Thos. Cavenah, Surveyed: 28 Feb.; Sec.: Thos. Downing, John Norriss; Surveyor: W. Haywood (Hofmann, pp. 98, 166; Bk. 5, p. 108, #2343; Clark, Col. Recds., v. 4,5., pp. 627, 674; Dd. Bk., p. 297; Pat. Bk 2, p. 224, Item #943); **?son:**
    1. **1750s** - **Thomas Carrell Jr.**, #11, Capt. Elisha Williams' Co., NC Militia (Clark, Col. Sldrs. ..., p. 674)

1748 Mar.25-16 Apr. - **William & John Carrol**, Granville Dist., chain carriers, surveyor James Alston, patent granted to James Cain, 260 acs on N. side of Tar River, joining mouth of a Great Branch and sd. river, 25 March 1749; wits.: W. Churton, Benj. Wynns; **1751** - **William Carrill**, sold 380 acs. bght in 1748 (Pat. Bk 2, p. 148, Item #630; Hofmann, Absts. ... 1748-1763, p. 66; Dd. Bk., p. 88)
1754 - **James Carrol**, Wallace/Wallis Jones wit. Hardy Cain will; 21 Dec./May 1755, wife Rachel; daus. Isobel & Peurity Cain, ld. in Johnston Co., dau. Sarah Cain, bro. James Cain (Williams & Griffin, Abst/wills, p. 63; Hathaway, NC Hist. & Gen. Reg., v. 1, no. 2, Apr. 1900, p.188)
1789 Feb. 2 Feb.Ct. - **John Curl/Curle** inventory; George Brownrigg, adm.; acct. of sale by Jacob Battle; acct. current w/exr. May Ct. 1791 sheriff; **1800** - **John Carrell** 2M10-, 1M10-16, 1M45+ 1F10-, 1F10-16, 1F45+ (21001-11001-00) (Watson, Est. Rcds., p.65; Census Roll 30, p. 190)
1790 - **Michael Carroll**, Halifax Dist. (Cens. Indx., p. 57) **[Did not find on cens.)**
1800 - No **Carroll** wills prior to 1800 in Edgecombe Co. (Courthouse Rcds. Office)
1811 Jan.3/May Ct. 1813 - **Willis Curl** inventory by Willie Bunn, exr.; acct. of sales 17 Jan./29 Aug. **1812**; **Sarah Curl**, the widow principal buyer and **Redmun Curl**; **1813** May Ct. - Leg. representatives: **Sarah Curl, widow; Redmon Curl, Caty Curl, Charity Curl, Seleter Curl, Patsy Curl**, 7 Aug.-Aug.Ct.1813; **c1808** - **Charity Curle**, dau. of **Willis Curle**, md. **Meedy Williford** (Watson, p. 65; Wms./Griffin, Marrs., p. 286); **ch:**
    1. **Redmun**, 2. **Caty**, 3. **Charity** md. **Meedy Williford**, 4. **Seleter**, 5. **Patsy**
1820 - **Sterling/Starling Carrol** (Cens. Indx. Roll 30, pp. 222, 223)

<u>**Northampton County**</u> was established in **1741** from **Bertie County** and in the Halifax Military Dist. in 1780.
1733 - **John Carroll**, wit. to John Jernagan will, Bertie Precinct, Ct.10 Jan.-Feb., wife Temperance Jernagan, exrx.; sons: Thomas, George, David, James; exr. Benj. Hill, other wits.: Barzilla Hewitt, Benj. Hill, Rt. Forster, CC; **1739**, - **John Carrell (Sr.)**, 300-ac. gt. by patent 21 Nov. 1739/25 July 1743; **John Carroll**, on panel of jurymen for Bertie & Edgecomb cos., 25 Feb.; **1742** - NC Taxpayer; **1743** - **John Carrell (Sr.) & (his brother) Millbre Carrell** of Northampton Co. sold to Joshua Cook of Charles City Co., VA 24 Nov. 1743 for 36p current money of VA, the tract of land and Plantation on Lizard Creek, joining the creek, all buildings, containing 300 acres granted by patent to **John Carrell** bearing date of 21 Nov. **1739**, **John Carrell** (Seal), **Millbre Carrell** (Seal), wits.: William Person, Charles Jones; Feb. Court 1743, F. W.(or J.) Edwards, Co. Clerk; **John Carrell & Millbre Carrell**, dd. to Joshua Cook of Charles City Co., VA, beginning on lower side of Lizard Creek, N60 degrees, E260 poles, W220, S60, being tract of land and plantation, 300 acs., gtd. to **John Carrell** 21 Nov. 1739, Feb. Ct. 1743, F. W. Edwards, CC; **1744** - **John Carroll** wit'd will of Wm. Prescott of Craven Co., 17 Mar. 1744-Sept. Ct. 1745, wife Mary, exrx.; sons: Moses, William, Richard, Job, dau. Mary, gddau. Elizabeth Prescott; other wits.: Daniel Conerly, Aaron Wood, Jno. Rice, CC; **1744**, Nov. 19 - Land grant of 200 acs. dd. to **John Carroll**; **1745**, Sept. 28 - ld. gt., 150 acs. on the N. easterly side of Lizard creek, joining his own lower corner, Francis Merrick's Mill, the Mill Pond and creek; **1746** - **John Carrol** wit'd. will of Andrew Simons of Beaufort Co., Beaverdam ld., 6 Jan. 1746-47/7 Apr. 1752, wife & exrx. Mary Simons w/exr. John Odeon; sons: William,

Thomas, John, Joshua, George, Levi; wits.: Robt. Cutler, Edward Byner, proven before Gab. Johnston at Bath Town; **1748** - **John Carroll** of Brunswick Co., VA, sold part of ld. gt. to **John Carrell** 28 Sept.1744, to Francis Myrick Sr. of Northampton Co. 24 Feb. 1748, 5p current money of VA, 150 acs on NE side of Lizard Creek, E40 poles, N80, E180, S10, E154, S80, W150 poles, a little below F. Myrick's mill and up various courses of mill pond & creek to the first station . . . with all houses and buildings, joining other lds. of **J. Carrell** and creek; wits. John Gillum, Anne Gillum, George Watts; Feb. Ct., 1748, J. Edwards, CC; **1751** Jan. 26 - Joshua Cook of Northampton Co. to Christopher Robertson of Johnston Co., 55p VA money, 300 acs. joining Lizzard Creek, all buildings etc. as by patent to **John Carrell** 21 Nov. 1739; wits.: Arthur Harris, Abraham Johnson, William Johnson, Susannah Harris, May Ct. 1751, J. Edwards, CC; **1756** - Charles Kimball of Granville Co., NC to **John Carrell** of Northampton Co., 17p10s VA money, 348 acs. joining James Hunt, Douglass and Robertson, all houses, orchards, fences etc; wits: Arthur Harris, John Irby, Benjamin Harris, Aug. 21/Feb. Ct. 1757, J. Edwards, CC; **1757** - **John Carrell, Sr.** of Northampton Co. **to John Carrell Jr.** of Northampton Co., 25 Aug. 1757 for 50p current VA money, 100 acres in Northampton Co., beg. at a Gum in the patent line hence along line of marked trees to a Red Oak at Kimbal's Road, then down the road to a red oak near Forsters Path, then along line of marked trees to Edward Robertson line back along line of marked trees to patent line. **John Carroll** (Seal) Aug. Ct. 1757, wits.: Thomas Green, Walter Clark, Arthyr Horry/Harris, J. Edwards, CC ; **John Carroll Sr.** of Northampton Co. **to Sterling Carroll** of Northampton Co., 25 Aug. 1757, 50p current VA money, 100 acres lying and being in the co. . . . beg. at a Red Oak tree on **John Carroll** line at the back of Dugg? frow? Breach? (?Pigg Pen Branch) to the county line to Douglass line then along the road back to the point of beg. **John Carroll** (Seal); wits: Thomas Green, Walter Clark/Walkers Clerk, Arthyr Horry/Art Harris, Aug. Ct. 1757; **John Carroll Sr.** sold ld. to James Cary Jr.; **1758** - Christopher Robinson of Granville Co. to Robert Taylor of Northampton Co., 22 May, 110p VA money, 300 acs. on Lizard Creek, all buildings etc as by patent of **John Correll** 21 Nov. 1739; wits.: William Johnson, John Lynch, Peter Kimball, July Ct. 1758, J. Edwrds, CC ; **1759** - **John Carroll (Sr.) will** dated 20 July 1759, proved Jan. Court 1760, **Wife unnamed**; **Ch: John Carroll Jr., Sterling Carroll, Charles Carroll, Thomas Carroll, daus. Agnes Jones, Betty Carroll, Tabitha Carroll, Sarah Carroll, Marthew Carroll (Martha)**; 7 slaves; Wits: James Linch, **Thomas Carroll**, John Linch, Clerk:

JOHN CARROLL WILL - 1760
Northampton Co., NC
Will Book I, Pp. 1-2

In the name of God amen. According to the Computation of the Church of Great Britain, I **John Carroll** being of perfect memory & the membrance praised be God Do make & ordain this my last Will & Testament in manner & form following.

First I bequeath my soul into the hands of Almighty God my maker hoping thus the meritorious Death & pasion (?,sic) of Jesus Christ my only saviour & redeemer to receive for pardon and forgiveness of all my sins; and ask for my Body to be Buried in a Christian manner at the discretion of my Executor hereafter nominated.

Item: I give unto my **son John** a negro Girl named Jam and two cows and calves.

Item: I give to my **son Sterling** a negro Boy named Nick two cows & calves, a pewter dish, & Basin two plates & a middle size ? pot, a bed & furniture

Item: I give to my **son Charles** & Moses Myrick a negro named Bob likewise a plantation joining James River both to be sold at the death of his mother or when he comes of age at publick auction; Likewise I give to my **son Charles** an Entry of Land joining William Huff: If my **son Charles** should die without heir Deem that his part may be equally divided between the rest of my Children

Item: I give my **son Thomas** the plantation wherein I now live & a negro Girl Judah desiring that it may remain in his mothers possession until her death or marriage

Item: I give to my **Daughter Agnes Jones** a Negro Girl named Ruth?, upon her husband's being an equal part with my three sons in paying my debts which may be twenty pound

Item: I give to my **Daughter Betty** a negro Girl named Nan to her and her heirs forever.

Item: I Lend to my **loving wife** a negro woman named Hannah during her natural life then to return to my **son Charles** I likewise give to my Loving Wife the Bed I now lie in & a horse and side saddle.

Item: I deem that the (issue?) of Judah may go to my three **Daughters Tabitha, Sarah & Marthew** (Martha) and five shillings Cash a piece, If she should have over three children the remainder to my **son Thomas**.

Item: I likewise appoint my **loving Wife** and my two **sons John and Sterling** Executors of this my last Will and Testament. In witness whereof I have hereunto set my hand & seal this **20th day of July Anno Dom 1759**; James Linch, John Linch, John Hunnicut; N'Hampton County ? **John Carroll** & a seal. **Proved in January Court 1760**

The preceeding Will of **John Carrell** Deceased was exh'd into Court & proved on the oath John Linch & Jno Hunicut, two of the subscribing witnesses, then to at the same time **John Carrell Sterling Carrell** were qualified Executors, thereof which a motion was ordered to be certified; Teste J Edwards, Clerk (Grimes, pp. 186, 301, 339; Dd. Bks.1 & 2, 1741-59, v. 1, p. 104; Clark, v. 4, pp. 521, 635; Radcliff, p. 36; Dd. Bk.1, p. 104, Box18; Col. Recds. Bk. 4, p. 947; Hofmann, pp. 21, 60, 76, 128, 134, 143, 235; NC Ld. Gts. Bk.1, p. 342, #3391; Dd. Bk. 1, pp. 370, 480; Dd. Bk. 2, p. 361, 401, 402, Box 18, 481; Cunningham, p. 29; Will Bk. 1, p. 1); **Ch.**:

   1. **John**

   2. **1760 - Sterling Carrell** to Arthur Atkins, 100 acs. from **John Carrell Jr.**'s line to branch, along Douglass line to Kimball's road, 28 Oct. 1760, signed: Hartwell Hunnicutt, **John Carrell**, Agnes Lynch, Nov. Ct. 1760; **1771 Oct. 16/Dec. 2, 1772** - **Sterling Carrell** sold land to Owen Myrick of Brunswick Co., VA, 80p current VA money, wits.: Sam Thompson, Thomas Reid (Dd. Bk. 3, p. 55; Dd. Bk. 5, p. 212) [Copies of dds from **Sterling Carrell** to Arthur Atkins, Dd. Bk.3, p. 55; to Owen Myrick, Dd. Bk. 5, p. 212; from **John Carrell** to Charles Kimball, Feb. 1757, Dd. Bk. 2, p. 361 can be obtained from Frank D. Gatton, Asst. Rcds. Adm., Div. of Archives & History, 109 East Jones St., Raleigh, NC 27611. [Name & address may be changed.]

   3. **1743 - Thomas Carril**, ld. patent applied for, 160 acs., 21 Mar. (Clark, v. 4, p. 627)

   4. **Charles,** underage in 1760

   5. **Agnes** md. ? **Jones**

   6. **Betty**

   7. **Tabitha**

   8. **Sarah**

   9. **Martha**

[North Carolina Ancestors, V. 2, p. 25 gives the same family code, #28500, to the following: **Milbrough Carroll**, b. c1710, ?VA, d. 1773 in ?Bute Co. (Will); **Sterling Carroll**, b. **1769**, ?**VA**, d. **1850** in Warren Co., md. twice, **1832** in Moore Co. to #2 **Elizabeth R. Moore**; **Thomas Carroll**, b. c**1745**, ?**VA**, d. **1813** Warren Co., md. **Rebecca**; **Sterling Carroll**, b. **1806** in Chatham Co., d. **1881** in TN, md. **1827** Chatham Co. **Winnie Tilman** (#60738); **Thomas Sterling Carroll** b. **1836** in Warren Co., d. **1916** in Wake Co., lived in Franklin Co., md. **1857** in Franklin Co. to **Minerva Viteria Green**]
1750 - William Scott of Southampton Co., VA to William Short of Northampton Co., 21 Sept. 1750, 40p, 640 acs. on N. side of Roanoak river and W. side of Occoneeche swamp . . . his brother Francis Scott, deceased of Williamsburg, VA, valued . . . by James Washington, Esq., sheriff of Northampton Co.; wits: Thomas Barrett, James Parram, **Daniel Connell?**, **William Carrell**, Nov. Ct., J. Edwards, CC (Dd. Bk. 1, p. 455; Hofmann, p. 72)
1753 Mar.29/Nov.Ct.1753 - David Douglass will, wife Elizabeth and sons William & John, exrs.; **daus.: Molley/Martha Carrill, Elizabeth Harwell, Susanah Douglass; gd.dau.: Elizabeth Carrol**, wits.: Christmas Ray & John Douglas; I. Edwards, CC (Grimes, Absts. NC Wills, p.101; Hathaway, NC Hist.& Gen. Reg., v. 1, no. 2, Apr. 1900, p. 198) [? - **Mrs. Mollie Carroll** & daus., **Elizabeth Douglas Carrill** & **Elizabeth Douglas Harwell** & **Neal Carroll** of Kent Co., MD removed to North Carolina (Source: ?]
1790 - **John Carroll**, Halifax Dist.; Army Accts. paid by John Armstrong (NC Army Accts., v. 2, Bk. AA, pp. 1-44; Radcliff, DAR Roster, p. 191)
1792-1816 - **No Carrolls** found in *Records of Estates, Northampton County, North Carolina*, v. 2, by David B. Gammon, 1988. **1800** - **No Carrolls** in county (1800 Cens.)
1911 May 4 - **O.S. Carroll** sold land to S. J. Kee (Tr) (Dd. Bk. 142, p. 406)
[Copies of deeds may be obtained from: Division of Archives & History, Attn: Search Room, 109 East Jones St., Raleigh, NC 27611]

Granville County, in Hillsboro Military Dist. #2, was established in **1746** from **Edgecombe County**. The county seat is Oxford, NC. (Carls,1st NC Cos, p. 6)
"In 1746, two years after Earl Granville came into sole possession of his slice of the American colonies, our county was established and named after him. It extended to present Warren on the east and present Caswell on the west, both included . . ." — F. B. Hays.
In **1746**, an act . . . authorizing a division of Edgecombe County in two parts, the upper to be called the Parish of Granville and the lower the Parish of St. John's, embracing a large territory containing present Warren and Franklin counties on the East and extending to the Pacific Ocean on the West. ... In 1769 an act ... to divide Granville into two counties, the Parish of Granville to be called Granville County, the Parish of St. John's as Bute County. (Mrs. E. G. Moss) [A notation states: A good deal of the above is inaccurate and misleading.]
1746/55 - **William Carroll, Fairfax Co., VA**, Papist in Lower Parish, b. c1720 in **VA**, d. **1781** in Granville Co., NC, md. c**1740** in VA **Elizabeth ?** (**Elizabeth ?Jewell** - see Goochland Co., VA; dau. Ann b. c1742 in Fairfax Co.,VA or **Elizabeth Raines**, see John Raines below); **1755** - **William Carol**, taxpayer; ?**1764** - James Moore of Granville Co. pd. 10s sterling, quit rents, etc for an Earl Granville gt. of 650 acs in parish of _____ in Gran. Co. on N. side of Tar River adj. to Haris, **Carrol** & the Spring Branch; Thomas Child Esq. was Earl Granville's agent, wits. Wm. Churton. J. Montfort, 1 Aug. 1762; proved by Joseph Montfort Esq., Halifax, 1 Sept. 1764,

Mont. Elbeck, A.J.; rcdd. 28 Sept. 1764, Sugan Johnson, P.R.; **1767** - **William Carrill**, Bute Co. planter, bght. 200 acs. on ss of Tar River in Granville Co., adj. to Hefford, pt. of tract bght. from Samuel Benton, Esq., from Wm. Chavis Sr. of Gran. Co. 18 Mar. for 10p VA money, wits. John Nevill, Geo. Stephenson, David Davis, delivered to **Wm. Carrell** 9 May **1770**; **1771** - taxpayer; **1772** - **William Carrol Sr.**; **1777** - **William Carroll**; **1780** - **William Carril** of Franklin Co. bght. 240 acs., 2000p, bdd. by James Weathers; dds. from Richard Bradford to John Huskey Sr. to John Huskey Jr. to Thomas Bridges to **William Carrill**, 27 May; **William Carrill** of Franklin Co., bght. ld. 27 May in Granville Co. from Thos. Bridges; **1781** - **William Carroll Sr.** will dated 26 Oct. 1781: a planter of Granville Co., d. **1782**; wife, **Elizabeth** 1 featherbed & furniture, 240 acs. bght. from Thomas Bridges; ch.: **Thomas**, 5p cash; **William Jr.**, equal part; **John**, equal part; **Spencer**, equal part; **Jesse**, plantation bght. from Thomas Bridges after he reaches 21 yrs. of age, saddle, 1 featherbed & furniture; **Anne Champion**, 5p cash; **Elizabeth Zarrard**, equal part; **Kezia Harp**, 5p cash; **Jenny**, 1 feather bed & furniture; **and Mary**, youngest dau., after she comes 18 yrs. of age or marries, 1 featherbed & furniture; exrs. wife **Elizabeth & son John**; bdsm. **John Carrel**, Bird Driver; wits. Bennet Searcy, John Pope Esq. & **William Carrol Jr.** ; **1782** - **Wm. Carroll**, taxpayer; **1785** - **Elizabeth Carroll**, taxpayer; **1786** - **Elizabeth Carrel**, Beaverdam Dist., 3F all ages; **1742** - **Ann(e) Carroll**, b. c1742/46 in Fairfax Co., VA?, md. **John Champion**, ch.: **Allen Champion**; ? - **Elizabeth Carroll** md. ? **Zarrard**; ? - **Kesia Carroll** md. ? **Harp** (Indx. NC Ancestors, p. 32; #17080; Early Amer. Series, v. 3, p. 38; Ratcliff, pp. 34, 36; Dd. Bk. A, p. 18; Kerr, Warren Co. Rcds., v. 2, pp. 3, 62; Dd. Bk. 3, p. 504; Will Bk.1, pp. 355, 356, 357; Dd. Bk. O, p. 99; Register, p. 159; Gwynn, p. 50); **Ch.:**

   1. **Anne**, born **1742** in Fairfax Co., VA, md. **John Champion**, son:
      1. **Allen Champion**
   2. **1771** - **Thomas Carroll**, taxpayer; wife, ?, son **Charles**; **1786** - taxpayer, Fork Creek Dist.; **?1789/1791/ 1799** - **Thomas Carroll**; **1796** - on tax list (NC Cens. Indx., NC Gen., Fall 1969, pp. 2408-9; Ear. Amer. Series, v. 1, p. 30)
   3. **William Carrill (Jr.)**, b. c1752 in Halifax Co., VA, d. **183?** in TN, md. **Keziah** ?, Sept. **1777**; **1777**, May Court - John Keziah bght. part of **William Sr.'s?** est.; **1781** - **William Carroll**, pvt., Hall's Co., out 10 Nov. 1782; **178?** - Army accts., NC Line, #2202, **William Carrell**, 19p7s received by John Sheppard in Warrenton; **1784** - **William Carroll**, taxpayer; **1785** - **Wm. Carroll**, taxpayer; Col. Martin Armstrong required to survey for **William Carroll**, NC ld. gt. in TN, 640 acs. within ... lands reserved by law for offrs. & sldrs. of NC Continental Line 23 Apr. 1785, #1754, Env. #2044, Davidson Co., TN, John Sheppard, signed: John Durham & **John Carrol**; to heirs **John, Charles & Nancy Sheppard**, 10 Sept. 1785, surveyed 20 Apr. 1786; **1786** - **William Carrel**, Beaverdam Dist., 1M21-60, 1F21-/60+, 1F, John Pope list; **1791** May 1 - in **Caswell Co., NC** ; moved to TN; **1787** - **William Carroll**; **1790** - **William Carril** from Thos. Bridge; **1793** - **William Carroll**, 640 acs. on waters of west fork of Mill Creek in Davidson Co., TN, ld. gt. #2064, 2 May 1793, heir: **John, his son**, assigned to **Nancy Sheppard**, his dau.; ? - **William Carroll** & Barnard Carter from NC were among A Revolutionary (War) Soldiers who flocked to Roane Co. (TN) in the Early Days around the Southwest Point ... as soon as lands there were available under various Indian treaties; **1833** - **Wm. Carroll**, pvt., pensioned 4 Mar. 1831, served in NC Line, living in Roane Co., TN #W6640; ? ch.: **Jess**, b. **1778**; **John**, b. **1779**; **Betsy** md. ? **Dover**, b. **1780**; **Elijah**, b. **1781**; **Henry**, b. **1783**; **Charles** (may be eldest who remained in Granville Co); **Nancy**, b. **1785**, md. ? **Dover**; **1850** - **Keziah Carroll**, widow of

William Carroll claimed he served in SC; his pension suspended for lack of proof of marriage and service by US Senate Resolution, 16 Sept. 1850 (NC St. Rcds., v. 2, pp. 370-380, v. 16; Clark, v. 17, p. 201, v. 22, p. 60; NC Cens. Indx.; Dd. Indx.; Ray, Tenn. Cousins, p. 453; Register, p. 159; Rev. War Pens. Appl. Rcds.; DAR Rev. War Rcds., p. 197, #306; Saunders, v. 22, p. 60; NC GT./TN; Radcliff, p. 36) [Did **Nancy** marry 1st **John Shepard** & later ? **Dover**?]; **Ch.:**
    1. **Jesse**, b. **1778**
    2. **John**, b. **1779**
    3. **Betty**, b. **1780**, md. **? Dover**
    4. **Elijah**, b. **1781**
    5. **Henry**, b. **1783**
    6. **Charles**, b. **?**; **1806** - **Charles Carral**; **1810** - **Charles Carroll/Carral**; **1820** - **Charles Carroll** (Early Amer. Series, v. 3, p. 38; Cens. Indx., pp. 23, 38, 42, 204; Cens. pp. 16, 658) [Wm. Jr.'s son?]
    7. **Nancy**, b. **1785**, md. **? Dover**
    4. **John** md. **Rebecca Huskey**; (Lost early info. on John, see sources below to retrieve) acs. on Horse Creek from John Champion, 27 Dec.; **1795** - **John Carroll** of Granville Co. sold ld. to Thomas Griffith/Griffin of Brunswick Co., VA , 177 acs. for 180p,10s, 14 Oct.; **1796** - on tax list, bght. 50 acs. from Thos. Roberts, $50, 30 Jan.; **1799** - bght. 50 acs from Richard Champion, $40, wits.: Wm. Husheth & Thos. Husketh, 30 Aug.; **1800** - **John Carrell** of Granville Co. bght. 65 acs. from Henry Cocke of Wake Co. at head of Buffaloe Creek no, of Thos. Bailey's line & corner, 40p, 17 Dec.; 1M45+, 1F10-, 1F10-16, 1F26-45, 3slvs.; **?1800** - **John Carrol**, 1M45+, 1F10-16, 1F45+; **1801/1805** - **John Carrell** bght. from Thomas Roberts ; **1804** Aug. - Henry Cooke to **John Carrell** for 65 acs, wit. John Cavener; **1808Aug.24/Nov.Ct.** - **John Carroll** wit. for Champion Allen petition for pay & bounty lands due from death of Samuel Allen and David Allen who died in service of Continental Line of the State, Champion Allen being their heir; **1810** - 1M26-45, 1F16-26, 1free person; **1814 May 20/Nov.Ct. 1814** - **John Carroll will** dated 20 May 1814, proved by Wm. Weathers and Elias Huskey, **Rebecca Carroll** qualified as exr., Nov. Ct. 1814: to dau. **Polley Harris** 115 acs on Buffaloe Creek forever; to dau. **Elizabeth Moore**, 115 acs. on Horse Creek forever; to **wife Rebecca** 50 acs whereon I live and all else I own; exrs. my wife & William Huskey; wits.: William Weathers, Elias Huskey; proved by William Weathers, Elias Huskey, **Rebecca Carrol**, wife, exrs., Stephen Sneed; **1820** - **Rebecca Carrol**, 000010-30100 probably had one daus' family living with her CC (M. Bk., p. 24; Holcomb, Granville Marriages, pp. 52, 93, 178, 233; Carroll Cables, July 1995, Apr. 1996; Radcliff, pp. 36, 56; Ear. Amer. Series, v. 1, p. 30; Cens.; NC Genealogy, Fall 1969, pp. 2408-9; Gwynn, pp. 57, 83, 140, 141, 148, 208, 255; NC; Cens. Indx., pp. 22, 23; Hds./ Fams., p. 89; Dd. Bk. R, pp. 334, 335; Dd. Bk. N, p. 106; Dd. Bk. S, p. 210; Dd. Bk. P, p. 339; Cens. Indx, Roll 31, p. 523, l. 12; Cens. Roll 40, p. 862; Cens., pp. 15, 121; Ct. Mins. Bk. 9, pp. 46, 47; Will Bk. 7, p. 468; Hummel, p. 34]; **Ch.:**
    1. **Polly** md. **John Harris**
    2. **1812** - **Elizabeth Carroll** md. **Charles Moore** 29 Jan. 1812, Bd. #987, John Harris, bdsm., W. M. Sneed, wit.
    5. **1785** - **Spencer Carroll**, b. 5 May **1756** in Goochland Co., VA, baptized 13 June **1756** in Goochland Co., md. **Sarah Huskey** 28 Apr. 1785, **John Carrel**, bdsm.; Bennet Searcy, wit.;

Spencer Carroll, taxpayer; **1786** - **Spencer Carroll**, Fork Creek Dist., 1M21-60, 1M21-/60+, 2F ; **1786/1787** - **Spencer Carroll** in court 20 Apr. 1786 says unfortunately, yesterday (he) did bit (bite) off the lower end of the right ear of John Rogers, for which I give my obligation to him, wits.: Capt. James Blackwell proved certificate from **Spencer Carroll** to John Rogers, Joseph McGehee, Wm. Gowing, John Pope; **?1789/1791/1799** - **Spencer Carroll**; **1796** - in county; **1800** - 1M10-16, 1M26-45, 2F10-16, 1F16-26, 1F26-45, 3sls (Ratcliff, p. 34; M. Bk., p. 24; Holcomb, p. 52; Carroll Cables, Apr. 1996; Ear. Amer. Series, v. 1, p. 30; Cens.; NC Gen., Fall 1969, pp. 2408-9; Register, p. 56; Ct. Mins. Bk. 1, p. 480; Gwynn, Absts./Granville Co., NC Ct. Mins. 1746-1789, p. 62, 64; Cens. Indx., Roll 31, p. 523, l. 15) [Probably moved to Williamson County, TN soon after]

    6. **Jesse**, underage in **1781**; **1781** - **Jesse Carroll** was under 21 (**Wm. Carroll's** will of **1781**); **1786** - **Jesse Carrel** 1M21-60+; **1787** - Jesse Carroll deeded property to John Dickinson, 240 acs, 180p; **1800** - **Jesse Carrott**, 1M26-45, F26-45, 1sl (Dd. Bk.; Cens. Roll 31, p. 523)

    7. **Elizabeth** md. ? **Zarrard**
    8. **Kesia** md. ? **Harp**
    9. **Jenny** was single in **1781**
    10. **Mary**, youngest daughter was under 21 in **1781**

[Note: See Goochland Co., VA, 1734 and Brunswick Co., VA, 1739 for deed from **William Carroll** of NC to Broadnax of Charles City Co., VA; lease and release, 200 acs., St. Andrews Parish, pt. of 570 acs. formerly granted to **Hannah Raines** Sept. 1732 and devised to **William Carroll** in **John Raines will**. See Fairfax Co., VA, Liber A 1742-1746, **Wm. Carroll's** lease of 100 acs. from Robt. Gates; **wife Elizabeth & dau. Ann.**, **Spencer Carroll's** baptism is rcd. in Douglas Register, p.168, **son of Wm. and Eliz. Carroll**, b. 5 May 1756, bapt. 13 June 1756. *Falls Church (VA) By Fence and Fireside*, p.526-527 under List of Tithables 1748-49: **William Carroll**, Papist, Lower Parish, "comes to church often;" **Dempsey Carroll**, Papist, "comes to church often." [Fairfax Co., VA dd. 1745: To **Demse Carroll, Frances Carroll his wife**, and **Daniel Carroll** his eldest son and heir, **Demse Carroll's** Loudoun Co., VA will of 1776; **Joseph Carroll** will **1765**, Fairfax Co., VA (Will Bk. 1, p. 405). **Daniel Carroll** Inventory, Fairfax Co., VA wills **1787**. How are these **Carrolls** related?]

1754 - **Benjamin Carrol**, pvt., #67, Muster roll of militia regt. under command of Col. William Eaton, Capt. Osborn Jefrey's Co., 8 Oct., Capt. Richard Coleman's Co., Granville Co., NC ; taxpayer; **1755** - Two **Benjamin Carols** on list of taxables 1-0-1 & 1-0; **1757** May 9 - Moses Myrick, 712 acs. in St. John Parish on E side of Stone House Creek, joining Macon's corner, a branch, Myrick's boundary, Simons corner, the meadow Branch, Persons corner, and the sd. Creek Or/S/Moses Myrick; wits.: Jno. Haywood, Thomas Smith, entered 21 Aug. 1751, surveyed 8 Apr. 1752, 8CC Moses Myrick, **Benj. Carrel**, Dan Weldon, survr.; **1771** - taxpayer, militia; **1772** - bght. 200 acs. on Little Creek (later in Warren Co.); **1774** - bght. Id.; **1776** - on Committee of Safety; **1777** - sold Id.; **1778** - sold to Benjamin McInvaile (M. Bk., p. 24; Holcomb, p. 53) **1754** - **Daniel Carrol**, pvt., #14, Muster Roll, Col. Wm. Eaton's Regt., Granville, Co., NC, 8 Oct., militia, Capt. Benjamin Simms' Co.; **1756 Sept.7/1Mar.1757** - **Daniel Carrol and wife Rebecca** v. James Brantly, trespass & James Brantly vs **Daniel Carrol & wife**; **1761** - **John Carroll** vs estate of **Daniel Carroll**, 10 Feb. **Rebecca**; **1762** - **Daniel Carroll** v. John Houchins, 11 May; **1763** Jan. 1 -Thomas Person, chain carriers: ..., **Daniel Carrill**, ... ; **1768** - **Daniel and Rebecca** wits. in court, John Hickins?; **1781/83** - **Daniel Carroll, Hannah**; **1785** - Congress proceeded to the election of three commissioners to treat with the Cherokees and all other Indians Southward of them within the limits of the US pursuant to the Act of the 15th of the present month, and the ballots being taken, (Col.) Benjamin Hawkins, Esq., **Daniel Carroll, Esq.** and William Perry, Esq. were elected, 21 Mar.; **1787** - **Daniel Carroll** assigned 228-ac.-ld. gt. in Sumner Co., TN to John Marshall; ?640-ac gt., Davidson Co., TN; **Daniel Carroll will** (Fairfax Co., VA), **son: Harwell** (Clark, Col./St. Rcds., v. 22, p. 494, Col. Sldrs. ..., p. 726, v. 17, p. 431; Ray, NC St. Rcds., v. 2, pp. 370-380, Col. Gran. Co. ..., pp. 287, 294; Ct. Mins. #s35, 43, 64, 72; Gwynn, pp. 51, 52, 57, 59; Pat. Bk. 14, p. 40, I #2608; Hofmann, The Granville Dist., v. 2, p. 140; NC Ld. Gts./TN, 1778-91) [Are there two **Daniels**; one md. to **Rebecca** and one to **Hannah**?]

1755 - **George Carroll** vs Philemon Hawkins, trespass, 3 June; **1779** - sold ld. to Moses Myrick (Ct. Mins. #20, Gwynn, p. 47)

1755 - **John Carrol** on list of taxables, 1-4-5; Negroes: Goliah, Primus, Nell, Hannah; **1756** - **John Carroll** v. Reuben Lawson est., 7 Sept./1Mar.1757; bght. 348 acs. from Charles Kimball; **1757** - **John Carrol** v. Hosea Easley, 6 Sept.; **1759** - **John Carroll**, 300-ac. gt., 20 Nov.; taxpayer; **1761** - **John Carroll** v. **Daniel Carrol** est., 10 Feb.; **1771** - taxpayer; **1772** - Pt. of 300-ac. gt. of 20 Nov. 1750 to **John Carroll** sold to Mark Moore of Northampton Co, NC by Joshua Taylor of Bute Co., on Lizard Ck. S. of Great Branch 31 July, wits. Matthew Myrick, Caleb Taylor, Robert Taylor; other pts. of gt. sold by Taylor's in 1769 (Ct. Mins. #36, 47, 64; Gwynn, pp. 51, 53, 57; Dd. Bk. 3, p. 504)

1761 - **Thomas Carroll**, wit. with John Dollar to William Moss will, wife Sarah Moss, 12 Mar./May Ct. 1762; **1795** - Deed & will prove **Thomas Carrol** md. **Rebecca Marshall**, dau. of John Marshall; **1813** - **Thomas Carroll** died, wife Rebecca, ch.: Sterling; Ezekiel; Tabitha; Miriam; Rebecca Lee; Thomas Jr.; Nancy Mize/Wize; Elizabeth Brooks Wade; Sally Read (Unrecd. Wills, 1746-1771, #41; Dd. Bk.18, p. 14; Will Bk. 3, p. 326; Gammon, p. 133); **Ch.**:
1. **Sterling**, 1794 - Sterling Carroll bght. part of Haynes est.; on **1820** Cens.
2. **Ezekiel**, on 1820 Cens.; **1824** - md. **Tabitha Moore**
3. **Tabitha** , 1826 - md. **John B. Shell**
4. **Mariam**
5. **Rebecca Lee**, 1814 - md. **Isaac Rainey**
6. **Thomas Jr.**, 1813 - **Thomas Carroll Jr.** sold ld. to **Tabitha**, his sister; on **1820** Cens.
7. **Nancy Mize/Wize**
8. **Elizabeth Brooks Wade**
9. **Sarah (Sally) Read**, 1798 - md. **James Read**

1762 - **Luke Carroll**, chain carrier, Augustine Bate, 6 Feb.; **Luke Carrill**, 315 acs., both sides of Meadow Spring Branch, OR:/S/**Luke Carel**; wits.: Jno. Linton James Martin, surveyed 17 July 1761, chain carriers: Sherwood Harris, Edw. Wood; surveyor Thos. Person; **1765** Feb. 21/**1768** - **Luke Carroll and wife Anne** sold ld. in Granville Co. to James Coffield of Halifax Co., NC for 30p sterling, money of England, parcel tract granted to **Luke Carroll** 6 Feb. 1762, 215 acs.; Robert Harris, wit.; M. Benton, register; **1771** - **Benjamin & Luke Carroll**, militia soldiers, Capt. Wm. Bueford's Co., taxpayer; **1774** - **Luke Carrol** bght. from Nicholas Holstein est., Nov. Ct. 1774 (Pat. Bk.11, pp. 331, 335; I #s1428, 1447; Hofmann, Granville Dist. ..., v. 2, pp. 15, 17; Dd. Bk. H, p. 34; Gwynn, p. 1; Clark, v. 22, p. 164; Ratcliff, p. 34; Ct. Mins. Bk.1, pp. 92-96)

1770 - **Benjamin Carrol/Carroll** md. **Charity Bonner** 27 Dec. 1770, Robert Harris, bdsm.;

wits.: Moses Bonner & Jesse Benton;**1770** - **Benjamin Carrol** (son of Stephen Carroll of Orange County) md. **Charity Bonner**, 27 Dec., bdsm. **Benj. Carrol**, Moses Bonner, Robert Harris, all of Gran. Co.; wit. Jesse Benton; **1771** - **Benjamin Carroll & Luke Carroll**, soldiers in Capt. William Bueford's Co.; **1781** - **Benjamin Carroll**, pvt., 12 mos. 10th Regt., Hall's Co., out 10 Nov. 1782, **#W10587**, b. in Orange Co., NC c1753, 80 in May 1833, md. Nancy Peeler, d. Jan. 1846, Nancy was in Orange Co. Home of Christian Peeler in July 1846 (Clark, v. 22, p. 373, Misc. List, p. 164, Col. Sldrs. ..., p. 720, v. 17; p. ?; NC St. Rcds., List of Earliest Inhabitants of Granville Co., v. 2, pp. 370-380, v. 16; Ray, Col. Gran. Co. ..., p. 292; Early Amer. Series, v. 3, p. 38; No. Carolinian Qtrly., Sept. 1959, p. 581; Ratcliff, p. 36; Pat. Bk. 14, p. 4, #2472; Hoffman, Absts. ... 1748-1763, p. 126; Marr. Bds.)

1773 - **Milbrough Carroll will** dated 1 Apr. 1773, proved May Ct. 1774, wife unnamed, **ch.: Thomas; Charles (ld. in Brunswick Co., VA); Betty Wilkins**; wits.: Stephen Shell, Sarh Brett, Rebekah Johnson (Bute Co. rcd., Bk. A, p. 275); **Ch.:**
    1. **Thomas**
    2. **Charles**
    3. **Betty Wilkins**

1776 - **John Carroll** enlisted in Bute (Warren) Co., Capt., **wife Ann**; ch.: **John Jr.**, and **Nancy**, b. **1782**, md. **John Patterson; 1778** - in Warren Co., NC; **1779** - entered 100 acs. (See Warren Co.); **1786** - bght. or sold 65 acs. to Henry Cooke (No. Carolinian Qtrly., Sept. 1959, p. 581; p. 5) Ch.: 1. **John Jr.**
    2. **Nancy**, b. **1782**, md. **John Patterson**

1778 - **Jepe/Jesse Carroll/Carrill** sold ld. on Beaverdam Creek, 210 acs. to John Dickerson for 180p; wits. James Bar, Joseph Peace, Feb./5 Oct.; **1787** - deeded 240 acs. for 180 pounds to John Dickinson (Dd. Bk. O, p. 550; Ct. Mins., #60; Gwynn, p. 18; Dds.)

1778 - **Douglass Carol**, pvt., ????, 3 yrs., mustered June 1778, 10th Reg., md. ?; **1787/1790** - **Douglass Carroll**, 428-ac.-ld. gt. in Davidson Co.,TN on N. Cross Creek, a military gt. assigned to Bennett Hill, #1614, #1342 issued 10 Dec. 1790 (Rev. War Pens. Rcds.; Clark, vs. 16, 23, pp. 507, 1034; Gt. Bk. 74, p. 379, #136; NC Ld. Gts., TN1778-1791)

1779 - **Hannah Carroll** insolvent (?) [May be Daniel's wife.]

1782 - **John W. Carrell**, 400 acs. in Washington Co., TN on Sinking Creek and waters of Nolochucky River (NC Ld. Gts./TN, 1778-91, MF Roll #68)

1800 - **Rebecca Carrol**, 000010-30100 (Cens. Indx. Roll 31)

1800 - **William Carroll**, 1M10-, 1M26-45, 3F10-, 1F16-26 (Cens. Roll 31, p. 531)

1800 - **William Carral**, 1M16-26, 1F26-45; **1800** July 24 - **Wm. Carnell** md. **Catherine Slaughter**, Wm. Fowler Bdsm., p. 25, #5678 (Cens. Roll 31, p. 581; Richard H. Thorton Library, Oxford, NC Courthouse, Male Marriage Record Book)

1800 - **Moses Carroll**, 3M10-, 1M10-16, 1M45+, 2F10-, 2F10-16, 1F45+, 2sls (Cens. Roll 31, p. 581); **?Son:**
    1. **1804 Aug. 21** - **Moses Carnell** md. **Sarah Meadow**, Wm. Carnel bdsm., #4159 (Richard H. Thorton Library, Oxford, NC Courthouse, Male Marriage Record Book)

1805 - **Patsey Carrel** md. **Kearney Bradford** 27 Sept., Isaac Husketh, bdsm.; Jas. Sneed, wit. (Holcomb, p.34; Hummel, v. 1, p. 26)

1830 - **Sally Carol** md. **James Fuller** 20 July, Thomas Leavister, bdsm.; David Laws, wit. (Holcomb, p. 120)

1809 - **Nancy Carrel** md. **Robert Bradford** 16 Dec. 1809, Chas. Moore, bdsm., Bennett Searcy, wit. (Hummel, p. ?)
1818 - **James Carnel** md. **Lucy Wood**, Wm. Terry bdsm. #6643, Jan. 11
1835 Mar. 9 - **Moses Carnel** md. **Margaret Dean**, Samuel A. Dean bdsm. #1605 (Richard H. Thorton Library, Oxford, NC Courthouse, Male Marriage Record Book)
1839 - **Jno W. Carnell** md. **Elizabeth Dean, Moses Carnell** bdsm. #1615, July 16 [W. Bk. 8, p. 366, Granville Co.; check out. What this has reference to is unknown.]

Johnston County, Newbern Military Dist., was established in **1746** from **Craven Co**. Earliest deeds and court records are **1759**. (Carls, NE Cos., p. 2)
1744 - **John Carroll** wit'd. will; **1750** - **John Carroll**, ld. gt., 200 acs in Craven Co., "joining Panther Creek and Barrow's line;" **1752** May 1 - **John Carrol**, 640 acs. both sides of Swift Creek, joining (a point) on sd. Creek above mouth of White Oak Swamp, OR:/S/mark; wits. Jno. Haywood, Joseph Bridges, surveyed 9 Feb. 1750; chain bearers: Richard Johnston, Sill Johnston Jr.; surveyor Richard Caswell; John Gaskins, chain bearer **John Carroll**, ...; **1756** May 11 - Major Samuel Smith, St. Patrick Parish, chain carrier **John Carrell**; **1763** Jan. 1 - N. Bryan, joining **John Carril**; **1763** - **John Carroll** died; **John Carroll** and his wife, name unknown and predeceased him, had at least five sons and daughters all born between 1742 and 1756. (NC Ld. Gts. Bk. 1, p. 411, #3724; Pat. Bk. 14, p. 194, I #33113, pp. 199, 208, I #s 3133, 3170, p. 233, I# 3307; Hofmann, The Granville Dist., v. 2, pp. 192, 194, 197, 211; Will Bk. 1, p. 163); **Ch.:**

1. **William Carroll**, b. ?c1731/1742 in ?Smithfield, NC/Craven Co., NC (two sources); **1763** - **William Carroll**, planter, paid 10p to James Jones, for 200 acs on Busby Branch "including the tract **John Carroll** formerly surveyed, running the old lines, including the whole," 22 Sept., wit. Needham Bryan Jr.; **1764** - **William Carroll** ordered with **Sill Johnson (Jr.)**, Caleb Penny, to work "upon the road where Simon Turner is overseer;" md. **Ann** ? c1765; **1770** - **William Carroll**, planter, and wife, **Ann**, sold 200 acs to Samuel Holloway for 30p, 21 Mar.; **1776** - **William Carroll**, 31 Dec., bght. 150 acs. on no. side of Swift Creek, which the late **John Carroll** had conveyed to his brother-in-law, **Sill Johnson, Benjamin Johnson**, son of **Elizabeth (Carroll) Johnson**, inherited the 150 acs., sold it to Benj. Clements, who moved to Wake Co. and sold it to **William Carroll** for 60p, dd. recorded Aug. **1777**, property description: beginning at a red oak on Swift Ck., running E. to a sweet gum, N. to a black jack, down Spring Branch to its mouth and down this ck. to place of beginning p1763; **1778** - **William Carroll**, 7 Mar., bght. 80 acs. at mouth of Cove Br. on Swift Ck. which **John Carroll Sr.** had bequeathed to **Benjamin Carroll** (**William's** brother); **William Carroll** bght. 80 acs. on Swift Ck. from his brother **John Carroll**, 7 Mar.; **1778** - **William Carroll and John Carroll** sold 240 acs. to Drewry Massey for 300p, 7 May; **William Carroll** entered 100 acs. "joining his own line and Sill Johnston, lying on the No. side of Swift Creek," 29 May; **1779** - **William Carroll** entered 100 acs. 11 Jan., on so. side of Swift Creek "joining Leven Coles and **John Carroll's** line; 100-ac. patent granted to **William Carroll** 30 Dec., **1780** - claim confirmed in County Court 24 Aug.; **1780** Aug./May **1782** - **William Carroll** to serve on jury panels; **1783** - Abraham Jordan sold ld. joining **William Carrell**, Wm. Bryan, Abner Jordan & Caleb Penny; **1784** - **William and Ann Carroll** sold 330 acs on Swift Ck. & Cove Br. To Cary Cox of Halifax Co. For 130p, adjoining Sill and Absalom Johnson, wits. Richard Rivers, Sion Wheless, John McCullers, JP, 31 Aug., Carey Cox sold the 330 acs.--"the line formerly called **William Carrol's** line" and "sd.

Carrols old line" 22 May 1786; **1784 - William Carroll**, Capt. Wm. Bryan Co.; **1790 - William Carroll**, Newbern Dist., 1M16+, 1M16-, 3F ; **1800** - 2M10-, 1M26-45, 2F10-, 1F26-45 ; **wife, Ann,** b. **c1734** in Smithfield, d. **c1790** (Dd. Bk. 1, p. 42, #562; p. 74, #512, p. 124, #516, p. 166; Ct. Order. Bk. 1, p. 199; Bk. 3, p. 350, #1024; Dd. Bk. 2, p. 7, #232, p. 171, #463, p. 204, #326, p. 255, #352; Carroll Cables, Jan. 1997; Ct. Ordr. Bk. 2, p. 262; Ct. Ordr. Bk. 3, p. 39, p. 84, #727, pp. 89, 146, 153, 203, 208, 264; Ent. Bk. 1, p. 38, #296, p. 82, #649; Dd. Bk. M1, p. 6, #6; Cens. Roll 2, p. 498; Hds. of Fams., p. 142; Tax List, NC Gen., Fall,1969, p. 2379; Cens. Roll 31, p. 767, l. 18)

William and Ann Carroll's children, all born in Smithfield:
    1.. **John**, b. **?1760/1766**, d. **1810**; **1786 - John Carroll**, Capt. Fishe's Dist., 2M21-60, 2M21-/60+, 4F; **?1789/1791/1799 - John Carrell**; **1790 - John Carrol**, Newbern Dist., 1M16+, 3M16-, 4F, 1Msl/0Fsl; **1800** - 2M10-, 1M10-16, 1M16-26, 1M45+, 2F10-, 2F10-16, 4sls (21101-22000-04); **1810 - John Carrell**; **1814 - John Carroll will**, Smithfield, dated 11 Nov.; **wife Aley, daus.**: Sally, wife of Mitchell Carroll; Lucy, wife of William Carroll; Delilah, wife of Warren House; Susanna, wife of Laban Griffith; Winifred, wife of Willis Johnson; Penny Carroll & Aly Carroll; sons: Benjamin; Matthew; Messill; Ranson; "that my Tennessee land which fell to me by death of my **brother Benjamin Carroll** ...;" exrs.: Simon Turner & Reubin Sanders; wits.: Jno McCullers, Brittian Barber & David Dodd; **1820 - Aley Carrell** (Cens. Indx., p. 39; Hds./Fams., p. 142; Cens. Roll 31, pp. 15, 766, l. 9; Cens. Indx., p. 276; Cens., p. 263; Ear. Amer. Series, v. 1, p. 30; Register, p. 79; Hds./Fams., p. 142; Cens., pp. 218, 276, 277, 751, 766; Cens.Indx., pp. 23, 42 Rcds. Comm. NS DAR of NC, 1958/59, p. 2)

        1. **1805 - Sarah (Sally) Carroll**, dau. of **John & Aly Carroll**, md. **Mitchell Carroll**, 3 Dec., b. **?1762/ 1782**, son of **William and Ann Carroll**
        2. **Lucy, wife of William Carroll**
        3. **Delilah Carroll** md. **Warren House** 28 Feb. ?
        4. **Susanna Carrell** md. **Laben Griffis** 16 Jan. ?
        5. **Winifred, wife of Willis Johnson**
        6. **Penny Carroll**
        7. **Aley Carrell** md. **Martin Nall** 7 Sept. **1823**
        8. **1830 - Benjamin Carroll**, 1M5-, 1M10-15, 1M20-30, 1M50-60, 1F5-, 1F5-10, 1F15-20 (Cens., p.260; Cens. Indx., Roll 31, p.9; Cens. Roll 122, pp.86,90) [Two Benjamins]
        9. **Matthew**
        10. **Messill**
        11. **Ransom Carroll** md. **Lucinda Stevenson**, 10 Aug. **1849**
            (Carroll Cables, July 1995, Apr.1996)

2. **James**, b. **1768**, Rev. War. **W6899**, BLWt. 86103-160-55; **1790 - James Carrol**, Newbern Dist., 1M16+; **1792 - James Carroll**, b.**1765**, d. 16 May **1834** in Johnston Co., NC, md. **Rhoda Stevens/Stevenson** 30 Jan. **1792** in Johnston Co.; **ch.: John; James Jr.**, b. 13 Sept. **1805**, d. 18 Aug. **1878**, wife **Pennie**, b.

Lenoir Co. NC, buried in Ozark, Dale Co., AL; **David; brother William Carroll;
1800 - James Carroll**, 1M10-, 1M16-26, 1F10-, 1F26-45, 1F45+; **1810 - James
Carrell; 1820 - James Carrell; 1830 - James Carroll**, 1M20-30, 1M60-70, 1F5-,
2F5-10,1F50-60; **1831 - James Carrell**, pvt., pension petition, age 69; **Margaret
(Peggy) Carrell** md. **Brittian Langdon Sr.** (his 1st wife), her 1st cousin once
removed, 7 Nov. **1815**; mentioned in her father, **James Carrell's** est. settlement
Feb. **1836** in Johnston Co., NC;(NC Cens. Indx, p. 142; Cens. Roll 31, p. 767, l.
2; Cens. Indx., pp. 11, 23, 42; Cens., pp. 217, 259, 261, 275; Hds./Fams., p. 142;
Cens. Roll 122, p. 88; Rev. War Pens. Rcds.; DAR Rcds., p. 439; Early Amer.
Series, v. 3, p. 38; Clark, v. 22, p. 60; Cens. Indx. Roll 31, p. 8fcp); **Ch.:**
   1. **John**
   2. **James Jr.**, b. 13 Sept. **1805**, d. 18 Aug. **1878**, md. **Pennie** ?
   3. **David 1830 - David Carroll**, 1M5-, 1M15-20, 1F5-, 1F5-10, 1F30-40
   (Cens. Roll 122, p.88)
   4. **Margaret (Peggy) Carrell** md. **Brittian Langdon Sr.** (his 1st wife),
   her 1st cousin once removed, 7 Nov. **1815**; **1820** - **Margaret Carrell**
   moved to Dale Co., AL
   4.- 8. **Four other daughters**
[**James Carrell**, b. **1765** in Ireland (DAR Recds.)]; was 69 when applied for Rev.
War Pens. 4 Mar. **1831**, d. 16 May **1834** in Johnston Co., md. **Rhoda
Stephenson**; James was bro. of **John & William** in Johnston Co.; no evidence
James was b. in Ireland; he had 5 daus in 17 Feb. **1836** est. division; Margaret
was paternal grandmother of Roberts children (Roberts, Notes on NC Ancs., p. 3]
[**1799 - Noah Carroll**, b. 30 Oct. **1799**, NC, mother was a **Murphree**, in
Covington Co., **AL** by **1821** when he md. **Elizabeth Mancill**, said he was related
to **James Carroll** of Johnston Co. (No. Carolinian Qrtly, June 1956, v. 2. no. 2,
#6, p. 191)]
   3. **William M.**, b. **?1768/c1770**, md. **Sarah Stevens/? Stevenson** 8 Feb. **1790**;
?**1800** - 20010-?23010/20010-00; **1810** - **William Carrell**); **1820** - **William
Carrell**; **1830** - **William Carroll Sr.**, 2M30-40, 1M60-70, 1F20-30, 1F30-40,
1F50-60, 1F80-90 (Cens. Roll 31, pp. 11, 767; Cens. Indx., p. 23, 42; Cens., pp.
212, 217, 261, 272, 275; Cens. Roll 122, p. 88)
     1. **1830 - William Carroll Jr.**, 1M5-, 1M30-40, 1F30-40, 1F70-80 (Cens.
     Roll 122, p. 88) [Went to Georgia]
   4. **Mary**, b. **?1756/1775**, md. **William Hunt**
   5. **Bethania**, b. **?1758/1778**, md. **Edward Prather**
   6. **Mitchell**, b. **?1762/1782**, md. **Sarah Carroll**, dau. of **John & Aly Carroll**, 3
   Dec. **1805**
   2. **1755 - James Carrell**, chain carrier with **John Carrell**; **1756 - Needham Bryan**, 338
acs. in St. Patrick Parish on N. side of Swift Creek, joining Busbys Branch, **John Carrell**,
Needham Bryan and the fork of Swift Creek and White Oak Swamp, May 11; wits: Sher
Haywood, Samuel Smith, entered 3 Aug. 1754, surveyed 22 Jan. 1755, chain carriers: **John
Carrell, James Carrell**; surveyor W. Haywood; **1763** - **James Carroll** sold 60 acs on so. side of
Swift Creek 20 Sept. 1763 for 9999p, "part of a tract granted to **Jas. Carroll** by deed by **John**

Carroll," to Needham Bryan Sr., wit. Needham Bryan Jr. (Pat. Bk. 14, p. 192, I. #3105; Hofmann, Granv. Dist./NC ... 1748-1763, v. 2, p. 194; Dd. Bk. 1, p. 40, #560)

    3. **Susannah**, in **1766**, to appear at next ct. session, when failed to, ordered to appear; **1767** Mar. - Chas. Bullock appt'd. grdn., **James Carroll** posted bond of 50p, Bullock resigned grdnship. and **Susannah** chose her bro., **Wm. Carroll** (posted bond, 40p); **1769** - Chas. Bullock filed against **John Carroll** est. for her care (Ct. Ordrs. Bk.1, p.242; Ct. Ordrs. Bk.2, pp.7,82,99)

    4. **Lucy**, in **1766** summoned to appear at next ct. session, failed to appear ... (Ct. Ordrs. Bk. 1, p. 242) [See Susannah]

    5. **John**, b. **1754**; **1764** - **John**, age 10, apprenticed to Wm. Jones until age 21; **c1770** - **John Jr.** made guardian of Caleb Penny, "bound apprentice ... to be taught the business of a cooper" (?); **1779** - **John Carroll Jr.** entered claim for ld. 11 Jan.; **1800** - **John Carrel**, 1M26-45, 2F10-, 1F26-45; **1800** - **John Carrel**, 1M16-26, 1M45+, 1F45+; **1817** - **John Carrell will** (Cens. Roll 31, p. 758; Ct. Ordrs. Bk. 1, p. 187; Ent. Bk. 1, p. 82, #648)

    6. **Benjamin**, b. **1756**; **1764** - **Benjamin**, age 8, apprenticed to Wm. Jones till age 21; **c1770** - **Benjamin**, age 14, "bound apprentice to **William Carroll (his brother)** to be taught the business of a planter" till 21 years old; **1790** - **Benjamin Carrell**; **1810** - **Benjamin Carrell**; **1820** - **Benjamin Carrell**; **1830** - **Benjamin Carroll**, 1M20-30, 1M50-60, 1F50-60 (Ct. Orders. Bk. 1, p. 194; Ct. Ordr. Bk. 2, p. 157; Cens., pp. 216, 275; Cens. Indx., pp. 23, 42) [1830 Benj. a different Benj.? "in TN before death of his brother, **John**, in **1817**"?]

    7. **Elizabeth Carroll** md. **Sill Johnson**, lived in Johnston Co.; **1763** - **Elizabeth Johnson** appointed guardian to orphans of **John Carroll** (her sibling), dec'd.: **William, Susana, Lucy, John, Benjamin**, bdsm; John McMullers, Dionysious Wright; **1763** - **Sill Johnson** d., Eliz. excx. of est.; their sons were **Benjamin** and **Sill Johnson Jr.**(Ct. Ords. Bk. 1, pp. 163, 165) **Ch.**:

        1. **Benjamin Johnson**
        2. **Sill Johnson Jr.**

1754 - **Heugh Carrell**, #43 on muster roll of Capt. Francis Mackelwain's Co., Johnston Co. (Clark, Col. Sldrs., p. 731)

1794 - **Jane Carrell** md. Ryas Johnson 28 Oct. 1794 (Carroll Cables, July 1995)

1797 - **William Carrell**, md. **Piety Fluellin, 1797**;[will dated 18 June 1853; **Ch.**:
    1. **Julia**
    2. **Seaborn Carrell** md. **Chasey Ivey/Ivy**; **Ch.**:
        1. **Marion/ Merrill Carroll**, b. Feb. **1846** in **AL**, d. **1870** in AL, md. **Nancy Singley**, b. May **1852**, in **MS**, d. 4 May **1920**, in Al, dau. of Simon Peter Singley & Elizabeth Cook; **Ch.**:
            1. **William Henry Carroll**, b. **1871** in AL, d. Jan. **1938** in Seagraves, **TX**, md. **1890** to **Nancy S. Bonner**, b. Dec. **1871/72** in AL, d. Plainview, **TX**, dau. of Robert James Bonner & Lucinda Slay; **Ch.**:
                1. **Hubert Eugene Carroll**, b. Apr. **1900** in Silas, **AL**, d. **1972** in Andrews, **TX**, md. **1922** to **Bertha Una Holston**, b. 4 Jan. **1906** in Buckatunna, **MS**, d. **1985** in Deming, **NM**, dau. of Noel DuBose Holston & Mary Elizabeth Giles
            2. **Bertha** md. 2nd to George Hike; **Ch.**:
(CarrollCables, Apr.1997)

1. **Noel DuBose Carroll Hike Sr.**, b. 3 Jan. **1931** in Tulia, **TX**, md. 25 Oct. **1985** to **Nancy Marie LaFerla**, b.29 Jan. **1932** in Omaha, NE
   3. **Henry**; 4. **Frances**; 5. **William (Jr.)**; 6. **Hedar**; 7. **Samuel**
   8. **Cathrine**; 9.**Alexander**; 10. **Hardy**
   [Carroll Cables, Apr. 1997; submitted by Nancy Hike]
1800 - **John Carrel**, 1M16-26, 1M45+, 1F45+; **1820** - **John Carrell** [**John Carroll 1833** (will dated 1833), md. **Rebecca ?**] (Cens. Roll 31, p. 758; Cens. Indx., Roll 31, p. 39)
1800 - **Thomas Carrell** 2M16-26, 1M16-45, 2F10-, 1F16-26, 1F26-45, 6sls (Cens. Roll 31, p. 751, l. 4)
1800 - **Elijah Carol**, 1M10-, 1M26-45, 1F10-, 1F26-45 (Cens. Roll 31, p. 749)
1820 - **Dwany Carrell**; **1830** - **Dwaney Carroll**, 1M10-15, 1M30-40, 1F5-10, 1F10-15, (Cens., p. 266; Cens. Indx, Roll 31, p. 20; Cens. Roll 122, p. 89)
1820 - **Dolly Carrell** md. **Calvin Smith** 17 Mar. 1820 (Carroll Cables July 1995)
1827 - **Beedy Carrell** md. **Elisha Lassiter** 9 Jan. 1827 (Carroll Cables, July 1995)
1830 - **Margaritte Carroll** (Cens. Roll 122, p. 88)
1830 - **Hannah Carroll** (Cens. Roll 122, p. 88)
1830 - **Reuben Carroll**, 2M5-, 1M20-30, 1F20-30 (Cens. Roll 122, p. 88)
1830 - **William Carroll**, 2M5-, 2M5-10, 1M40-50, 1F40-50 (Cens. Roll 122, p. 88)
1830 - **John Carroll**, 2M5-, 2M5-10, 2M10-15, 1M30-40, 1F5-, 1F40-50 (Cens. Roll 122, p. 88)
1830 - **John Carroll**, 1M5-10, 2M20-30, 1M50-60, 1F5-10, 1F10-15, 1F15-20, 1F20-30, 1F40-50 (Cens. Roll 122, p. 89)
1830 - **William Carroll**, 1M5-, 1M20-30, 1F20-30 (Cens. Roll 122, p. 89)
1832 - **Rhoda Carrell** md. **Joseph Matthews** 14 July (Carroll Cables, July 1995)
1836 - **Gincy Carrell** md. **Henry Dean** 9 May (Carroll Cables, July 1995)
1836 - **Sarah Carrell** md. **Levy Stevens** 28 June (Carroll Cables, July 1995)
1842 - **Sintka Carrell** md. **Matthew Hall** 31 Mar. (Carroll Cables, July 1995)
1846 - **July Carrell** md. **Wesley Fowler** 22 Jan. (Carroll Cables, July 1995)
1853 - **Marry Jane Carrol** md. **Gaston Johnson** 14 May (Carroll Cables, July 1995)
1859 - **John Carroll** md. **P. A. Jones**, 2 Mar. (Carroll Cables, Apr. 1996)
1859 - **Rixy Carroll** md. **Bennett Wall** 2 July (Carroll Cables, July 1995)
1860 - **Joseph Carroll**, b. **1806**, wife, **Mittie**, b. **1809**, Ch. (all b. in New Berne, Craven Co.):
   1. **Mary F.**, b. **1839**
   2. **Sarah**, b. **1842**
   3. **Elizabeth**, b. **1844**
   4. **Josephine**, b. **1847**
   5. **George H.**, b. **1849** (Source: ?)
1862 - **Ellen Carroll** md. **Atless Hocut** 9 Oct. (Carroll Cables, July 1995)
1866 - **Mary Carroll** md. **Counsel Ayres** 30 Apr. (Carroll Cables, July 1995)
1866 - **Raiford Carroll** md. **Courtney Sanders**, 31 Dec. (Carroll Cables, Apr.1996)
1866 - **Joseph Carroll** md. **Cazilla Tomlinson**, 27 Sept. (Carroll Cables, Apr.1996)
1895 - **Rev. John Lemuel Carroll**, DD, b. in Duplin Co., NC Dec. 21, **1836**, d. June 26, **1895**, pastor of Baptist Church at Chapel Hill, NC (NC Original Marriage Bonds of Mecklenburg and Johnston Counties, DAR, NC Genealogical Records Commission, p. 12)

Duplin County, established in **1750** from **New Hanover County**, took in all of **Sampson Co.** in **1779**. It is thought by some that **Carrolls** migrated to Duplin (later Sampson) county in the early 1730s from Craven County and settled along Six Runs and the Black River near what later became Lisbon. They cleared land for farming and developed a naval store operation using the river as a means of shipping goods and supplies (Mary Shell MacArthur English, a **Carroll** descendant and native of Sampson Co., NC). Ray states in *Old Albemarle and Its Absentee Landlords*, that **Carrolls** were early settlers of Duplin County (p. 678).
1760 - **John Carrill will**, Duplin Co., dated 12 Jan. **1760**, probated 23 Mar. **1761**; wife **Mary Carroll**, exr.; **sons: John Carroll**, exr., plantation where now live after d. or remarriage of wife, Mary; **Joseph Carroll**, moveable est.; daus.: **Dorcas/Darios & Rachel Carroll**; wits.: Dempsey Benton, Henry Hollingsworth, John J. Bachus; Reg. of Wills, John Dickson; wife **Mary Carroll** was the dau. of John Thomas of Albemarle, Granville Co.(Will Bk. A, p. 84; Will Bk. C, p. 100, #95; Dd. Bk. 3, p. 124; Ray, ... and Its People, p. 204) [See Sampson Co.] **[John Carroll Sr.'s** wife, **Mary, was the dau. of John Thomas** of Albemarle, Granville Co., NC (Ray, Col. Granv. Co. ..., p. 224); **or was Mary** the dau. of Michael Thomas Henderson who patented lands in Albemarle c1745; this **Mary md. a Carroll and had a son John.] John & Mary's children:**
    1. **1762** - **John Carroll** bght. ld. deeded to **Thomas Carroll** (will 1757) of Brunswick Co., VA , wit. **Thomas Carroll**, Feb.; **1764** - **John Carroll** bght ld. from **Thos. Carroll**; **1767** - **John Carroll** bght. 100 acs. bounded by **John Miller Carroll's** property 13 Jan.; **John Carroll** sold ld. on Six Runs to **Jesse Carroll**; **1775** - **John Carrol**, 28 Feb., 100 acs. W. side Six Runs between Chas. Gavin, **Jesse Carrol** ...; **1779** Feb. - **John Carell** signed petition "to be in the House of Commons ...;" **1781** - **John Carrol**, tax list; **1790** - **John Carrol Sr.**; **1800** - **John Carrol, Dorcas Carrol** (Chas. Carroll Letter, 24 Jan. 1764; Dd. Bks.; Pat. Bk. 26, pp. 171, 172; NC Leg. Papers 1729-1935; Johnson, v. 11, no. 1, pp. 1781, 1782; Censuses; Carroll Cables, July 1995)
    2. **Joseph**
    3. **Dorcas** md. **Thomas Braddy** 20 Dec. **1801**
    4. **Rachel**
c1749/1750 - **Jesse Carroll Sr.**, b. **c1750** in NC, d. **1802** in NC, md. **1769** ; **1767** - sold ld. on Six Runs; **1768** - **Jesse Carrol**, 28 Apr., 200 acs. W. side Six Runs, Gavin's Mill Branch above Samuel Gavin . . .; **1769** - **Jesse Carrol**, 16 Dec., 100 acs. E side Crain Creek ... joining **Thomas Carrol**; **Jesse Carroll Sr.**, NC Militia and Rev. War, b. **c1749**, Granville Co. (Don't think he was born in Granville Co., confused w/Wm. Carroll's [d.1781] son, Jesse.), d. near Kenansville (Sampson Co.), NC 16 Aug. **1801**, md. **c1769** to **Mary Rachel Gavin**, b. **1751**, dau. of Samuel Gavin and gddau. of Chas. Gavin of Duplin Co.; she d. at family home 19 Feb. **1811**; **1774** - **Jesse Carrol**, grant, 22 July; **1775** - **Jesse Carroll** property, 28 Feb., in relation to **John Carroll**; **1779** Feb. - **Jesse Carell** signed a petition (probably to establish Sampson Co. separate from Duplin) "to be put in House of Commons ...;" service from 17 Oct.1781 to 19 Apr.1782, had **brother, Edwin Carroll, whose eldest son was James A. Carroll**; lived in Sampson Co. after formed from Duplin; **1781** - **Jesse Carrol**, tax list; **1790-1800** - **Jesse Carrol** (Indx. NC Ancestors, v. 1, p.32, Mrs. J. E. Paulk, #17080; Dd. Bk; Pat. Bk. 23, p. 186; Hofmann, Crown . . ., v. 1, pp.167,481; Pat. Bk. 20, p.528; Rev. War Pen. Appl. Rcds.; Pat. Bk. 26, p.171; NC Leg. Papers 1729-1935; Johnson, v. 11, no. 1, pp. 1781, 1782; Pioneers, pp. 42, 43; Cens.)
Jesse & Mary's ch.:

1. **John**, b. 3 Sept. **1770**, d. 6 Dec. **1826**, Milltown, GA, md. 1st **Elizabeth Hollingsworth**, b. c**1775**, d. **1802**; md. 2nd her sister **Ann Nancy Hollingsworth**, b. 16 Feb. **1778**, d. 16 June **1861**, daus of James Henry Hollingsworth
2. **Thomas**, b. 10/20 Jan. **1772**, md. **Mary Ryall**, their dau. **Elizabeth**, b. 25 Dec. **1806**, md. her cousin **James Carroll**
3. **Mary**, b. 4 June **1773**, md. **James Hollingsworth**, son of James H. & Betsy (Merritt) Hollingsworth & bro. to Eliz. & Ann, moved to MS
4. **Jesse Jr.**, b. 19 Oct. **1774** in NC, d. **1828** in NC, md. **1801** to **Margaret (Peggy) Merritt**, dau. of Robert Merritt (Indx. NC Ancestors, v. 1, p. 32, Mrs. J. E. Paulk, #17080) **ch.:**
    1. **Jesse Carroll**, b. **1803**, md. **Margaret Chestnutt**, moved to Lowndes Co., Georgia **1848**; **1847** - **Jesse Carroll** witnessed Paterck Exxell will (Mrs. J. E. Paulk, #17080) (Will #162, p. 48) **Ch.:**
        1. **Ann**, 2. **Elizabeth**, 3. **Francina**, 4. **Theresa**, 5. **Margaret**
    2. **Lewis Carroll**, b. **1808** in Sampson Co., NC, d. **1872**, md. **Catherine Eliza Lamb** in **1832** (NC Ancester Indx. #17080)
    3. **Priscilla** md. **Henry Edw. Smith**; [Jesse Carroll's **1802** will mentions **dau. Priscilla Carrel**] [Rev. War Pens. Appl. Rcds.; Family History; Descendant Mrs. Billie Spells Gibbs admitted to DAR, 1951, descended through Jesse's son John and his dau., Mrs. Marg. Lamb (Pioneers, pp. 42, 43) **ch.:**
        1. **Edward**, 2. **Christopher**, 3. **Yancey**, 4. **Amos**, 5. **Thomas**, 6. **Margaret** (Mrs. Alvin Royal Sr.), 7. **Mary** (Mrs. Robt. Howard), 8. **Henry Smith**(1800-1877)
5. **Joseph**, b. 23 Feb. **1776**, md. 1st **Nancy Carr**, 2nd **Miss Chesnutt**; **ch.:**
    1. **William**, 2. **James** 3.**Thomas**, 4. **John**, 5. **Margaret**, 6. **Charity** md. ? **Bass**
6. **Rachel**, b. 12 Nov. **1777**, md. **Ira Tucker**
7. **Margaret**, b. **1799**, md. **William Lamb**, in **1848** moved to So. Georgia
    ch.: 1. **John Carroll Lamb** (1832-1863);2. **Edwin Lamb**; 3. **Ann Lamb**; others
8. **James**, b. 6 Mar. **1801**, d. 29 June **1883**, md. 24 July **1822**, 1st **Elizabeth Carroll** [his cousin, dau. of **Thomas and Mary (Ryals) Carroll**], Eliz. d. 10 Nov. **1864**; md. 2nd **Mrs. Sophronia E. Raneau** (nee Chastain); moved to Lowndes Co., GA in **1848**; **ch.:**
    1. **John Thomas Carroll**, b. **1824** in NC, md. **Catherine Maria Lamb**
    2. **James Henry Carroll**, b. **1827** in NC, d. 29 June **1883**, md. **Sarah Catherine Huffman**
    3. **Daniel Bunyan Carroll**, b. **1829** in NC, md. **Theresa Harris**
    4. **William Joseph Carroll**, b. **1831** in NC
    5. **Elizabeth Ann Carroll**, b. **1832** in NC, md. **James S. Harris**
    6. **Martha Jane Carroll**, b. **1834** in NC
    7. **Charity Marie Carroll**, b. **1837** in NC, md. **Andrew J. Liles**
    8. **Edwin Benajah Carroll**, b. **1839** in NC, Capt., CSA from Berrien Co., GA, md. **Julia Chastain Hayes**
    9. **Margaret U. Carroll**, b. **1841** in NC, md. **Elijah Carter**
    10. **David Thompson F. Carroll**, b. **1845** in NC
    11. **George Washington Carroll**, b. **1848** in GA
    12. **Bessie Carroll** (b. to 2nd wife, Sophronia)

1753 - William Carrell, 100 acs., 17 Nov. **1753**, on the Great branch of Cape fear, joining the swamp; **1787 - William Carrel**; **1790 - William Carroll** (Pat. Bk. 2, p. 82; Hofmann. Crown to Colony NC, v. 1, p. 467; Cens.)
1756 - Patience Carroll/Carrel md. **Samuel Gavin** 22 Sept. **1756**; **1762 - Samuel Gavin** will, wife **Patience (Carroll) Gavin**; **Thomas Carroll**, exec. [Patience Gavin, wife of Samuel (#78), **Thomas Carroll** had 5 daus. (#79-DAR File Case, Duplin Co. 1762), one was **Patience**] (Bass. Marr. Bds.; Carroll Cables, July 1995; North Carolinian Qrtly., Mar. 1957, p. 271; Cumb. Co. Marr. Bds. 1808-1868; Will Bk. 1, p. 1; Will Bk. 2, p. 95, #180A; DAR File Case, Duplin Co., NC, Sam'l Gavin Will)
1761 - Demsey Carroll bght. 239 acs on No. side of Rowan swamp from James Jonakin; wit.: **Thomas Carroll**; **1762 - Demsey Carroll**, S32161, b. 22 Dec. **1762** in Duplin Co., was 16 when he entered service and on muster roll; volunteered in Duplin Co. in Capt. Michael Kenian's Co. at age 17 under commanders: Gen. James Kinian and Col. Richard Clinton for 6 mos. duration; was in 2-hr. skirmish between Duplin Co. and Wilmington, then marched to Wilmington, to Fayetteville and to Bluford Bridge to guard against expected British invasion; moved to **South Carolina** – report left in SC that he was a minister of the gospel and a family Bible record of his birth if not destroyed, and to **Wilcox Co., AL**, an invalid; sons: **Elias and Demcy Carroll** witd. his testimony; recd. $20 7 June 1832 and pd. Mar. 1837-4 Sept.1838 pd. Mar.1828-4 Sept.1838 ; **1769 - Demsey Carrol** joined Hardie Stephens, Six Runs where **Jesse Carrol** is, 4 May; **1770 - Demsey Carroll**, 168 acs. W side Six Runs; **1771 - Demcy Carroll** bght. ld. from Garret Williams, at Charles Gavin corner on Six Runs ..., 100 acs., 30p, wit. **John Carroll**, 8 Oct.; **1779 - Demcy Carell** signed a petition "to be put in House of Commons ...;" **1781 - Demcy Carrol**, tax list; **1787 - Dempsey Carrell**, 100 acs. on Crane Creek to **Alex. Carroll's** corner; **1790-1800 - Demcy Carrol**; (Dd. Bk. 3, p. 207; Rev. War Pens. Appl. Rcds.; Pat. Bk. 20, pp. 444, 638; Hofmann, Crown ..., v. 1, pp. 125, 217; Dd. Bk. 4, p. 483; NC Leg. Papers1729-1935; Johnson, v. 11, no.10, pp. 1781, 1782; Dds., p. 137; Cens.) **Ch.**:
    1. **Elias**, 2. **Dempsey**
1761 - Thomas Carroll witnessed **Demsey Carroll's** buy of 239 acs on No. side of Rowan swamp from James Jonakin; **1765 - Thomas Carroll**, 16 Apr.; **1769 - Thomas Carroll**, joined **Jesse Carrol**, 16 Dec., 100 acs. E side Crain Creek ...; **1770 - Thomas Carrol**, deceased
1770 - Thomas Carrol, 100 acs., 7 Apr., 150 acs, E. side Crain's Creek including his improvements, joining the Marsh, Wm. Gainey, David Duncan and side of creek; 24 Dec., E. side Crain Creek joining **Carrols** old line and ld. that belonged to **Thomas Carrol, deceased**; **1787 - Thomas Carroll**; **1800 - Thomas Carroll** (Pat. Bk. 18, p. 159; Hofmann, Crown ..., v. 1, pp. 12, 177, 217; Pat. Bk. 20, pp. 547, 638; Cens.)
1779 Feb. - Alexander Carrell, signer of petition "To be put in House of Commons ...;" **1781 - Tax List**; **1783 - Alexander Carroll** md. **Lucy Ryals**, Apr. 7., Demcy Carroll bdsman; CC W.W. Dickson; **1785 - Alexander Carrell**, 200 acs; **1787 - Dempsey Carrell**, 100 acs. on Crane Creek to **Alex. Carroll's** corner; **1790 - Alexander Carrol** (NC Legislative Papers 1729-1935; Johnson, v. 11, no. 1, pp. 1781, 1782; Bass, Marr. Bds.; Dds., p. 218; Cens.) **Alexander and Mary's ch.**:
    1. **Major Hardy Carroll**, b. c1769; **1775 - Hardy Carroll**, b. 17 Oct. **1760**, md. **Lydia Hollingsworth** c1775, dau. of Henry, b. 1741, son of Zebulon & Mary (Murray) Hollingsworth; NC; #S41469; "On the 17th day of Oct. 1820," he (Hardy) was 60 years old moved to Stokes. NC

[letter from **Robert G. Carroll**, 4 Sept. 1965]; Rev. War, **S41469** NC,; **1786** - **Hardy Carrol**, HH49, Capt. Kenan's Dist. 2M21-60, 1F; Daniel Hicks, cens. taker; **1790** - **Hardy Carrell**, Wilmington Dist., 1M16+, 1M16-, 3F; **?1789/1791/1799** - **Hardy Carrol**; **1800** - **Hardy Carrel**, 1M10-, 1M10-16, 1M16-45, 3F10-, 1F16-45; **1806** - **Hardy Carol**; **1810-1820** - **Hardy/Hord Carroll** (Pens. Appl.; So. Carolina Heritage; Family Histories, #682, p. 437; Ear. Amer. Series, v. 1, p. 30, v. 3, p. 38; Register, p. 34; Hds./Fams., p. 190; Cens., pp. 3, 632; Cens. Indxs., pp. 17, 23, 27, 42; Cens., pp. 180, 192; Cens. Roll 31, p. 400, l. 21)
    2. **Wylie** [Shinn: **Mary E. Carroll**, **dau. of Wylie & Polly Hunnicutt**, was 2nd wife of **Josephus Cuffman** of Sumner Co.,TN]
    3. **Reason**, 4. **Rebekah**, 5. **Phanney Bridges**, 6. **Mary Ann Tedder**, 7. **Betsy Ann Royal** (Notes of **James Milton Carroll**; Folks, vs. 1-3)
1779 Feb. - **Stephen Carrell** signed a petition "to be put in House of Commons ...;" **1781** - **Stephen Carrell**, tax list; **1790** - **1800** - **Stephen Carrell** (NC Leg. Papers 1729-1935, v. 11, no. 1, pp. 1781, 1782; Cens.)
1784 - **James Carrel** 1; **1790** - **James Carrell**; **1793** - **James Carrell**, 184 acs.; **1800** - **James Carroll** (Dds., p. 233; Cens.)
1784 - **Moses Carrell**
1786 - **Elisha Carrol**, HH21, Capt., Bowden's Co., 1M21-60, 3M21-/60+, 3F, Francis Oliver, census taker; **?1789/1791/1799** - **Elisha Carrol**; **1800** - **Elisha Carroll**; **1810** - **Elisha**; **1817 Apr. 5** - **Elisha Carroll** md. **Sarah Brown**, bdms: Wm. Brown & Wm. Stoakes; wit: Wm. Dickson, CC; **1820** - **Elisha Carroll** (Ear. Amer. Series, v. 1, p. 30; Register, p. 33; Cens., pp. 16, 192, 658; Cens. Indxs. pp. 23, 27, 42; Bass, Marr. Bds.)
1787 - **Hannah Carroll** [Daniel Carroll's wife?]
1803 - **Elizabeth Carrol** md. **Philip Coley** 9 June 1803 (Carroll Cables, July 1995)
1805 - **Benajah Carroll**, b. **1805**, md. 12 Sept. 1829 to **Mary Eliza Mallard**, bdsm. **James Carrell**; wit.: James Pearsell, CC; **1840** - moved to **Mississippi**; then to Drew Co., **AR**, then to **TX**; ?- **Benajah Carrol** will (Bass, Marr. Bds.; Dd., p. 233; Will #185) **ch.**:
    1. **Rebecca Ann**; 2. **John William**; 3. **Richard Baxter**; 4. **Margaret**; 5. **Andrew Fuller**; 6. **Benajah Harvey**; 7. **Laban Joseph**; 8. **Charles Aliene**; 9. **Francis Wayland**; 10. **Mary Emma**; 11. **James Milton**; 12. **Mary Eliza Mallard Carroll**
1807 - **Laban Carroll**, b. **1807**, md. 1st **Sally Ann Fillyaw**; **ch.**:
    1. **John Cullen**; 2. **Laban**; 3. **Benajah** md. **Martha** ? & their dau. **Mollie Black Carroll** was 2nd wife of Geo. Washington Carroll; 4. **Isaiah**; 5. **Augustus**; 6. **Thomas Owen Carroll**
?- B. V. Carroll will (Will #163)
?- Eda Carroll will (Will #19)
1809 - **John Durham Carroll**, b. 3 Jan. **1809**, d. 23 Mar. **1885**, md. **Zilpha Chestnutt**, b. 25 Apr. **1811**, d. 25 Oct. **1890**, both buried in **George Carroll Cem.** near Magnolia, ½ mi. east of U.S. 117; **John and Zilpha's children**:
    1. **George Washington Carroll**, b. 20 Sept. **1833**, d. 15 Sept. 1912 (Will Bk. 4, p. 247), md. **Mary White Houston**, b. 25 Aug. **1836**, d. 11 Jan. **1894**, postmaster of Six Runs 11 June 1888 (Ref. 26S, p. 26), buried in George Carroll Cem. **ch.**:
        1. **Annie Estelle Best**, b. **1889**, 2. **Herman Randall**, b. **1891**, 3. **Mary W. Ledbetter**, b. **1894**, 4. **Charles F.**, b. **1900** (LL.D) [Chas. b. 1900, mo. d. 1890?]

2. **James Thomas**, b. 8 July **1835**, d. 6 June **1887**, buried **George Carroll Cem.**
3. **Rev. John Lemuel Carroll**, DD, b. in Duplin Co., NC 21 Dec. **1836**, d. 26 June **1895**, pastor of Baptist Church at Chapel Hill, NC (NC Original Marr. Bds. of Mecklenburg and Johnston Counties, DAR, NC Genealogical Records Commission, p. 12)
4. **Luther Rice Carroll**, NC senator, b. **1838** (Tomlinson, p. 115)
5. Owen Judson, 6. **Mary Ann**, 7. **Martha Jane**, 8. **Margaret Elizabeth**, d. young
c1813 - **Charity Marie Carroll**, b. **c1813**, md. 1st **W. J. McGowan**; 2nd **William Moore**; moved to FL; buried in **George Carroll Cem.**
c1815 - **Rachel Jane Carroll**, b. c1815, buried in George Carroll Cem.
? - **Edwin Joseph Carroll** md. **Sarah Eliza Wilson**; moved to Carroll Co., MS; ch.:
    1. John Bunyan; 2. Ann Judson; 3. Edwin Carroll, d. in Army
1810 - 1820 - **Charles Carroll** (Cens., pp. 16, 38, 204)
1820 - **Eden Carroll** (Cens., p. 192; Cens. Indx., p. 27)
1820 - **Willis Carroll** (Cens., p. 204; Cens. Indx., p. 38)
1822 - **Mary Carroll** md. **Jesse Brown** 29 Mar. (Carroll Cables, July 1995)
1822 - **Elizabeth Carrol** md. **James Corrol** 24 July (Carroll Cables, July 1995)
1825 - **Ann Carrol** md. **William Gray** 29 Mar. (Carroll Cables, July 1995)
1825 - **Mary Carrol** md. **Anthony Drew** 18 July (Carroll Cables, July 1995)
1828 Sept. 23 - **Thomas Carroll** md. **Sarah Kelegraves**, bdms. Bass Beasley, wit.: James Pearsall, CC (Bass, Marr. Bds.; Carroll Cables, Apr. 1996)
1852 Sept. 16/Apr. Ct. **1864** - **James G. Carroll will**, slave to brother **William C. Carroll**; exr. Gibson Carr (Will Bk. 3, p. 89)
1856 - **Malcolm Carrell** md. **Mary E. Murray** 24 Feb., bdsm. Alfred Grey (Bass, Marr. Bds.)
1866 - **Martha Carroll** md. **Thomas Friar** 5 Apr. (Carroll Cables, July 1995)
1868 - Daniel **Carroll** Dickson, **son of Sanders & Juna (Carroll) Dickson**, md. **Margaret Burton Pickett**, dau. of Handy & Rachel (Burton) Pickett; Robt. N. Cole, JP; wit. Walter R. Bell, CC (Bass. Marr. Bds.)
1884 - **William C. Carroll** will (Will Bk. 4, p. 236)
1885 - **John D. Carroll** will (Will Bk. 4, p. 247)
1887 July 11 - **Mrs. Susan C. Carroll**, postmistress of Harrells' P.O. in SE co.

<u>**Anson County**</u> was established in **1750** from **Bladen County**.
1800 - **Roan Carrel** 00010-20100-00 (Cens. Roll 29, p. 213, l. 14; Bentley Indx., p. 41)
1800 - **Abraham Carrolle**, 40010-12010-00 (Cens. Roll 29, p. 217, l. 6)
1810 - 1820 - **John Carell**, 220001 -00010 (NC Cens. Indx., p. 21; Cens. Indx., p. 19)

<u>**Orange County**</u> was established **1752** from **Johnson, Granville and Bladen counties**.
Three brothers, Scots Irish, natives of Ireland, came to Wilmington, NC via London about **1750**. **Stephen Carroll** settled in Orange Co, NC; **John** settled in Duplin/Sampson Co.; and the **other brother** settled in Carroll Co., VA. **(Robert C. Carroll**, *Orange County Carrolls?*)
1750/1760 - **Stephen Carroll**, Orange Co., NC; 1790 - **Two-Stephen Carrols**, Hillsborough Dist., St. Mary's Dist., no enumeration given; 1800 - **Stephen Carrel**; 1810 - **Stephen Carrall**; 1820 - **Stephen Carrell**; 1827 - **Stephen Carrel** will, probated 1828, md. **Elnor**; (Cens. Roll 34, p. 557; Cens. Indx., p. 23; Cens., pp. 151, 396; Will Bk. E, p. 173) **ch.:**

56

1. **Benjamin**, b. **c1753**, d. **31 Jan. 1846**, Rev. War pvt. under Cmdr. Green, 10th Regt.; **Benjamin Carroll** md. **Nancy Peller** ?**13 Jan. 1786**; b. **c1753/1756** in **Orange Co., NC**; **1790** - **Benjamin Carroll**, Hillsborough Dist., 1M16+, 1M16-, 3F; **1800** - **Benjamin Carral /Carrill**, 3M10-, 2M10-16, 1M16-26, 1M45+, 1F16-26, 1F26-45; **1810** - **Ben. Carroll**; **1820** - **Benjamin Carroll**; **1833** - **Henry Benjamin Carrell**, **80** yrs. old in Orange Co., b. **c1753**, d. **1846**, md. 1st **Charity Bonner** in **1770**, md. 2nd **Nancy Peeler** in **1786**; ch.: **Eli**, b. **1783**; and **Benjamin**, b. **1796**; Rev. War Final Settlements; **Nancy** testified they were md. in **1783/84 in Wake Co.** at house of Nancy's father, her brother was Jacob Peeler; **Benjamin** d. ?**31 Jan. 1846**; **1846** - **Benjamin Carroll will** (Rev. War Pens. Appl. Rcds.; No. Carolinian Qtrly., Sept. 1960, p. 754; Indx. NC Ancestors, p. 25, #60795; History compiled by Mrs. Lynne W. Belvin of Garner, NC; Hds./Fams.; Cens. Roll 498, p. 97; Cens., pp. 167, 948, 394, 613; Cens. Roll 34, p. 614; Jackson Cens. Indx., p. 41; Bentley Cens. Indx., pp. 41, 42, 89; Will Bk. F, p. 274); **Ch.**:
    1. **Eli Carroll**, b. **1783** in Orange Co., d. **1846**, moved to **Davidson Co., NC**, md. **Catherine Burrage** in **1808/1810**; **1846** - **Eli Carrell will** (Orange Co., NC Rcds.; Will Bk. 1, p. 493 - Davidson Co.)
        1. **Nancy**, b. **1809**, md. **Mathew Varner**
        2. **Benjamin Carroll**, b. **1811**, md. **Laney Noah**; **ch**:
            1. **Jesse**, b. **1828**; 2. **Elen**, b. **1830**; 3. **Daniel**, b. **1832**, 4. **Nancy**, b. **1839**
        3. **Sarah**, b. **1814**, md. **Jacob Huffman**
        4. **Rebecca**, b. **1822**, md. **Rev. A. D. Storker**
        5. **Catherine**, b. **1824**, md. **Zachariah Coggins**
        6. **Eli Jr.**, b. **1826**, died young, wasn't on 1850 Census
    2. **Alsey Carroll**, b. **c1792**, d. **c1882** in Orange Co., md. **1825** in Orange Co. **Nancy Elizabeth Scarlett**; **1810** - **A. Carrol** (Indx. NC Ancestors, p. 25, #60795; Cens., p. 148, 861; Cens. Indx, p. 42)
    3. **Archibald Carroll** md. **Ester Warren** 22 Dec. **1808**; **1810** - **Arch Carroll** (Cens., p. 167, 948; Cens. Indx., p. 42); **ch.**:
        1. **Charles** married **Catharine Raney** 8 Apr. **1824**
    4. **1800** - **Three-Charles Carrel/Carrell/Carril**, 20100-00100-08 (p.503); 20100-00100-00 (p.553); 20110-00100-00 (p.557); **1810** - **Charles Carral** (Cens. Roll 34, pp. 503, 553, 557; Cens., p. 105, NC Cens. Indx.)
    5. **Benjamin Carroll**, b. **1796**, d. **1884**, md. **Nancy Riley**, dau. of Peter Riley; **1810** - **Ben Carroll**; **1820** - **Benjamin Carroll (Jr.)** moved to Davidson Co., NC/TN (Cens. Indx., pp. 91, 167; Cens., p. 396) **ch.**:
        1. **Rebecca**, b. **1823**, d. **1900**, md. **Andrew Smith**
        2. **Elie**, b. **1825**, d. **1895**, md. **Matilda Rush**; **ch.**:
            1. **Nancy**, b. **1849**, d. **1900**, md. **W. P. Kenny**
            2. **Dora**, b. **1852**, md. **David Kenney**
            3. **Pless**, b. **1855**, moved to High Point, NC
            4. **Rubin**, b. **1859**, d. **1900**, his children went to High Point, NC
            5. **Burrel**, b. **1866**, d. **1940**, moved to High Point, NC.
        3. **Peter**, b. **1828**, md. **Mary Bean**, Civil War, moved to TN in **1867**
        4. **Stephen**, b. **1830**, md. **Sarah A. Cameron**, Civil War, moved to TN **1870**
        5. **Rachel**, b. **1833**, md. **? Bean**

6. **Nancy**, b. **1835**, md. **Wyatt Davis**
7. **Benjamin**, b. **1840**, d. **1920**, Civil War, md. **Mary Newsom**; ch.:
   1. **Cicero**, b. **1862**, d. **1931**, md. **Loise J. Hodge**, ch.:
      1. **Sally**; 2. **Ann**; 3. **Van**; 4. **Olin**.
   2. **Benjamin John**, b. **1863**, d. **1944**, md. **Sarah Peacock**, ch.:
      1. **Nora**, 2. **Bill**, 3. **May**
   3. **Betty**, b. **1866**, d. **1955**, single.
   4. **Leach**, b. **1867**, d. **1941**, md. **Jane Bean**, ch.:
      1. **Genie**, 2. **Dela**, 3. **Alice**.
   5. **Roby A.**, b. **1869**, d. **1943**, md. **Mary Ann Peacock**, ch.:
      1. **Duckery**, 2. **Cleo**, 3. **Pallie**, 4. **Benjamin**, 5. **Ella**, 6. **Mary Lee**, 7. **John**
   6. **Eula**, b. **1874**, d. **1899**, md. **Jim Davis**, ch.: 1. **Bertha**, 2. **Roy**
   7. **Dora**, b. **1875**, md. **Frank Davis**, ch.:
      1. **Gurney**, 2. **Wyatt**, 3. **Mary**, 4. **Maude**, 5. **Dewey**
   8. **Duckery Carroll**, b. **1888**, d. **1947**, md. **Emma Lou Ward** in **1909**; ch.: 1. **Robert C. Carroll**, b. 3 Nov. **1909**
8. **Alsey**, b. **1845**, did not return from Civil War
6. **Clement Carroll**
7. **1790** - **Stephen Carroll (Jr.)**, Hillsborough Dist. (Cens. Indx., p. 97)
8. **Ilia Carroll**; 9. **Luvice Carroll**; 10. **Decy Carroll**
11. **1790** - **Michael Carroll**, Hillsborough Dist., St. Thomas Dist.; **1800** - **Michael Carrel** 01010-00001-00 ; **1810** - **M. Carroll**; **1820** - **Mical Carrell** (Hds./Fams. Cens. Roll 498, p. 97; Cens.Roll 34, p. 58; Cens., pp.147, 858, 382; Smith Cens.Indx., p.23; Bentley Cens. Indx., p. 42)
12. **1790** - **Robert Carroll**, Hillsborough Dist. (Hds./Fams. Cens. Roll 498, p. 95); **1810** - in Adams Co., MS

1754 - **Daniel Carroll** (militia, Granville Co.), **wife Rebecca**, still in co. in 1768, d. 1787, inventory in **Fairfax Co., VA**; **son Harwell**; **1779** - **Hannah Carroll**, insolvent (?)
1769 - **Jas. M. Carroll** on list of petitioners For Remedy ... (and) mutual Benefit of the Trades, & the Industrious Laborer & Planter that a Publick Inspection may be established at the Town of Hillsborough, Sept. (Clark, Col. & St. Rcds., v. 8, p. 80a)
1790 - **Henry Carroll**, Hillsborough Dist., Orange Dist., no enumeration (Cens. Roll 198; Hds./Fams., p. 95) [**1800,1810** - **Rockingham Co.**]
1790 - **James Carroll**, 1M16+, 2F; **1800** - **James Carrel**, 12010-20010-00; **1810** - **Jas. Carroll**; **1820** - **James Carrell**; **1842** - **James Carrell will** (Cens. Roll 498, p. 158; Cens. Roll 34, p. 615; Cens., p. 152, 868, 384; Cens. Indx., p. 42; Will Bk. F, p. 136)
1792 - **Dolly Carrell** md. **John Williams** 8 Sept. (Carroll Cables, July 1995)
1799 - Cane Creek Monthly Meeting (Orange Co., now Alamance) 6, 1, **Phebe Carrol** (from Gilbert) dismov.? (Marshall, p. 377)
1800 - **William Carrell** (Cens.)
1804 - **Lemuel Carroll** md. **Elizabeth Lloyd** 27 July; **1820** - **Lemuel Carrell** (Carroll Cables, Apr. 1996; Cens., p. 384): ?ch.:
   1853 - **Lemuel Carroll Sr.** md. **Elinor Smith** 2 Aug. (Carroll Cables, Apr. 1996)
1807 - **Nimrod Carrolle** md. **Rebecca Cole** 21 Dec.; **1810** - **Nimrod Carroll** (Carroll Cables,

Apr. 1996; Cens., p. 151, 867; Cens. Indx., p. 42)
1810 - John Carral; **1820 - John Carrell** (Cens., pp. 151, 386; Cens. Indx., pp. 23, 42)
1810 - M. Carroll; **1820 - Moses Carrell** (Cens. Indx., p. 147; Cens., p. 388)
1810 - Nelly Carroll md. **Will Cole** 18 Sept. (Carroll Cables, July 1995)
1811 - Polley Carroll md. **William McCollum** 12 Jan (Carroll Cables, July 1995)
1812 - Candis Carrel md. **John Andrews** 4 Nov. (Carroll Cables, July 1995)
1818- Patsey Carrol md. **William Andrews** 12 Mar. (Carroll Cables, July 1995)
1822 - Sarah Carroll md. **William Barton** 16 Jan. (Carroll Cables, July 1995)
1822 - Rachel Carroll md. **Duke Glenn** 21 Oct. (Carroll Cables, July 1995)
1825 - Salley Carroll md. **William Dollar** 21 May (Carroll Cables, July 1995)
1826 - Elizabeth Carroll md. **Azariah E. Reeves**, 7 July, bdsm. Thomas Clancy, wit. **Dickson Carroll** (Holcomb, p. 252; Carroll Cables, July 1995)
1827 - Charlotte Carroll md. **William Hinchey** 13 Aug. (Carroll Cables, July 1995)
1828 - Stephen Carroll md. **Nancy Glenn** 24 Sept. (Carroll Cables, Apr. 1996)
1829 - Sally Carroll md. **James Hutchins** 16 Nov. (Carroll Cables, July 1995)
1832 - Nelly Carroll md. **William Browning** 24 June (Carroll Cables, July 1995)
1832 - Anne M. Carrell md. **David Kirkland** 24 July (Carroll Cables, July 1995)
1841 - Catharine Carroll md. **James Carrington** 5 Jan. (Carroll Cables, July 1995)
1845 - Martha Carrel md. **Thomas S. Cates** 9 Sept. (Carroll Cables, July 1995)
1846 - Elizabeth Carroll md. **William Baldwin** 10 July (Carroll Cables, July 1995)
1847 - Mary Carrell md. **John Desern** 18 Nov. (Carroll Cables, July 1995)
1849 - Elenor Carrel md. **Barnnerd Cates** 2 July (Carroll Cables, July 1995)
1850 - Elizabeth Ann Carroll md. **Joseph C. Alvin Cates** 15 Oct. (Carroll Cables, July 1995)
1853 - Nancy Carrol md. **Henry Woods** 3 Feb. (Carroll Cables, July 1995)
1858 - Elizabeth Carroll md. **James Rhew** 13 Mar. (Carroll Cables, July 1995)
1861 - Nancy J. Carroll md. **James M. Wells** 12 Jan. (Carroll Cables,July1995)
1865 - John L. Carroll md. **Sarah G. Mitchell** 2 Nov.; **1895 - John L. Carroll** will (Carroll Cables, Apr. 1996; Will Bk. C, p. 458, recorded copy in Buncombe Co.)

Rowan County was established in **1753** from **Anson County**.
1756 - Jas. Carrel, Nov. 12, chain carrier, John Rhodes, St. Luke Parish, both sides of N. fork of Haw River; **1775 - James Carroll** has leave to bring suit against James Brooks for a debt under 5p, 10 Nov.; **1790 - James Carroll**, tax list, Salisbury Dist.; **1800 - James Carnell**, 1M16-26, 1F10-, 1F16-26; **1818 - James ?Carrick** will (Orig. Recds. S.S.L.G. 127-E,129-E, NC St. Archives, Raleigh; Hofmann, Gran. Dist. ..., v. 3, pp. 99, 107, I #s4852, 4921; Clark, v. 10, p. 317; Radcliff, p. 40; Cens., p. 441, l. 5; Mitchell Indx, Will Bk. G, p. 494)
1760 - John Carrol, pvt., #14, Payroll, Lt. Alex. Dobbin's Co. of NC Militia, Rowan, Col. Alex. Osburn, 16 Apr.; **1820 - Two John Carrels** (Clark, Col. Sldrs. ..., p. 851; Cens. pp. 234, 242; Indx., pp. 9, 15) **ch.**:
    1. **1820 - John Carrel Jr.** (Cens., p. 234; Indx., p. 9)
1761 - Joseph Carrell, Will Reed, . . ., wits., Dec. 21, John Patterson, 628 acs. on waters of Sills Creek ...; **1790 - Joseph Carroll**, Salisbury Dist. (S/S/L/G/126-F; Hofmann, v. 3, p. 95; Radcliff, p. 40)
1768 - William Carroll, tax list; **1800 - William Carwell**, 1M10-, 1M10-16, 1M16-26, 1M45+,

1F10-, 1F10-16, 1F16-26, 1F26-45, 1F45+ **1800 - William ?Carwell**, 11101-11111-00 (Radcliff, p. 34; Cens. Roll 33, p. 364, l. 2; Cens., p. 362or364, l. 2))
1768 - Thomas Carroll, tax list (Radcliff, p. 34)
1778 - Daniel Carnell?, 320 acs., 11 May (Dd. Bk.11, p. 10; Edmunds, Hist. of Halifax . . ., v. 2, p. 766)
1790 - Benjamin Carroll, Salisbury Dist. (Radcliff, p. 40)
1800 - Richard ?Carnell, 3M16-26, 1M45+, 2F10-, 3F10-16, 1F16-26, 1F45+ (Cens. Roll 33, p. 441, l. 4)
1818 - Catharine Carell md. **Michael Freeze** 8 Aug. (Carroll Cables, July 1995)
1820 - Two-Jacob Carrels (Cens., p. 234; Cens. Indx., p. 9)
1820 - Phillip Carrell (Cens., p. 234; Indx., p. 8)

Cumberland County was established in **1754** from **Bladen County** and named for William Augustus, Duke of Cumberland. Fayetteville is the county seat. The first courthouse was at Linden, second at Campbellton, third at Fayetteville, fourth at Fayetteville in 1893 and the present courthouse was completed in 1926. When the Cumberland was spoken of as late as **1781**, Moore County was included in the county. (The Hist. Rcds. of NC, v. 2, p.25)
1751 - In Bladen Co., Gov. Gabielle Johnston bequeathed 7000 acs. on Deep River to his brother John's two sons, Samuel & John Johnston, saying his brother would allow his creditors to get it. Samuel, oldest and of Edenton, was elected gov. in 1787 and senator in 1789, held his share until 1763 when he conveyed his half of 6500 acs. to his bro.-in-law, Geo. Blair, an Edenton merchant, for 525p. Blair and his bro.-in-law, John Johnston II, began to convey portions of the grant to settlers. Records show conveyances of 1,418 acs. to six purchasers, usually of 100 acs.: beginning in **1763** to Powell Benbow; **Sterling Carroll** 400 acs. for 200p; Joshua Hancock; William Brazier; James Barnes buyer of largest tract of 663 acs. for 180p proclamation money; Cornelius Tyson; and Elisha Hunter. (Robinson, p. 15)
1762 - Sterling Carroll, dd. from Dennis McLendon, 200 acs., 19 Feb.; **1762 - Sterling Carroll**, dd. from Charles Findley, 80 acs.; **Sterling Carroll** prv'd. dd. from James Russell to Gabriel Hardy, 15 May; **1763** - dd. from Dennis McClendon to **Sterling Carroll**, prvd. by Francis McClendon, 17 Feb.; Following grand jury, defaulters fined: Abm. Branson, Benjn. Grimes, Joel McClendon, Archd. McKay, Sam'l Lorimer, Wm. Hodges, Gilbert Bouy, Francis James, Stepn. Gardner, Richd. Smith, **Sterling Carroll**, Charles Findley, 18 May; **1764 - Sterling Carroll**, dd. to Gabriel Harden, 80 acs., May; **1765** - Johnston and Blair dd. to **Sterling Carroll**, 7 Feb.; **1765** - Dd. to **Sterling Carroll** from George Blair and John Johnston, prvd. by Jas. Russell, 20 Aug.; **1766 - Sterling Carroll** dd. to James Russell, 100 acs., 15 Nov.; **1767 - Sterling Carroll** dd. to **John Carrol**, 200 acs., 14 Jan.; **1767 - Sterling Carroll**, taxpayer; **1768** - ... the Sandy Creek Baptist Assn. records note that "the church on Deep River" was moved to Bear Creek, in Chatham County in 1768, "leaving only two of its members in Cumberland (Moore) county" ... Connor Dowd and **Amy Carrol**. This church was probably in the vicinity of Carbonton, where both Dowd and the **Carrols** lived, and could have been in either Moore or Chatham [Is **Amy** the wife of **Sterling or John**?]; **1770 - Sterling Carroll** dd. to James Russell, 300 acs, 14 May; **Sterling Carroll** dd. to Hartwell Hunnicutt, 200 acs., 1 Nov.; **Sterlon Carroll**, 11 Dec., 200 acs., upper prong Governors Creek S. of Deep river, joining S. branch above mouth of a small branch said to be near John Messus; **1771 - Sterlon Carroll**, 18 Nov., Anthony Seale Jr. pat.: **1772** -

Sterling Carroll & wife, dd. to Jas. Russell, prvd. by Randolph Hunneycut, 28 July; **Sterling Carroll** taxable in Jacob Duckworth's dist.; **1777** - **Sterling Carroll**, taxable in Jacob Duckworth's Dist., 100 acs. along Deep River below the Horseshoe and along McLendon's Creek; **1790** - **Carrol** owned ld. N. of Deep River in vicinity of Horseshoe or Haw Branch (Dd. Bk. B, pp. 121, 180, 358, 563, Bk. C, pp. 92,142, Bk. E., p. 44; Wellman, pp. 18, 19, 34, 35, 36, 66, 117, 314, 461; Fields, pp. 107, 118, 181, 202; Early Amer. Series, v. 3, p. 38; Radcliff, p. 36; Pat. Bk. 20, pp. 611, 717; Wicker, p. 461; Hofmann, Crown ..., v. 1, pp. 205, 252) [See Chatham Co.] **1755** - **John Carrel**, 1-0-0, tax list; **John Carrol**, #26, Field return of Cumberland Co. Militia, commanded by Col. James Rutherford, both items undated; **1761** - Two dds. from John Newberry & wife Elizabeth to Messrs. Dyer & **Carrell**, prv'd by Isaiah Parvisol, 18 Nov.; **1764** - **John Carrell & Sterling Carroll** on grand jury with Wm. Lee, Jas. Naper, Hugh Gilmore, Gabriel Harden, John Smith, John Martinleer, Robt. Love, Sam'l. Kennedy, Stepn. Gardner, Patrick Moore, Richd. Stringfield, Edd. Dunfield, Archd. Homes, John Grimes, John Gilmore, James Muse, Wm. Gilmore, John Buie, 16 May; **1765** - **John Carroll**, John Gilmore and Dan'l. McGill fined 20s each for non-attendance on petty (sic) jury, 21 Aug.; **?** - **Capt. Carrill's Co.**, #24, James Russell, Ensign, Cumb. Co., NC Militia, Return of Officers; Leaven Ainsworth apptd. constable in **Capt. Carroll's** Dist., Wm. Manus in Capt. Cheney's dist., 21 May; **1766** - **Capt. John Carrol(l)**, Cumb. Co. Militia officers, Feb.; **1767** - **Sterling Carrol** dd. to **John Carol**, 200 acs., 14 Jan.; **John Carroll**, taxpayer; **1769** - **John Carroll**, on Deep River, 4 May, 1, Duckworth patent; **1770** - **John Carrell** grant, 100 acs., 5 Feb.; **1770/1771** - **Capt. John Carrol** Sr., #36 on list **Carrel's Dist.**, 8th Co., Regt. of Militia, foot soldiers commanded by Capt. William Whittfield Nov.; **Capt. John Carrol, Carrol's Dist.** 8th Co., the War of the Regulators, offrs. recommended as Captain; on list of Cumberland officers; Enough men had settled . . . along Deep River and below to take part in Regulator's War of 1771 in which some Piedmont colonists refused to pay exorbitant taxes. They handled officials roughly and gathered in armed bands. Gov. Wm. Tryon led NC militia against the malcontents. Two companies from Moore Co.: Chas. Herd at fork of Little River and James Chaney who lived west of Cabin Creek. Two captains did not report for duty but **Capts. John Carroll** and James Collins did with the following: Lt. Thomas Matthews, Lt. Hugh Gilmour, Ens. Stephen Gilmour for Herd's Co. and Capt. Wm. Garner, Lt. James Muse Jr., Ens. Joel McLendon and Maj. Thomas Collins for Chaney's Co. The two cos. marched with the militia and on 16 May 1771, fought and scattered 2,000 armed Regulators; **1772** - **John Carrell**, garnishee in suit, Richd. Lyon & Co. v. Jas. Collom, 30 Oct.; **1774** - **John Carell** dd. to John Overton, prvd. by Hartwell Hunnicut, 27 Apr.; **John Carrel** dd. from Cornelius Tyson, 300 acs., 15 July; **1775** - dd. from Cornelius Tyson to **John Carrel**, prvd. by Conner Dowd, 26 Apr.; **1777** - **John Carroll**, taxable in Jacob Duckworth's Dist., 700 acs. along Deep River below the Horseshoe and along McLendon's Creek; **1778** - Daniel Goald, #24, entered 300 acs. on N. side of McLendon's Creek adjoining **John Carrol's** line where it crosses said creek, 29 Jan.; Isaac Pennington, #120, entered 500 acs on both sides of Deep River, adjoining **John Carrel** and Joseph Duckworth above mouth of White Lick Branch, 14 Sept.; **1779/1781** - **John Carrel** signed a petition; **1781** - **John Carrell**, tax list; **1790** - **John Carroll Esq.**; **Carrolls** owned ld. N. of Deep River in vicinity of Horseshoe or Haw Branch; **1790** - **Four: 2 John Carrols, John Carrol, Esq.** 60+, lived in Fayette Dist. [? - **Col. Wade**, a Whig, ... 100 dragoons under Capt. Bogan to avenge death by Tories (Robinson,p.70); **Sterling Carroll and John Carroll's** sisters married Wades and Martins,

found on Cumberland Co., NC censuses from 1800-1850; Wades from 1820-1840; see Northampton Co.] (Early Amer. Sers., v. 3, p. 38; Wicker, pp. 458, 461; No. Carolinian Qtrly., Mar. 1960, p. 645; Radcliff, p. 36; Fields, pp. 101, 148, 175, 182, 212, 221, 253; Clark, Col. Sldrs. ..., pp. 783, 790, 791, 835, v. 22, pp. 411, 413, 473, 494, v. ?, p. 812; Radcliff, p. 36; Pat. Bk. 20, p. 421; Hofmann, Crown ..., v. 1, p. 116; Wellman, pp. 11, 39, 62, 314, 461; Pruitt, pp. 2, 8; Johnson, Jour., pp. 1781, 1782; Cens.; Cens. Indx.) **Ch.:**
 1. **1770** - **John Carrol Jr.**, foot soldiers commanded by Capt. William Whittfield, Nov.; **1781** - **John Carroll Jr.**, tax list; **1790** - **John Carroll Jr.**, Fayette Dist. (Clark, Col.& St. Rcds., v. 22, p. 494; Cens. Indx.)
1757 - **James Carrell**, John Thomas vs Robert Love, ?, John Martileer, ?, Joseph Reinboult, Andrew Shepheard, Samuel Howard, Esq., William? 10 Oct.; **1773** - **James and Lucy Carrel** dd. to John Morris, 27 Jan.; **1778** - **James Carrol** est., Abraham Perry, admr. with 400p bond, Alexr. Avera & Joshua Gist, Esqs., bdsm., 30 July; **Jas. Carrol** est. inventory rendered by Abram Perry, 27 Oct.; **1779** - Abraham Perry entered 350 acs., #235, on N. side of Black River near Indian ford, bordering **James Carrol** and Alexr. Avera, 20 Jan.; **1784** - **Carrol**, Nedham Bryant, Virginia Alexander Avera, Robt. Perry border John Perry, #2943 (?134), who entered 200 acs, 18 Nov., old line, #s 2943, 134; **1787** - Alexr. Avera, #1056 (?497), entered 200 acs. on Black R. Swamp adjoining Ryal, Dean, **Carrol** and his own line, 29 Sept.; **1790** - **James Carrol**, ?20, Fayette Dist., Fayetteville Town, 1M16+ **1790** - **Two: James Carrols**, Fayette Dist. (Cumb. Co. Ct. Mins. 1755-1782, vs. A, B, C, D; Fields, pp. 66, 185, 217, 302, 308; Pruitt, p. 15; Clark, v. 22, p. 60; Cens. Indx.; Gwathney, p. 63; Hds./Fams., p. 41)
1761 - **William Kerrill** appt'd. constable from Sandy Bluff to lower end of co. NE side of Cape Fear Rr., 21 Aug.; **1762** - **William Kirrell** appt'd. constable from Taylor's Hole to lower end of co.; Constables **Wm. Kirrill** and Isaiah Powell ordered to make lists of taxable inhabitants in their districts, Alex'r. McAlister, Esq., 19 May; **1765** - **William Carroll**, Walter Gibson and Edmond Fanning ackd. indebtedness to King for 10p ... on condition that **Wm. Carroll** shall make his personal appearance ..., 22 Aug.; **1772** - **William Carrol** apptd. constable in place of Neil McArthur (crossed out, noted error), 2 May; **William Carrol** died before **1775** - **Margaret**, 8, and **Sophia**, 6, **ch. of William Carrel**, bound as apprentices to Charles Stevens; **Susannah**, 10, bound to Moore Stevens (marked in error), 25 Jan.; **Susannah Carrel**, 13, **orphan of Wm. Carrel**, formerly bd. to Moore Stevens late decd., to be bd. to Easter Stevens (Fields, pp. 98, 109, 186, 201, 248, 257)
1762 - **Richard Carroll** on Grand Jurors' list incldg. Geo. Robards, Adam Killen, Arthur Danelly, John Harvile, Wm. Gilmore, Stepn. Gardner, Dun. Patterson, Wm. Tomlinson, Alex'r. Campbell, John Harper, John Willcocks, Wm. Moore, Christopher Yeaw, 17 Feb.; **Richard Carroll** prv'd. dds. from John Newbery and wife, Elizabeth, to Robt. Brennerman, and from John Stevens to Robt. Bennerman, 19; **Richard Carroll** on Grand Jury w/Matthew Porterfield, John Gilmore, Joel McClendon, Wm. Lee, Wm. Tully, John Donahoe, Hugh McLauchlin, Neill McFall, Duncan McAfee, John Clark, Hector McNeill, James McNeill, 17 Aug./May; **1763** - **Richard Carroll** ack'd. a dd. and an assignment of his est. and effects to Wm. Mouat, Esq. and assignees Robt. Mackie and John Rand, apptd. for use of his creditors, 20 May; **Richard Carroll** and James Dyer dd. to Wm. Park, prvd. by John Stewart, 19 Nov.; **1764** - **Richard Carroll**, Wm. Mouat, Robt. Mackie dd. prvd. by Isaiah Parvisol, 23 Nov.; **1765** - **Richard Carroll**, dds. read and recorded, 19 Feb., dds. from exrs. of John Nesfield est., late of Bladen Co., and dd. from

Richard Carroll to John Robinson, all prv. by Richard Grove, 21 Feb.; **1772** - **Richard Carrel** est., Robt. Rowan, Esq., adm., 1 Feb. (Fields, pp. 104, 108, 113, 126, 140, 166, 169, 170, 196) **1765** - **James Carrell**, b. **1765** in **Ireland**, pvt., NC, Rev., under Col. Raiford, pensioned under Acts of 1818 & 1832, **W6899**, BLWt #86103-160-55, vol'd in Cumberland Co. where resided until about 40 yrs. old, moved to Johnston Co., placed on pension roll, md. **Rhoda Stevenson/ Stevens** 1 Feb. **1792** (marr. bd., Smithfield, NC), d. in **Johnston Co.** 16 May **1834**, brother **William Carrell** of Johnston Co.; **1832**, Rhoda and sons: **James, Lazarus and Mathew** moved to **AL** where "all the **Carrells** from **Maryland**" within one to three miles, A. Coates, JP. **ch.**:
    1. **Margaret**, b. spring **1793**, d. **c1836**, md. **Briton Langdon**
    2. **John**, eldest son b. **1794**, age 64 in **1858**, moved to Dale Co., **AL** in **1836**
    3. **David**, b. **1800**, d. **1863**, md. **1822 Mary Mathews**, b. **1802**, d. **1863**; **ch.**:
        1. **Willis**, b. **1832**, d. **1907**, md. **1857 Sarah Marge Barnes**, b. **1841**, d. **1883**, moved to Dale Co., **AL** in 1835
        2. **Mary Elly Carroll**, b. **1861**, md. **1879 William Garner**, b. **1853**, d. 1911; **ch.**:
            1. **Allie Garner**, b. Ozark, AL (Family #146417, DAR Lineage Bk., v. 147, p. 137)
1772 - **Mitchel Carril**, among panel of 12 to lay out road: Greer's old field to bridge between Carlton Atkinson's and Isom Carver's, 2 May; **Mitchel Carrol** ackd. dd., Robert Rowan, sheriff, 29 July; **1773** - **Mitchel Carrol** prvd. dd., Frederick Gregg & Richard Lyon, Esqs. to Charles Campbell, 29 Jan.; **Mitchel Carroll** & Jas. Gilmore, evidences, court at Campbellton, the King v. Joseph Hall, horse stealing, John Hawkins, prosecutor, 22 July; **1774** - **Mitchel Carrol** est., Archd. Maclaine, atty. for Jos. Morris of Philadelphia, the largest creditor, applied for letters of adm. on est., granted, bond 1,000p, bdms.: Richd. Lyon, Esq. & Robt. Rowan, 29 Apr.; **Mitchel Carrol** est. Acct. exhibited in ct. by Archd. McLaine, adm., 30 Oct.; **1785** - Deed recorded 28 Jan., from John and Sarah Stevens to Thomas White, handwriting of **Mitchl. Carroll**, one of witnesses, proved by Wm. England; **1778** - **Mitchel Carrol** est., suit: Archd. McLean, adm. v. John Linton, jury sworn and assessed damages to plaintiff for 20p and costs, 29 Apr. (Fields, pp. 201, 204, 218, 225, 244, 329, 296, v. 2, p. 81)
1779/1781 - **Jesse Carell** signed a petition; **1781** - **Jesse Carell**, tax list; **1790** - **Jesse Carroll**, Fayette Dist. (Johnson, Jour., pp. 1781, 1782; Cens. Indx.) **ch.**:
    1. **Jesse Carroll (Jr.)**, b. **1803**, md. **Margaret Chestnutt**; **1847** - **Jesse Carroll** witd. Will of Paterck Exxell (Will Bk., p. 48, #162; Murphy); moved to Lowndes Co., **GA** in **1848**; **ch.**: 1. **Ann Carroll**, 2. **Elizabeth Carroll**, 3. **Francina Carroll**, 4. **Theresa Carroll**, 5. **Margaret Carroll** (Notes of James Milton Carroll; Folks, vs. 1-3)
1779/1781 - **Alexander Carroll** signed a petition; **1781** - **Alexander Carroll**, tax list; **1783** - **Alexander Carroll** md. **Lucy Ryals** 7 Apr., bdsm. **Demcy Carroll**, W.W. Dickson, CC; **1789** - **Alexander Carrol**, Bladen Co., md. **(unnamed)** 1 Jan.; **1790** - **Alexander Carrol**, Fayette Dist. (Johnson, Jour., pp. 1781, 1782; Bass, Marr. Bds.; NC Gen. Soc J., v. 3, p. 150; Cens. Indx.) **ch.**:
    1. **1775** - **Hardy Carroll**, Maj., **#S41469**, NC, b. 17 Oct. **1760**, md. **c1775**, **Lydia Hollingsworth**, "On the 17th day of Oct. 1820" **Hardy Carroll** was 60 yrs. old; **1790** - **Hardy Carroll**, Fayette Dist. (Rev. War Pens. Appl., Sampson County Heritage; Family Histories, p. 437, #682; Cens. Indx.) ch.: 1. **Hardy Carrell**, b. **1791**
    2. **Wylie Carrell** md. **Mary E. Hunnicutt**, dau. of Wylie and& Polly Hunnicutt & 2nd wife of Josephus Cuffman of Sumner Co., TN (Shinn)

3. **Reason Carrell**, 4. **Rebekah Carrell**, 5. **Phanney Bridges**, 6. **Mary Ann Tedder**, 7. **Betsey Ann Royal**
1779/1781 - **Demcy Carell** signed a petition; **1781** - **Demcy/Demsey Carell**, tax list; **1790** - **Demcy/Demey Carrol**, Fayette Dist. (Johnson, Jour. pp. 1781, 1782; Cens. Indx.)
1779/1781 - **Stephen Carrell** signed a petition; **1781** - **Stephen Carrell**, tax list; **1790** - **Stephen Carrol**, Fayette Dist. (Johnson, Journal, pp. 1781, 1782; Cens. Indx.)
1781 - **William Carrell**, 4 Free Persons, tax list; **1790** - **William Carrol**, 21, Fayette Dist., Fayetteville Town, 1M16+, total 1; **1800** - **William Carroll**, 00100-00100-00 (Hds./Fams., p. 42; Bentley Cens. Indx. Roll 31; Cens., pp. 351, 353, 394; North Carolinian Qrtly., March 1958, p. 754)
1781 - **Elizabeth Carrell**, tax list; **1790** - **Elizabeth Carroll**, Fayette Dist. (Cens. Indx.)
1789 - Andrew Armstrong, 20 June/July, residue of lds in Davidson and Sumner cos. (TN) on Cumberland river known to Maj. James Cole Mount-florence, exr. with Augustine Ceeaty, to be sold to discharge debts (see Armstrong will); to **Joannah Cannole?**, **Charles Carroll** and Augustine Ceeaty/Cicaty; wits.: Philip Raiford, Isaac Burkloe, John Elwell (Lepine, p.3)
1790 - **Elisha Carrol**, Fayette Dist.; **1817** - **Elisha Carroll** md. **Sarah Brown**, 5 Apr., bdms. Wm. Brown & Wm. Stoakes, wits. W. Dickson, CC (Cens. Indx.; Bass, Marr.) [Alexander's son?] **?Son:**
    1. **1868** - **Elisha Carroll** md. **Elizabeth Smith**, 10 Jan., bdsm. Daniel J. Baker, wit. Edw. L. Winslow (Cumb. Co. Marr. Bds.- 1868, p.53; North Carolinian Qrtly., March 1957, p. 271)
1790 - **Thomas Carrol**, Fayette Dist. (Cens. Indx.)
1791 - Deed from **Dennis Kerral** (i.e. **Kerrell**) to Wm. Avera, proved by John Warner, recorded 27 Jan. (Field, p. 315)
1791/1792 - **John Carrell** of Nash Co., NC, lately soldier in NC Line, gave power of atty. appointing Solomon Cotten, atty. to receive of Francis Child, comptroller, a final settlement certificate, wit.: Redmun Bunn, 29 Mar. 1792 (NC Gen. Soc. J., v. 3, p. 212, I. 20) [See **John Carroll** & Thomas Child, Franklin Co.]
? - **William Carral**, Rev. War, Final Settlements; **1791/1792** - **William (C) Carrel**, Beaufort Co., sol., NC Line, gave p/a, Solomon Cotten to receive of F. Child, compensation, a final settlement certificate, wit.: Robert Tripp, 25 Apr. 1792; **1792** - **William (C) Carrel** of Cumberland Co., late a sol., NC Line, p/a, Philemon Hodges, atty. to obtain a final settlement, sworn statements of Jas. Pearl, Lt., Cont. Line, Cumb. Co.: **William Carrel** served 9 mos. in Southward Army commanded by Gen. Linchhorn (NC Gen. Soc. J., v. 3, pp. 20, I. 22, p. 212, I. 21)
1805 - **Benajah Carroll**, b. 1805, md. **Mary Eliza Mallard**, **1840** moved to **MS**, then to **Drew Co., AR**, then to **TX**, **ch.**:
    1. **Rebecca Ann Carroll**
    2. **John William Carroll**
    3. **Richard Baxter Carroll**
    4. **Margaret Carroll**
    5. **Andrew Fuller Carroll**
    6. **Benajah Harvey Carroll**
    7. **Laban Joseph Carroll**
    8. **Charles Aliene Carroll**

9. **Francis Wayland Carroll**
10. **Mary Emma Carroll**
11. **James Milton Carroll**, lived 5 miles from Kenansville on Elder Creek, later sold to his brother
12. **John Durham Carroll** and moved into Kenansville
13. **Mary Eliza Mallard Carroll**

1870 - **Laban Carroll**, b. **1807**, md. 1st **Sally Ann Fillyaw**, ch.:
    1. **John Cullen Carroll**; 2. **Laban Carroll**; 3. **Benajah Carroll** md. **Martha ?**, dau., **Mollie Black Carroll** was 2nd wife of **George Washington Carroll** (Will Bk. ?, #185; Murphy Indx.); 4. **Isaiah Carroll**; 5. **Augustus Carroll**; 6. **Thomas Owen Carroll**

1809 - **John Durham Carroll**, b. 3 Jan. **1809**, ?d. **1885** (Will Bk., 4, p. 247) md. **Zilpha Chestnutt**, ch.:
    1. **George Washington Carroll**, b. 20 Sept. **1833**, d. 15 Sept. **1912**, postmaster of Six Runs Post Office 11 June **1888** (Folks, p. 26, #26S), md. 1st **Mary White Houston**, b. 25 Aug. **1836**, d. 11 Jan. **1894**, md. 2nd **Mollie Black Carroll**, ch.:
        1. **Annie Estelle Best**, b. **1889**
        2. **Herman Randall Carroll**, b. **1891**
        3. **Mary W. Ledbetter**, b. **1894**
        4. **Charles F. Carroll**, b. **1900**, LL.D;
        5. **James Thomas Carroll**
        6. **John Lemuel Carroll**
        7. **Luther Rice Carroll**
        8. **Owen Judson Carroll**
        9. **Mary Ann Carroll**
        10. **Martha Jane Carroll**
        11. **Margaret Elizabeth Carroll**, d. young

c1813 - **Charity Marie Carroll**, b. c**1813**, md. 1st **W. J. McGowan**, 2nd **William Moore**, in FL
c1815 - **Rachel Jane Carroll**, b. c**1815**
? - **Edwin Joseph Carroll**, md. **Sarah Eliza Wilson**, moved to Carroll Co., MS, ch.:
    1. **John Bunyan Carroll**
    2. **Ann Judson Carroll**
    3. **Edwin Carroll**, d. in Army

1820 - **Brother Carroll** (Cens., p.177; NC Cens. Indx., p. 49)
1823 - **James Carroll** md. **Lydia Moore** 7 Jan., bdsm. Duncan McCall, Jno. Armstrong; **1839** - **James Carrol** md. **Elizabeth Sikes** 27 June, bdsm. John Newberry, wit. J. McLaurin Jr.; **1850** - **James Carrell**, Western Dist.; **1890** - **James Carroll** will, dau. **Amelia**, Holly/Hawly ld. and Steel ld. int.; son **J. Wesley Carroll**, exr. and Jenkins ld.; **James A. Carroll**, Peace ld. bght. from Warren, Carver; Drieslow, McLeod, **Carroll**, Lillerlah tract; Maria Peace, RS Huske ld.; **Sallie Ann Dickes?**, clothing and schooling; exrs.: Henry S. Cook, **J. Wesley Carroll**; wits.: W. J. Ayers and E. E. Ayers (Cumb. Co. Marr. Bds., p. 53; NC Cens. Indx., pp. 46, 55; Ingmire, p. 18; Will Bk. E, p. 485) **ch.**:
    1. **1850** - **John W. Carrell**, Eastern Dist.; **1855** - **John W. Carrol** md. **Elizabeth Ann Porter**, 19 June, by D.G. MacRae, JP, bdsm. James Sewell, wit. Rob. B. Gilliam; **?** - **John**

Wesley Carroll, Co. B., 13 NCL Artillery, CSA, b. Block #26 in Cross Creek Cemetery #1, Fayetteville, NC (NC Cens. Indx., p. 80; Cumb. Co. Marr. Bds.-1868, p.53; Sherman, Anna S. and Kate J. Lepine, Cross Creek Cemetery #1, Fayetteville, NC, 1988, p. 24)
    2. **Sallie Ann Dickes?**
    3. **Amelia**
    4. **1882 - James Carroll**, son of **James and Elizabeth**, md. **Mary Ellis**, 15 Feb. by Rev. J. P. McPherson, Presb. Mins., wit. A. M. Campbell (Cumb. Co. Marr. Bds.-1868, p. 53)
1823 - Philip Carroll md. **Alge Willis** 6 Sept., bdsm. Duncan McCall, wit. Chas. Rhodes (Cumb. Co. Marr. Bds., p.54; Ingmire, p. 18; Carroll Cables, Apr. 1996)
1828 - Thomas Carroll md. **Sarah Delegraves** 23 Sept., bdsm. Bass Beasley, wit. James Pearsall, CC (Bass, Marr.)
1830 - Jerritt Carroll, Rockfish (NC Cens. Indx., Cens., p. 39)
1833 - Jesse Carrol md. **Catharine Wilson** 19 Dec., bdsm. James Snipes, clk. A. McLean Jr. (Cumb. Co. Marr. Bds., p. 53)
1840 - Ellen M. Carroll (NC Cens. Indx., p. 302)
1840 - Hetty Carroll md. **William DeFever** 1 June, bdsm. Wm. W. Winn, wit. D. McLaurin (Cumb. Co. Marr. Bds.-1868, p. 78; Carroll Cables, July 1995)
1840 - Mary Carroll md. **Walter Bane** 5 Sept., bdsm. Thos. Js. Bulla, wit. D. McLaurin (Cumb. Co. Marr. Bds.-1868, p. 14; Carroll Cables, July 1995)
1845 - Eliza Carroll md. **Shipman Jones** 7 Apr. by D. G. McRae, bdsm. Amosa Barnhill, wit. J. McLaurin, D. G. MacRae, JP; **1870 - Eliza Carroll**, Rock Fish Twp. (Cumb. Co. Marr. Bds.-1868, p. 151; Carroll Cables, July 1995; NC Cens. Indx., Cens., p. 153)
1847 - Mary Ann Carroll md. **Russel Bagley** 10 Oct/4 Nov. by J. McKethan, bdsm. G. R. Gaughtery, wit. John McLaurin (Cumb. Co. Marr. Bds.-1868, p.11; Carroll Cables, July 1995)
1850 - Mary Ann Carroll, Fayetteville (NC Cens. Indx., p. 12)
1850 - Rhoda Carroll, Fayetteville (NC Cens. Indx., p. 15)
1850 - Joseph Carrell, Eastern Dist. (NC Cens. Indx., p. 70)
1852 - James G. Carroll, d. c1864; 16 Sept. **1852**, Apr. Ct. **1864**, willed slave to **brother William C. Carroll**, exr. Gibson Carr (Will Bk., p. 28, #96; Murphy Indx.) [**William C. Carroll** will, **1884** (Will Bk. 4, p. 236) (See previous p. 64]
1853 - Catharine Carroll md. **Riley Starling** 31 June/July by Alfred Jackson, JP, wit. J. T. Warden (Cumb. Co. Marr. Bds.-1868, p. 286; Carroll Cables, July 1995)
1859 - John H. Carroll md. **Elizabeth Ann Beard** 25/30 July by William Alderman, JP, bdsm. & wit. Henry Huske (Cumb. Co. Marr. Bds.-1868, p. 53; Carroll Cables, Apr. 1996)
1859 - Thomas Caroll/Carroll md. **Nancy Gay** 7 Sept., bdsm. William J. Monroe, wit. Henry Huske; md. 7 Aug. 1862, by John P. Leonard, JP, bdsm. J. W. Baker Jr., wit. Wm. J. McDonald, clk. J. T. Warden; **1862 - Thomas Carroll** md. **Nancy Gay** 7 Aug.; **1870 - Thomas Carroll**, Seventy Firs (Cumb. Co. NC Marr. Bds.-1868, pp. 53, 54; Carroll Cables, Apr. 1996; NC Cens. Indx., Cens., p. 83 or 88)
?- B. V. Carroll will (Will Bk.?, #163; Murphy Indx.)
?- Eda Carroll will (Will Bk. ?, #19; Murphy Indx.)
1866 - Joseph Carroll md. **Aly McAlister** 3 Jan., bdsm. Wm. McAlister, wit. & clk. J. T. Warden; **1867 - Joseph Carroll** md. **Harriet Pepper** 4 May; **1870 - Joseph Carrol**, Rick/Rock Fish Twp.; (Marr. Bds.-1868, p. 54; Carroll Cables, Apr. 1996; NC Cens, Indx., Cens., p. 152)

1868/?1869 - Mary Carroll md. **John McAlister** 20 July **?1868** (Carroll Cables, July 1995)
1868 - Daniel Carroll, son of **Sanders and Juna Carroll**, md. Margaret Burton, dau. of Handy and Rachel Burton Pickett, 20 Feb.; Robt. N. Cole, JP, wit. Walter R. Bell, CC (Bass, Marrs.)
1868 - William Carroll, md. **Jennetta Bryant** 23 Dec., by M. N. Leary Jr., JP, wit. John Frey, RD; **1870 - William Carroll**, Rock Fish (Cumb. Co.Marr. Bds.-1868, p. 54; Carroll Cables, Apr. 1996; NC Cens. Indx., Cens., p. 153)
1870 - James Carroll md. **Catharine Johnson** 16 Jan., by H. W. Cole, MG, wit. A. McPherson Jr. DC; **James Carroll**, Rock Fish Twp. (Cumb. Co. Marr. Bds.-1868, p. 53; NC Cens. Indx., Cens.p.161) [?Son of David md. **Cherry Carroll**; ?dau. of **Jannett** md. David Johnson]
1870 - William H. Carroll md. **Sally Gainey** 7 Dec., by David Williams, bdsm. A. M. Campbell, DC (Cumb. Co. Marr. Bds.-1868, p. 54; Carroll Cables, Apr. 1996)
1870 - Aurella Carroll, Rock Fish Twp. (NC Cens. Indx., Cens., p. 161)
1870 - Hugh Carrol, Cedar Creek (NC Cens. Indx., Cens., p. 223)
1870 - Maulsey Carroll, Rock Fish Twp. (NC Cens. Indx., Cens., p. 65)
1874 - Annie Carroll md. **George Murphy** 5/8 Nov., by James Bryant, MG, wit. W. W. Autry, RD [Afro-Americans] (Cumb. Co. Marr. Bds.-1868, p. 227; Carroll Cables, July 1995)
1887 - Mrs. Susan C. Carroll, postmistress of Harrells' Post Office in SE county, 11 July
1932 - Rachel Carroll, b. **1826**, Sampson Co., md. **Isham Royall** in Sampson Co. in **1855**, lived in Duplin Co., d. in Cumberland Co. in **1932** (Indx. NC Ancestors, p. 32) [**Rachel**, 106 yrs. old!]

<u>Halifax County</u> was established **1758** from **Edgecombe County**.
1739 Feb. 11 - Abraham Carnell? of Upper Parish, Nansemond Co., Colony of VA, and **wife Charity**; grandson **Thomas Carnell** whose mother is **Charity Carnell**, land in Edgecomb Co., NC (Absts. of Dds., Bk. 1, p. 384)
1783/85 - William Carrol, #300, military pay settlements in Halifax Co.; **1786 - Warrenton, Warren Co.** (DAR Roster, p. 226)
1790 - John Carroll, 1M16+,2M16-, 2F, taxpayer (Cens. Roll 498, p. 59; Radcliff, p. 40)
1790 - Thomas Carroll, taxpayer; **1795 - Thomas Carrol's** wife was **Rebecca**, dau. of John Marshall; **Thomas Carrol** md. **Rebecca Marshall**, dau. of John Marshall (Dd. Bk. 18, p. 14; Will Bk. 3, p. 326; Gammon, p. 133; Radcliff, p. 40)
1790 - Joseph Carroll, 3M16+, 2M16-, 2F, 2 sl (Cens. Roll 498, p. 158)
1827 - William Carroll, bdsm., marriage of Charles Lynch and Temperance Richardson
1857 - John A. Carroll md. **Nancy Grant** 8 Aug. (Carroll Cables, Apr. 1996)
1858 - William S. Carroll md. **Louisa King** 14 Sept. (Carroll Cables, Apr. 1996)
[**1821 - William Carroll** & Perina Ellis, NC, moved to Indiana; **Jane Carroll Davis**, b. **1839**, d. **1866**, was their dau. or a relative; letter from Ellen Cato, dated 16 Jan. 1992]

<u>Dobbs County</u> was established in **1758** from **Johnston County** and no longer exists.

<u>Hertford County</u> was established in **1759** from **Chowan, Bertie and Northampton counties**. In 1780 it was in Edenton Military Dist. No information found on **Carrolls** in this co.

<u>Pitt County</u>, established in **1760** from **Beaufort County**, was in Newbern Military Dist. #5. (Carls, NE Cos., p. 1)

1784 - **Isaac Carroll**; **1786** - Capt. Robert Hodge's Dist., 1M60+, 2M16-60, 2M16-, 1F60+, 2F16-, 1Fsl 16-?, 8 total; **1787** - Tax List; **?1789/1791/1799** - **Isaac Carrel**; **1790** - **Isaac Carrill**, Newbern Dist., 38, b. **c1742**, 3M16+, 4M16-, 5F, ; **1800** - **I. Carroll Sr.**, 1M10-, 1M10-16, 3M16-26, 1M45+, 2F10-, 1F10-16, 1F16-26, 1F45+, 1sl; **1810** - **I. Carrell**, Newbern Dist., 3M16+, 4M16-, 5F (Ear. Amer. Series, v. 1, p. 30; Register, pp. 32, 136; Tax List; Hds./Fams. Indx., p. 148; Cens. Indx., pp. 23, 32, 42; Cens., p. 507; Cens. Roll 32, p. 251, l. 6) **Ch.:**
    1. **1822 Mar. 20/ Sept. 29, 1823** - **Elizabeth Carrell**, dau of Isaac and Sally Carrell md. **Benjamin Buck**, 20 Mar. **1822**, widow's dower (CC-268, item #781, CC-60, #783; Kammerer, p. 59)
1810 - **John Carrell** (Cens. Indx., pp. 23, 42; Cens., pp. 231, 468)
1810 - **1820** - **Joshua Carrell** - (Cens. Indx., pp. 39, 42; Cens., pp. 477, 559, #39)
1810 - **Thomas Carrell** (Cens. Indx., pp. 23, 42; Cens., pp. 237, 479)
1819 - **Adam Carrel (Sr.)**, b. 18 Nov. **1789**, d. 25 Aug. **1829**, md. **Hollen Brooks**, b. 7 Mar. **1798**, md. ?22 Dec. **1819**; **1820** - **Adam Carrel** (Cens. Indx., p. 37; Cens., p. 556, #37) **ch.:**
    1. **Arena Carrel**, b. 7 Oct. **c1820**
    2. **Patsy Carrel**, b. 2 Jan. **1822**
    3. **Southey Carrel**, b. 2 July **1823**
    4. **John G. Carrel**, b. 3 Dec. **1826**, md. Sarah Jane Edwards, ch.:
        1. **Wm. Francis Carroll**, b. 6 Mar. **1851**, ch.:
            1. **Ida Brooks Kellam**
        2. **Joseph G. Carroll**, b. 2 July **1852**
        3. **Emily Louisa Carroll**, b. 24 Nov. **1853**
    5. **Nancy Carrel**, b. 2 Feb. **1828**
    6. **Adam Carrel**, b. ? Feb. **1829** [info submitted by Ida Brooks Kellam for NC Bible Records, NC DAR, Stamp Defiance Chap., Wilmington, from family Bible of Adam & Holland; in 1959, the Bible was owned by **Annie Carroll**, Greenville, NC]
1897 - **John Carroll** will (Will Bk. 3, p. 121)

Mecklenburg County, established in **1762** from Anson County, included what was to become Rutherford County.
1732-1774 - **John Carrell Sr.**, #24 on undated list of Capt. Thos. Neel's Co. of NC Militia; **1770** - Dd. to **John Carroll** of Mecklenberg Co. from Wm. Neely, same co., for ld. W. side of Catawba, S. side of north fork of Fishing Creek, wits.: John Anderson & Thomas McWhorter (Clark, Col. Sldrs. ..., p. 839; Holcomb, p. 13) **?Son:**
    1. **1732-1774** - **John Carrell Jr.**, #25 on list of Capt. Thos. Neel's Co. of NC Militia (Clark, Col. Sldrs. ..., p. 839)
1732-1774 - **Joseph Carroll Sr.**, #26 on list of Capt. Thos. Neel's Co. of NC Militia; **1766** - **Joseph Carrol**, 25 Sept., 200 acs. at forks of Allison's Creek, joining John Barr, Wm. Mackelmurray, John Venable and **Carrol's** own lines; **1767** - **Joseph Carrol** ld., 25 Apr., Samuel Willson patent; **1790** - **Joseph Carroll**, 30, Salisburg Dist. #1, 3M16+, 2M16-, 2F, 3sls/0sls; **1800** - **Joseph Carroll**, Salisbury Dist. #1, 3M16+, 2M16-, 2F16+, 3sls (Clark, Col. Sldrs. ..., p. 839; Pat. Bk. 18, pp. 254, 363; Hofmann, Crown ..., v. 1, pp. 49, 88, 534; Hds./Fams. Cens. Indx., p. 158; Ray, p. 357; Cens.)

1767 - **Jonans Carrol**, 26 Oct., ld. of Robert Marrs patent (Pat. Bk. 23, p. 122; Hofmann, Crown..., v. 1, p. 534)
1768 - **James Carrol**, 29 Apr., 200 acs. on N. fork Tygar river; **1790** - **James Carroll**, 25, Salisburg Dist. #1, 1M16+, 2F; **1800** - **James Carroll**, Salisbury Dist. #1, 1M16+, 2F16+ (Pat. Bk. 23, p. 310; Hofmann, Crown..., v. 1, p. 519; Hds./Fams. Cens. Indx., p. 158; Ray, p. 357; Cens.)
1769 - **Doctor Carrol** owned ld. in co. 4 May (Pat. Bk. 20, p. 432; Hofmann, Crown..., v. 1, p. 120)
1790 - **Henry Carrell**, 45+; **1800** - **Henry Carrell**, 10001-10010 (Ray, p. 357; Cens. Roll 33, p. 606, l. 4; Bentley Indx., p. 41)
1800 - **James Carroll** md. **Martha Williams**, 11 June (Clemens, p. 56; Holcomb, p. 36)
1800 - **Dennis Carrill** 00010-?10310-10010-00 (Jackson Cens. Indx., Cens. Roll 33, pp. 492, 606)
1831 - **Nathan B. Carroll** md. **Jennett Graham**, 13 Oct. (Clemens, p. 56; Holcomb, p. 36; Carroll Cables, Apr. 1996)
1895 - **Rev. John Lemuel Carroll** died (Source ?)

<u>Bute County</u>, was established in **1764** from Granville County and no longer existed after **1779**.
1753 - **Benjamin Carroll**, b. **1753**, md. Nancy Peeler; **1771** - **Benjamin Carol**, taxpayer; **1772** - **Benjamin Carroll** bght. from Wm. Duke, both of Bute Co., 30p Va money, 200 acs in Bute Co. where said **Carroll** now lives, where cart path crosses and along old cart path to new road, adj. Thos. Christmas, Charles Burk and Wm. Reddock/Reddick, Ben McCullock, CC, Aug. Ct., regd. 9 Nov., Jas. Johnson; **Benjamin Carroll** leased to Benj. McIvaile, both of Bute Co., 25p proclamation money, 50 acs. in co. on Little Ck. adj. to Chas. Burk and Thos. Christmas, wits.: Wm. McInvaile, Jas. McInvaile, Aug. Ct. 1777, Thos. Machen, CC; regd. 28 Oct. by Jas. Johnson, PR; **1774** - **Benjamin Carol** leased ld. to Wm. Park, 15p procl. money, 125 acs. in Bute Co. on Little Creek from Benj. McInvale line up on Cart Way to another Cart Way from line of John Jackson to Thos. Christmas, wits. Thos. Machen, CC, Obed Greene, Wm. Weldon, Feb. Ct., regd. 9 May 1777 by Jas. Johnson, P.R.; **1776** - **Benjamin Carrel**, member of Committee of Safety; **1778** - **Benjamin Carrell's** property line mentioned in sale of ld. from Wm. Reddick to Thos. Robins, both of Bute Co., 220p VA money for 250 acs. between Little Creek and Thos. Christmas to O'Possum Quarter Ck., up Possum Q. Ck. from Allan Love & Co. and **Ben Carrell**, wit. Thos. Miller Jr., Wm. Miller, regd. 1 Feb. 1780 by Jas. Johnson, P.R. (Early Amer. Series, v. 3, p. 38; Radcliff, p. 36; Dd. Bk. 4, p. 15; Kerr Absts., p. ?; Dd. Bk. 6, pp. 131, 213) [See Warren Co.]
1759 - **John Carrell**, 300-ac. grant, 100 on East Lizard Ck., 150 on E. Lizard Ck. mouth of Great Branch, sold to Robert, Caleb & Joshua Taylor; **1766** - **John Carroll**, taxpayer; **1771** - **John Carroll**, taxpayer; **1772** - **John Carroll**, pt. of his 300-ac. gt. sold by Joshua Taylor to Mark Moore of Northampton, wit. Matt. Myrick (Radcliff, pp. 34, 36; Early Amer. Series, v. 3, p. 38) [See Warren Co.]
1778 - **John Carroll**, 130 ac. grant... 12 Dec.; **1804/1816** - **John Carroll** bght. & sold ld. (NC Ld. Gts., p. ?; Dds.) [See Warren Co.]
1765 - **Mary Carroll and Elizabeth Carrel**, wits. (?)
1767 - **William Carroll** bght. 200 acs. on south side of Tar River (later in Franklin Co.), wife

Elizabeth, sons: John, William and Thomas; 1771 - **William Carol**, taxpayer (Dd.; Early Amer. Series, v.3, p. 38) [See Warren Co.] **Son:**
 1. **William Carroll** [Note: **Wm**. md. **Keziah** ? - **1777** - **John Keziah** among others who purchased parts of Wm. Baker, decd., est., May Ct.; **1782** - **William Carroll** returned from serving in war (Kerr, p. 53) [See Warren Co.]
1768 - **Daniel Carrill and Rebecca Carrill** wit'd. ld. transfer of Wm. Eaves Sr. to Benjamin Eaves, both of Bute Co. on Tar River, S. side Mill Ck. down a Spring Branch, up Linche Ck. to Mill Ck., 50 p, 200 acs., Halifax, 7 Jan./12 Oct.; **1779** - **Daniel Carroll**, 24, b. **(1755)** in VA, Bute Co., NC, 1778, "Balloted Men and Volunteers" from Bute Co. to serve 9 mos. as Continental Soldier beginning 1 Mar. **1779**; **1781** - **Daniel Carrell**, **R1726**, b. 17 Oct. **1748**, d. 20 Apr. **1837** in **Lincoln Co., TN.**; resident of Bute Co. in **1781** when he enlisted under Capt. Daniel Jones, served under Capt. Jacob Turner, Lt. Alsay High & Sgt. Maj. David Speer, discharged in Halifax Co., NC, md. 11 Nov. **1793** in **Union Co., SC**; **1820** - **Daniel Carrell**, 72 yrs. of age, living in **Lauderdale Co., AL** with wife **Hannah** (dau. of Edward & Ester Inslo/Insoe, age 42, b. **1778**, d. 12 Apr. **1840** without bearing a child, buried on Ebenezar Rickett's Plantation, Fayetteville, **Lincoln Co., TN**), had a brother in GA; another statement: "**Alabama 1825**, Limestone Co. md. here Mar. **1822**." Grief Carrell swore:
 1. **Daniel George Carrell**, b. 16 Feb. **1780**; **Daniel Carrell**, 8 Nov. **1819**; **1846**, **Wayne Co., NC**, petition for his pension (Dd. Bk. 2, p. 130; Kerr Absts., p. ?; No. Carolinian Qtrly., Sept. 1960, p. 727; Rev. War Pens. Rcds., letter of July **1820**, Lincoln Co., AL; Rev. War Pens. Appl. Rcds.) [Daniel's son]
1771 - **Thomas Carol**, taxpayer (Early Amer. Series, v. 3, p. 38; Radcliff, p. 36)
1773 - **Milborough N. Carroll**, b. c1710 in ?VA, d. **1773**, will in Bute Co. dated 1 Apr. 1773 (Indx. NC Ancestors, p. 25, #28500; Warren Co.,Will Bk. 1, p. 275): **wife unnamed**, probably deceased, probated May **1774** : **Milbrough Carrole** of **Bute Co** of the Province of North Carolina, 1 April 1773
Item I give and bequeath to my **two sons Thomas Carrole and Charles Carrole** all my stock of cattle and hoggs to be equally divided between them, to them and their heirs and assigns forever.
Item divided house hold goods and furniture between **Thomas Carrole, Charles Carrole and Betty Wilkins.**
Item to son **Charles Carrole** 200 acres of land in Brunswick Co. Va and my horse saddle and briddle
Item to **Betty Wilkins** 10 pounds cash and my side saddle
Item to son **Thomas Carrole** 4 pounds cash
Item I hereby appoint my two sons **Thomas Carrole** and **Charles Carrole** and John Mosely executors
Milbrough N Carrole
In presence of Stephen Shell, Sarh Brett, Rebekah Johnson [See Warren Co.]
1778 - **George Carroll** bght. 268 acs. from Wm. Shearin, both of Bute Co., 143p6s8d procl. money, 268½ acs. in co. on E. side Little Ck., adj. exam, wits.: Sarah Johnston, Jane Haynes, Thos. Miller Jr., 30 Mar., regd. 8 Jan. 1780; **1779** - **George Carroll** sold ld. to Moses Myrick (Dd. Bk.6, p. 426; Dd. Bk. ?, p. ?) [See Warren Co.]
1807/1810 - **Ann Carroll** bght. ld. (Dd. Bk. ?, p. ?) [See Warren Co.)

Brunswick County was established in **1764** from **New Hanover and Bladen counties.**
1750 - **John Carrell**, Wm. Holloway and Wm. Moseley wits **Mar. 1/Feb.Ct.1751** for John Johnson, St. Andrews Parish, Brunswick Co.; son and exr. William; daus.: Amey Mitchell, Ann Jelks; gddaus.: Martha and Anne, daus.; **1784** - **John Carroll**, taxpayer; **1790** - **John Carrol**, Wilmington Dist., 1M16+, 1M16-, 3F (Grimes, Abtsts. of NC Wills, p. 188; Ratcliff, p. 34; Hds./Fams., p. 189) [Two Johns with same enumeration on same page]
1790 - **Hardy Carrel**, Wilmington Dist., 1M16+, 1M16-, 3F; **1800** - **Hardy Carrel**, Wilmington Dist., 1M16+, 1M16-, 3F (Hds./Fams., pp.189,190) [For 1790, see Duplin Co.]
1800 - **Ann Carrol**, Wilmington Dist., 10000-10010-00 (Cens. Indx., p. 37; Cens. Roll 29, p. 14)
1820 - **Frederick Carrol**, Wilmington Dist. (Cens. Indx., p. 5, #6)
1820 - **Joab Carrol**, Wilmington Dist. (Cens. Indx., p. 5, #6)
1850 - **William Carroll**, b. **1812** in NC, wife **Mrs. Rebecca Carroll**, b. **1814, ch.:**
  1. **Robert A., b. 1833**
  2. **William I., b. 1835**
  3. **Mary A., b. 1837**
  4. **Ann, b. 1839;**
  5. **Thomas, b. 1841**
  6. **Caroline, b. 1841**
  7. **Nathaniel, b. 1842** (Cens.)
1866 - **Dorcas Carroll** md. **Dougald M. Turner** 6 Oct. (Carroll Cables, July 1995)

Tyron County, established in **1768** from **Mecklenburg County**, no longer exists.
1768 - **John Carrol** ld, 22 Dec., Wm. Patrick patent; **1769** - **John Carrol**, 4 May, 100 acs., Fishing Creek, including part of improvement **Carrol** now lives on, joining Peter Keykendale and the waggon road; ? - from Wm. Neely of Mecklenburg Co. to **John Carroll** of same, ld. on W. side of Catawba on S. side N fork of Fishing Creek, wits. John Anderson, Thos. McWhorter; **1772** - **John Carrol**, 22 May, 200 acs. S. side Catauba River, including **Carrol's** improvements, joining Patterson's ld. and some rocks; **1774** - **John Carrol** of Tyron Co., to Alex'r. Patterson (Pat. Bk. 23, p. 346; Hofmann, Crown ..., v. 1, pp. 124, 287, 534; Pat. Bk. 20, p. 442; Holcomb, pp. 13, 64; Pat. Bk. 22, p. 79)
1769 - **Joseph Carrol** and **Thomas Carrol** of Tyron Co. to James Logan of same, 16 Nov., Catawba, wits. John Venables, **Joseph Carrol, Samuel Carrol** (Holcomb, p. 12)

Wake County was established in **1770** from **Cumberland, Orange and Johnston counties.**
1771 - **Suckey Carrell** md. **Thomas House, 1771** (North Carolinian Qrtly., June 1957, p. 308; Cumberland Co. Marr. Bds. 1808-1868; Carroll Cables, July 1995)
1797 July 2 - **John Carrol**, buyer, E. Strickland est. sale; **1797** Dec. 8 - **John Carroll** bght. ld. from James Tate est.; **1798** May 4 - **John Carrell**, buyer, Mary Stevens est.; **1800** May - **John Carroll** owed Britain Sander's est., inv.; **1801** Aug. - **John Carrell** paid in B. and E. Sanders' Acct. Current (Bk. D, p. 197; Wynne, pp. 124, 146, 158, 191, 220; Bk. E, pp. 7, 138; Bk. F, pp. 68,290)
1808 - **Delilah Carrell** md. **Joseph Baccus** 8 Apr. (Carroll Cables, July 1995)
1817 - **Matthis Carroll** md. **Polley Ivey/Ivy** 20 Feb., Wm. Ivey, bdsm. (Holcomb, p. 50; Carroll Cables, Apr. 1996)

1819 - **Merrel Carroll** md. **Stancey/Stanny House** 15/18 Nov., Warren House, bdsm.; **1820 - Merrell Carroll** (Holcomb, p. 50; Carroll Cables, Apr. 1996; Cens. Indx. supplemented/tax list)
1820 - **Frederick Carrol** (Cens. Indx., p. 6)
1820 - **Joab Carrol** (Cens. Indx., p. 6)
1822 - **Delilah Carroll** md. **Thomas Mosley** 2 Jan. (Carroll Cables, July 1995)
1825 - **William Carroll** md. **Peaty/Piety Hobby** 1 Dec., John Young, bdsm.; **1856 - William Carroll** (Holcomb, p. 50; Carroll Cables, Apr. 1996; R. Bk. 30, p. 79)
1828 - **James Carroll** md. **Clary Leopard** 25 Mar., John Johnston, bdsm. (Holcomb, p. 50)
1845 - **Betsey Carroll** md. **Dennis House** 10 Apr. (Carroll Cables, July 1995)
1846 - **Jane Carrol** md. **Turner Honeycut** 22 Aug. (Carroll Cables, July 1995)
1852 - **John Carroll** md. **Ann Beemer** 29 Dec. (Holcomb, p.50; Carroll Cables, Apr.1996)
1853 - **Hardy Carroll** md. **Emily W. Tample** 6 Dec. (Holcomb, p. 50)
1853 - **Julia Carrol** md. **Olonso Poole** 27 Dec. (Carroll Cables, July 1995)
1856 - **Howell Carroll** md. **Thula Earp** 12 June (Holcomb, p. 50)
1860 - **James Carrol** md. **Lucinda King** 31 Jan. (Holcomb, p. 50)
1860 - **S. H. Carroll** md. **M. R. Barnett** 24 Dec. (Holcomb, p. 50)
1860 - **Mary Carroll** md. **William Wall** 28 Dec. (Carroll Cables, July 1995)
1865 - **Eliza Carroll** md. **Thomas Pulley** 18 Nov. (Carroll Cables, July 1995)
1867 - **Mathew Carrol**, son of **John and Lila Carroll**, md. **Nancy Wheeler** 20 Apr. (Holcomb, p. 50)
1867 - **Major Carroll** md. **Candice Jones**, 5 Feb. [Afro-American] (Holcomb, p.50; Carroll Cables, Apr. 1996)

Chatham County was established in **1770** from **Cumberland, Orange and Johnston counties.**
1790 - Starling Carrot (Sic), Hillsborough Dist., 1M16+, 2M16-, 3F; **1800 - Sterling Carrol** 3M16-26, 1M45+, 1F10-, 1F10-16, 1F16-26, 1F45+, 1 sl; **1813 - Sterling Carrel** (Hds./Fams. Cens. Indx., p. 85; Cens. Roll 31, p. 222, l. 12, p. 223, l. 8; Will Bk. A, p. 239) **?Son:**
    1. **1830 - Sterling Carroll**, Pittsbon (NC Cens. Indx., Cens., p. 447)
[Martins in Chatham Co., censuses 1800-1850 at least. Sterling's sister married a Martin.]
1800 - John Carrol, 2M10-, 1M26-45, 3F10-, 1F16-26, 1F26-45, 1 sl (Cens. Roll 31, p. 136)
1800 - William Curl, 2M10-, 3M16-26, 1M45+, 1F10-, 1F10-16, 4F16-26, 1F45+ (Cens. Roll 31. p. 192 [297])
1800 - Thomas W. Carrol, 1M10-, 1M10-16, 2M16-26, 1M16-45, 1F10-, 1F26-45, 11sls ; **1840 - Thomas Carrol** (Cens. Roll 31, p. 331, l. 6; NC Cens. Indx., Cens., p. 194)
1805 - Emily C. Carroll, b. 11 Oct. **1805**, d. 11 Jan. **1873**
1810 - Alexander Carrol (Cens. Indx., pp. 23, 42; Cens., p. 200)
1810 - James Carrol; **1820 - James Carrell** (Cens. Indx. pp. 23, 42; Cens., p. 214; NC Cens. Indx., Cens., p. 53)
1810 - Daniel Carrol; **1820 - Daniel Carrol** (Cens. Indx., pp. 23, 38, 42; Cens., pp. 196, 197, 215)
1830 - Edward Carroll, Pittsbon; **1840 - Edward W. Carroll** (NC Cens. Indx., Cens. pp. 56, 446)
1830 - Mary Carroll, Pittsbon; **1840 - Mary Carrol**; **1850 - Mary Carroll**, Upper RE (NC Cens. Indx., Cens., pp. 186, 420, 447)

1835 - **Lydia B. Carroll** md. **Philip Wilson** 12 Jan. (Carroll Cables, July 1995)
1836 - **Robert D. Carroll**, b. 25 May **1836**, d. 8 Jan. **1845**
1840 - **Daniel Carroll** (NC Cens. Indx., Cens. p. 155)
1852 - 14 Aug., **Nancy Paterson**, 70 yrs. old, **dau. of John and Ann Carroll**; John, a resident of Mecklenburg Co., VA when he entered service, pvt.; raised to Capt. and commanded a company; moved to Warren Co., NC where he d. 13/15 Oct. **1832; widow Ann (Crowder) Carroll** d. in Warren Co. 25 Dec. **1844**; Nancy claimed to be only child; **Fanny Carroll**, 78, gave testimony for **Nancy, the wife of John Patterson** of Chatham Co., NC (Rev. War Pens. Appl. Rcds.)
1870 - **Noah Caroll**, Bear Creek Twp. (NC Cens. Indx., Cens. p. 10)
1870 - **Wesley Carroll**, Gulf Twp. (NC Cens. Indx., Cens. p. 64)
1904- **C. W. and M. A. Carroll; Ch.:**
  1. **Lydia J. Carroll**, dau. b. 26 July **1904**, d. 11 Aug. **1906**
  2. **Clarence C. Carroll**, son, b. 13 Dec. **1908**, d. 15 Aug. **1909**; Emily-Clarence C., buried in Williams & **Carroll Cemetery** on Williams property, RFD1, Goldston, NC (Misc. Gen. Recds., Guilford Battle Chap. NSDAR, Greensboro, 1961, p. 291)

<u>Guilford County</u> was established in **1770** from **Orange and Rowan counties**.
1790 - **Elizabeth Carrel**, Salisbury Dist., 1M16-, 5F; **1798** - **Elizabeth Carrel** md. **John Winchester Sr.** 21 Mar. (NC Cens. Indx.; Hds./Fams., p. 154; Carroll Cables, July 1995)
? - **James Carroll**, buried, Antioch Bapt. Ch. Cemetery (Miscellaneous General Recds., Guilford Battle Chap., NCDAR, Greensboro, NC, 1961, p. 203)
? - **Mary Carroll**, b. Antioch Bapt. Ch. Cem. (Same ref. as James)
? - **Charlie Carroll**, b. Antioch Bapt. Ch. Cem. (Same ref.)
1814 - **Sally Carrell** md. **Hugh Mathews** 4 Feb. (Carroll Cables, July 1995)
1817 - **Famey Carrol** md. **Armsted Holloway** 29 Oct. (Carroll Cables, July 1995)
1822 - **Bettsey Carrell** md. **Samuel Helton** 16 Nov. (Carroll Cables, July 1995)
1826 - **Sally Carrol** md. **Joshua Frost** 16 Feb. (Carroll Cables, July 1995)
1829 - **Arenia Carrell** md. **William Johnson** 12 Dec. (Carroll Cables,July1995)
1843 - **Elizabeth Carroll** md. **David Marshall** 25 Sept. (Carroll Cables, July 1995)

<u>Surry County</u> was established in **1770** from **Rowan County**.
1782 - NC gt. to David Allen, 640 acs., Big Elkin Creek, branch of Yadkin River, mouth of Big Elkin, div. line between Surry & Wilkes counties, agreed line with **William Carrel** ... (Absher, I. #215)
1786 - **Thomas Carral**, Capt. Love 1 Dist., 1M21-60, 2F, Robert Walker census taker (Register, p. 143)

<u>Martin County</u>, established in **1774** from **Tyrrell, Edgecombe and Halifax counties**, was in Halifax Military Dist. #3 in 1780. (Carls, NE Cos., p. 2)
1779 - **Thomas Currel**; **1780** - **Thomas Carrell**, son-in-law and exr. of William McKey est., 16 July, wife **Susanna (?McKey) Carrell**, other ch.: **Sarah (?McKey) Spanell**; **Margrite (?McKey) Jones**; son-in-law George Walker; gddau. Susanna McKey; **1787** - Dist. 7, 1M21-60,

4M21-/60+, 1F, 2blks12-50. 4blks12-50+; **1787** - **Thomas Carrell** will, dated 3 July **1787**, proved Sept. Ct., wife **Elizabeth** and others bght. ld. from exr., oldest son **William, John and Thomas**, other ch. unnamed; wits.: Thomas Hunter, Stephen Miller; **ch.**:
    1. **1800** - **William Carrell**, 1M16-26. 1F10-, 1F16-26. 1 sl (Cens., p. 391, l. 12)
    2. **1820** - **John Carrol**; **1830** - **John Carrol** (Cens. Indx., p. ?; Cens. Indx.)
    3. **Thomas Jr.**;   4. **Others**   (Early Amer. Series, v. 3, p. 53; Will Bk. 1, pp. 73, 135; Register, p. 95)

Camden County, established in **1777** from **Pasquatank County**, was in Edenton Military Dist. in 1780. No info on **Carrolls** in this co.

Nash County, established in **1777** from **Edgecombe County**, was in Halifax Military Dist. in 1780.
1800 - **William Carrell**, 20 (Cens. Indx.)
1841 - **Delila Carroll** md. **Robert Jones** 7 Oct. (Carroll Cables July 1995)

Caswell County was established in **1777** from **Orange County**. The **James Ruffin Carroll** family Bible reveals: "... **Carrolls** were Johnston County, N.C. people." They came with Barnes and Hinnants. (John Burch Baylock, reg'r. of deeds, Caswell Co., 12 Mar. 1945.)
1777 - **Richard Carroll**, Gloucester Dist. taxpayer; **1786** - **Richard Carrol**, Gloucester Dist. (Radcliff, p. 36; Kendall, p. 27)
1781 - **Mary Carroll** md. **Thomas White** 8 Jan. (Marr. Bds., p. 198; Ray, ... and Its People, p. 3)
1781 - **John Carroll** on list of Elephaz Shelton's Co. with F. Barrat, J. Barratt, M. Sims, J. Adams, W. McGhee, T. Harrisby, J. Arnols, T. Hudson, S. Barrett, H. Harris; St. of VA, County of Henry: appeared J. G. Penn, 12 Mar. 1896, to certify a true copy of the original muster roll of Col. Abram Penn's Regt. in Rev. War. Militia was ordered to march from Henry Co., VA to Hillsborough, NC to be under command of Gen. Stevens, to avoid a surprise attack by enemy, by the best route. Order of 11 Mar. 1781, Abraham Penn, Col. H.C. (Source ?)
1782 - **William Carral** md. **Sarah Bryant** 5 Jan., William Reed, bdsm.; **1783/1789** - **William Carrol** and Thomas Graves, wits. to power of attorney from Bazilla Human to John Graves, right and title to ld. on Reedy Fork, 200 acs., 18 Dec. 1783/July Ct. 1789; **1784** - **William Carroll**, Gloucester Dist., tax list, 100 acs., 1 polled; Hillsborough, Gloucester Dist. south east part of co., 1M21-60, 1M21-60+, 3F all ages; **1786/1787** - **William Carroll**, tax list; **?1789/ 1791/1799** - **William Carrel**; **1790** - **William Carrell**, Hillsborough, Gloucester Dist.; **1792** - **William Carroll** sold livestock to **George Carroll**, wits. Jesse Carter, James Gilaspi, 25 Feb./June Ct.; **1800** - Jan. Ct., allotment of ld. to Thomas Graves to said legatees ...William Moore, land called **Carol's tract**, North fork Country line Creek and Mill Creek; **1815** - **William Carroll**, insolvent; **1820** - **William Carroll**   (Bk. B, p. 279; Kendall, pp. 4, 27, 37, 41, 67, 138; Register, p. 23; Early Amer. Series, v. 1, p. 30; Radcliff, p. 34; Hds./Fams., p. 79; NC Cens. Indx., p. 48; Bk. C, p. 2; Bk. ?, p. 428; Bk. G, p. 65; Cens., p. 50; Indx., p. 9)
1783 - **Salley Carrell** md. **James Bryan** 22 Jan., Joseph Smith, bdsm. (Kendall, p. 16; Carroll Cables, July 1995)
1784/1787 - **Hannah Carrell**, 2M21-60, 4F all ages, Gloucester Dist., William Gooch Jr.;

?1789/ 1791/1799 - Hannah Carrell; **1812 - Hannah Carrol** md. **John Kennon**, 1 Nov., bdsm. William Evans, (Ear. Amer. Series, v. 1, p. 30; Register, p. 23; Marr. Bds.; Kendall, p. 80; Carroll Cables, July 1995)
1784 - George Carrol, St. Lawrence Dist., tax list, 0 acs., 1 white polled, 0 blacks; **1790 - George Carriol**, Hillsborough Dist., Richmond Dist.; **1792 - William Carrol** bill of sale to **George Carroll**, livestock, wits. Jesse Carter, James Gilaspi, 25 Feb./ June Ct.; **1797 - George Carroll**, "a list of taxable property of Richmond Dist., 265½ acs., 1 polled, 0 blks.; **1800 - George Carrell/ Carrol**, 1M10-, 2M10-16, 1M16-26, 1M26-45, 1M45+, 1F10-, 1F26-45; **1802 - George Carrol** bght. from sale of William Stephens est.; other buyers: R. Willson, S. F. Stephens, A. Stephens, J. Samuels, H. Tucker; **1803 - George Carrel**, Richmond Dist., 265 acs.; **1806** - Bonded to Geo. **Carrole** orphans **John Carrole**, 9 yrs. old and **Edward Carrole**, 6 yrs. old, 29 Oct.; **1810 - George Carrall**; **1819** - Geo. **Carroll** on long list of those buying property from Geo. Willson, 3 Nov. (Kendall, pp. 35, 41, 42, 49, 79, 141, 277; Hds./Fams., p. 81; Bk. C, p. 2; Co. Hist. Newsletter; Cens. Roll 31, pp. 109, 112; Bk. D, pp. 94; 278; Cens., p. 470; Indx. p. 42; Bk. H, p. 226) **?Son:**

1. **1800 - George Carrels/Carrell**, 1M10-16, 2M16-26, 1M45+, 1F10- 1F10-16, 1F26-45 (Cens.Roll 31,p. 698)

1784/1787 - Thomas Carroll, tax list; **1800 - Thomas Carrels**, 2M10-, 1M10-16, 1M16-26, 1M45+, 1F10-, 2F10-16, 2F16-26, 1F45+ (Register, p. 23; Cens. Roll 31, p. 111)

1790 - James Carrol md. **Sarah Bruce** 29 Nov., bdsm. James Hays; **1795 - James Carrell** owed money to wife of Robert Bruce (will); Bruce will: dau. Betsy, sons Thomas, William, John, Robert Bruce; ld. adj. to **James Carroll** and Joseph Bush; wits. John Payne (Taylor,) **James Carroll**, 16 Oct. Ct.; **1797 - James Carrel**, bdsm.; **1800 - James Carrol**; **1801 - James Carrol**, **Starling Carroll**, Jan. Ct., sale of Robert Bruce est., parts to **James and Starling**, **James Carroll**, adm.; **1803 - James Carrol**, Gloucester Dist., 100 acs.; **1804** - Joseph Bush, decd. (Will): wife Mary Ann, son Zenas Bush, exr., ld. adj. to Robt. Martin and **Jas. Carroll**; friends B. Graves Sr., S. Graves Sr., wits. B. Yancey; **1804 - James Carrol** (2) insolvents, Sam'l. Johnston, high sheriff, each assessed for 1 poll unless ... July Ct. 1805; **1804/1806** - 15 Sept. 1804, **James Carrole**, adm. of Elizabeth Bruce est., cash pd. to Francis Smith, Elijah Graves, Wm. Muzzall, Chas. Turner, Robt. Mitchell; sale in 1801, legacies to Wm. Hall, John Travis for David Tolloch, John Payne (Taylor), James Hayes, **James Carrole**; apprd. by Jas. Yancey and Alex Murphey; **1810 - J. B. Carrol** (Marr. Bds.; Kendall, pp. 16, 21, 42, 50, 74, 98, 117, 281; B. C, p. 137; Bk. M; Bk. D, p. 27; Bk. F, p. 85; Ccns., p. 57)

1790 - Ellis Carrol, no enumeration given; **1817 - Ellis Carrell** md. **Cathy Whitlow** 14 May, William Lyon, bdsm.; **1820 - Ellis Carroll** (NC Cens. Indx., p. 50; Kendall, p. 21; Cens., p. 52; Indx., p. 11)

1790 - Lemuel H. Carrol, no enumeration given; **1819 - Lemuel H. Carroll** md. **Salley Hooper** 11 Sept., William W. Lyon Jr., bdsm.; **1820 - Lemuel A./Samuel H. Carrl/Carroll**; **Lemuel H. Carroll**, bdsm. (NC Cens. Indx., p. 50; Kendall, pp. 21, 128; Carroll Cables, Apr. 1996; Cens., p. 49; Indx., p. 10)

1790 - Sterling Carrol, no enumeration given; **1792 - Starling Carrol**, bdsm.; **1793 - Polly Carroll** md. **Joshua Beaver** 5 Oct., **Sterling Carroll**, bdsm.; **1800 - Two-Starling Carrells** 3M10-, 1M26-45, 1F16-26, 11 sis; 1M10-, 1M26-45, 1F10-, 1F16-26; **1801** - Jan. Ct., sale of Robert Bruce est., parts to James Carroll and Starling Carroll, 5 Nov.; **1808 - Starling Carrol**

bght. pt. of John Gomer est; Jeremiah Beaver, adm.; other buyers: John and Robert Foster, Mar. Ct.; **1810 - Starling Carrole**; **1815 - Sterling Caroll**, insolvent; **1820 - Sterling Carroll** (Cens., p. 514; Indx. pp. 23, 42; NC Cens. Indx., p. 52; Kendall, pp. 4, 6, 16, 74, 111; Cens. Roll 31, pp. 112, 128, l. 20; Bk. D, p. 27; Bk. ?, p. 409; Bk. G, p. 65; Cens., p. 51; Indx., p. 11)

1793 - **Rebeccah Carrol** md. **James Hamlett** 9 Feb., Tobias Williams (Kendall, p.61; Carroll Cables, July 1995)

1798 - **Nancy Carrell** md. **Levin Roberts** 14 Nov., **George Carrell**, bdsm. (Marr. Bds., pp. 128, 428; Carroll Cables, July 1995)

1800 - **Joseph Carrell** 2M10-, 1M26-45, 3F10-, 1F16-26, 1F26-45, 1sl (Cens.Roll 31, p. 120, l. 9)

1801 - **Daniel Carrel** md. **Suckey Jones** 5 Jan., William Jones, bdsm; **1803 - Daniel Carrel**, Richmond Dist.; **1810 - Daniel Carroll** (Marr. Bds.; Kendall, pp. 21, 42; Cens. p. 470; Indxs., pp. 23, 42)

1802 - **Patsey Carrol** md. **Peter Powell** 31 Aug., Vincent Roberts; **1810 - Patsey Carroll** (Marr. Bds.; Kendall, p. 120; Carroll Cables, July 1995; Cens., p. 470; Cens. Indxs., pp. 23, 42)

1804 - **Betsy Carrol** md. **?Robert Elam** 14 Mar., bdsm. Benjamin Ingram and Sol. Debow (Marr. Bds.; Kendall, p. 41, Carroll Cables, July 1995)

1804 - **Betsey Carrol** md. **?John Terry** 14 Apr., Leavin Roberts (Marr. Bds.; Kendall, p.151, Carroll Cables, July 1995)

1820 - **Samuel H. Carroll** on long list of those buying property of Wm. Lyon, decd. (Bk. H, p. 365; Kendall, p. 46; Cens., p. 52, #10) [Was there a Samuel or is this **Lemuel H. Carroll**?]

1820/1821 - **Jackson Carrol**, orphan, age 12 last month, bound to Noel Read; Elijah Withers, Ch. Co. Ct., 9 Oct. 1820; **1838 - Jackson Carrol** md. **Martha Shelton** 12 Apr., Benjamin Evans, bdsm.; **Jackson Carroll**, SO34166, alleged: Capt. James L. Henderson's Co., 21st U.S. Troops (Bk. H, p. 398; Kendall, pp. 21, 48, 49; Indx./War1812 Pens. Appl. File, MC313, Roll 16)

1824/1825 - **Hezekiah Carrol** and others bght. ld. (Bk. 1, p. ?; Kendall, p. 69)

1825 - **Tabitha T. Carrel** md. **William F. Russell** 24 Nov., Robert White (Marr. Bds.; Kendall, p. 132; Carroll Cables, July 1995)

1826 - **Edward Carrol** md. **Polly Ferrell** 19 June, John C. Harvey, bdsm.; **1827 - Edward Carrol** md. **Delilah Baxter** 9 Jan., Thomas Ware Jr., bdsm.; **1830 - Edward Carrell**, bdsm. (Kendall, pp. 21, 40)

1827 - **James R. Carroll** md. **Polly Hubbird** 10 Aug., Thomas Johnson, bdsm. (Kendall, p. 21); ch.:

    1. **1835 - James Ruffin Carroll**, b. 15 June **1835**, md. #1 **Maryann Barnes Hinnant** (md. 1st James Hinnant), b. 11 Oct. **1838**, d. 15 Mar. **1890**; md. #2 **Cora Crowder** 10 Feb. **1895**; ch.:

        1. **Alice**, b. 2 Apr. **1870**, d. Aug. **1896**, md. **C. E. Wall** 16 Dec. **1890**

        2. **Francis M.** (son), b. 18 Aug. **1873**, d. 24 May **1876**

        3. **Ida**, b. 8 May **1875**, md. Jas. Jasper Ferrell, d. 19 Nov. **1943**, 4 June **1894**, buried in Clayton NC

        4. **Charles**, b. 18 Sept. **1877**

        5. **Essa** (dau.), b. 18 June **1882/1883**

        6. **Lattie Mozell**, b. 2 Dec. **1895**

  7. **Dan Hugh**, b. 10 Nov. **1898**
  8. **Sonora**, b. 6 Sept. **1901**
   (**Jas. Ruffin Carroll Bible**)
1849 - **Sarah A. Curls** md. **Franklin Keirsey** 2 Nov., Thomas S. Poore (Kendall, p. 80)
1858 - **William Carroll** md. **Polly ?**, b. **1834**, d. 19 Mar. **1911**, in **1858**; had 8 children, 3 living at her death, member of Fellowship Church (Mrs. J. Loyd Stephenson, dau., published 1 Oct. 1911 in Zion's Landmark, a Primitive Bapt. pub. in NC; Bk. 2, pp. 403-404; Blaylock) [1900s lineage traced from **Eli Carroll** to **Ruben Henderson Carroll** to **Pleasant Carroll**-according to **Carroll** descendant's spouse working in Caswell Co. Ct. House when info obtained.]

  <u>Wilkes County</u> was established in **1777** from **Surry County**.
1777 - **William Carrell**, Bedford Co., VA, indenture to Joseph Hardy, wits.: Robert. Ewing, Joseph Dickson, Thomas Campbell, Stephen Dooley, Thomas Martin; **1778** - **William Carrell**, **#39187**, pensioned, **#993**, entered 400 acs N. side Yadkin River, below mouth of Little Elkin including improvement where said **Carrell** now lives ... 22 May; **William Carrel** entered 100 acs. both sides Elk Branch at **Wm. Careel's** own line, 23 Dec.; **1779** - Thomas Sisk entered 100 acs. N. side Yadkin River at **William Carrel's** corner to **Wm. Carrel's** line to Gabriel Loveing's line, 11 Feb.; David Allen Jr. entered 640 acs. on county line joining **William Carrel's** line, 15 Feb.; **William Carrel**, 300 acs. on Little Elkin Creek above Loveing Mill near Cattail Marsh, including improvement whereon said **Carrell** now lives ... 29 May; **1780** - Richard Gwin entered 640 acs. on little Elkin & Yadkin waters joining entry made by Gabriel Loveing, John Parks Jr., Memucan Hunt, **William Carrel** and Simon Carter ... 18 Aug., entry withdrawn; **William Carrell**, 150 acs. on Peach Bottom Mountain (Tax List); **1784** - **William Carrel**, 1M21-60, 1M21-60+, 3F all ages; **1786** - **William Carrell**, **Capt. Carrell's Dist.**, 3M21-60, 4F, 1sl12-50+; **1787** - **William Carrel**, 1WM21-60, 1M21-60+, 8F all ages, **Capt. Carrel's List**, taken by Wm. Terrell Lewis July 3; **?1789/ 1791/1799** - Two **William Carrels**; **1790** - Morgan Dist., 7th Co., 3M16+, 4F, 7sls; **1795/1797** - taxable, 470 acs. ?Sebastion, Capt. R. R. Gwyn's Dist. (?, p. 4); **1800** - **William Carrel** 00001-00120-01; **William Carrell**, b. c**1725**, wife **Mary; Ch.:**

  1. **William Jr.**, b. c**1752**; **1784** - **William Carrel (?Jr.)**, 1M21-60, 3M21-60+, 1F; **1787** - **William Carrell**, **Capt. Carrel's Dist.**, 3M21-60, 4F all ages, 1sl 12-50+; **1797** - **William Carroll**, 1 polled, 150 acs., Capt. Toliver's Dist. (?, p.15); **1800** - **William Carrel** 00001-00120-01; **1805** - **William Carroll**, Capt. Holloway's Dist., 1 polled, 30 acs. (Cens., p. 159; Ear. Amer. Series, v. 1, p. 30; Cens., p. 34, I. 1; ?, p. 31)

  2. **James**, b. 31 Mar. c**1765**, pvt., NC, son of **William and Mary Carrell**, d. 17 Apr. **1841**, md. 23/24 Dec. **1802/1805** (bdsm. Richard Parks, Jno. Jones, Dep. CC) **Sally Parks**, b. 28 Apr. **1771**, d. 17 Aug. **1838**; **1850** - **James Carroll** and wife **Sally** (Cens.,p. ?); **Ch.:**
   1. **Mirah**, b. 25 Apr. **1807**, d. 28 Jan. **1813**
   2. **William**, b. 14 Oct. **1808**, md. **Eleanor Shelby** Mar. **1831**, **ch.:**
    1. **John Parks**, b. 24 June **1833**
    2. **Sally Martha Ann**, b. 14 July **1835**
    3. **Naomi Louise**, b. 19 June **1838**
    4. **James Meredith**, b. 28 July **1840**
    5. **William Grayson**, b. 24 Apr. **1843**
    6. **Mary Elizabeth**, b. 21 July **1845**

3. **Elizabeth**, b. 21 Sept. **1810**, d. 19 Apr. **1818**
4. **John Parks**, b. 30 Apr. **1813**, d. 31 Jan. **1838**
(Family Bible Rcds. sent by Mrs. May Shearer Stringfield, Thomasville, NC; Memory Aldridge Lester, p. 64; Pens. Rcds.; Marr. Bds.; Sidden) [See Burke Co.]

3. **John and son John**, **1780** - 60+ (tax poll); William Tolby entered 150 acs, 1 Mar., at foot of Peach Bottom Mountain including the cabbin made by Julius Bunch, a little above the house (Wm. Tolby marked out; **John Carrell** written in; **1782** - **John Carroll**, tax list); **1795** - **John Carrel/Carrol**, 1 polled, Capt. Toliver's Dist. (?, p.9); **1797** - **John Carroll**, 1 polled, Capt. Toliver's Dist. (?, p. 19); **1800** - **John Carrel**, 01001-00100-10; **and William Carroll** (Land Entry Bk.1778-1781, p. 97; Tax List; Radcliff, p. 34; Cens., p. 33, I. 18; Hds./Fams; No. Carolinian Qrtly., v. 11, 1965, p. 1411), **son;**

1. **1795** - **John Carroll**, 1 polled, Capt. Toliver's Dist. (?, p. 9); **1797** - **John Carroll**, 1 polled, Capt. Toliver's Dist. (?, p. 19); **1800** - **John Carrell** md. **Mary Ferguson** 18 Oct., bdsm. John Parker, Wm. B. Lenoir; **1800** - **John Carroll /Carrel** 00100-00100-00 (Marr. Bds.; Sidden; Cens. Roll 33, v. 5, p. 34, I. 22)
4. **Rachel**, b. **1771**
5. **Naomi**, b. **1772** (single?)
6. **Mary**, b. ? , md. **Thomas Willard**, wit.?: **Daniel Carrell** (Bk. A-1, pp. 7, 37, 95; Land Entry Bk.1778-1781, pp. 7, 8, 37, 50, 51, 108; Lester, Old So. Bible Rcds.; Register, pp. 178, 179; Ear. Amer. Series, v. 1, p. 30; NC Cens., p. 3; Hds./Fams. Cens. Indx., p. 122; Cens. Roll 33, p. 34, I. 1; No. Carolinian, v. 11, 1965, p. 1411; ?, p. 4; Fam. Hist.) [Mrs. Stringfellow: **William Carrell had brothers Daniel Carrell** (lived with Wm. in 1810), **and James Carrell** of Burke Co.]

?- **Thomas Carrel**, militia, Salisbury Dist., #1290); **1786** - **Thomas Carral**, Capt. Lovel Dist., 1M21-60, 2F, 1sl12-50 (DAR Roster, p. 329; Register, p. 143)
?- **Peter Currell**, militia, Salisbury Dist., #2423 (DAR Roster, p. 329, under Cooper Family)
1784/1787 - **Hannah Carrell**, 2M21-60+, 4F all ages (Cens., p. 3)
1792 - **Elizabeth Carrel** md. **Benjn. Thurston** 24 Jan. (Carroll Cables, July 1995)
1793 - **Elizabeth Carrel** md. **John Parker** 9 Jan. (Carroll Cables, July 1995)
1793 - **Charles Carrell**, Morrow Dist., tax (Early Amer. Series, v. 1, p. 30)
1793 - **Britton Carril**, Newsom's Dist., tax (Early Amer. Series, v. 1, p. 30)
1793 - **Anthony Carrole**, Newsom's Dist., tax (Early Amer. Series, v. 1, p. 30)
1800 - **Stephen Carrolle** (Cens., p. 34, I. 19)
1801 - **Charity Carrel** md. **John Livingston** 17 Dec. (Carroll Cables, July 1995)
1806 - **Samuel Carrel** md. **Sally Kaylor** 2 Apr., bdsm. John Parker, Wm. B. Lenoir, CC (Marr. Bds.; Sidden)
1807 - **Samson Carrol** md. **Nancy Livingston** 23 Nov., bdsm. John Livingston, R. Martin, CC (Marr. Bds.; Sidden)
1814 - **Archibald Carrell** md. **Suana Bell** 19 Nov., bdsm. Wesley Swanson, W. W. Martin (Marr. Bds.)
1820 - **John C. Carrill** (Cens. Indx., p. 17) [**1820** - **John C. Carrill**, Wayne Co. (Cens., p.506)]

Burke County, in the Morgan District, was established in **1777** from **Rowan County**. In **1810**, according to Smith's NC. Census Index and Roll 39, pgs. 300-357, the population of Burke Co.

was 11,007. There were 542 looms working to make 77,025 yards of wool, of which 7,700 were sold at $1 per yard; 69,325 yards of cotton and linen at 50 cents per yard; 100 stills made 20,400 gallons "of spirits" at 50 cents per gallon; six iron works (bloomeries & forges) provided 234,800 quantity of iron at $6.25 per 100 lbs. and 25,200 lbs. at 20 cents per lb. of iron; and three tanners made 1,200 yards of hides at $4 per hide.

According to Mrs. Stringfield, below, there were **three Carroll brothers** in Burke Co.: **William, Daniel and James**. [See Wilkes County]

1777 - **William Carrell**, wife **Mary**, indentured to Jos. Hardy, sold 90+ acs. to Hardy; **1780** - **William Carroll**, tax list; **1790** - **William Carrell**, Morgan Dist., 3M16+, 4F; **1800** - **William Carrell** (Cens.); **1810** - **William Carroll**; 5 Dec., census taker; E. Sharp; **1820** - **William Carroll**, 1M45+, 1F26-44, 1F45+, 9 in agri., 4 in manf., 4 sls (Hds./Fam., p. 110; Smith, Cens., p. 110; Bentley, Cens., p. 315; Cens. Roll 33, v. 4, p. 23, #16) [Mrs. Wilma Williams, Three Mile, NC near Newland or Linville Falls, NC, gt.granddaughter of **William Carrell** of Burke Co., NC through his dau. **Naomi**, owns the family Bible. Mrs. Stringfield says **Naomi** was never married. See Wilkes Co.] **ch.**:

    1. **William Jr**

    2. **1780** - **James Carrell**, tax list; **1790** - **James Carroll**; **1800** - **James Correll**, 00110-00000-20; **1802** - **James Carrell**, b. 31 Mar. **176?**, d. 17 Apr. **1841**, md. **Sally Parks**, b. 28 Apr. **1771**, d. 17 Aug. **1838**; **1810** - **James Carroll**; **1820** - **James Carrell** (Stringfield, Williams Bible; Hds./Fams., p. 110; Cens., p. 735, l. 2; Cens. Indxs., pp. 23, 42; Cens., p. 316; Cens. p. 23, #16);

        1. **Mirah**, b. 25 Apr. **1807**, d. 28 Jan. **1813**

        2. **William**, b. 14 Oct. **1808**, md. **Eleanor Shelby**, b. 5 Dec. **1802**; **Ch.**:

            1. **John Parks**, b. 24 June **1833**

            2. **Sally Martha Ann**, b. 14 July **1835**

            3. **Naomi Louise**, b. 19 June **1838**

            4. **James Meredith**, b. 28 July **1840**

            5. **William Grayson**, b. 24 Apr. **1843**

            6. **Mary Elizabeth**, b. 21 July **1845** (Stringfield, Williams Bible) [Records of Mrs. May Shearer Stringfield, Thomasville, NC, 1960, from Bible owned by Mrs. Wilma Williams, Three Mile, NC, gt-gddau. of William Carrell of Burke Co. through his dau. Naomi. Info. included: Bedford Co., VA, Wm. Carrell with wife, Mary, in 1777 made indenture with Jos. Hardy, witd. by Robt. Ewing, Jos. Dickson, Thos. Campbell, Stephen Dooley & Thos. Martin. 90+ acs. sold to Hardy. Wm. Was in VA Militia, Rev. War #29187 993, Capt. Jonathan Hanby's Co., pensioned. Wilkes Co., NC, Bk. A-1, p. 95, ld. gt. to Wm. C 1778-1779; Lester, p. 64]

        3. **Elizabeth**, b. 21 Sept. **1810**, d. 19 Apr. **1818**

        4. **John Parks**, b. 30 Apr. **1813**, d. 31 Jan. **1838**

    3. **Rachel**; 4. **Naomi**; 5. **Mary**

1780 - **Daniel Carroll**, tax list; **1790** - **Daniel Carol**, Morgan Dist., 13th Co., 1M16+, 1F ; **1810** - **Daniel Carroll** in **William Carroll's** household (Hds./Fams., p. 110; Cens., Bentley Indx., p. 315)

1790 - **Jno./Jonathan Carrol**, Morgan Dist.,12th Co., 1M16+, 2M16-, 4F (Hds./Fams., p.110)
1790 - **George Carol** Morgan Dist., 1M16+, 1M16-, 8F (Hds./Fams., p. 106)
1790 - **Sterling Carol**, Morgan Dist., 1M16+, 1F16+ (Hds./Fams., p. 106)
1790 - **Charles Carroll**; 1810 - **Charles Carroll** (H./Fs.,p.106;Cs.Indx.,pp.23,42;Cens., p. 308)
1820 - **Eady/Pedy Carrell** (Cens., p. 21, #14)
1824 - **Lurena Carrell** md. **David Street** 17 Nov. (Carroll Cables, July 1995)
1850 - **James Carroll** (Cens. Indx., p. 160)
1850 - **Sally Carroll** (Cens.Indx., p. 162)

<u>Jones County</u> was established in **1778** from **Craven County**.

<u>Franklin County</u>, established in **1779** from **Bute County**, was in the Halifax Military Dist. In 1780, Halifax Military District encompassed the counties of Northampton, Halifax, Martin, Warren, Franklin, Nash and Edgecombe. (Map by L. Polk Denmark with districts added).
1764 Sept. 28 - Earl Granville grant: Thomas Child Esq., agent of Earl Granville to James Moore of Granville Co., 1 Aug. 1762, 10s sterling, Quit Rents, ... for a grant of 650 acs. in Parish of _____, Granville Co., on N side of Tarr River adjacent to Harris, **Carrol**, Spring Branch; wits.: William Churton, J. Montfort; proved by Joseph Montfort Esq., Halifax 12 Sept. 1764, Sugan Johnson, PR (Warren Co., NC Rcds.; Dd. Bk. A, p. 18; Kerr, p. 3)
1764 Oct. 9 - Land transaction from John Ferrell Jr. to Thomas Stuard of Halifax Co., 50 pounds VA money for 550 acs "where I now live on BS Mill Swamp known as Dears Branch" adjacent to Thomas Davis and Vinson, land granted by Thos. Child; wits: Elizabeth Doolling, **Mary Carell**, Denis Bradley, George Sorrell, Bute Co., Nov. Ct.; Ben McCullock, CC; Reg.: 12 Jan. 1765, Sugan Johnson, PR (Warren Co. Rcds., p. 6; Dd. Bk. A, p. 52; Kerr, p. 3)
1765 Mar. 2 - **Elesebeth Carrel** witness with Green Duke, land from William Partin to William Duke, 21p12s VA money for 100 acs "where I now live" bought from Theo. Burk; proved by Green Duke, Bute Co., Oct. Ct.; Ben McCullock, CC; Reg.: 29 Aug. 1766, William Johnson, PR (Warren Co. Rcds., p. 28; Dd. Bk. A, p. 312; Kerr, p. 28)
1767 - **William Carroll Sr.** bought land; **1771** - **Two Williams** taxpayers; - **William Carroll's sons named: John, William and Thomas**; **1779/80** - **William Carroll Sr.**, 200 acs. to Alexuis Mador Foster, **1780** Oct. 18, S. of Tar River adjacent to Hefford, 2,500 pds., wits: Thomas Going and **John Carrel** (1781) part of tract granted to William Chavous Sr. by deed from Samuel Benton Esq. (Real Est. Indx.,W, p. 106; Dd. Bk., p. ?; Ratcliff, p. 36; North Carolinian, v. 11, 1965, p. 1450, 1458; Dd. Bk. 1, pp. 22, 23, #148); **Ch.:**

    1. **1771** - **Two John Carrolls**, taxpayers; **1778** - NC entry; **1786** - taxpayer, Halifax Military Dist.; **1790** - **John Carroll**, Halifax Dist., 1M16+, 2M16-, 2F16+, 5 sls; **1795-99** - **John Carroll** (?); **1800** - **John Carroll**, 1M10-16, 2M26-45, 1M45+, 2F16-26, 2sls (01011-00200-02) (Ratcliff, p. 36; North Carolinian, v. 11, 1965, p. 1510; Real Est. Indx. Conveyances, Bk. W, p. 106; Hds./Fams., p. 34; Cens. Indx., pp. 15, 45, 59; Cens. Roll 31, p. 34)

    2.**1771** - **William Carroll (Jr.?)**, taxpayer; **1790** - **William Carroll Jr.**, Halifax Dist.; **1810** - **William Carrell**, 1M10-, 1M16-26, 1M26-45, 5F10-, 1F26-45; **1820** - **William Carroll**, tax list (Ratcliff, p. 36; Cens. Indx.; Cens., p. 34; Cens. Roll 40, p. ?; NC Cens. Indx., p. 474, supplemented from tax lists)

3. **1771** - **Thomas Carroll**, taxpayer; **1790** - **Thomas Carroll**, Halifax Dist.; **1800** - **Thomas Carroll** (Ratcliff, p. 36; North Carolinian, v. 11, 1965, p. 1504; Cens. Indx., pp. 15, 45; Cens., p. 34) **son:**
    1. **1771** - **Charles Carroll**, taxpayer (Ratcliff, p. 36)
1771 - **Benjamin Carroll**, taxpayer (Ratcliff, p. 36; North Carolinian, v. 11, 1965, p. 1510)
1784 - **Douglas Carroll** bought from George Richards; **1791** Feb. 14 - **Douglas Carrell** and wife **Elizabeth**, dau. of David Vinson of Franklin Co., sold to Joseph Nash of Franklin Co., 40p VA money, 100 acs. on branch adjacent to George Bledsoe, the Glebe line, Thomas and Seawell, it being part of tract laid out to John Thomas; wits.: Thomas Caloard & Stephen Richards; **1810/1812**, Nov. 6 - **Douglas Carrell** & wife **Elizabeth Carrell**, dau of David Vinson, deceased, of Randolph Co., GA, sold interest in Vinson est. in GA to Jas. Collins of Franklin Co. (Dd. Bk. 4, p. 83; Dd. 137, #1003, p. 66, Watson Absts.; Dd. Bk. 16, p. 36; Watson Kinfolk, p. 83)
1780 - **Daniel Carroll**, tax list; **1790** - **Daniel Carol**, Morgan Dist., 13th Co., 1M16+, 1F ; **1810** - **Daniel Carroll** in **William Carroll's** household (Hds./Fams., p. 110; Cens., Bentley Indx., p. 315)
1786 Mar. 13 - **Daniel Carrel** witnessed with Caleb Dossey and James Murphey a dd. of Marcus Gilliam of Franklin Co. to Mary Noakes of Franklin Co., adjacent to John Leonard, Jas. Murphey and Vinson; Frances Gilliam, wife of Marcus Gilliam, signed the deed.; **1789** - **Daniel Carroll**, pvt., assigned his grant to John Marshall, Sumner Co., TN on Mancy fork creek (Dd. Bk., p. 173, #519; Watson Absts., p. 68; NC Ld Grants in TN)
1790 - **Joseph Carroll**, Halifax Dist., 3M16+, 2M16-, 2F, 2sls (Cens. Indx, Cens., p. 34)
1790 - **Polly Carrel** md. **William Bush** 8 Sept. (Carroll Cables, July 1995)
1799 - **Grip Carroll** bght. from Ezekiel Fuller Sr.; **1800** - **Grief Carrell**, 45+, 5M10-, 1M16-26, 2M45+, 1F26-45 (50102-00010-00); **Grip Carroll** bght. from John Pearce; **1801** - **Grip Carroll** sold to John Finch Sr.; **1820** - ?**Grus Carrol** 50102-00010-00 (Cens., p.460) (Dd. Bk. 9, p. 99; Dd. Bk. 11, p. 172; Cens. Indx., pp. 15, 45; Cens. Roll 31, p. 15, 460, I. 2; Dd. Bk. 3, pp. 42, 100) [See Daniel, mil. pens. appl. testimony]
1800 - **David Carrell/Carrol**, 18, 1M16-26, 2sls (00100-00000-02) (Cens. Roll 31, p. 45, I. 6, J.1, 490)
1813 May 25 - **William Carrell** md. **Mary Pope**, Sec. Allen Minnis, wit. N Long ; **1820** - taxpayer (Cens. Roll 40, p.789; Ingmire, Marr. Rcds.; Cens. Indx., p. 474)
1825 Feb. 9 - **Dickson Carrell** md. **Latitia May**, Sec. **William Carrell**, wit. N. Patterson (Ingmire, Marr. Rcds.)
1830 Oct.25 - **James Carrell** md. **Mary Foster**, Sec. James St. John, wit. N. Patterson (Ingmire, Marr. Rcds.)
1830 - **Ezekiel Carroll** deed of trust from Jesse Reid; **1830** Jan. 27 - **Ezekiel Carroll** of Warren Co., NC was about to move out of the state and appointed Alfred A. Reid as trustee in his stead; **1831** - **Ezekiel Carroll** sold to Jesse Reid; **Ezekiel Carroll Sr.** sold to John L. Walkins (Dd. Bk. 26, pp. 76, 264, 333; Watson Kinfolk, p. 193)
1833 - **William Carroll** md. **Elizabeth Swanson**, 4 Mar., Sec. William Leonard, wit.: S Patterson; **1834** - **William Carrell** bill of sale to Nancy Swanson for token amount, Dec. 8 (Igmire, Marr. Rcds.; Carroll Cables, Apr. 1996; Dd. Bk. 27, p. 98; Watson Kinfolk. p. 211)
1834 Dec. 30 - **William Carroll** md. **Nancy Cooper**, Sec. John M Patillo, wit. S. Patterson;
1850 - **William Carroll** b. 1806, wife **Nancy**, (Igmire, Marr. Rcds.; Carroll Cables, Apr. 1996;

Census) **ch. all born in Franklin Co.:**
  1.**James Carroll, b. 1837; son:**
    1. **Peter Carroll** md. **Henrietta Pernell** (Luther Carroll letter dated 3/4/1988)
    2. **1875 - J. E. Carroll and wife** to W. H. Edwards (Dd. Bk. 43, p. 101)
    3. **Addie (Carroll) Mosley**, b. **1896** to **Peter & Henrietta Pernell Carroll**, grew up in Franklin Co. one of 13 brothers and sisters, md. **Herbert Mosley** who d. 1952, d. 16 Feb.**1988**, age 92, three living **ch.: Anni Edwards, Doris Hale** (husb. **Ben Hale), & Lynell Mosley**, seven grand children and 13 gt-grand children (Obit., Franklin Co. newspaper,1988)
  2. **Mary, b. 1839**
  3. **William, b. 1840; 1875 - William R. Carroll**, guardian with Power of Attorney to Jos. J. Davis (Bk. 41, p. 338)
  4. **Robert Z., b. 1842; 1865** Oct. 1 - **Robert Z. Carroll** md. **Sarah (Sallie) A. Mustian**, **ch:**
    1. **Robert Archie Carroll** md. **Iva Ball, ch.:**
      1. **Robert Dee Carroll**, father of **Louise Carroll Ayschue**
      2. **Lucy Bell Carroll**
      3. **Luther Allen Carroll**
      4. **Sarah Carroll**
      5. **Grace Carroll**
      6. **Mildred Carroll**
      7. **William (Bill) Carroll**
      8. **Benjamin Carroll, Ch.:**
        1. **Louis**, 2. **George**, 3. **E.**, 4. **Mae**, 5. **Virginia**, 6. **Daisy**
(Fam. Rcd. Carroll Reunion, Warrenton, NC, 1987) [Luther Carroll letter dated 4/30/89 stated his gt.grandmother Ball's mother was a Shearin.]
  5. **Benjamin, b. 1844; 1885 - B. J. L. Carroll and wife** to **O. P. Carroll** (Dd. Bk. 71, p. 142); **son:**
    1. **? - Willie S. Carroll**, age 81, d. at home in Franklinton, NC, the **son of Benjamin L. and Betsy Ann (Segram) Carroll**, md. **Georgia Marshall** who survived him with 4 **daus.:**
      1. **Mrs. Everett Carroll (Lucille)** of Warrenton, NC
      2. **Mrs. W. T. Carroll** of Henderson, NC
      3. **Betsy Ann**, at home
      4. **Auth Carroll**, at home
      5. **Thurman Carroll** of Washington, DC
    2. **Louis Carroll** of Nashville
    3. **Mrs. R. H. Dalehite** of Durham, NC
    [Willie S. had two grandchildren] (Willie S. Carroll Obit., Fam. Rcd.)
  6. **Oliver, b. 1845; 1885 - O. P. Carroll** from **B. J. L. Carroll**; **O. P. Carroll** to W. L. McGhee; **1885/1889 - O. P. Carroll & wife** to E. G. Davis (Dd. Bk. 71, p. 142; Md. Bk. 69, pp. 25, 528; Md. Bk. 80, p. 108) [**Oliver** d. p. to his brother **Benjamin** (Lucille Carroll Letter, 10 Nov. 1989)
  7. **Martha, b. 1846** (Cens.)

1847 - **Betsey Carroll** md. **William Sanders** 31 March, H(enry) G. Williams, bdmn. or wit. (M. Bds, p. 152; Carroll Cables, July 1995)
1859 Dec. 14 - **Thomas T. Carrol** md. **M. V. Green**, by T. H. Joyner, Sec. Robert Rodwell, wit. N. S. Patterson (Ingmire, Marr. Rcds.)
1862 Sept. 3 - **James Carrell** md. **Martha E. Crowder**, John G. Leonard, JP; Sec. H. W. Nash, wit. T. C. Horton (Ingmire, Marr. Rcds.)
1866 - **Sarah A. Carroll** md. **William J. Smith** 9 Aug. 1866; wit.: T. C. Horton, CC; bd. or license issued 11 July 1866 by W. A. Brame, JP (Marr. Bds., p. 156)
1869 - **T. S. Carroll** bght. from Mary Hicks; **1879** - **T. S. Carroll Jr.** to Henry Wright Jr.; **T. S. Carroll Jr.** to Haywood Meeting House, church; **1883** - **T. S. Carroll Jr. and wife** to J. A. Williams; **T. S. Carroll Jr. and wife** to D. J. Fuller; **1884** - **T. S. Carroll Jr. and wife** to W. H. Pleasants; **1885** - **Thomas Carroll** to Hamilton Steward; **1888** - **Thos. S. Carroll and wife** to E. E. Reavis (Dd. Bk. 35, p. 56; Dd. Bk. 49, p. 534; MD. Bk. 62, pp. 414, 448; MD Bk. 63, p. 582; MD Bk. 66, p. 382; Dd. Bk.79, p. 419)

Warren County, established in **1779** from **Granville and Bute counties**, was in Halifax Military Dist. in 1780.
1755 - **William Carroll** (?); **1767** Mar.18/MayCt.1768 - **William Carroll**, planter, of the S. province in Bute Co., bght. 200 acs. in Bute Co., S. side Tar River, adj. to Hefford, part of a tract bght from Samuel Benton Esq., 10p VA money to William Chavers Sr. of Granville Co. of Province of North Carolina; wits.: John Nevill, George Stephenson, David Davis, Ben McCulloch, CC, recd. 30 Aug.1768 by Wm. Johnson, PR; marginal note: delivered to **Wm. Carrell** 9 May 1770; **1770** - **William Carroll Sr.** of Franklin Co. sold 200 acs. on S. side of Tar River, adj. Hefford to Alexius M. Foster for 2,500p, wit. **John Carrel**, 9 May; **1771** - **William Carrell**, taxpayer; **1777** - **William Carroll & sons: John, William (Jr.) and Thomas** (Dd. Bk. 2, p. 62; Radcliff, p. 36; No. Carolinian, v. XI, 1965, "Father-Son Relationship," in Franklin, Warren, Vance Cos. Area, pp. 1450, 1458) [See Granville County] **Ch.:**
    1. **Anne, c1742** in VA, md. **John Champion**
    2. **Thomas; 1771** - **Thomas Carroll**, taxpayer; **1777** - **Thomas Carroll & son Charles**; **1781** - **Thomas Carroll** taxpayer; **1783** - (?); **?1789/1791/ 1799** - **Thomas Carrel**; **1790** - Halifax Dist., 1M16+, 4M16-, 6F, 6others, 17sls +; **1792** - bght. from **Allen Champion**; **1800** - Halifax Dist., 1M10-, 2M16-26, 1M45+,2F10-, 1F16-26, 1F45+, 10sls; (No. Carolinian Qrtly., v. XI, 1965, p. 1504) [A **Thomas Carroll** will, **1833**, in Raleigh Archives: "... to daughter ..."unnamed, ended abruptly as if rewriting a will but never finished.] **Son:**
        1. **1771** - **Charles Carrell**, taxpayer (Radcliff, p. 36)
        2. **1771** - **William S. Carroll**, taxpayer (Radcliff, p.36) [Thomas' son?]
    3. **William Jr.**; **1781** - **William Carroll Jr.**, son of planter, Capt. Hall's Co., substituted for **brother George** of Warren Co., returned from war service to Warren Co.,1782, removed to Caswell Co., then to Hawkins Co., TN for 10-12 yrs., then to Roane Co., TN where he was age 77 on 2 Oct. 1832; wife **Keziah**, removed to Caswell, Lincoln cos. in NC and Hawkins, Roane cos. in TN; **1783/ 1785** - **Wm. Carrol**, #300, pay settlements in Halifax Co., pvt., 640 acs., service during 23 Apr. 1783/ 1784, Maj. Dixon Continental Line, gt. #1753 to heirs; **1786** - **Wm. Carrol**, #2202, 19p7s1d, received by John Sheppard in Warrenton for military pay; **1790** -

Halifax Mil. Dist.; **1810** - bght. from Philemon Kinneman, decd., est., 26 May/Feb.Ct.1812; **1820**; **1832** - **William Carroll**, #263, pvt. Pens. Acts. 1818 & 1832; **1833** - **William Carroll**, #W6640, b. in Fairfax Co., VA, md. **Keziah**, substituted for his **bro. Jesse**; moved to Granville Co., NC; to Warren Co., NC; Caswell Co, NC; moved to Hawkins Co., TN, **d. in Roane Co., Sparta, White Co., TN** 28 Dec. **1835** (Rev. War Pens. Appl. Rcds.; NC DAR Roster, pp. 226, 269, 479, 573; Clark, v. 17, p. 201, v. 22, pp. 55-92; Hds./Fams., p. 76; Kerr, p. 206; Cens. Indx., pp. 11, 42; Cens., pp. 765, 800; K. K. White, p. 156) [**William Carroll** of Lincoln Co., pensioned by NC in 1833, testimony given after William's death. 1777 - **John Keziah** among others who purchased parts of Wm. Baker (dec'd.) est., May Court (Kerr, v. 1, p. 53) William's wife's name was Keziah. Is there a connection?] **ch.:**
    1. **Jesse**, 2. **John**, 3. **Elijah**, 4. **Henry**, 5. **Betty**, 6. **Nancy**
    4. **1771** - **John Carroll**, taxpayer;**1778** - NC Entry; **1783** - **John Carroll** insolvent; **1784** - **John Carroll**, taxpayer; **1786** - **John Carroll**, Halifax Mil. Dist.; **1790** - in Halifax Dist., 1M16+, 2M16-, 2F; **1833** - **John Carroll**, Halifax Dist., sol., Continental Line, #1018 (Radcliff, pp. 36, 40, v. 2, p. 34; No. Carolinean Ortly., v. 11, 1965, p. 1510; Kerr, p. 11; Cens.; Harvey Family, NC DAR Roster, p. 366)
    5. **Spencer** [See Granville Co. and look in Williamson Co., TN for Spencer.]
    6. **Jesse** [Wasn't legal age when his father died in 1781. See Granville Co.]
    7. **Elizabeth** md. ? **Zarrard**
    8. **Kezia** md. ? **Harp**
    9. **Jenny** [Under legal age in 1781]
    10. **Mary** [Under legal age in 1781]
1755 - **Benjamin Carroll** (?); **1771** - **Benjamin Carrell**, taxpayer; **1772** Dec. 25/Aug. Ct. 1777; **Benjamin Carrl** of Bute Co. sold partial of ld. to Benjamin Melvaile of Bute Co. for sum of 20 pounds, ld. on Little Creek, Charles Burke's Line and Thomas Christmas line; **1772** - **Benjamin Carroll** bght. William Duke ld.; **1774** - **Benjamin Carrol** of Bute Co., sold 125 acs along Little Creek bordering cart way to John Jackson's and line of Thomas Christmas for sum of 15 pounds to William Park; wits: Thomas Machem, Abed Green and William Weldon, 19 May; **1776** - **Benjamin Carrel** member of Committee of Safety; **1777** - **Benjamin Carroll and John Carroll**; **1778** - **Benjamin Carroll** sold to Benjamin Vale/McInvaile; **1781** - **Benjamin Carroll**, pvt., Hall's Co., 25May1781/10Nov. 1782, 10th Reg., Col. Abraham Shepard, 12 mos.; **1831** - **Benj-amin Carroll**, #316, pvt., Pens. Acts of 1818 & 1832; Continental Line, #807; **1833** - NC Line, #2435, 32p10s recd. by Will Lytle, Warrenton Settlements; #1091, by B. McCullock, Warrenton Settlements (Radcliff, p. 36; No. Car. Qtrly., v. XI, 1965, p. 1510; Dd. Bk. 6, pp. 131, 213, 302, 426; Dd. Bk. 4 or 5, p. 15; Hist. Soc., Hist. of Co., p. 30; NC Army Accts., NCO, Pvts. & Misc., v. 4, p. 3; Harvey Family, NC DAR Roster, pp. 116, 205, 515, 574)
1759 - **John Carroll**, 200 ac. grant, 20 Nov.; **John Carrell**, 300 ac. grant, 4 May; **John Carrell**, 100 acs. on East Lizard Ck., mouth of Great Branch, sold to Robt., Caleb and Joshua Taylor, 8 May; **1769** - **John Carrel**, 100 acs. of grant in Bute Co., sold by Robt. Taylor to Caleb Taylor, both of Bute Co., E. side Lizard Ck...., 4 May; wits.: John Linch Sr., James Linch, Joshua Tayler, Ben McCulloch, CC, recd. 9 Aug. by Wm. Johnson, PR; 150 acs. of **John Carrel** gt. in Bute Co., sold 8 May by Robt. Taylor to Joshua Taylor...recd. 9 Aug., Wm. Johnson, PR; marginal note: delivered to Ma. Myrick Feb. 1771; **1772** - 150 acs. of 300-ac. grant to **John Carrell** sold to Mark Moore of Northampton Co. by Joshua Taylor of Bute Co., 130p, E. side Lizard Ck., mouth

of Gt. Branch, up branch to Robt. Taylor's Spring Branch, wits.: Matt Myrick, Caleb Taylor, Robt. Taylor, Ben McCulloch, CC, 31 July 1772, recd. 29 Oct., Jas. Johnson, PR; **1777 - Benjamin Carroll and John Carroll** (Dd. Bk. 2, pp. 1, 203, 204; Dd. Bk. 3, p. 504) **1765 - Luke Carroll** (?)
1784/1786/1787 - Thos. Carroll, (b. c1728) Granville Co., 60+, taxpayer, wife **Rebecca**, 60+, 3M21-, 3sls12-50, 4sls 12-50+, Halifax Dist., Capt. Clanton's Dist.; **1786** - taxpayer, Capt. Clanton's Dist., 1M21-60, 3M21-60+, 5F, 3 sls12-50, 4sls12-50; **1804** - bght. from Samuel Bell, decd., est., Aug. Ct.; and sold to Thomas Hunt; **1807** - sold to Francis Jones; **1810** - sold ld. to Ezekiel Blanch; **1810/1816 - Thos. Carroll** to J. B. Rice and Wm. Warwick; **1811 - Thomas Carrol Sr.** taxable in River Dist.; **1812 - Thomas Carrol Sr.**, James Carrol, Ezekiel Carrol, **Thomas Carrol Jr.**, Aug. Ct.**1813/14 - Thomas Carrol Sr.**,b. c1728, will: dated 20 Jan. **1813**, May, devisees **Thomas Carroll, Rebecca Carroll,** probated in May, wife & exrx. **Rebecca**, lds. and slaves; **ch.: Sterling (& son James Carrol); Ezekiel (& son Thomas); Tabitha; Miriam R.; Rebecca Lee; Sally Read**; **1810** - sold ld. to **Tabitha Carroll**, his sister; **1816** - sold to Ezekiel Blanch, to **Tabitha Carroll** his sister, to J. B. Rice & Wm. Warwick; **1820 - Thomas Carroll**, Warrenton; **1820/1821 - Thomas Carroll** to Richard Daverson; to Francis Jones; to **Tabitha Carroll; Thomas Jr.**, exr.; **Nancy Mize/Wize; Elizabeth Brooks; & grandson Solomon Shell Carrol, son of Sally Read**; wits.: F. Jones, William Shell, Pleasant Shell **1820 - Rebecca Carroll**, Warrenton (No. Carolinean Qrtly., 1965, v. XI, p. 1504; Register, p. 166; Radcliff, pp. 34, 36; Ear. Amer. Series, v. 1, p. 30; Hds./Fams., p. 62; Bentley, Cens. Roll 31, p. 798; Kerr, v. 1, pp. 143, 199, 219, 226; Dd. Bk. 17, p. 426; Dd. Bk. 18, p. 224; Dd. Bk. 19, pp. 27, 399, 405; Cens., pp. 181, 763, 806, 816; Cens. Indx., p. 29, 32, 42; Dd. Bk. 21, pp. 9, 28, 125, 202; Will Bk.17, pp. 143, 147); **Ch.:**

1. **1794 - Sterling Carrell** bght. Harbert Haynes (dec'd) est., Feb. Ct.; **1813** - in Six Pound Dist.; **1820 - Sterling Carroll**, Warrenton; **1832 - Sterling Carroll** md. **Elizabeth R. Moore** 19 Dec., bdsm. Amos White, wit. M. M. Drake (Kerr, pp. 58, 226; Cens., p. 818, #31; Indx., p. 31; Utah Gen. Soc. M. Bds., p. 37; Carroll Cables, Apr. 1996) **?Son:**

    1. **James**; **1802 - James Carrol** bght. part of Robt. Alexander (dec.d) est., May; **1805 - James Carrell** md. **Patsy Shell** 27 Feb., bdsm. Stephen Ellis, M.D. Johnson, CC; **1810 - James Carrle/Carple**; **1811** - taxable in River Dist.; **1812** - Aug. Ct.; **1813** - in Six Pd. Dist.; **1814** - in Six Pd. Dist.; **1818/1821 - Jas. Carroll** bght. from James Shell; **1820 - James Carroll**; **1829/ 1835 - Jas. Carroll** from **Thos. Carroll**, Warrenton; **1831/1832 - Jas. Carrell**, pvt. NC Militia, pd. $99.99, 69 yrs. old, 4 Mar. 1831; #264, Pens. Acts 1818 & 1832; **1833/1834 - James Carroll** will dated 3 Dec. **1833**: wife and exr. **Martha Carroll**, ld. & slaves; dau. **Lucy Mosely**, slave Nancy; son and exr. **William**, slave & horse; dau. **Martha Mosely**, slave; dau. **Mary**, slave & furniture; son and exr. **Jordin**, slave, horse & furniture; dau. **Rebecca L.**, slave & furniture; Feb. Ct., wits: G. W. Blanch Jr., Wm. Ellis and Stephen Ellis; **1834 Feb. 24 - Martha Carroll** and Clack Robinson bound to David L. Swain Esq., gov. of st. for sum of $2,000; **Martha** appointed guardian of minor orphans, **Jordan W. Carrole and Rebecca L. Carroll**; **1834** Mar. 3 - John Moseley and Hartwell Moseley are named in inv. of est. given by **Martha Carroll**, exrx.; **1850 - James Carroll, wife Martha**; ch.: **William G.**, exr.; **Martha**; **Mary**; minors **Jordon W.** 12-; **Rebecca L.** 12-; **Lucy**;

1852 - wife **Martha Carroll** d. 1852, est. acct. of sales, Edmund Shell bght. ld., 15 Dec. 1852 (Kerr, v. 1, pp. 126, 199, 219, 226, 239; Utah Gen. Soc. M. Bds., p. 37; Jackson Cens. Indx.; Cens., p. 175, 816, #29, Cens., Index., p. 29; Dd. Bk. 21, p. 369; Dd. Bk. 26, p. 122; NC DAR Roster, pp. 439, 573; Clark, v. 22, pp. 55-92; Will Bk. 34, pp. 381, 382; Will Bk. 35, p. 11; Will Bk. 42, pp. 173, 174) **Ch.:**
 1. **William G. Carroll** md. **Nancy Jett,** 1835; 1850; 1852 Aug.Ct. - **William G. Carroll,** Abner Mosly & William Duncan made inv. of **Martha (& James')** est.; **William Carroll,** son of **James Carroll,** gave inv. 7 Sept. 1852, Nov. Ct.; **1852 - William G. Carroll,** wife, Nancy in Warren Co. with child?; **1853** Feb. Ct. - Acct. of sales of est. of **James Carroll, William Carroll,** exr.; **1854** Aug.Ct. - Final acct. of **Martha Carroll** est. by **William Carroll** (Cens.; Will Bk. 42, pp. 68, 90, 173, 174; Will Bk. 43, pp. 179, 180) [**Robt. Carroll** may be his son.]
 2. **1830 - Lucy Carroll** md. **John Moseley** 24 Dec., wits.: John Kirkland, C. Drake,CC (Utah Gen. Soc. M. Bds., pp. 120, 166; Car. Cbls, July 1995)
 3. **1831 - Martha Carrol** md. **Hartwell Moseley,** 26 Dec., wits. Jas. Maxwell, & E. D. Drake (Utah Gen. Soc. M. Bds., p. 165, Carroll Cables, July 1995)
 4. **1836 - Mary J. Carrol** md. **Martin F. Lambert,** 10 Dec., wit. **Jurdan W. Carroll,** E. D. Drake, CC (Utah Gen. Soc. M. Bds., p. 145; Carroll Cables, July 1995)
 5. **Jordon W. Carroll**
 6. **Rebecca L. Carroll**
2. **1812 - Ezekiel Carroll** taxable; **1820 - Ezekiel Carroll,** Warrenton; **1824 - Ezekiel Carroll** md. **Tabitha Moore** 7 July, bdsm. Joseph Carter, wit. C. Drake, CC; **1829/1835 - Ezekiel Carroll** to Anthony Dowlin, trustee; to F. J. Juakins, trustee; **1830** - bght. from Jesse Reid; **1831** - sold to Jesse Reid and John L. Wilkins (Franklin Co.) probably removed from state (Cens., p. 798, #9; Indx., p. 9; Utah Gen. Soc. M. Bds., p. 37; Dd. Bk. 26, p. 91, 172) **ch.:** son
 1. **Thomas**
 3. **1826 - Tabitha Carroll** md. **John B. Shell** 17 Jan., wit. **Thos. Carrol (Jr.)** & M. M. Drake (Utah Gen. Soc. M. Bds., p. 227; Carroll Cables, July 1995)
 4. **1813 - Miriam R. Carroll** md. **James Edwards,** 20 Sept., wits. James Robinson and Jno. H. Green (Utah Gen. Soc. M. Bds., p. 69)
 5. **1814 - Rebecca Lee Carroll** md. **Isaac Rainey,** 26 Feb., wits.: **Thomas Carrol** and Wm. Green (Utah Gen. Soc. M. Bds., p. 202; Carroll Cables, July1995)
 6. **1798 - Sarah (Sally) Carrall** md. **James Read** 11 Nov., wit. Hillery Capps, M.D. Johnson, CC (Utah Gen. Soc. M. Bds., p. 203; Carroll Cables, July 1995)
 1. **Solomon Shell Carrol**
 7. **1811 - Thomas Carroll Jr.** taxable in River Dist.; **1812 Thomas Carrol Jr.,** Aug. Ct. 1827 - **Thomas Carrell (Jr.)** md. **Sarah A. Robinson,** 10 Dec.; **1835/1840 - Thos. Carroll** bght. ld. from Clack Robinson (Utah Gen. Soc. M. Bds., p. 37; Dd. Bk. 26, p. 215)
 8. **Nancy Carroll** md. **?Mize/Wize**
 9. **1802 - Elizabeth Carroll** md. **Wade Brooks** 14 Apr., wits.: Jas. Blazly & Gideon Johnson (Utah Gen. Soc. M. Bds., p. 17)

1850 - **William Sterling Carroll**, b. Franklin Co. in **1806**, md. **Nancy Cooper** 30 Dec. **1834**; owned 1,000 acs. lost by **Benjamin Carroll** in a poker game (Luther Carroll, oral) **ch.:**
   1. **James Carroll**, b. Franklin Co. in **1837**, lost an arm in Civil War, one of many children: **George**, lived in Henderson, NC, d. of stroke; **Louis**, decd.; **Peter** (L.Carroll letter 6/8/1989); **ch:**
   1. **James/Jimmy** 2. **Peter** 3. **Mollie** (Lucille Carroll Letter, 10 Nov. 1989]
   2. **Mary Carroll**, b. Franklin Co. in **1839**, never married
   3. **Robert Z. Carroll**, b. Franklin Co. in **1842**, md. **Sarah (Sallie A.) Mustian** 25 Sept.1865/1Oct.**1865**, T. Page Ricaud, bdsm. Thomas J. Judkins, wit. William A. White, CC (Utah Gen. Soc., M. Bds., p.37; Carroll Cables, Apr. 1996); **Ch.:**
      1. **Robert Archie Carroll**, b. **1875**, d. **1936**, md. 1st **Lucy Stevenson**, 2nd **Iva Thomas Ball**; **ch.:**
         1. **Leona Carroll** (by 1st wife), md. **Roy Dee**, decd., md. 2nd **? Simon**, **ch.:**
           1. **Evelyn**
         2. **Robert Dee Carroll**, decd., md. **Ida Collins**; 15 **ch.:**
           1. **Louise C.** md. **? Ayscue**, (of Warren Co., granddau. of **Robert Archie Carroll**)
           2. **Florence Bell** md. **? Overton**
           3. **Shirley** (only living twin of 4 sets of twins) md. **? Lynch**
           4. **Iva Jean** md. **? Burton**
           5. **Betty Joanne** md. 1st **? Floyd**, 2nd **?**, 3rd **Pat Register**
           6. **Robert**
           7. **Judy** md. **? Ross**, 2nd **?**, 3rd **John Cameron**
           8. **Anthony**
         3. **Lucy Bell** md. **John Allen Felts** who d. July **1986**; she lives in Wise, NC; ch.: 1. **Lois Bell** md. **? Hawks**; 2. **John Thomas Felts**
         4. **Roy Melvin Carroll Sr.**, ?decd., md. **Helen Curl**; **ch.:**
           1. **Elizabeth** md. **? Watson**; 2. **Barbara**; 3. **Roy M. Jr.**
         5. **Luther Allen Carroll**, called Zack by an "old lady" in his youth, was b. 27 Nov. **?**, d. ?Sept. **1996/97**, told of helping his mother raise flowers and build chicken coops. Her many chickens roamed the yard. His daddy taught him to make many things with a pocket knife. Luther recalled carloads of old **Carroll** men visiting, chewing and spitting tobacco while partaking from a jar of moonshine beneath a large oak tree at his Grandpa's house. **Luther** md. **Mary Felts** 12 Jan. **?**. He farmed tobacco until felled by strokes in the **1970s** which left him childlike and confined to wheel chair. He was a keen-minded Bible reader and loved to tell jokes. **Mary** resides in Norlina, NC. **Ch.:**
           1. **Alice Ruth Carroll** md. 1st **Elton Shearin**, 2nd **William (Billy) Franklin Pearce Sr.**; **ch.:**
              1. **Lester Thomas Shearin Pearce** (adopted) md. **Temple Ann Price**; ch.: 1. **Christopher**, 2. **Kimberly Ann**, 3. **Timothy Sean Pearce**
              2. **William Franklin Pearce Jr.** md. **Renee Porter**; ch.: 1. **Wm. Franklin Pearce III**

  2. **Peggy Faine Carroll** md. **Robert (Bobby) Vincent Allen**
  3. **Luther Allen Carroll Jr.** md. **Cecilia Reardon**; ch.:
    1.. **Luther A. Carroll III** md. **Jill Lewis, ch.:** 1. **Joy Nicole Carroll**; 2. **Ann Marie**; 3. **Michael Scott Carroll**
  4. **Delores Ann Carroll** md. **Robert Myrick Stegall, ch.:**
    1. **Robert M. Stegall Jr.**
 6. **Mildred Carroll** md. **Melvin Choplin**, resided in Richmond, VA; ch.:
  1. Harold Jackson
  2. **Bonnie** md. **? Hopkins**
  3. **Jane** md. **? Wortham**
  4. **Bobbie Jo** md. **? Bay**
  5. **Mac Ray Choplin**
 7. **Sarah Carroll** md. **Weldon D. Adams** who d. ?1997, resided in Richmond, VA, **ch.:**
  1. **Clarence D. Adams** md. **Lynda ?; ch.:** 1. **Kathryn Adams**
  2. **Ronald R. Adams** md. **Linda ?, ch.:** 1. **Angie Rogers**, 2. **April Lee**;
  3. **William D.** md. **Ellen ?**; 4. **Grace Carroll** md. **?**, lived in Garner, NC
 8. **Ben Holt Carroll** md. **?**
 9. **William T. (Bill) Carroll** md. 1st **Helen Carroll**, 2nd **Rachel ?**, d. Oct. **1989**; Bill resided in Norlina, NC
(Info on **Robert Z. Carroll** family given in oral interviews of **Luther & Mary Carroll** (22 Jan. 1991)

4. **William Carroll**, b. Franklin Co. in **1840**, d. ?
 1. **William Louis**, died in Rocky Mount Hospital of gallbladder surgery, md. **Martha (Nannie) Ball** (sister to Luther's mother), lived at Gold Sand near Louisburg, NC, **ch.:**
  1. **Helen Arlene**, md. **Herrian Frazer, ch.:**
   ch.: 1. **Gladys**, 2. **Crawford**, 3. **Essie**, 4. **Martha**, 5. **Robert**
   6. **Infant son**, d. young, 7. **Everett Carroll**, md. **Lucille Carroll**
   8. **Ethel** md. **Richard Green, ch.:**
    1. **Thelma Leigh Carroll**
  2. **Della** md. **Clifton Spain/Span, ch.:** 1. **C. A. Jr.**, 2. **William**, 3. **Roy or Roger**
5. **Benjamin Lee Carroll**, b. Franklin Co. in **1844**, d. **1928/1929**, md. **Betsey Ann Pegram**, d. **1920 ch.:**
 1. **George**
 2. **Lewis**
 3. **William Sterling Carroll**, b. 3 Feb. **1876**, d. 13 Feb.**1958**, md. **Georgia Washington Marshall**, b. 27 Aug. **1893**, d. 21 Feb. **1970**; **ch.:**
  1. **Lucille Buxton Carroll**, b. 22 Apr. **1919**, md. **Everett Elmore Carroll** (son of **William Carroll**) 1 Oct. **1955** (Lucille Carroll letter,10 Nov.1989)
  2. **Betsy Ann Carroll**, b. 18 Aug. **1920**

3. **Willie Ruth Carroll**, b. 17 Oct. **1922**
4. **Martha Helen Carroll**, b. 8 Dec. **1923**, d. 28 Sept. **1959**, md. **W. T. (Bill) Carroll**
5. **Thurman Kinlaw Carroll**, b. 10 Aug. **1928**, md. 1st **Essie Mae Frazer**, ?md. 2nd **Ann Jones**; ch.:
   1. **Thurman Kinlaw Jr.** md. **Kathey Huff**, ch.: 1. **Robie**, b. in 1989; 2. **Mike**, b. in 1989; 3. **Benjie** d. in **1970s**
   2. **Georgia Arlene** md. **Wyatt Pegram**, ch.:
      1. **Patric**, b. in **1989**
      2. **Suzann**, b. in **1989**
[I don't know under what name(s) the following belong: **Thurman Lee; Mildred Roy; Ruth Ann; Peggy Lyn; Meria Louis (Lula); Shelley; Sallie Bet; Ida; and Lucy**]
6. **Oliver Carroll**, b. Franklin Co. in **1845**, md. ? **Cefrees**, ch.:
   1. **Lizzie** (gddau. Fannie Davis lives at Gold Sand, NC)
7. **Martha Carroll**, b. Franklin Co. in **1846**, never married
(Some of above info. from Luther Carroll's letter and Lucille Carroll's letter, 10 Nov. 1989)
1785 - **Warren Plains Baptist Church** was originally known as Tanner's for Elder John Tanner who lived near Snow Hill. He donated land on which the church stands. It is located two miles from Warrenton and a few hundred yards west of the Warrenton-Norlina highway.

Buried in the cemetery are: **Robert K. Carrol**, b. 7 Feb. **1878**, d. 4 May **1951** and his wife, **Alberta R. Umberger Carroll**; **Elnora Carrol** (dau. of J. P. and Elnora Shearin), b. 22 Sept. **1890**, d. 11 Jan. **1919**; infant **Carroll**, d. **1942**; **Iva Ball Carroll**, b. **1890**, d. **1936**; **Robert A. Carroll**, b. **1875**, d. **1936**; **James A. Carroll**, b. **1930**, d. 9 June **1939**; **John William Carroll**, b. 9 Feb. **1910**, d. 10 Aug. **1926**; **Julia Louise Carroll**, b. 16 July **1942**, d. 30 July **1946**; **Margie Louise Carroll**, b. 15 June **1918**, d. 20 June **1919**; **Martha Ann Ball Carroll**, b. 13 Mar. **1874**, d. 24 Feb. **1942** (wife of **Wm. Lewis Carroll**); and **Samuel H. Carroll**, b. 21 June **1917**, d. 30 Oct. **1917**.

Stained glass windows memorialize past members. **R. K. Carroll Sr.** gave in memory of **John William Carroll**. Robert K. Sr.'s widow, **Alberta U. Carroll**, born 1 Oct. 1887 to the Robert Umbergers of Wytheville, VA, one of six sisters and one brother, d. 10 Nov. 1962. She was a graduate of East Radford Teachers College and taught in Virginia elementary schools. She visited her sister, Mrs. Lettie Daniel, in Macon, NC, and met Robert K. They married in Apr. 1921 and had four children. **R. K. Carroll Jr.** made a memorial gift, and **Mark P. and Dora Lou Carroll** memorialized the R. K. Carrolls with a stained window.

Luther and Mary Carroll donated a window and pew in memory of **Robert A. and Iva (Ball) Carroll**. Vacation Bible School flags are in memory of **Gary Dean Carroll Jr.** Among deacons were: **Luther Carroll, R. K. Carroll Sr. a R. K. Jr.** Superintendent of Sunday School: **Edward Rooker Carroll** (1985). Church Committee: **Mrs. Luke Carroll, Luther Carroll, R. K. Carroll**. Sunday School teachers: **Bobby Carroll, Mrs. Mary Carroll, Mrs. Gus Carroll**. WMU president: **Mrs. Lucille Carroll** (1977 & 1984). [White Plains Baptist Church History]
1773 - **Milbrough Carrole/Carroll**, of Bute Co., will, 1 Apr. **1773**/MayCt.1774/Apr.1, 1778; sons: **Thomas Carroll, Charles Carroll** (200 acs. in Brunswick Co., VA, horse & tack); **Betty Wilkins** (?dau., not indicated, 10p cash & side saddle); exrs.: sons **Thomas Carroll** (4p cash) & **Charles Carroll** and John Moseley; wits.: Stephen Shell, Sarah Brett, Rebekah Johnson; **1774** -

Milborough Carrole/Carroll, devisee Charles Carroll, May 1774, Thomas Carroll (ld. in Brunswick Co., VA); Charles Carroll; Betty Wilkins (Will Bk. 1(A), pp. 275, 276; Kerr, p. 39) [Wm. Carroll, d. 1781 in Granville Co., was son of Anthony Sterling Carroll, b. 1700 in Prince George's Co., MD, d. p1760 in Northampton Co., NC, md. 1722 in VA to Elizabeth Millborough, b. 1705 in ?VA, d. c1773 in Warren Co., NC. Deeds prove John, Benjamin and Milborough Carroll were brothers. Was Anthony Sterling Carroll their brother? Who was the father of John, Benjamin and Milborough? It's believed William, Thomas, Daniel also brothers. Info from Michael S. Cole on his wife's lineage.]
1776 - John Carroll, #R1737 ?1733 SC, 13 Oct. 1832, Capt., lived in Wake Co., enlisted in Warren Co., NC/Edgefield Dist., SC; father John Carroll; 1777 - John Carol; 1804 - John Carrell bght. from Jonathan Wilson, decd.; 1800 - moved to Warren Co., from Mecklenburg Co., VA, bght. from Henry Cocke of Wake Co.; bght. from Anderson Paschall; 1807 - John Carroll, wife Ann/e or Amey, no children named, 27 Nov., Edmund Mayfield, adm., bd. 500p to Thomas Eaton, bdsm.: Joseph Hawkins & Kemp Plumber; inv. given 29 Dec., Edmond Mayfield, adm.; - John Carroll est. ld. sold to Ames Carroll; 1808 - provisions for Amey given Feb. Ct.: to Ames (Ann) Carroll, widow Carroll Est., stock and provisions on hand for her support for one year; wits: John Harwell, James Powell, Dickey Neal, B.; 1810 - Anne Carroll bght. John Carroll est. (Ann Carroll from John Carroll Est.), Davis; 1810 - Anne Carrell; 1832 - Ann Carroll died in Warren Co.; (NC DAR Roster, p. 114; Kerr, pp. 139, 167; Dd. Bk. 17, p. 146; Dd. Bk. 18, p. 268; Will Bk. 14, pp. 178, 181; NC Gen. Indx., p. 268; Cens. Indx., pp. 168, 737; Cens. Indx., pp. 23, 42) ch.:

    1. 1813 - Nancy J. Carroll md. John Patterson, 4 May, wits. Charles Palmer and Jno. H. Green; 1852 - Nancy Patterson in Chatham Co., NC, age 70 (Utah Gen. Soc. M. Bds., p. 187; Carroll Cables, July 1995; Rev. War. Pens. Appl. Rcds.)

    2. 1818 - John Carroll md. Sally Wright 13 June, bdsm. Robt. Tally, wit. W. A. K./A. H. Falkoner; 1820; 1852 - John Jr. lived in Lincoln Co., GA (Utah Gen. Soc. M. Bds., p. 37; Carroll Cables, Apr. 1996; Cens. Indx., p. 18; Pens. Rcds.)

1776 - Douglas Carroll, pvt., enlisted, 3 yrs., Capt. Clement Hall's Co., 2nd Batalion, Col. John Patten, White Plains, 1 June; 1777 - NC soldier, Rev. Army Accts, 18 July/June 1778, 10th Regt., Col. Abraham Shepard; 1783 - Douglass Carrol, Mil. Ld. Wrnts, C L, #135, 428 acs., 36 mos., Col. Murfee, 22 Oct. (Clark, St. Rcds.; NC DAR Roster, pp. 114, 184, 235, 607)
1777/1782 - Laniel/?Daniel Carroll, Continental Line, #1338, Halifax Dist.; 1785 - Daniel Carrell, #1600, pvt., 228 acs., 30 mos., 12 Mar., J. Marshall; 1833 - Daniel Carroll, #506, CL, Warrenton, #762, recd. by H. Montfort (Cooper Family, NC DAR Roster, p.329; NC DAR Roster, p.266; Harvey Family, NC DAR Roster, pp. 368, 514) [Daniel Carroll assigned his NC ld. gt. in Sumner Co., TN, Maney Fork, to John Marshall - NC Land Gts. In TN.]
1778 - George Carroll bght. ld. from William Shearin; 1779 Nov. 22/June 25, 1780 - George Carrell of Warren Co., 1000p VA money, sold to Moses Merrick/Myricke, ld. East of Little Creek, partial of 168½ acs., wits.: Francis Myricke Jr., John Meakons, James Mattory; 1813 - taxable in Capt. Turner's Dist.; 1814 - taxable in Nutbush Dist., Richard Bullock, JP; 1818 - George Carroll md. Eliza Tucker 10 Nov., bdsm. Edward Birchett, wit. Will Green, CC);
1820 - George Carrol, Warrenton (Dd. Bk. 6, p. 426; Dd. Bk. 7, p. 302; Kerr, v. 1, pp. 230, 240; Utah Gen. Soc. M. Bds., p. 37; Cens., p. 816; Cens. Indx., p. 30)

1778 - Britton Carol, pvt., Hogg's Co., 9 mos., 20 July/2 Nov.; **Britian Carol**, militia, #629, Newbern Dist.; **1833 - Britton/Brettor Carrol/Carroll**, Contential Line, #804, Warrenton Settlements, #1091, B. McCullock (NC DAR Roster, pp. 114, 191, 366, 515; Harvey Family)
1779 - Hannah Carroll, insolvents (Kerr, v. 1, p. 4)
1780 - Polly/Holly Carroll md. **Bereud Decicaty/Decilaty**, 6 Dec. (Utah Gen. Soc. M. Bds., p. 58; Carroll Cables, July 1995)
1786 - Joannah Carril will, **ch.: James**; **1786** - Wm. Johnson, JP, binds **"James Carril**, 13-year-old ... base(bastard) son of **Joannah Carril** to James Cannon" to learn trade of taylor (sic), apprenticeship till 21, must be taught to read and write (Will Bk.5, p. 160; Kerr, p. 36); **Ch.:**
    1. **James**, b. **1773**
1790 - Joseph Carroll, (Hds./Fams.)
1790 - Thomas Carrol, Halifax Dist., 1M16+, 2F (Hds./Fams.)
1810 - Benjamin Carroll md. **Frances Rottenberry** 19 Apr., bdsm. Matthew Bolton, wit.: M. Duke Johnson, CC (Utah Gen. Soc. M. Bds., p.37)
1813 - Mecham Carrol md. **Susan Williams** 8 Aug., bdsm. James Edwards, wit. Wm. Green, CC (Utah Gen. Soc. M. Bds., p. 37)
1813 - Mariam Carrell md. **James Edwards** 20 Sept. (Carroll Cables, July 1995)
1818 - Grief Carrol md. **Polly Nanney** 29 Aug., bdsm. Allon Rainey, wit. Wm. Green, CC; **1824 - Grief Carroll** md. **Elizabeth Taylor** 2 Dec., bdsm. Edward Lambert, wit. C. Drake, CC (Utah Gen. Soc. M. Bds., p. 37)
1819 - Betsy Carrell md. **John Brewer**, 4 Oct., wit. James Jeffres, Cas. Drake, CC (Utah Gen. Soc. M. Bds., p. 25)
1820 - William Carrel md. **Nancy Capps** 24 May, bdsm. Moses Bennett (Utah Gen. Soc. M. Bds., p. 36)
1820 - John Carroll, Warrenton (Cens., p. 806, #18)
1823 - Minerva Carroll md. **William King**, 26 July, wits.: John Gossee & Edwin D. Drake (Utah Gen. Soc. M. Bds., p. 143; Carroll Cables, July 1995)
1823 - Lucy Carroll md. **Wiley Hicks** 25 Nov. (Carroll Cables, July 1995)
1825 - William Carroll will, 13 Oct. **1825**, probated Feb. **1828**, wits.: Drury Andrews, John Dowling, Chastain Allen, ? J. Smith; wife **Mary, ch.:**
    1. **Winifred/Winney**, md. **Nimrod Williams** 27 May **1809**, wit. Littlebury Tucker, Jno. C. Johnson, DC (Will Bk. 31, p. 148; Utah Gen. Soc., p. 272; Carroll Cables, July 1995)
    2. **George**
    3. **Edmond Carroll** md. **Rebekah Burton** 7 July **1825**, bdsm. Reuben Newman, wit. Burl. Pitchford; **1825/1827** - **Edmd. Carroll** to Jas. Scoggin, trustee (Utah Gen. Soc. M. Bds., p. 37; Dd. Bk. 24, p. 497)
    4. **Sally**
    5. **Lucy**
    5. **1822 - Elizabeth Carrol** md. **Rueben Newman**, 18 July, wit. **Edmund Carrol**, Cas. Drake, CC (NC Gen. Soc. M. Bds., p. 173; Carroll Cables, July 1995)
1828 - Joel Carrol md. **Catharine Rottenberry**, 5 Feb., bdsm. Ruben Newman, wit. Burl. Pitchford (Utah Gen. Soc. M. Bds., p. 37)
1828 - William Carroll md. **Mary Barner** 25 Feb., bdsm. John Robinson (Utah Gen. Soc. M. Bds, p. 37; Carroll Cables, Apr. 1996)

1833 - Jonathan Carrell, #3121, Timothy Mcarthy recd. Warrenton Settlements (NC DAR Roster, p. 518)
1833 - William Carroll md. **Rebecca A. Edwards** 24 Apr., bdsm. Augustin C. Pattillo, wit. C. Drake, CC (Utah Gen. Soc. M. Bds., p. 37; Carroll Cables, Apr. 1996)
1841 - William Carral/Carrell md. **Sarah Cleton** 10 Jan., wit. John R. Roberts, Burl Pitchford, JP (Utah Gen. Soc. M. Bds., p. 36)
1851 - Mary A./Maryya E. Carroll md. **Robert Clarey**, 16 Jan., wit. William Clary, Richard B. Robinson, JP (Utah Gen. Soc. M. Bds., p. 44; Carroll Cables, July 1995)
1853/1858? - James H. Carroll md. **Diomysia F. Bartlett** 21 Jan., bdsm. William A. Walch; wit.: William A. White; md. by J. B. Solomon (M. Rcds.; Utah Gen. Soc. M. Bds., p. 36)
1853 - Joseph W. Carroll md. **Sarah E. Carroll** 24 July; Geo. W. Holloman, bdsm.; Jno. W. White, wit. (Utah Gen. Soc. M. Bds., p. 37; Carroll Cables, Apr. 1996)
1859 - Mary Carroll md. **Nathaniel Kimball** 19 Feb., wits. Jos. J. Haithcock and Jno. W. White, J. B. Solomon, MG (Utah Gen. Soc. M. Bds., p. 138; Carroll Cables, July 1995)
1860 - Mary N. Carroll md. **George W. King**, 5 Apr., wits. Allen E. Rainey and Jno. W. White, N. A. Purefory, MG (Utah Gen. Soc. M. Bds., p. 141; Carroll Cables, July 1995)
1866 - Ellen Carroll md. **George Allen** 4 Aug. (Carroll Cables, July 1995)
1866 - Ann Carroll md. **Beckham Paschall** 20 Dec. (Carroll Cables, July 1995)
1866-67 - James A. T. Carroll (Col.) md. **Mariah Jefferson**, 19 Dec./13 Jan., William W. White, CC; R. D. Paschall, JP (M. Rcds., p. 33)
1866 - Samuel Carroll (Col.) md. **Chany Paschall**, 15/25/28 Dec., William W. White, CC; Thomas T. Paschall, JP (M. Rcds., p. 34; Carroll Cables, Apr. 1996)
1866 - William H. Carroll md. **Pattie Capps** 24/26 Dec., J. M. Brame, JP, wit. Wm. A. White, CC (Utah Gen. Soc. M. Bds., p. 37; Carroll Cables, Apr. 1996)
1867 - Reubin Carroll md. **Minerva Wheeless**, 14 May, Rev. P. H. Joyner, bdsm.; William A. White, wit. (M. Rcds., p. 34; Carroll Cables, Apr. 1996)
1867 - Sarah Carroll md. **Jacob Johnson** 21 Feb. (Carroll Cables, July 1995)
1867 - Missoura Carroll md. **Henry Ball** 13 July (Carroll Cables, July 1995)
1867 - Lizze Carroll md. **Henry Christmas** 7 Nov. (Carroll Cables,July1995)
1867 - Charlotte Carrol md. **Boson Somerville** 9 Nov. (Carroll Cables, July 1995)
1991 - Griffin Roy Carroll, 78, died Sat., ? Jan., at Heritage Meadows Nursing Home in Oxford, NC, native of Warren Co., a farmer, buried Tues., 11 a.m. in Greenwood Cemetery, Rev. Joey Anthony, officiating; **surviving sisters: Mrs. Virgie Seagroves and Mrs. Mamie Vanderburg**, both of **Durham, NC, Mrs. Lena Marsh** of McKeesport, PA, **Mrs. Ethel Carter** of Henderson, NC, **Mrs. Jessie Hicks** of McLeansville, NC, **Mrs. Rebecca Pryor** of River Ridge, LA; six brothers: **Rooker Carroll, Richard Carroll, Gus Carroll** and **John Carroll** of Warrenton, **Jimmy Carroll** of Springfield, OH, and **Milton Carroll** of Scotland Neck, NC (Henderson Daily Dispatch, obit., 21 Jan. 1991)

<u>Randolph County</u> was established in **1779** from **Guilford County**.
1800 - Edward Carroll, 26, 00010-30101-01, 1M26-45, 3F10-, 1F16-26, 1F45+, 1sl; **1810 - Edward Carel** (MF Cens. Roll 32, p. 305, l.16; Cens. Indx., p. 160)
1834 - Huldah Carroll md. **Andrew Jackson Craven** 20 Dec. (Carroll Cables, July 1995)

1839 - **Dicey Carrol** md. **Silas Presnall** 22 Apr. (Carroll Cables, July 1995)
1854 - **Nancy Carroll** md. **Eli Pugh** 15 July (Carroll Cables, July 1995)
1864 - **John H. Carroll** md. **Kisiah J. Trogden** 2 June (Carroll Cables, Apr. 1996)
1867 - **John H. Carroll** md. **Isabelle Clapp** 21 Feb. (Carroll Cables, Apr. 1996)

Rutherford County, established in **1779** from **Tyron County**, was part of **Mecklenburg County** in **1762**.
1790 - **John Carrick?**, Morgan Dist., 3M16+, 1M16-, 7F, 6sls; **1810** - **Three John Carrells** (Hds./Fams., p. 119; Cens., pp. 93, 163[2], 359; Cens. Indx., pp. 23, 42, Jackson Cens. Indx.) [See Sampson Co.]
1790 - **Joseph Carroll**, Dist. 1 (Cens. Indx.)
1790 - **James Carroll**, Dist. 1; **1800** - **James Carroll** md. **Martha Williams** 11 June (Cens.)
1800 - **Dennis Carrel** 2M10-, 1M45+, 1F10-, 1F10-16, 1F26-45; **1820** - **Dennis Carrell** (Cens. Roll 33, p. 101, l. 24; Cens. Indx., p. 33)
1800 - **Willis Carrel** 01010-01010-00 (Cens. Roll 33, p. 102)
1807 - **John Carroll** md. **Elisabeth Pruett** 27 Jan. (Carroll Cables, Apr. 1996)
1810 - **Jesse Carroll** (Cens. Indx., p. 163)
1810 - **Leah Carrill** (Cens., p. 363; Cens. Indx., p. 42)
1810 - **Manson Carrol** (Cens.,p. 152; Cens. Indx., p. 23; Jackson Cens. Indx.) [See Sampson Co.]
1810 - **Two Edmond Carrolls** (Cens.p. 157;Cens.Indx.p. 23,Jacks.Cens.Indx.)[See Sampson Co.]
1810 - **Joseph Carroll** Cens.p. 163;Cens.Indx.Smith, p. 23; Jacks. Cens.Indx.)[See Sampson Co.]
1810 - **Thomas Carroll** (Cens., p. 163; Smith, Cens. Indx., p. 23) [See Bladen Co.]
1810 - **Sarah Carroll** (Cens., p. 156; Smith, Cens. Indx., p. 23) [See Bladen Co.]
1831 - **Nathan B. Carroll** md. **Jennett Graham** 13 Oct. (?)
1856 - **William H. Carroll** md. **Susannah Bostick** 2 July (Query - Carroll Cables, Apr. 1997)
1865 - **Thomas Carroll** md. **P. Bostick** 8 Dec. (Carroll Cables, Apr. 1996)

Lincoln County, in Salisbury Military Dist, was established in **1779** from **Tyron County**.
1768 - **John Carroll** leased land from Wm. Naely; **1774** - **John Carrell** (R. E. Indx., Bk.1, pp. 174,175, Bk. 2, p.37)
? - **John Carrel**, 16; **1781** - **John Carrel**, pvt., Raiford's Co., 10th Regt., Col. A. Shepard, enlisted for 12 mos. 11 June 1781, out 11 June 1782? (Clark, v. 16, p. 1035)
1769 - **Joseph Carol and Thomas Carol** deed to James Logan; **1820** - **Joseph Carrel** (Dd. Bk. 1, p. 158)
1769 - **Thomas Carol** and **Joseph Carol** deed to James Logan; **1789** - **Thomas Carrell**, grantor, Real Estate conveyance (Dd. Bk. 1, p. 158; R. E. Indx., Bk. 4, p. 25)
1777 - **Butler Carrall**, enlisted 19 Apr., 10th Regt., Continental Line, Col. Abraham Shepard, ensign, Jarvis' Co., died May **1780** (in war) (Clark, v. 16, p. 1033)
1780 - **William Carroll**, patent; **1787** - **William Carrell**, grant of 40 acs. 12 Sept. (?); **1790** - **William Carrot**, 2M16+, 1M16-, 1F; **1800** - **William Carrell**, 1M10-16, 1M45+; **1803** - **William Carrel Sr.** transferred to **William Carrel Jr.** 23 July for $20, Potts Ck. . . . 40 acs. granted to **William Carroll** by the state 12 Sept. 1787 (#357), wits.: John Yoder and John

Frederick Cool, proved Oct. 1804, John Dickson, CC; **1804 - William Carrell to Nathaniel Carrell; 1810 - William Carrel; 1824 - William Carrell**, grantees, Real Estate conveyance; **1830 - William Carroll**, 1M70-80, 1F60-70 (Hds./Fams., p. 112; Cens., p. 901, 1. 12; Dd. Bk. 21, p. 291; R. E. Indx., Bk. 21,p. 299; Bk. 25, p. 512; Jackson Cens. Indx., p. 23, Cens., pp. 162, 335; R. E. Indx., Bk. 31, p. 381); **Son:**
    1. **1803 - William Carrel Jr.; 1810 -** (Cens. Indx., pp. 42, 326; Cens., p. 418)
1777 - Nathan Carroll, born 17 Sept. **1777**, died 4 June **1870**, (?father **David Carroll** of SC) md. **Mary A.** ?; **1800 - Nathaniel Carrol**, 2M10-, 1M26-45, 3F10-, 1F26-45; **1804 - Nathaniel Carrell** from **William Carrell Sr.**; **1810 - Nathl. Carrol/ Nathaniel Carrell**, 2M10-, 1M26-45, 3F10-, 1F26-45; **1812 - Nath. Carrel** of Lincoln Co. and George Mosbiller, 78p, indenture, Mary W. Williams, wit.: Vardey McBridle 12 Dec./Jan.1813 Ct. (Carroll Cables, Oct. 1996; Cens. Roll 40, p. 495; R. E. Indx., Bk. 21, p. 299; Dd. Bk. 25, p. 512; Cens. Indx., pp. 23, 42; Cens., pp. 374, 495; R. E. Indx., Bk. 29, p. 148)
1794 - James Carroll wit'd. dd. of sale from John Sloan to Alex'r Lackey, wit. Mark Bird, 3 Sept.; **1800 - James Carrett**, 2M10-, 1M10-16, 1M26-45, 3F10-, 1F26-45; **1804 - James Carrol** bght. 250 acs. from Henry Levengood, wit. John McNemarr, 26 July; **1808 - James Carrel**, juror, John Huffman v. David Hanks, Henry Shell, Henry Hoover, Adam Costner, Jan.-Apr.; **1810 - James Carrel; 1819 - James Carrell**, grantee, Real Estate conveyance; **1820 - James Carrell**, 3M10-15, 2M16-25, 1M45+, 1F16-25, 1F45+, 5 in agriculture; **1821 - James Carrell**, grantee; **1830 - James Carroll**, 3M20-30, 1M60-70, 1F5-, 1F50-60 (Dd. Bk.; Dellinger, pp. 42, 71; Dd. Bk. 21, p. 388; Sullivan, pp. 128, 129, 130; Cens., pp. 330, 335, 336, 421; Indx., pp. 23, 28, 42; Jackson Cens. Indx.; R. E. Indx., Bk. 29, p. 145; Cens. Roll 83, p. 326; R. E. Indx., Bk. 30, p. 77; Cens. Roll 122, p. 217); **Son:**
    1. **1820 - James Carrell Jr.**, 1M26-44, 1F16-25, 4Msls; **1830 - James Carroll**, 1M5-, 1M10-15, 1M40-50, 1F5-, 2F5-10, 1F30-40 (Cens. Roll 83, v.4, p. 308; Cens. Roll 122, p. 218)
1819 - Susannah Carrol md. **James McClurg** 27 Feb. (Carroll Cables, July 1995)
1822 - Esther Carrol md. **William Aderholt** 4 July (Carroll Cables, July 1995)
1826 - Martha Carrol md. **Christian Eaker** 1 Nov. (Carroll Cables, July 1995)
1830 - John Carrol, Martin poll (Cens. Indx.)
1830 - Alfred Carroll, 1M5-, 1M20-30, 1F30-40 (Cens. Roll 122, p. 160)
1830 - Green Carroll, 1M5-, 1M20-30, 1F15-20 (Cens. Roll 122, p. 162)
1830 - William Carroll, 1M70-80, 1F60-70; **1831 - William Carol; 1832** June 7 - **William Carroll**, pvt., **W6640**, "appeared in open court of Lincoln Co., NC," age "about **80 years**" to make "following declaration in order to obtain ..." of pension. "... lived in ... NC near **Tar River** in the **county of Granville**," when he "enlisted (in) the service of the US" ... drafted (1781) ... 15 or 18 months before the close of the Revolutionary War "but was prevented from going into the service at that time ... Afterwards called out and joined ... near ? Springs in state of SC" command of Col. Little, Major Donoho and Capt. Hall, command Gen. Green, "served as a guard ... never was in any engagement ...," born in **Fairfax Co., VA**, moved to Tar River in Granville Co., served 12 months, signed **Wm. X Carrol**; drafted **1781**, 12 mos., pvt., Gen.Green, Col. Little, Maj. Donoho, Capt. Hall; **William Carroll** ... "The King's Mountain Men," pvt.; **William Carroll** was pentioned by NC in **1833**; at the time he was in Roane Co., TN; **1844** June 17 - **White Co., TN, Kessiah Carroll**, resident of said county and state, aged **83**, (William) entered service in

Granville Co., received pension in Lincoln (where resided) $40, md. by a minister of the gospel in **Granville Co. in Sept. 1777**, "knows of no person now living by whom she can prove the marriage," **William d. 28 Dec. 1835** (in TN); she heard him say he served first under Capt. Hall and Gen. Green, then Capt. Armstrong, Maj. Donoho and Col. Little; **Elijah Carroll** gave sworn statement in Sparta, TN; **1846** June 22 - Cleveland Co., NC, **Joseph Carroll**, acting JP: "**Betsy Dover**, dau. of **William and Keziah**, appeared before me" swore (her mother), who d. **9 Feb. 1845** in TN, had family record in her possession for many years and believes it to be the ? Record and her father's own handwriting. Richard Champion, clk.; certified **Joseph Carroll**, an acting JP (Rev. War Pens. Appl. Recds., National Archives, Washington, DC; White, pp. 479, 573; Cens., Roll 122, p. 162; Ear. Amer. Sers., v. 3, p. 38; Roster of Soldiers 1833, pp. 156, 263) Submitted page of record shows in handwriting: "Family Record of **William Carroll** and **Keziah Carroll**:"

    1. **Jessy Carroll**, b. 14 Nov. **1778** (testimony by John Steward: **Jesse, oldest son, was left in Granville Co.**)

    2. **John Carroll**, b. 3 Aug. **1779**; **1820** - **John Carrol**; **?1830** - **John Carrol**, Martin list

    3. **Betsy Carroll**, b. 13 Dec. **1780**

    4. **Elijah Carroll**, b. 7 April **1781**; **1830** - **Elijah Carroll**, 1M5-, 1M20-30, 1F5-, 1F20-30 (Cens. Roll 122, p. 162)

    5. **Henry Carroll**, b. 26 ? **1783**; **1830** - **Henry Carrol**, 2M5-, 2M5-10, 1M30-40, 1F30-40, 4sls (Cens. Roll 122, p. 153)

    6. **Nancy Carroll**, b. 21 Sept. **1785**

[Payment made to John Huske, Fayetteville, NC for the above heirs]
1831 - **Joseph M. Carrell** md. **Elizabeth Endsley** 31 May, wit.: Silas Williams, M. Hull, JP (Bynum, p.28; Carroll Cables, Apr. 1996); **?son:**

    1. **1832** - ???son **Joseph Martin Carroll**, b. 8 Jan **1832**, d. 16 July **1889** in MO, 20 Apr. **1856** md. **Martha Jane Biggs**, b. 13 Aug. **1832**, d. 27 Oct. **1892**, b. Mount Carmel Cem., Miami Station, **MO** (Carroll Cables, Oct. 1996); **Son:**

        1. **1862** - ?son **Hugh Riley Carroll**, b. 15 Mar. **1862** in Henryville, **IN**, d. 17 Jan. **1927** in Carroll Co., **MO**, md. **Malinda J. Finley** (Carroll Cables, Oct. 1996)

1837 - **James Carroll** md. **Ann ? Lusk** 14 Mar., wits.: Henry Huss, M. W. Abernathy (Bynum, p. 28)

1839 - **Henry W. Carroll** md. **Nancy Lavina Wethers** 15 Aug., wits.: Thos. K. Pursley, Eli Hoyl (Bynum, p. 28)

1839 - **Susanah D. Carrol** md. **William Ferguson** 16 July (Carroll Cables, July 1995)

1840 - **John Carroll** md. **Sary Delany Baker** 4 Oct., wits.: John Baker/Eaker, C. Stroup, JP (Bynum, p. 28, Carroll Cables, Apr. 1996)

1867 - **Joseph Carroll** md. **Catharine Mullin** 26 Sept. (Carroll Cables, Apr. 1996)

1914 - **Correll** estate, accts. and settlements, Frank Julia applicant (Index, Accts. & Settlements)

Gates County, established **1779** from **Hertford, Chowan and Perquimans counties**, was in 1780 in Edenton Military Dist.
1810 - **Elizabeth Curl**, 1M10-, 1F10-, 1F16-26, 1F26-45, 1F45+ (Cens. Roll 40, p. 852)
1810 - **John Curl**, 1M10-16, 1M45+, 1F10-, 1F10-16, 2F16-26, 1F26-45, 2slvs (Cens. Roll 40, p. 852)

Montgomery County was established in **1779** from **Anson County**.
1781 - **William Carroll**, tax list; **1790** - **William Carrill**, Salisbury Dist., 1M16+.4M16-, 2F;
1790 - **Jane/James Carrill**, Salisbury Dist., 3F; **1800** - **Jane/James Carrill**, 25, 3F16+ (Hds./Fams. Cens., p. 188; Cens. Roll 33, p. 165)
1800 - **William Carrell/Carrill**, Salisbury Dist., 1M16+, 4M16-, 2F16+ (Cens. Roll 29, p. 901; ?, p. 165; Hds./Fams. Cens. Indx., p. 165)
1800 - **Dennis/Denise Carrell/Carrill**, 30, 1M26-45,1M45+,1F26-45 (Cens. Roll 33, p.490, l.6)
1810 - **Ann Carrol** (Cens. Indx., p.2 3, Jackson Cens. Indx.; Cens., p. 56)
1810 - **Two John Carrols** (Cens. Indx., p. 23, Jackson Cens. Indx., Cens., pp. 55, 56)
[Census Indx. doesn't list James Sr. and Jr. under any spelling of Carroll, but notation advised "see Charrel" since they were probably in county.]

Richmond County was established in **1779** from **Anson County**.
1800 - **Archibald Carroll**, 1M16-26, 1M45+, 2F10-16, 1F16-26, 1F45+ (Cens. Roll, p. 260, l. 16)

Wayne County was established in **1779** from **Dobbs County**.
1820 - **John C. Carrell**, 3M10-, 2M10-15,1M45+, 1F26-44, 1 in agri. (Cens.Roll 83, v. 4, p. 506)
1820 - **Samuel C. Correll**, 1M10-15,1M26-44,3F10-, 1F26-44, 3 in agri. (Cens. Roll 83, p. 535)

Sampson County, in the Fayette Military Dist., was established in **1784** from **Duplin County**. It is located in South Central NC on the Black River which runs into the Atlantic Ocean at Cape Fear. In **1779**, Duplin Co. took in all of Sampson Co. (Johnson, pp. 1781, 1782)
1756 - **Patience Carroll** md. **Samuel Gavin**; lived on Cedar Hill plantation one mi. So. of Turkey, NC, **ch.**: **Mary Rachel Gavin**
1767 - **Jesse Carroll Sr.**, b. **c1749/c1750** in Granville Co., d. 10 Mar. **1802** in Sampson Co., lived in Franklin Co., sol., NC unit, md. **1769** in Sampson Co. **Mary Rachel Gavin**; sold land on Six Runs; Rev. War; obtained three ld. grants in Duplin and Sampson counties; **1781** - taxpayer; **1784** - 1105 acs.; **1790** - **Jesse Carol/Carrol**, Fayette Dist./Newbern Dist., b. **c1750**, 3M16+, 4M16-, 4 females, 5sls; **1800** - 1M10-15, 2M16-26, 1M45+,1F10-16, 1F26-45, 1F45+, 10sls; **1802** - **Jesse Carrell Sr.** will, d. 10 Mar. **1802**; wife Rachel; sons: Jesse, John, Thomas, Joseph; daus: Mary Hollingsworth, Priscilla Carrell, Rachel Carrell, exrs.: sons John & Jesse; wits.: **John Carrel**, David Chesnutt, Alexander Chesnutt [This Jesse cannot be the son of William who died in Granville Co. in 1781. That William's will indicates his Jesse was under legal age. Perhaps Jesse and William were brothers.] **1820** - **Rach Carrell**, 1M10-, 2M10-15, 1M16-25, 2F10-15, 1F16-25, 1F26-44, 3F45+ (DAR Patriot Indx, 1776; Indx. NC Ancestors, p. 32, #17080; Gwathney, p. 63; Deeds; NC Rev. Accts., v. 5, p. 40; NC Tax List; Hds./Fams., p. 126; NC Cens. Indx. p. 51; Cens. Roll 32, p. 511, l. 17; W. Bk. A, p. 34; Absts./Wills 1784-1895, p. 3; Cens. p. 280); **Ch.** of Jesse Carroll Sr. and Rachel:

    1. **Thomas Carroll** md. **Mary Royal**; **1800** - **Thomas Carrel** [Their Thomas?] (Cens., p.530; Bentley Indx, p.41)

    2. **Mary**, b.**1807**, d. **1889**, md. 1st **John K. Smith**, one son; md. 2nd **Henry Hollingsworth** in **1825**, moved to Kosciusko, MS, 10 ch.

    3. **John**, b. **1770**, d. **1826**, md. 1st **Ann Hollingsworth**, 2nd **Elizabeth Hollingsworth**;

1790 - John Carrol Sr., 2M16+, 3M16-, 5F; **1800 - John Carrel Jr.** 2M26-45, 1M10-, 1F26-45, 1sl (NC Cens. Indx., p. 52; Cens. Roll 32, p. 512, l. 6; Bentley Indx., p. 41)
    4. **Jesse Jr.**, b. **19** Oct. **1774** in Duplin Co., d. **1828** in Sampson Co., md. **1801** in Sampson Co. **Margaret (Peggy) Merritt**, Six Runs plantation; **1800 - Jesse Carrel**; **1810 - Jesse Carroll** (Indx. NC Ancestors, p. 32, #17080; Hds./Fams., p. 51; Cens. Roll 32, p. 511; Bentley Indx., p. 23, Cens., p. 473); **ch.**:
        1. **Margaret** md. **Wm. Lamb**, moved to GA
        2. **James** md. **Eliz. Carroll**, 9 children
        3. **Benajah** md. **Mary Mallard**, 12ch., TX
        4. **Laban** md. **Sallie Ann Fillyaw**, 6 ch.
        5. **John Durham** md. **Zilpha Chesnutt**; 8 ch., a son: Rev. **Rice Carroll**
        6. **Edwin Joseph** md. **Eliza Watson**, went to Carroll Co., MS
        7. **Charity** md. 1ˢᵗ **Mr. McGowen**;; 2ⁿᵈ **Wm. Moore**, lived in FL
    4. **Joseph** md. 1ˢᵗ **Margaret Chesnutt**, 2ⁿᵈ **Miss Carr**; **1810 - 1820 - Joseph Carrell** (Cens., p. 472; Bentley Indx., p. 23; Cens., pp. 21, 22, 294; Cens. Indx.); **ch.**:
        1. **Caleb**
        2. **Joshua**
        3. **Curtis**
        4. **Joseph**
        5. **Elizabeth**
        6. **Jesse**
        7. **John**
        8. **Margaret**
        9. **Charity**; moved to TX
    5. **Rachel** md. **Ira Tucker**, moved to AL
    6. **Priscilla** md. **Henry Edward Smith**, 6 ch.
    7. **Lewis**, b. **1808** in Sampson Co., md. **Catherine Eliza Lamb** in **1832**; **1872 - Lewis Carroll** will, plantation on Six Runs, so. of Turkey, NC (Indx. NC Ancestors, p. 32, #17080; Will Bk. 3, p. 55) **ch.**:
        1. **Wm. Joseph** lived in Portsmouth, VA; **4 ch.**:
            1. **Cornelius Tate** md. **Addie Chesnutt**, went West
        2. **James** md. **Ellen Barden**, lived Turkey, NC, 6 ch.
        3. **Geo. Washington** md. **Frances Williams**, 6 ch.
        4. **Mary E.** md. **Geo. Herring**, lived Harrells, NC, 5 ch.
        5. **Rachel**, b. **1826** in Sampson Co., d. **1932** in Cumberland Co., md. **1855** in Sampson Co. Prof. **Isham Royal**, lived in Duplin Co. (Indx., NC Ancestors, p. 32, #17080); 6 ch.
        6. **Rebecca** md. 1ˢᵗ **Mr. Merriman**, 2ⁿᵈ **Mr. Hamblin**, 3ʳᵈ **John Stokes**, d. in Magnolia, NC, 3 ch.
        7. **Francis Marion**, b. 5 Oct. **1841**, sol. CSA, md. **Eloise Jane Taylor**, lived Turkey, then Clinton, NC where buried, 5 ch.
        8. **Amma B.** md. **Martha Barden**, moved to Lenoir Co., NC, then OK, then TX, 11 ch.
        9. **Adelaide (Addie)** md. **John Southerland**, 2 ch.

[For the remaining lines of the Jesse Carroll Sr. family, suggest: *The Forefathers of James Williams Bryan and Irene Carroll Bryan and Their Descendants*, compiled by Claude Hunter Moore, Prof. of History, Mount Olive College, 1978, pp. 27-36]
1761 - **John Carroll** to wife, **Mary** . . ., to **John** the plantation where I now live . . ., son **Joseph Carroll**, dau. **Dorcas Carroll** (NC Wills) **Ch.:**
    1. **1762** - to **John Carroll**, witness **Thomas Carroll**; **1767** Jan. 13 - **John Carroll** bought 100 acs. bounded by **John Miller Carroll**; and **John Carroll** sold land to **Jesse Carroll**; **1781** - taxpayer; **1784** - **John Carrell**, tax list; **1790** - **John Carrol Sr.**, Fayette Dist., 2M16+, 3M16-, 5F; **1800** - **John Carrel**, 110-16, 2M16-26, 1M45+, 1F10-, 2F16-26, 1F26-45; **1814** - **John Carrell** d. 22 May **1814**; son **Raeford**; **other children** mentioned but not named; exr. **Rashel Carrell**; wits. Hiram Blackburn, **Raiford Carrell** (Deeds; Hds./Fams., pp. 52, 59; Cens. Roll 32, p. 526, l. 14; Absts./Wills 1784-1895, p. 3; Cens., pp. 294, 512, l. 7) **Ch.:**
        1. **1790** - **John Carroll**, 1M16+, 2M16-, 2F; **1800**- **John Carrel**, 01201-10210-00 [two Johns, Jackson Indx., same #s]; **1800** - **John Carrel**, 1M26-45, 1F16-26; **1810** - **John Carroll**; **1820** - **John Carrell**, 1M10-, 3M10-15, 1M16-18, 1M16-25, 1M45+, 3F10-, 2F10-15, 1F16-25, 1F26-44 (Bentley Indx., p. 23; Cens., p. 473; Cens.; Cens., p. 22)
        2. **1820** - **Raiford Carroll**; **1848** - **Raiford Carroll** will (Cens., pp. 8, 282; Will Bk. A, p. 169)
        3. **1820** - **Joseph Carroll**, 2M10-, 1M10-15,1M26-44, 1M45+, 2F10-, 1F10-15, 1F16-25, 1F26-44, 1F45+ (Cens.)
        4. **Dorcas**,
        5. **other children** not named in will
1768 - **Thomas Carroll** sold to Samuel Watkins; **1784/1787** - **Thomas Carroll**, tax list; **1784** - **Thomas Carroll**, 8 Nov., ?; **1800** - **Thomas Carril**, 3M10-, 1M10-16, 1M45+, 1F10-, 1F10-16, 1F16-26, 1F45+; **1810** - **Thomas Carroll** [Thomas the son of Jesse and Mary Rachel or Jesse's brother?] (Deeds; Register, p. 56; Clark, v. 19, p. 428; Cens. Roll 32, p. 513, l. 12; Smith, p. 163; Bentley Indx., p. 473)
1781 - **Alexander Carrell**, taxpayer; **1790** - Fayette Dist., 1M16+, 2M16-, 3F; **1800** - 2M10-, 1M10-16, 1M26-45, 2F10-, 1F10-16, 1F26-45; **1827** - **Alexander Carrell**, d. 25 Feb. **1827**; wife **Lucey**; sons: **Hardy, Wylie, Reason**; daus.: **Rebekah Carrell, Rhanney Bridges, Mary Ann Tedder, Betsey Ann Royal**, exrs. wife and Hardy Royal; wits.: Daniel Williams, Nathan Williams, Thomas Maxwell (Hds./Fams., p. 51; Cens. Roll 32, p. 536, l. 4; Will Bk. A, p. 125; Absts. Sampson Co. NC Wills 1784-1895, p. 3); **Ch.:**
    1, **1790** - **Hardy Carroll**, Wilmington Dist., 1M16+, 1M16-, 3F; **1800** - **Hardy Carol** (Hds./Fams., p. 59; Cens.)
    2. **Wylie**
    3. **Reason**
    4. **Rebekah**
    5. **Rhanney Bridges**
    6. **Mary Ann Tedder**
    7. **Betsey Ann Royal**
1781 - **Demcy Carell**, taxpayer; **1784** - **Demey Carrell**, tax list; **1790** - **Demcy Carrol**, Fayette Dist., 1M16+; 2M16+, 3F [**1790** - **Demey Carrol**, Fayette Dist., 2M16+, 3F]; **1800** - **Dempsey**

Carril, 1M10-16, 1M45+, 1F16-26, 1F45+, 2 sls (Hds./Fams., p. 52; Cens. Roll 32, p. 527, l. 9)
1781 - Stephen Carrell, taxpayer; **1790 - Stephen Carrol**, Fayette Dist., 1M16+, 1M16-, 4F, 1 sl; **1800** - 3M10-, 1M26-45, 3F10-, 1F26-45, 2sls (Hds./Fams., p.51; Cens. Roll 32, 529, l.5)
1784 - James Carrell, tax list; **1790 - James Carrol**, Fayette Dist., 3M16+, 1M16-, 7F, 1 sl; **1800 - James Carrel**, 3M10-, 1M16-26, 1M45+, 2F10-16, 2F16-26, 1F45+ (Hds./Fams., p. 51; Cens. Indx., p. 142; Cens. Roll 32, p. 525, l. 10)
1784 - Moses Carrell, tax list
1784/1787 - William Carrel, 1M21-60+, 1M21-60, 3F; **1790 - William Carroll**, Fayette Dist., 1M16+, 4F (Register, p. 56; Hds./Fams., p. 51)
1784/1787 - Hannah Carroll, 2M21-60+, 4F (Register, p. 56)
1790 - Elisha Carrol, Fayette Dist., 1M16+, 2M16-, 4F; **1800 - Elisha Carrel**, 2M10-, 1M16-26, 1M45+, 1F10-, 2F10-16, 1F26-45 (Hds./Fams., p.53; Cens. Roll 32, p. 535, l. 2)
1790 - Elizabeth Carroll, Fayette Dist., 1M16-, 2F (Hds./Fams., p. 53)
1800 - Thomas Carrel/ Carril; 1M10-, 1M26-45, 1F10-, 1F26-45 (Cens. Roll 32, p. 527, l. 10)
1800 - Fedrick Carrel 1M16-25 (Cens. Roll 32, p. 512, l. 18)
1800 - Williby Carell, 2M10-, 1M26-45, 3F10-, 1F26-45 (Cens. Indx., p. 679, l. 1)
1810 - Edmond Caroll; **1820 - Edmund Carrell** (Bentley Indx., p. 42, Cens., pp. 2, 485)
1810 - Manson Carrol; **1820 - Manson Carrell**, 4M10-, 2M10-15,1M26-44, 1F26-44 (Bentley Indx., p. 23, Cens., pp. 294, 494)
1810 - Sarah Carroll; **1820 - Sarah Carroll**, 1M10-15, 1M16-18, 1M16-25, 1M45+, 1F10- ,1F10-15,1F16-25,1F26-44,1F45+; **1855 - Sarah Carroll** will (W.Bk. 1,p. 476; Bentley Indx. p. 23, Cens. p. 487; Cens. p. 276)
1820 - Rebecca Carroll, 1M26-44, 3F10-, 1F16-25 (Cens.)
1820 - Gradeless Carroll (Cens., p.4,276; Cens. Indx., p. 4)
c1885 - L. R. Carroll will (Copy in NC Archives)
1891 - James G/L. Carroll of Sampson Co. md. **Marcella Jackson** of Sampson Co., June at Franklin A. Jackson's residence by Josiah Baggett, Esq. (NS DAR of NC, Cornelius Harnett Chap., p. 36) **ch.:**
    1. **1892 - Thaddious Troy Carroll**, son of **James L. and Marcella Carroll**, b. 20 May 1892 (NS DAR of NC, Cornelius Harnett Chap., p. 37)

<u>**Moore County**</u> was established in **1784** from **Cumberland County** and named for Alfred Moore, a Revolutionary patriot and associate judge of the U.S. Supreme Court. Carthage is the seat of government. The first courthouse was built shortly after 1784, replaced in 1820, burned in 1889 and was rebuilt in 1890. The present courthouse was built in 1922. (The Historical Records of NC, v.2, pp. 538-555)

    First settlements in the Moore County area were **c1745**. Settlers were predominantly of English, Ulster, Scot, and Irish descent, and a few Germans, French and Pennsylvania "Dutch," the latter of whom were largely Quakers.

    On 16 May **1751**, Gov. Gabriel Johnston bequeathed 7,000 acs. on Deep River (then in Bladen Co.) to his brother John's two sons -- Samuel and John Johnston -- saying "his brother would allow his creditors to get it." Samuel, of Edenton and older of the two, was elected governor of the state in 1787 and was North Carolina's first senator in 1789. The area around Carthage was settled from **1754 to 1774**. "Land had value now." (Robinson, pp. 11, 15, 16, 17)

In **1763** Samuel Johnston conveyed "the one half or a moriety" of his 6,500 acres to his brother-in-law, John Blair of Edenton, for 525p. Blair and the younger John Johnston began selling land to the new settlers streaming into the area. From **1763 to 1765**, they sold 1,418 acres to six purchasers. James Barnes bought the largest tract, 663 acres for 180p proclamation money. **Sterling Carroll** paid 200p for 400 acres, perhaps more desirable land. Cornelius Tyson, who had bought John Tyson's Horseshoe tract, added 383 acres more for 100p. Smaller tracts went to Joshua Hancock, William Brazier and Elisha Hunter. This most fertile clay land lay along Deep River and its creeks. (Wellman, p. 10)

. . . the Sandy Creek Baptist Association records note: "the church on Deep River" was moved to Bear Creek in Chatham county in **1768**, "leaving only two of its members in Cumberland (Moore) county" ... Connor Dowd and **Amy Carrol**. This church was probably in the vicinity of Carbonton, where both Dowds and **Carrols** lived, and could have been in either Moore or Chatham. (Wicker, p. 117; Wellman, p. 117) [See Cumberland Co.]

"Enough men had settled in the area along Deep River and below to take part in the so-called Regulator's War of **1771**. A number of Piedmont colonists refused to pay" what seemed exorbitant taxes. They handled officials roughly and gathered in armed bands. Gov. William Tryon led the NC militia against these malcontents. From present day Moore County came two companies, that of Charles Herd at the fork of Little River and that of James Chaney, who lived west of Cabin Creek. ... Other officers from the area were **John Carroll** and James Collins. The two companies marched with the militia which, on May 16, **1771** fought 2,000 armed Regulators and scattered them. " ... Not long afterward, Philip Alston, a member of a rich and influential family in Halifax County, appeared in Horsehoe Bend. ... he was personable, gifted and sometimes violent and unscrupulous." (Wellman, p.11)

In **1785**, county voters elected Philip Alston to the state senate, and **John Carroll** and John Cox (**1785-1788** gts.,450 acs. plus small amts. in TN) to the House of Commons. When North Carolina called a convention in **1788** to accept or reject the United States Constitution, Cornelius Doud (son of Conner Dowd, a banished Tory) was a delegate from Moore County along with **John Carroll**, John Cox, and **William Martin** (son of a banished Tory, House of Commons **1788-1791**, state Senate **1793**, slave owner). They were the Anti-Federalist delegation (Wellman, pp. 36, 38).

An examination of Moore County deeds and wills reveals that these men were certainly among the largest landowners of the county. The Federalists, led by Samuel Johnston, James Iredell, and William R. Davie, waged a relentless campaign in favor of the adoption of the Constitution and succeeded in calling a second state convention to meet in **Nov. 1789** at Fayetteville, and despite a statewide swing to Federalism, Moore County continued to adhere to Anti-Federalism. Its representatives voted as a bloc against adoption of the Constitution. (Robinson, pp. 108, 109).

When the Cumberland is spoken of as late as **1781**, Moore County (middle NC) is included. Moore County Census of **1790** shows 3,770 residents in 639 households; 355 were black slaves belonging to 81 of the households. Only 11 households had 10 or more slaves (Wellman, p. 39).

Moore County wills were received from **1794**. Will Book A also contains court minutes, bonds, etc. Page numbers in record volumes were assigned at a later date. The book appears to consist of several separate volumes combined and bound together. After **1868**, original wills were placed in special proceedings files. In Sept. **1889**, the courthouse burned, and nearly all loose records burned, including original wills proved prior to **1868** as well as special proceedings files were destroyed. Will books survived as did other records in bound form. Many original wills are missing, a few are in state archives ... (Mitchell, v. 1, p. XXIX, Code #068)

In **1814**, "Concerning the beginning of Methodism in Moore County ... great deal of obscurity, but before the Revolution pioneers of Methodism had preached at the home of Jerry Phillips, on Indian Creek in Chatham County, about four miles NE of the church of Fair Promise, on Deep River." First members of the Methodist Church in the county were Jerry Phillips, his wife, Susan, John Phillips, **Amy Carroll** and John Seal. This small nucleus did not survive the stress of the Revolutionary War [Did Robinson mean the War of 1812?]. Charles Dickerson, a native of Moore, returned in 1814 as a Methodist minister from Georgia to his old home on Deep River. He "preached at a 'school hut' which stood on or near the site of Fair Promise; at a place near Gulf; and at another near the Siler camping-ground, on the old Rhodes place, about five miles southeast of Carthage." The church historian continued: "At the 'school hut' he had evidently organized a society, for under the ministry of his successor the membership there was increased in 1816 by the addition of **Polly Carroll**, Polly Barnes, and George Stewart and his wife." (Robinson, pp. 181, 182).

"It is evident that the Methodists were largely in the majority in the **1850** period, while the Baptists were surprisingly few. Although the Quakers were probably here first."

1755 - **John Carrel** of Cumberland Co. (Moore Co.), "true list of Taxables in Cumberland Co., ..., 1 polled;" **1765** - Apr. 23, witness to mortgage deed from James Muse to John Overton; **1766** - **John Carroll, Sr.**, J. P. [Justice of the Peace], Deep River, at mouth of McLendon's Cr.; July 10 - Witness to deed, Cornelius Tyson to Connor Dowd; **1767** - **Sterling Carrol** gave deed to **John Carrol**, 200 acs on so. side of Deep River, beg. at mouth of Buck (McLendon's) Creek; runs thence up said creek to a red-oak thence N. 164 poles to a pine, a corner tree; thence E. 114 poles to a black walnut on the river bank; thence down said river to the beginning; wits: John Hunnicutt and Randolph Hunnicutt, 14 Jan.; witness with Connor Dowd to deed from Cornelius Tyson to Robert Cheek, 6 Feb.; **1768**, Mar. 11 - witness to deed from Geo. Blair to Cornelius Tyson; Sept. 23 - **John Carrell** surveyed; **1770-1788** - (See Cumberland Co.); Grant to **John Carrell**, 100 acres, lower side of Deep River, beg. at white oak by a Spanish oak on bank, said to be Joel McLendon's or Gabriel Harden's corner, running thence as an old, marked line, N 59 W, 25 chains; thence . . . 80 W, 6.10 chs; thence S 32 West, 38.20 chs to Joseph Duckworth's upper line; thence as it, S 30 E 31 chs to a hickory on the bank; thence up to beg. Wm. Tyron, Governor, 5 Feb. 1770 [Dd. from **Carrell** to Hunnicutt not of record]; **1772** - **John Carrell** witnesses deed to Elisha Hunter from Philip Alston, 22 Feb.; witnesses deed from Mary and Robt. Dickenson to John Overton, 24 Feb.; **1773** - **John Carrol** deed to John Overton 300p procl. money, 200 acs., So. Deep River, above mouth of McLendon's Creek, tract of ld. gtd. to Jacob McLendon (200 acs. bght. Jan. 14, 1767), wits: Hartwell and Randolph Hunnicutt; **1774** - Deed from Cornelius Tyson to **John Carrel**, 300 acres, 10 pounds proclamation, on s. side of Deep River, being part of Cornelius Tyson's 400-acre grant, wits: Benjamin Tyson and Connor X Dowd, 15 July; **1777** - **John Carroll**, 700 acs., same as location for **Sterling Carroll**, below in 1777; **1785** - **John Carrel**, a Justice of the Peace, elected to House of Commons, ". . . difficult to determine his property interests because of similar names in records . . .;" the county's voters elected Philip Alston to the state senate, and **John Carroll** and John Cox to the **House of Commons**; Tues., Nov. 22, the House met according to adjournment. Mr. **John Carroll**, one of the members for Moore County, appeared, was qualified and took his seat. Voted between above date and ?, "the

House met, ordered **Mr. Carroll** and Mr. McDaniel have leave to absent themselves from the service of this House for three Days and Mr. Singleton until Tuesday next." Vote on keeping principal offices of State in the Town of Hillsborough ... **Carroll** voted yea. Bill on incorporating Protestant Presbyterian Church of Wilmington. **Carrol**, yea. Vote on currency for pound weight of tobacco. **Carrol**, nay. Duty of Jurors to establish Damages ... **Carroll**, nay. 20 Dec. - Bill on courts. **Carroll**, yea. State Superior Court. **Carrol**, yea. Tax raise for 1786. **Carrol**, nay. **John Carroll Esquire** and John Kendrick took oath before Committee on Memorial of Philip Alston who commanded corps of Militia and testified for Alston. Alston should be brought to trial for death of Thomas Taylor. Griffith Rutherford, Chrm. **1785**, Dec. - When Philip Alston went to the state senate, he headed for deep trouble. Charged in Dec. with the murder of Thomas Taylor, apparently during the retreat of Greene's army before Cornwallis in 1781, Alston argued that Taylor had been a Tory "and was ... guilty of misprision of Treason for a few minutes before he fell." A senate committee of review majority recommended that Gov. Caswell pardon Alston, but three dissenting members felt Taylor should have been captured instead of killed, and spoke sternly of Alston's "strong passions." Caswell pardoned him, but the newspaper denounced him and the investigation continued for a time. Living as a neighbor to Philip Alston in 1791 was Captain Benjamin Harrison. Gen. Rutherford, from the Committee to whom was referred the Memorial of Philip Alston, Reported as followeth, vizt: That from the testimony of **John Carroll, Esquire**, 19 Dec. 1785, and Mr. John Kendrick, taken on oath before your Committee, it appears that Thomas Taylor had long been, and continued to be an Enemy to this State, and was actually guilty of misprision of Treason for a few Minutes before, if not at the very instant he fell in the re-encounter with Colonel Philip Alston. That the said Alston then commanded a Corps of Militia in the service of this State for the express purpose of suppressing the Tories, the situation of the County, (Gen. Greene being at that time under the necessity of retreating before the British Army) and every circumstance considered, Your Committee is of opinion that Col. P. Alston should not be brought to tryal on account of the death of the said Thomas Taylor, and they beg leave to suggest that a recommendation from the Honorable, the Gen. Assembly to his Excellency the Governor to issue a pardon to the said Colonel Alston would be the best method to close the enquiry: – all which is submitted. Griffith Rutherford, Chn. Currency Bill. **Carrol**, yea. **John Carrol** gave reason with others concerning salt brought into Country as ballast (tax on it) would discourage and price of salt will be very much enhanced. Protest against taxing of land by the hundred acres as unproductive and impolitic and unjust and oppressive to the poor. **John Carrol**. Allowances for members and clerks, etc. recommended they be reduced. **Carrol**, yea. **1787** - **John Carrol Sr. and John Carrol Jr.** in company of Foot Soldiers commanded by Wm. Whittfield (?); **1788** - **John Carroll** ...when North Carolina called a convention in 1788 to accept or reject the United States Constitution, Cornelius Dowd was a delegate from Moore (county). Another delegate, like Dowd, son of a banished Tory – William Martin. **John Carroll** and John Cox – had served in the Assembly, also represented Moore County at the Convention ...; July 25, **John Carroll**, Cornelius Dowd, Thomas Tyson and William Martin of Moore Co. certified as only elected members of Convention at Hillsborough for purpose of resolution deliberating Federal plan for fixing state seat of government; 1 Aug., **John Carrel** took his seat, voted nea to amendment to Constitution binding vessels, one against other, or paying duty; voted yea on fixed state of government; voted yea on Convention concurrence with report of whole convention; 2 Aug. voted yea to Congress shall pass a law for collecting an impost in aforesaid states and this state to enact law for collecting a similar impost on goods into state, and appropriate money arising from to the use of Congress; the Convention shall fix on a particular place for holding future meetings of General Assembly, and residence of chief officers of state ratified. **1790 - John Carrol Sr.**, North of Deep River, in vicinity of Horsehoe or Haw Branch; **John Carroll Esq.**, Fayette Dist., 3M16+, 3M16-, 5F, 2sls [3M16+, 3M16-, 5F, 3sls; NC Cens. Indx.p.44]; **1793** - 100 acs. gt. #417, "Know ye that we have granted unto **John Carrel** ... land in our County of Moore beginning at a post oak by a branch in Thomas Agurtous Line" runs ... N. 20, W. 23 chains to a pine, S. 70 W. 43 chains & 48 Links, S. 20, E. 23 chains to Peter Smiths Line, N. 70, E. 43 chains & 48 Links with said Line to the beginning to Hold to the said **John Carrel** his heirs and assigns forever ... 26 Nov.; Secr.: J. Glasgow, wit.: Richd. Dobbs Spaight; Carrol lived No. of Deep River, in the vicinity of Horseshoe or Haw Branch; **1800** - 3M16-26, 1M45+, 1F16-26, 1F26-45, 1F45+, 3sls (00301-00111-03); **1810 - John Carrol Sr.**, 1010-31001-0-0/00011-00001-04; **1820 - John Carroll**; **1821/1822 - John Carrell** will dated 3 Sept. 1821, codicil dated 14 Sept. 1821, **wife unnamed**; ch: Charlotte Carrell (dau); Alexander Carrell (son); Starling Carrell (son); Huldah Wade (dau.) md. to Edmond Wade; Jane Wade (dau) md. to Finsley Wade; John Carrell (son) & his ch.; James B. Carrell (son); Polly Martin (dau) md. to John Martin; Jesse Carrell (son), dec'd.; Susannah Carrell (dau) md.? Myrick; exr: Archibald McBryde, atty.; wits: James Hardin & Hugh Hardin; 1821, Moore Co., Devisor **John Carrolle**; Devisees: **John Carrell, Alex Carrell, James B. Carrell, Starling Carrell, Charlotte Carrel**; Devisor **John Carroll**; Devisees: **Polly Carrell, Tensley Wade, Jesse Carrell, Susannah Myrick, Atlas Jones (his sister, Agnes Jones?)**, Richard Street, Archie McBryde (Will Bk. B, p. 21); Codicil (Will Bk. B, pp. 23, 24)

John Carroll - 1821 Will
Moore Co., NC, Will Bk. B, pp. 21-24

... I **John Carroll** publish and release my last will and testament. My wish: one half of my hoggs and all my cattle (Except cows and calves or yearlings to be Selected by my **Daughter Charlotte**,) one half of my Hoggs and all the Homespun Cloth on hand at my death and two of the best bed quilts be sold by Executor on that Credit as he May deem ? with any other personal property which my **daughter Charlotte** May think can be ? and the proceeds applied to Discharge of my funeral Expenses and payments of my Last debts. My Will farther is: Horses I now own and other half of Hogs and ? Cows and Calves or Yearlings reserved together with all my household and ? furniture (Subject to the Exception) and My farming tools and Impliments of Husbandry together with all my slaves shall remain on the plantation whereon I now live and in the possession of my **Daughter Charlotte** for three years after this season (if State of my afairs will Admit of it) until the 24th of December 1824 during which time if **Charlotte Carroll** Mannage the Negroes She is to imploy a stutable (suitable) person to Superintend them and the Surplus produce of all Kind on Plantation to be Sold and applied towards discharge of my debts, and during the three years My sons **Alexander Carroll and Starling Carroll** and sons in law **Edmond Wade and Tinsley Wade** and their families in the Event of death of Either of them Shall remain in possession of lots or parts they Now respectively acupy (occupy) if they Choose to remain but are not to rent Same, and they or my Negroes during the three years. May Clear Land but Commit No wast by Cuting wood or otherwise Except what is Necessary for firewood and Expense? of their respective Farms at Experation of the three years or at any time after the 24th of December 1824. My will: my Land and all personal property on Land Except Negroes be Advertised by Executor and sold on such Credit and on such Conditions as he may deem most presedant? and Advantages to My Estate, and after paying my just Debts Ballance of price of Land and personal Property together with all my Negroes (Except My Negro Hannah) be Equally devided among **my Nine Children** or their Heirs or representatives. Towd, the Children of my son **John Carroll** deceased., one Share, **Alexander Carroll** one Share, **James B. Carroll** one Share, **Sterling Carroll** one Share, **Charlotte Carroll** one Share, **Daughter Polly Martin wife of John Martin** and if she should be dead her Surviving Children one Share. **Hulday Wade wife of Emond Wade** one Share, **Sister (Jane) Wade wife of Tinsley Wade** one Shair, and the **Children of My Son Jesse Carroll deceased.** one Shair, But My Negro girl Hannah is Excepted in above division. My Will: **My Daughter Charlotte** Shall have her services? and remain in possession of her during her life, and at her death Negro Hannah will go to Children of **Son John Carroll** or Survivors of them or their heirs? and if Hannah should have Children after My death and before death of **Charlotte** My Will: they be Equally divided among My Nine Children or their legal representatives. I will and bequeath to **My Daughter Susannah** the Sum of one Dollar in full of her part of Shair of My Estate She having already been Advansed by Me, and my will: Each of my Nine Children shall take their parts of shairs Clear of all deduction for former Advancement or on any Other Amount whatever, lastly nominate and appoint Archibald W Bryde (or McBryde?) Attorney at Law Executor of My last will and testament, revoking all former wills by me and testifying this only as **my last will and testament my hand and seal this third day of September 1821** Signed Sealed published as my last will and testament in the presents of James Hardin, Hugh Hardin, A W Bryde (or McBryde)

I **John Carroll** do make publish and declare the following to a **Codicil** to my last will and testament . . . made **14 Sept. 1821**: Thereby invoke and annull the <u>absolute</u> gift made on My above Will to **My Sons Alexander Carroll, James B. Carroll and Starling Carroll** and to **my Sons in law ? their ?, Hulday, wife of Edmond Wade and Sister, wife of Tinsley Wade** and I hereby Will and bequeath the shairs Mentioned in my Will to others Jonas Richard Street: and Archibald McBryde and their Heirs. But intrust ? that trustees pay annually or soon as may be to Each of my Sons and Sons in Law ? above Mentioned profits or proceeds of their respective shairs as set forth in my Will and balance or other ? of Each Son or Son in Law Shall be ? and Valued discharge to Such trustees or Survivors or Exec. or Admr. of Such Survivor and on death of Either of my Sons in Law will: their Share or part be delivered by trustees or survivor to his Wife if alive but if both should die before Husbands respectively their Shares of Each or Either of my two daughters is to go to their Heirs at Law. at death of any these **Sons ? Alexander, James B. & Sterling**, my will: Exec. or survivor of them or Exec. or Admrs. of survivors deliver to Heirs of son or sons their respective shair or to Guardian or Guardians of their Children. my will: at end of three years as stated in my will for **daughter Charlotte** to have Land and Negroes to use and possess for five years and my Sons and Sons in Law mentioned in will Hold their lots on same term mentioned in will for five years Next after my death and until they can compleat five Crops if sale of any part of my Estate becomes Necessary before Expiration of five years I will: my Lands be Sold by Executor and my debts paid from proceeds reserving and subject to use of five years. At Expiration of five years if a division of my Negroes Cannot be Effected according to direction of will and sale if Necessary my will: Executor Sell them in Such Manner as to Consult My Negroes by giving them Opportunity of Choosing their Masters so far as Can be done without Material prejudice to my Estate.

I . . . declared it to be a Codicil to My last Will and testament this 14th of September 1821 In presents of Wm McIver?, A McBryde, **Jane (X her mark) Wade**

Moore County Court Feby Term 1822, The preceeding Will was duly proven in Open Court by the Oaths of James Hardin and Arch. McBryde and the Codicil by Arch. McBryde and **Jane Wade** and Ordered to be recorded and it is recorded in Book B. Pages 21, 22, 23 & 24; Corn. (Cornelius) Dowd (E. Amer. Ser., v. 3, p. 38; Wicker, pp. 19, 21, 37, 39, 62, 65, 306, 314, 458, 461; Dd. Bk.B, pp. 34, 35, 544; Wellman, pp. 11, 36, 37, 38, 186; Dd. Bk. C, pp. 16, 36, 59, 65, 142, 167, 266; Dd. Bk. F, pp. 21, 111, 333, 353, 397; Dd. Bk. E, pp. 19, 30, 62; Robinson, pp. 108, 225; Clark, v. 17, pp. 227, 335, 354, 359, 365, 366, 368, 391, 394, 395, 399, 406, 409, 410, 425, v. 20, p. 73, v. 22, pp. 2, 6, 26, 27, 30, 32, 34; Cens. MF Roll 7, v.2, p.158; Hds./Fams., p. 43; Radcliff, p. 40; Dd. Bk. 81, #428; Gt. Bk.1; Cens. Roll 32, p. 42, l. 8; Cens. Roll 41, pp. 597, 598, 599; Bentley Indx., p. 23; Cens. Indx., p. 55; Cens., p. 311, #29) **John Carroll Sr.'s children:**

    1. **1787 - John Carrol Sr. and John Carrol Jr.** in company of Foot Soldiers commanded by Wm. Whittfield (?); **1790 - John Carrol** , Fayette Dist., 2M16+, 4M16-, 3F; **1793 - John Carrel (Jr. or his father, John Sr.?)** granted 100 acres, #417, "beginning at a post oak by a branch in Thomas Agurtous Line S. 70 W 43 chains & 48 links, S. 20 E. runs" ... N. 20 W. 23 chains to a pine, 23 chains to Peter Smiths Line, N. 70 E. 43 chains & 48 links with said Line to the beginning to Hold to the said **John Carrel** his heirs and assigns forever; . . . Secretary: J. Glasglow, Sec.; Wit: Richard Dobbs Spaight, 26 Nov.; **1800 - John Carroll Jr.**, 28, 1M26-45, 2F10-, 1F26-45, 1sl (00010-20010-01); **1810 - John Carroll Jr.**, 31010-31010-0, 00011- 00002-0-4; **1820 - John Carrol** 1M45+, 1F26-45; **1821 - John Carroll Jr.** d. prior 3 Sept. 1821 (See John Carroll Sr.'s will) [Appears to be 3 John Carrolls: Fayette Dist. (Cens., p. 44; Radcliff, p. 4; Hds./ Fams., p. 43, 44; Wicker, p. 306; Gt. Bk. 81, #428; MF Cens. Roll 32, p. 43, l. 8; Cens. Index., p. 599; Cens. Roll 41, p. 598; Bentley Indx., p. 42; Cens., pp. 56, 311; Cens.; Jack.-Teep., p. 24, #29); **John Carroll Jr. had children**

    2. **Alexander Carroll** md. **Phebe** in ?; **1800 - Alexander Carrell**, 30, 1M26-45, 1F10-, 1F26-45, 0sl (00010-10011-00); **1806 - Alexander Carrell** entered 100 acs., state grant #2571, 17 Oct.: beg. at stake his 3rd corner of 75 acs. in line of **John Martins** 200 acs. about S 20, E 7 chs & 60 lks from forked Beach on S bank of Richland Creek in line of his 75 acres, N 35, E 24 chs & 40 lks to line of his 100 acs., S 45, E 10 chs to 4th corner of 100 acs., thence with 3rd line N 45, E 31 chs & 63 lks to 3rd corner then S 25, E 14 chs & 50 lks to stake then S 45 W 58 chs to Martins line of 200 acs. thence to beg. . . . To hold to the said **Alex. Carrell** his Heirs and assigns forever, 24 Dec. 1822, Secr: Wm. Hill; Wit: Cabl. Holmes; **1810 - Alexr. Carrell**; **1815 - Alexdr. Carrell**, Moore Co. landowners, 375 acres, $400; **1820 - Alex'r Carrol**, Jameston, 2M10-, 1M10-16,1M16-26, 1M26-45, 1M45+, 1F10-, 1F10-16, 1F16-26, 1F26-45; **1830 - Alexander Carrol**, Jameston; **1840 - Alexr. Carroll**; **1850 - Alexander Carrell**, 75 and **Phebe**, 73, Real est. $250, 16 Nov. (Cens. Roll 32, p. 42, l. 3; Dd. Bk. 135, p. 73; Cens. Roll 41, p. 599; Wicker, pp. 278, 464; The No. Carolinian Qtrly., Ju./Sept./Dec.1960, p. 692; Cens., p. 311, #29; Jack.-Teep., p. 24; NC Cens. Indx, p. 180; Cens., p. 458; Census, HH #1159, p. 243; Wellman, p. 278)

    3. **James B.**; **1790** - Fayette Dist/Fayetteville Town, **James Carrol**, 1WM16+; **1810 - J. B. Carrol** 00020/12010/05 (Hds./Fams., p. 21; Cens. Indx., p. 23; Cens. Roll 41, p. 600)

    4. **Sterling**; **1820 - Stutive/Stirtive Carroll (Sterling?)** - 2M10-, 1M10-16, 1M45+, 1F10-, 1F10-16,1F16-26; **1832** - **Sterling Carroll**, b. **1769** in **VA**, d. **1850** in Warren Co., NC, md. **1832** in Moore Co., 2nd wife **Elizabeth R. Moore** (Cens., p. 310, #27; Jack.-Teep.; Indx. NC Ancs., p. 25, #28500)

    5. **Charlotte Carroll**, single in 1821; **1820-1831 - Charlotte Carroll**, inv. (Newletter. v.

2, no. 6, Mar.10, 1986, p. 6, Moore Co. Gen. Soc., Inc.; Moore Co. Vertical File)
   6. **Polly md. John Martin**, probably the son of Capt. John Martin in ? (See John Carroll Sr.'s will); **1768** - John Martin a wit., 2 Dec.; **1771** - **John Martin** arrived to clear 40 acres on McLendon's Creek, ... "... he built a grist mill, bought more land and became well-to-do;" **1773** - wit. 6 Jan.; **1774** - grants of 150/250/350 acs. 21 July (Josiah Martin, gov. of NC), 250 acs. 16 Nov. and 200 acs. 3 Mar. 1775; **1775** - Thos. McLendon dd. to **John Martin**, 12 Jan., 100 acs.; dd. to John McRae, 150 acs., 22 Apr. **He ?Capt. John Martin** and his wife returned to Scotland ... (Bk. F, pp. 42, 229, 327, 351; Wicker, pp. 62, 74, 101, 102); **1815** - **John Martin**, taxable landowner, 440 acs, $300; 500 acs, $750; 385 acs, $30; 100 acs., $50; **1820-1831** - John Martin, inv.; **1820** - **Margaret (?Polly) Martin** 3M10-16, 1M16-26, 1M26-45, 1F10-, 1F10-16, 1F16-26, 2F26-45 (Wicker, p. 465; Newsletter, v. 2, no. 6, 10 Mar 1986, p. 6, Moore Co. Gen. Soc. Inc.) [Capt. John Martin's mother was a Bethune. "The Martins of Moore are doubtless the descendants of Captain John Martin" who was captured at Moore's Creek. Capt. John Martin was in the county in the 1770s, and his family remained in Moore Co., where there are many descendants. Martin was one of the Highland officers. "A little known document" titled: A Narrative of the Proceedings of a Body of Loyalists in North Carolina, written by a participant, probably Alex'r McLean, relates in detail the rising and the battle at Moore's Creek Bridge. The Martins were loyalist to Britian. John Martin, native of Scotland came to America in 1771. Capt. John Martin of the late Royall North Carolina Regiment was living in Inverness, Scotland in June 21, 1787 when called upon to declare what he knew of deceased relatives of Kenneth Campbell. **c1765-1819** - **William Martin**, son of Capt. John Martin, wife Flora Martin; dau. Flora Jr. md. Archibald Black; **1815** - William Martin on list of taxable landowners, 1080 acs, $2400; 100 acs, $100; 500 acs, $50; 50 acs, $50; William Martin d. 7 May **1819**; **1820-1831** - William Martin, inv.; a merchant, William Martin, son of Capt. John Martin and father of William Pinckney Martin of Civil War days, was last merchant of this family of merchants **William**, perhaps ... eldest of his **sons**, **died April 24, 1819**, aged 51 years, ... (headstone). His will dated July 11, 1818, names Murdoch and John Martin executors (assumed to be his brothers). (Will Bk. B, p. 1;] Newsletter, v. 6, no.5, Jan. 1990, Moore Co. Gen. Soc., Inc., p.70; Wicker, pp. 455, 464, 478; Newsletter, v. 2, no. 6, 10 Mar. 1986, p. 6, Moore Co. Gen. Soc., Inc.)
1777 - Angus Martin, 100 acs., Capt. Wm. Seal's Dist. (Wicker, p. 460)
1815 - Randol Martin, 350 acs. $350, taxable landowner in county
1815 - Murdoch Martin, 200 acs., $670; 200 acs., $200; 30 acs., $1, taxable landowner in co.; **1820** - Murd. Martin 1M26-45, 1M45+, 3F16-26, 1F45+ (Wicker, p. 469)
Daniel Martin 1M26-45, 1F16-26 (Cens.) [Probably family Polly Carroll married into.] [Josiah Martin, ?bro. to Capt. John Martin and governor of North Carolina in 1771-21, Nov. 1783, raised the Highlanders ... of North Carolina to 1500 fighting men in 1745-1746. (Wicker, pp. 75, 90, 91, 108, 371, 377, 383) [Martins found on Moore Co., NC censuses from 1790-1850 at least, when research ended.]
   7. **Hulday md. Edmond Wade**; **1820** - **Edward Wade**, 45+, 1F45+ (Cens.) [Wades found on Moore Co., NC censuses from 1800-1840]
   8. **1790** - **Jesse Carroll**, 1M16+,1F; **1800** - **Jesse Carrell**, 37, 1M16-26, 1M26-45, 2F10-, 1F16-26, 1sl (00110-20100-01); **1810** - 1M10-, 1M26-45, 1F10- 2F10-16, 1F26-45, 5sls (10001-12001-02); Jesse, deceased in **1821** (See John Sr.'s will above) [**Jesse Carroll** moved his family to **Williamson Co., TN** between **1810 and 1820** and died there around Jan. **1820** when his widow, Sally, gave inv. In Williamson Co., TN, 12 July 1828, Sally stated that she was his lawful

widow, that they had three children, to wit: **Deborah** who has married **Jonathan Gore, William Carroll** and **Elizabeth Carroll, Sally** who this day issued a power of attorney to Cornelius ?Cavid Jr. in Moore County, NC. These are his **(Jesse's)**, the reputed **son of John Carroll**, decd. of Moore Co., NC, **only heirs** (Radcliff, p. 49; MF Cens. Roll 32, p. 243, l. 13; Cens., p. 600; Cens. Roll 41, p. 57; Bentley, p. 599; Cens. Indx., p. 42; Williamson Co., TN Ct. Mins. Bk. 10, p. 44; Fischer, v. 1, p. 63); **Ch.:**
    1. **Deborah**, Williamson County, TN, md. **Jonathan Gore**
    2. **William**, Williamson County, TN, md. **Lockey Walton**
    3. **Elizabeth Carroll**, Williamson County, TN
  9. **Susannah md. ? Merrick**

Jane (Sister) Carroll md. **Tinsley Wade; 1781** - Wade & Culp came from Anson to avenge a massacre at Piney Bottom; **1815** - **Tinsley Wade**, 420 acs, $500, taxable landowner (Wicker, pp. 312, 464); **1820** - **Tensby Wade**, 45+, 2M10-16, 2M16-26, 1F10-, 1F16-26, 1F26-45 (Cens.) [I believe Jane (Sister) Carroll could be John Carroll Sr.'s sister-in-law, a widow who md. Tinsley Wade. According to John's father, John who died in Northampton County in 1760, John Sr. did not have a sister named Jane, unless she was left out of the will.]

1762 - **Sterling Carrol**, to him a deed from Dennis McLendon, 200 acs, 500p Being in the Mountas? fork of Deep River and McLendon's creek; wits: Thomas Knight, Joel McLendon and Francis McLendon, 19 Feb.; **Sterling Carroll** witness to deed from Jas. Russell to Gabriel Harding, 28 Apr.; witness to deed from Jas. Findley to Connor Dowd; also, witness to deed with other wits., Charles & Susana Findley, date unknown, 3 May 1762; Deed from Charles Findley to **Sterling Carroll**, 80 acs., being part of land that did belong to James Barton on the so. side of Deep Rr., 50p proclamation money (Description of parcel given); "James Barton to James Muse . . ." this part of the above Joel McLendon grant of 300 acs. was home of James Muse, Sr. The Rocky Ford mentioned was later known as Dickerson's ford and was the site where David Fanning crossed the river when he besieged Phil Alston in the Horseshoe. Charles [X] Findley; wits: James Muse and Isaac Ramsey, 15 May 1762; **1764** - **Sterling Carroll** deed to Gabriel Hardin, 80 acres, Beginning at Rocky Ford . . . down the river, 50 pounds proclamation money, 15 May; **1765** - Johnston and Blair to **Sterling Carroll**, 200p, 400 acres, beginning at hickory on Governor's Creek ... thence West, 20 chs to south bank of Deep River; thence down river to mouth of creek; thence up said creek to beg. Wits: James Russell, Elisha Hunter and **John Carroll**, 7 Feb.; **1766** - **Sterling Carroll**, Horseshoe of Deep River; **Sterling Carroll** deed to James Russell, 100 acs., 50p procl. money; part of 400 acs. conveyed by Blair to **Sterling Carroll** on 7 Feb. 1765; wits: ? McLendon and ? Dowd, 15 Nov. 1766; **1767** - **Sterling Carrol** deed to **John Carrol**, 200 acs on so. side of Deep River, beg. at mouth of Buck 87(McLendon's) Creek; runs thence up said creek to a red-oak thence N. 164 poles to a pine, a corner tree; thence E. 114 poles to a black walnut on the river bank; thence down said river to the beginning; wits: John Hunnicutt & Randolph Hunnicutt, 14 Jan.; **1770** - **Sterling Carroll** deed to James Russell, 150p, 300 acres . . . land said **Sterling Carroll** bought of Geo. Blair and John Johnston 14 May; deed to Hartwell Hunnicutt, 200 acs on upper prong of Governor's Creek; wits: John Overton, John Hunnicutt and Randolph Hunnicutt, 1 Nov.; **1771** - gt. to Anthony Seal bordering **Sterling Carrol's** corner"... 18 Nov.; **1777** - 100 acres, along Deep River below Horseshoe and along McLendon's Creek in Jacob Duckworth's Dist. (Dd. Bk. B, pp. 64, 121, 123, 140, ?, 180, 358, 563; Wicker, pp. 17,18, 19,24,

34, 35, 36, 64, 66, 88, 108,[Co. Highway #100 leads to the Horseshoe,] 355, 461; Wellman, p. 186; Dd. Bk. C, pp. 92, 142; Dd. Bk. E, p. 44; Dd. Bk. D, p. 294) **[Sterling and John Sr. are brothers.]** (See John Carroll will, Northampton Co.)
1790 - William Carrol, 1WM16+; **1800?** (Hds./Fams., pp. 41, 42; Cens., p. 43)
1800? - Stephen Carrol
1800? - Thomas Carrol
1814 - Amy Carroll and Polly Carroll: "Concerning the beginning of Methodism in Moore (Co.), (there is a) great deal of obscurity, but before the Revolution pioneers of Methodism had preached at the home of Jerry Phillips, on Indian Creek in Chatham (Co.), about four miles northeast of the church of Fair Promise, on Deep River." The first members of the Methodist Church in Moore were Jerry Phillips, his wife, Susan, John Phillips, **Amy Carroll** and John Seal. This small nucleus did not survive the stress of the Revolutionary War. ... not until 1814 that Charles Dickerson, a native of Moore, returned as a Methodist minister from Georgia to his old home on Deep River. He "preached at a 'school-hut' which stood on or near the site of Fair Promise; at a place near Gulf; and at another near the Siler Camping-ground, on the old Rhodes place, about five miles southeast of Carthage."

The church historian of Moore Co. continued: "At the 'school-hut' he had evidently organized a society, for under the ministry of his successor the membership there was increased in **1816** by the addition of **Polly Carroll**, Polly Barnes, and George Stewart and his wife." **1850 - Amy Carroll** . . . Sandy Creek Baptist Assn. (Robinson, p. 181; Wicker, p. 117) [Polly is John Sr.'s daughter. Was Amy his wife or Sterling's?]
1870 - Mary Carrol, Sheffield Twp. (NC Cens. Indx., Cens., p. 609)
[An account of Hugh McDonald, regarding th Alston event: Hugh McDonald, age 14, was taken by his father to the battle of Moore's Creek where he was taken prisoner . . . He later entered American army till end of the war. An account of Tory army and Battle of Moore's Creek: the Expedition took place in Feb. 1776. Around 1 June, a report circulated that a company of light horse were coming into the settlement. Col. Alston had sent 4 to 5 men to cite all to muster at Henry Eagle's on Bear Creek. People took refuge in swamps. Daniel Buie and ? Gaster were among light horsemen. Thomas Graham lived near head of McLennon's Creek. They took me (Hugh McDonald) to houses of Daniel Shaw, John Morrison (shoemaker), Alexander McLeod, father of merchant John McLeod who died in Fayetteville, Alexander Shaw (blacksmith) and Hugh McSwan. Col. Phillip Alston appeared at muster at Eagle's house the next day. David McQueen, a noted bard, took me home to my father (p. 831). **William Carrol**, in the company of George Dudley, found me (after enlisted in brigade commanded by Gen. Frank Nash (6 regts.) . . . Capt. Lyttle was from Orange, Capt. McRee from Bladen, 3rd Capt. was George Doherty, Hanover Co. (Clark, v.11, pp. 828-837, extract from Rev. Journal, University Mag.)

Fayette County was established in **1784** from **Cumberland County** and it no longer exists.

Rockingham County was established in **1785** from **Guilford County**.
1790 - Henry Carrot (sic), Salisbury Dist., 2M16+, 4M16-, 4F; **1800 - Henry Carrell/Carroll**, 02110-11101-00; **1810 - Henry Carrol** 02110-11101-00; **1820 - Henry Carroll**; **1835 - Henry Carrell** will (Hds./Fams., p. 167; Cens. Roll 32, p. 446, l. 2; Cens., pp. 26, 221; Cens. Indx., pp.

23, 42; Cens., p. 622, #36; Will Bk. B, p. 137) [See Daniel below]
1800 - Benjamin Carral/Carrol, 1M10-, 1M16-26, 2F10-, 1F10-16, 1F26-45; **1810 - Benjamin Carrol** (Cens. Roll 32, p. 471, l. 2; Cens., pp. 14, 197; Cens. Indx., pp. 23, 42)
1800 - Joseph Carl?, 3M10-, 1M10-16, 1M16-26, 1M26-45, 1F10-16, 1F26-45, 1F45+ (MF Cens. Roll 32, p. 660, l. 18)
1800 - Margaret McCarrol, 1M10-16, 1M16-26, 1F10-16, 3F16-26, 1F45+ (MF Cens. Roll 32, p. 644, l. 9)
1800 - Israel McCarrol, 3M26-45, 3F10-, 1F26-45, (MF Cens. Roll 32, p. 644, l. 10)
1800 - William McCarroll, 3M10-, 1M10-16, 1M16-26, 1M45+, 2F10-, 1F10-16, 2F16-26, 1F45+ (MF Cens. Roll 32, p. 653, l. 13)
1811 - Nancy Carroll md. **Owen Overby** 1 Oct. (Carroll Cables, July 1995)
1818 - Sarah Carroll md. **John Barber** 24 Dec. (Carroll Cables, July 1995)
? - J. E. Carrel md. **Turner F. Barber** 21 Aug. ? (Carroll Cables, July 1995)
1819 - William Carroll md. **Sarah Cantrell** 30 Mar.; **1820 - William Carrol**; **1850 - William Carroll** (Carroll Cables, Apr.1996; Cens., pp. 598, #19, 285)
1820 - Daniel Carroll; **1865 - Daniel Carrell**, b. 13 Oct. **1789** in VA, moved from **Caswell Co.** to **Rockingham Co.**, md. 6 Feb. **1812 Frances Elizabeth Thomas**, b. 12 Oct. **1793** in NC, d. 7 Dec. **1865** in Rockingham Co., may be buried in same plot as **Henry Carrell** on old 29 By-Pass along Wentworth St., Reidsville, NC. **Frances** d. 11 April 1863, may be buried there, too; **ch.**:
  1. **James Carrell**, b. 12 Dec. **1812**, d. 24 Dec. **1812**
  2. **Laney Carrell**, b. 16 Jan. **1814**, d. 3 Dec. **1814**
  3. **Charlotte Carrell**, b. 2 Nov. c**1815**, d. Nov. **1896**; **1862 - Charlotte Carrell** md. **Capt. Charles Mattlock** 19 Nov. 1862 (Carroll Cables, July 1995)
  4. **Sarah Lamesea Carrell**, b. 28 Feb. **1818**, d. p**1887**; **1853 - Salley Carrell** md. **Jarratt Wall** 7 Nov. (Carroll Cables, July 1995) [If same person, she would be 35.]
  5. **Nancy Carrell**, b. 17 May **1820**, d. ?, **1841 - Nancy Carrell** md. **Robert Baily** 22 July; **1843 - Nancy Carrell** md. **William McCollester** 2 Nov.; **1845 - Nancy Carrell** md. **Nelson Bailey** 8 Dec. (Carroll Cables, July 1995) [Nancys may not be same person.]
  6. **John L. Carrell**, b. 25 Oct. **1822**, d. 17 July **1895**
  7. **Mary Emily Carrell**, b. 4 May **1825**, d. 29 Sept. **1907**; **1868 - Emily Carrell** md. **Leonard R. Fry** 12 Oct. (Carroll Cables, July 1995) [If same Emily, she would be 43.]
  8. **Thomas Daniel Carrell**, b. 29 May **1828**, d. 27 Feb. **1914**
  9. **Jannette Elizabeth Carrell**, b. 25 May **1831**, d. ?
  10. **Levinia Ann Frances Carrell**, b. 8 Sept. **1833**, d. a**1893**; **1859 - Frances Carrol** md. **Robert Wray** 10 Nov. (Cens., p.598; will - W. Bk. F, p.31; Carroll Cables, July 1995) (Daniel Carroll info, Family Bible; **J. Frank Carroll**, p. 5)
1820 - Peter Carrol (Cens., p. 616, #30)
1821 - Rachael Carrell md. **Alexander Dlay** 16 July (Carroll Cables, July 1995)
1862 - Elizabeth Carrell md. **Joshua North** 11 Dec. (Carroll Cables,July1995)
1865 - Easter Carrell md. **Daniel Bailey** 24 Apr. (Carroll Cables,July1995)

Robeson County was established from **Bladen County** in **1787**.
1790 - Jesse Carrill, Fayette Dist., 1M16+, 1F, 1 sl.; **1800 - Jesse Carrill**, Fayette Dist., 1M26-45 (00010-00000-00) (Cens. Indx., p. 369; Cesn. Roll 32, p. 369)

1790 - **Thomas Carrill**, Fayette Dist., 2M16+, 1M16-, 4F, 5 sls.; 1800 - **Thomas Carrill**, Fayette Dist., 1M16-26, 1M45+, 4F10-, !F26-45 (00101-40010-00) (Cens.Indx., p. 369; Cens. Roll 32, p. 369)
1790 - **James Carrol**, Fayette Dist., 1M16+ (Hds./Fams., p. 41)
1790 - **William Carrol**, Fayette Dist. (Hds./Fams., p. 42)
1790 - **John Carroll, Esqr.**, Fayette Dist. (Hds./Fams., p. 43)
1790 - **John Carrol**, Fayette Dist.; 1790 - **John Carroll**, Fayette Dist. (Hds./ Fams., p. 43, 44) [1810 cens. wasn't researched; no Carrolls on 1820 Cens. Index.)

Iredell County was established in **1788** from **Rowan County**.
?1789/1791/1799 - **Thomas Carral** (Early Amer. Series, v. 1, p. 30)
1800 - **Luke Carrol** 50010-00100-00; 1810 - **Luke Carrol** (Cens. Roll 29, p. 643, l. 14) (See Adams Co.,MS]
1800 - **John Carrell**, 01200-12100-1; 1810 - **John Carrell** (Cens. Roll 29, p. 638, l. 14; Cens. Indx., pp. 23, 42, 161; Cens., p. 246) [See Adams Co., MS]
1810 - **Samuel Carrell** (Cens. Indx., pp. 23, 42; Cens., pp. 161, 246) [See Lenoir Co.]

Stokes County was established in **1789** from **Surry County**.
1790 - **Benjamin Carroll**, Salisbury Dist., 1M16+, 1F (Hds./Fams. Cens. Indx., p.178)
1790 - **John Carroll**, Hillsborough Dist. (Hds./Fams.)
1790 - **William Carroll**, Gloucester Dist., 1M21-60+, 1M21-60, 3F (Hds./Fams., p. 79)
1797 - **John Carroll** md. **Nancy King** 21 Dec. (Carroll Cables, Apr. 1996)
1820 - **Sterling Carrell** (Cens. Indx., p. 336, #12)
1820 - **Hardy Carroll** (Cens., p. 337, #13)
1838 - **Mary Ann Carrell** md. **Landon Southern** 12 Nov. (Carroll Cables, July 1995)
1852 - **John H. Carroll** md. **Selina Jane Johnson** 28 Feb. (Carroll Cables, Apr. 1996)
1899 - **Calvin J. Carroll** will (Will Bk. 6, p. 496)

Buncombe County was established in **1791** from **Burke and Rutherford counties**.
1800 - **John Carrel** 42010-22010-00; 1810 - **John Carrel** (Cens. Roll 29, p. 164, l. 11; Cens. Indx., p. 255)
1810 - **Dennis Carrel** (Cens. Indx., p. 185)
1810 - **Willis Carrel** (Cens. Indx., p. 285)
1810 - **Nancy Carrel** (Cens. Indx., p. 250)
1820 - **William Carroll**, 101200-00100 (Cens., p. 125; Cens. Indx., p. 57)
1820 - **David Carell** (Cens., p. 96; Cens. Indx., p. 57)
1838 - **Sarah M. Carroll**, b. 23 Sept. **1838**, d. 18 Aug. **1912**, wife of **Rev. J. L. Carroll**, b. in Riverside Cemetery, Asheville, NC (WPA Index, prior to1914 graves)
1895 - **John L. Carroll** will; **John L. Carroll**, DD, b. **1837**, d. 26 June **1895**, age 58, b. Riverside Cem., Asheville, NC (Recorded copy, Will Bk. C, p. 458)
p1914 - **Eugene Carroll** b. Riverside Cem., Asheville, NC (WPA Indx., prior 1914 graves)

Lenoir County was established in **1791** from now-extinct **Dobbs County**.
1800 - **Samuel Carroll**, 0021?-10010-02 (Cens. Roll 32, p. 2, l. 12)

1800 - Benjamin Curl, 02001-00000-00 (Cens. Indx. Roll 32, p .2, l. 11) **1820** - No **Carrolls**)

Person County, in Hillsboro Military Dist., was established in **1791** from **Caswell County**.
1800 - Capt. Richard Curnol, 1M10-, 1M10-16, 1M26-45, 2F10-, 1F16-26, 5sls (Cens. Roll 32, p. 609, l. 10)
1800 - Hubbard Curnal, 1M10-, 1M16-26, 1M26-45,1F10-, 1F16-26, 3sls (MF Cens. Roll 32, p. 609, l. 13)
1800 - Pettriark Curnal, 3M10-, 1M26-45, 1F10-, 1F16-26, 3sls (Cens. Roll 32, p. 610, l. 10)
1800 - Archibal Curnal, 1M16-26, 1F10-, 1F16-26, 5sls (MF Cens. Roll 32, p. 610, l. 19)

Glasgow County was established in **1791** from **Dobbs County**, both no longer exist.

Cabarrus County was established in **1792** from **Mecklenburg County**.
1800 - William Carell, 30, 30010-10010 (Cens., p. 699, l. 17)
1804 - Peggy Carroll md. **Jacob Steward** 11 July (Carroll Cables, July 1995)
1810 - Beny Carrell (Smith Indx., p. 23; Cens., p. 100)
1820 - John Carrele (Cens., p. 139, #2)
1868 - **S. L. Carroll** md. **Martha E. Caldwell** 14 Sept. (Carroll Cables, Apr. 1996)

Ashe County was established in **1799** from **Wilkes County**.
1800 - James Carrel, 35, 11010-30010/30010-00 (Cens. Roll 29, p. 75, l. 22)
1800 - John Carrel Jr., 20, 10100-00100-00 (Cens. Roll 29, p. 75)
1800 - John Carrel Sr. 10100/00100 (Cens. Roll 29, p. 75, l. 12)
1820 - John C. Carroll (Cens. Indx.)
1800 - William Carrel, 30, 40100-00100-00 (Cens. Roll 29, p. 75, l. 15)

Washington County was established in **1799** from **Tyrrell County**.
1782 - John W. (J. W.) Carrell, 400 acs., Washington Co., TN, Sinking Creek and waters of Nolachucky River (Cook, NC Ld.Gts., p. 127; NC Ld. Gts.1778-1791, Roll M68, #130)
1787 - Harwell Carroll, pvt., **heir Daniel Carroll**, assigned 1782 ld. grant 640 acs. in Davidson Co., TN to John Marshall (NC Ld. Gts./TN 1778-1791; Cook, p. 127)
1789 - Daniel Carroll, pvt., assigned 1782 ld. grant 228 acs. in Sumner Co., TN to John Marshall (NC Ld. Gts./TN 1778-1791; Cook, p. 127)
1810 - Milly/Willy Carroll (Smith, Cens. Indx., p. 23; Cens., p. 223)

Greene County was established in **1799** from **Lenoir County**.
1800 - Elijah Carnell, 1M10-, 1M16-26, 2F10-, 1F16-26 (Cens. Indx., p. 29, l. 16)

Haywood County was established in **1808** from **Buncombe County**.
1820 - John Carrel (Cens., p. 217, l. 8)
1820 - Nathanel Carrel (Cens., p. 215, l. 4)
1820 - William Carrel (Cens., p. ?, l. 5)
1839 - Martha Carrol md. **John S. Gipson** 29 Aug. (Carroll Cables, July 1995)
1843 - Elizabeth Carroll md. **James M. Campbell** 1 Dec. (Carroll Cables, July 1995)

Columbus County was established in 1808 from Bladen and Brunswick counties.
1938 - John Richard Carroll, b. 1854 in Bladen Co., NC, md. 1st Leanna Elizabeth Jones 1881, md. 2nd Senie R. Clewis in Columbus Co. in 1915, d. in Columbus Co. 1938 (Indx. NC Ancs., v. 2, p. 25)
1943 - Andrew Albert Carroll, b. 1892 in Columbus Co., NC, md. 1st Della Register in Columbus Co. 1911, md. 2nd Omer Gambill in N. Y. 1919, d. 1943 in TX [Indx. NC Ancs.,v. 2, p. 25, gives family Code #28767 to Andrew Albert Carroll/Carell, b. 1892 in Columbus Co., d. 1943 in TX, and John Richard Carroll/Carell, b. 1854 in Bladen Co., d. 1938 in Colb. Co.]

Davidson County was established in 1822 from Rowan County.
? - Ellen Carroll md. Jesse A. Park, ? (Carroll Cables, July 1995)
1845 - Rebeca Carrel md. Ambers P. Stoker 18 Dec. (Carroll Cables, July 1995)
1846 - Eli Carrell will (Will Bk. 1, p. 493)
1864 - Martin Carroll md. Polly A. Baker 11 Feb. (Carroll Cables, Apr. 1996)
1865 - Lovenia Caroll md. Jesse G. Newsom 16 Nov. (Carroll Cables, July 1995)
1880 - Katharine Carroll will (Will Bk. 3, p. 302)
1890 - Mary J. Carroll md. J. W. Whiteheart 27 Dec. (Carroll Cables, July 1995)
1893 - Wesley R. Carroll md. Mattie Hiatt 1 Aug. (Carroll Cables, Apr. 1996)

Macon County was established in 1828 from Haywood County.
1842 - Polly Carrell md. Nipper Adams 29 Dec. (Carroll Cables, July 1995)
1847 - Margarett Carroll md. William Hooper 17 Mar. (Carroll Cables, July 1995)
1847 - Elizabeth Carroll md. Isaac Peek 22 Dec. (Carroll Cables, July 1995)

Yancey County was established in 1833 from Burke and Buncombe counties.

Davie County was established in 1836 from Rowan County.

Henderson County was established in 1838 from Buncombe County.

Cherokee County was established in 1839 from Macon County.

Caldwell County was established in 1841 from Burke County.

Stanly County was established in 1841 from Burke and Buncombe counties.

Cleveland County was established in 1841 from Rutherford and Lincoln counties.
Joseph Carroll, father of Margaret Dellinger, Shiloah Bapt. Ch., Dumas, MS (Dellinger,p.85)

Catawba County was established in 1842 from Lincoln County.

McDowell County was established in 1842 from Burke and Rutherford counties.

Union County was established in 1842 from Mecklenburg and Anson counties.

Gaston County was established in **1846** from **Lincoln County**.
1798 - **Christopher Carpenter**, b. **1798**, d. **1883**, 3rd wife **Caroline Carroll**, b. **1828**, d. **1907**, b. St. Paul's Meth. Ch. Cem., 5 mis. No. of Cherryville, NC
1844 - **James Carroll Jr.**, b. ?, d. 19 Nov. **1844**, b. Mt. Zion Bapt. Ch. Cem., Cherryville, NC
1847 - **Wilson J. Carroll**, b. ?, d. 6 Oct. **1847**, b. Mt. Zion Bapt. Ch. Cem., Cherryville, NC
1847 - **James Carroll**, b. ?, d. 11 June **1847**, b. Mt. Zion Bapt. Ch. Cem., Cherryville, NC (Cherryville Cem. info. Source: Dellinger, pp. 84, 107, 111)
1876 - **Margaret Carroll** will (Will Bk. 2, p. 109)
1898 - **Lottie May Correll**, b. 12 May **1898**, d. 28 June **1900**, b. Mt. Zion Bapt. Ch. Cem., Cherryville, NC (Dellinger, p. 107)
1900 - **E. I. Carroll** will (Will Bk. 3, p. 70)
1900 - **S. M. Carroll** will (W.Bk. 3, p. 71)

Alexander County was established in **1847** from **Iredell, Wilkes and Caldwell counties**.

Alamance County was established in **1849** from **Orange County**. 1799 - Cane Creek Month Meeting, 6, 1, **Phebe Carroll** (from Gilbert) dismov.? (Marshall, p. 377)

Forsyth County was established in **1849** from **Stokes County**.

Watauga County was established in **1849** from **Ashe, Wilkes, Caldwell and Yancey counties**.

Yadkin County was established in **1850** from **Surry County**.

Jackson County was established in **1851** from **Macon and Haywood counties**.

Madison County was established in **1851** from **Buncombe and Yancey counties**.

Harnett County was established in **1855** from **Cumberland County**.

Polk County was established in **1855** from **Rutherford and Henderson counties**.

Wilson County was established in **1855** from **Nash, Edgecombe and Johnston counties**.

Alleghany County was established in **1859** from **Ashe County**.

Clay County was established in **1861** from **Cherokee County**.

Transylvania County was established in **1861** from **Jackson and Henderson counties**.

Mitchell County established in **1861** from **Caldwell, Watauga, Yancey and McDowell cos.**

Dare County was established in **1870** from **Tyrrell, Currituck and Wickham counties**.
[See Currituck Co. - **Milberry Carrell**, **Malachi Carral** and **Mary Carroll**]

Swain County was established in **1871** from **Macon and Jackson counties.**

Pamlico County was established in **1872** from **Beaufort and Craven counties.**

Graham County was established in **1872** from **Cherokee County.**

Pender County was established in **1875** from **New Hanover County and Cumberland cos.**
1838 - Isaiah Carroll, b. 14 Aug. **1838**, d. 21 Apr. **1909**, buried in Mt. Holly Cem., Burgaw, NC, member of Co. I, 18th Reg., NC Vols., CSA (WPA Index, Pre-1914 graves)
    wife #1 - **Chanly R. Carroll**, b. 19 Sept. **1842**, d. 7 Oct. **1878**, wife of **Isaiah Carroll**
    wife #2 - **Mary E. Carroll**, b. 23 Dec. **1833**, d. 6 Jan. **1891**, wife of **Isaiah Carroll**, buried Mt. Holly Cem., Burgaw, NC (WPA Index, Pre-1914 graves)
        Son: **Chas. T. Carroll**, b. 16 Jan. **1874**, d. 18 Feb. **1874**, son of **Isaiah & C. R. Carroll**, buried Mt. Holly Cem., Burgaw, NC (WPA Index, Pre-1914 graves)
1836 - Benajah Carroll, b. 18 Apr. **1836**, d. 28 Oct. **1905**, buried Mt. Holly Cem., Burgaw, NC
1836 - John C. Carroll, b. **1836**, d. **1908**, buried Burgaw Cem., Burgaw, NC
1836 - Lavina J. (Dobson) Carroll, b. 26 Jan. **1836**, d. 14 Mar. **1914**, wife of **James T. Carroll**, buried Mt. Holly Cem., Burgaw, Ch.:
    1. **John Adams Carroll**, d. 15 Feb. **1850** is buried in the John Dobson Cem. 5 ½ mis. So. of Kenanville
    2. **Ashley J. Carroll** (son), b. 15 June **1862**, d. 16 Feb. **1876**, buried in J. Dobson Cem.
1846 - Susan R. Carroll, b. 10 Jun. **1846**, d. 26 Aug. **1911**, wife of **Augustus Carroll**, buried Mt. Holly Cem., Burgaw, NC NC
[Query from Carroll Barton in Sept.1960, The North Carolinian Qtrly., p. 765: **William or John Barton** md. **Sally Carroll** of NC, c1810-12, moved to TN, 3 of their **children** moved to LA **(Louisiana) in c1840: Eleanor, Elijah & Luvinia Barton.**]
? - **T. A. Carroll**, b. ?, d. ?, Co. C. 13th NC, Army of CSA
1881 - John C. Carroll, b. **1881**, d. 8 Feb. **1932**, age 51, buried Mt. Holly Cem., Burgaw, NC
(All information from the WPA Indx., Pre 1914 graves)

Durham County was established in **1881** from **Orange and Wake counties.**

Vance County was established in **1881** from **Granville, Franklin and Warren counties.**

Scotland County was established in **1899** from **Richmond County.**

Lee County was established in **1907** from **Chatham and Moore counties.**

Hoke County was established in **1911** from **Cumberland and Robeson counties.**

Avery County was established in **1911** from **Caldwell, Watauga and Mitchell counties.**

SOURCES

Absher, Mrs. W. O. and Mrs. Robert K. Hayes, compilers. *Surry County, North Carolina Abstracts, Record of Deeds 1770-1783.*
Abstract of Early Deeds of Franklin County.
Barber, Henry Rev., M.D., F.S.A. *British Family Names: Their Origin and Meaning.* London: Elliot Stock, 1903.
Bell, Mary Best. *Colonial Bertie Co, North Carolina.* "Abstracts of Deed Books D & E 1730-1739." 1964; *Colonial Bertie County, North Carolina.* V. 6. "Abstracts of Deed Book H 1753-1757." 1968.
Belvin, L. Harriette Riggs, eds. *The Heritage of Wake County, North Carolina.* Winston-Salem: Hunter Pub. Co., 1983.
Bentley, Elizabeth Petty. *Index to the 1800 Census of North Carolina.* Baltimore: Gen Pub. Co., Inc., 1977.
Bible Records. N.S.DAR of North Carolina. Cornelius Harnett Chapter. Dunn, NC: 1965.
Bicentennial Committee, compiler. *A History of Warren Plains Baptist Church.* Warren Plains, NC: 1985.
Black, J. Anderson. *Your Irish Ancestors.* New York: Paddington Press Ltd., 1974.
Blaylock, J. B., compiler. *Miscellaneous Records.* Yancyville, NC: Caswell County Courthouse.
Bockstruck, Lloyd Dewitt. *To Virginia 1674-1702.*
Boyer. *Historical Journal of American Irish Society.* P.188 13 (1914) 177-187 Lancour No. 66?????
Burgess, Louis A. *Virginia Soldiers of 1776.* V. 3, Copy 2; *Virginia Revolutionary War Applicants.* V. 2.
Burke, Sir Bernard, C.B., LL.D. *Landed Gentry of Ireland.* Rev. Ed. London: Harrison & Sons, 1912. (Carrolls, p. 99)
Burns, Annie. *North Carolina Genealogical Records.* "Craven County, North Carolina Marriage Records." Washington, DC: 1943.
Bynum, Curtis, Abstractor. *Marriage Bonds of Tryon and Lincoln Counties, North Carolina.* Newton, NC: Catawba County Historical Association, Inc., 1929.
Carroll, R. Francis. *The Heritage of Our Children.* 1981. (Family History)
Cartwright, Betty Goff Cook. Lillian Johnson Gardiner. *North Carolina Land Grants in Tennessee 1778-1791.* Memphis: I. C. Harper & Co., 1958.
Caswell County Historical Association Newsletter. P. O. Box 278. Yanceyville, NC 27370
Censuses: National Archives Microfilm Pubs., Roll 34, Microcopy 32, 2nd Census, 1800, North Carolina, Vol. 6, GSA, Washington, D. C, 1957.
Census Indexes. National Archives, Washington, D. C.
Clark, Murtie June. *Colonial Soldiers of the South 1732-1774.* Baltimore: Gen. Pub. Co., Inc., 1986; *Pension Roll of 1835.* Vs. 3, 4. Southern States. (Lib. of Congress).
Clark, Walter, ed. *The Colonial Records of North Carolina.* Goldsboro, NC: Nash Bros. Book & Job Printers, 1899; *The State Records of North Carolina.* Vs. IV, XVI, XVII, XXII. "Abstracts of Army Accounts of the North Carolina Line, Army Pay and Miscellaneous List 1781-1785. *North Carolina State Records, 1782-1783.* (unpublished records). V.16. " [V. XXII is reprint of 1907 ed.] NY: AMS Press, 1970.]

Clemens, William Montgomery. *North Carolina and South Carolina Marriage Records: From the Earliest Colonial Days to the Civil War.* NY: E. P. Dutton & Co., ?; rpt. Baltimore: Gen. Pub. Co. Inc., 1973.

Coldham, Peter Wilson. *The Complete Book of Emigrants 1607-1660.* Baltimore: Genealogical Publishing Co., Inc., 1987; *History of Transportation 1615-1775.* Vs. 1 & 2.

Colonial Records of North Carolina: Higher Court Records, County Court, 1687.

Conservation Commission. *Inventory of Church Archives of Virginia.* V. 1. Richmond, VA: The Historical Records Survey of Virginia, Aug. 1941.

Cook, Betty Goff. Lillian Johnson Gardiner. *North Carolina Land Grants in Tennessee 1778-1791.* Memphis, TN: I.C. Harper & Co., 1958.

Cumberland County, North Carolina Marriage Bonds to 1868. Genealogical Society of Utah, 1937.

Cunningham, Caroline, compiler. *Migrations: Actual and Implied.* Vol. 1. 1968. (NC Archives, Raleigh, NC)

Dandridge, Danske Bedinger. *American Prisoners of the Revolution.* Charlottesville, VA: The Michie Co., printers, 1911.

(The) North Carolina Daughters of the American Revolution. *North Carolina Original Marriage Bonds of Mecklenburg and Johnston Counties.* North Carolinal Genealogical Records Commission; *Roster of Soldiers From North Carolina in the American Revolution.* 1932.

Dellinger, Paul. *Cemetery and Death Records.* (Archives, Genealogy Sec., Raleigh, NC)

Donaldson, Mary Frances Kerr. *Caswell County 1777-1877; Historical Abstracts of Minutes of Caswell County, NC Index.* 1977.

Dunstan, Edythe Smith, compiler. *The Bertie Index for Courthouse Records of Bertie County, NC 1720-1875.* 1966. (Sec. III, Index for Grantee Deeds 1720-1800, p. 23.) (Located in Jackson, NC Public Library)

Early American Series. "Early North Carolina 1600-1789-1791- 1799." Vs. 1, 3, AIS Census Report. Accelerated Index System Census Report. 1981.

Edmunds, Pocahontas Wight. *History of Halifax County, Virginia.* V.2.

English, Mary Shell (MacArthur). Carroll research and oral interviews.

Fields, William C., ed. *Abstracts of Minutes of the Court of Pleas and Quarter Sessions of Cumberland County, Oct. 1755- Jan. 1779*, V.1. Bicentennial Committee, 1978; *Apr. 1779- Jan. 1791*; V.2. Cumberland County Bicentennial Committee, 1981.

Fischer, Marjorie Hood. *Tennessee Tidbits 1778-1914.* V.1. Easley, SC: Southern Historical Press, Inc., 1986.

Foley, Louise Pledge. *Early Virginia Families Along the James River: Their Deep Roots and Tangled Branches.* V. 1. Richmond, VA: 1974.

Foster, Austin P., A.M., Dept. of Education, Div. of History. *Counties of Tennessee.* "Heads of Families ... 1790, St. of Tenn." Baltimore: Gen. Pub. Co., Inc., 1973.

Fouts, Raymond Parker. *Bertie County Marriages 1762-1868.* 1982.

Fowler, Malcolm. *Valley of the Scots*, rpt. by Wynoma Fowler. Raleigh, NC; Edwards & Broughton Co., 1986.

Gammon, David B. *Abstracts of Wills, Bertie County, North Carolina 1722-1774.* (Wills held by the Secretary of State); *Marriage Records of Halifax County, North Carolina 1757-1872.*

Genealogy Society of Utah. *Warren County Marriage Bonds 1779-1868.* Salt Lake City, Utah: 80 N. Main St., 1943-44.

Grantee and Grantor Indices to Real Estate, North Carolina, 1776-1895.

Greer, George Cabell. *Early Virginia Immigrants, 1623-1666.* Baltimore: Gen. Pub. Co., Inc. 1960.

Grimes, John Bryan, Sec. of St. *Abstract of North Carolina Wills.* Raleigh, NC: Trustee of the Public Libraries; E. M. Uzzell & Co., St. Printers & Binders, 1910; rpt., *Abstract of North Carolina Wills 1690-1760.* Baltimore: Gen. Pub. Co., 1967.

Guilford County, North Carolina: Miscellaneous General Records. N.S.DAR. Battle Chapter. Greensboro, NC: 1961.

Gwathney, John H. *Virginians in Revolution.* Richmond, VA: The Dietz Press, 1938.

Gwynn, Zae Hargett. *Kinfolks of Granville County, North Carolina 1765-1826.* Rocky Mount, NC: Joseph W. Watson, 1974; *Abstracts of the Wills and Estate Records of Granville County, North Carolina 1808-1833.* V. II. Rocky Mount, NC: Joseph W. Watson, 1976. *Court Minutes of Granville County, North Carolina 1746-1820.* Rocky Mount, NC: James W. Watson, 406 Piedmont Ave., 1977 (GR 929.3N8 gra N867C)

Hathaway, J.R.B., ed. *The North Carolina Historical & Genealogical Register.* Vs. 1, 2, 3. Baltimore: Gen. Pub. Co., 1970.

Haun, Waynette Parks. *Bertie County, North Carolina County Court Minutes 1724-1739, Book 1.* 1976; *Old Albemarle County, North Carolina Miscellaneous Records 1678-c1737.* North Carolina Genealogy Society, 1982; *Abstracts of Johnston County, North Carolina Deeds 1759-1794; Abstracts of Johnston County, North Carolina Court Minutes 1759-1826; Abstracts of Johnston County, North Carolina Land Entries 1778-1805.*

Hays, Francis B. *Who Was Earl Granville?* (Bk. or periodical?)

Heads of Families at the First Census of the United States taken in the year 1790, North Carolina. Baltimore: Gen. Pub. Co., Inc., 1973, 1978.

Hofmann, Margaret M. *Crown to Colony of North Carolina 1735-1764.* Abstracts of Land Patents. V. I. 1982. (Libr. of Congress); *The Granville District of North Carolina 1748-1763.* Abstracts of Land Grants. Vs. 1, 2, 3. Weldon, NC: The Roanoke News Co., 1986, rpt. 1987; *Abstracts of Deeds, Northampton County, North Carolina.* (Public Registry 1754- 1759, Dd. Bks.1 & 2)

Holcomb, Brent H. *Deeds Abstracts of Tyron County, Lincoln County and Rutherford County, North Carolina 1769-1786, Tyron Wills and Estates.* Easley: S.C.: Southern Historical Press, 1977; *Marriages of Granville County, North Carolina 1753-1868.* Baltimore: Gen. Pub. Co., Inc., 1981; *Marriages of Orange County, North Carolina 1779-1868.* Baltimore: Gen. Pub. Co., Inc., 1983; *Marriages of Wake County, North Carolina 1770-1868.* Baltimore: Gen. Pub. Co., Inc., 1983.

Hotten, John Camden, ed. *The Original Lists of Persons of Quality 1600-1700.* Baltimore: Gen. Pub. Co., Inc., 1978.

Hummel, Elizabeth Hicks. *Hick's History of Granville County.* V. 1. "Marriage Bonds." Oxford, NC: Coble Printing Co., 1965.

Index of North Carolina Ancestors. North Carolina Genealogical Society. 1984.

Index of Revolutionary War Pension Applications. Rev. Bicentennial Ed. Washington, D.C.: National Genealogy Society, 1976.

Ingmire, Frances T. *Cumberland County, North Carolina Marriage Records 1803-1878.* 1984; *Franklin County, North Carolina Marriage Records, 1789-1868.*

Jackson, R. V. C. R. Teeples. *North Carolina 1800 Census Index* (F253.J22.LH&G); *North*

Carolina 1810 Census Index, 1976.
Johnson, William Perry. *Journal of North Carolina Genealogy*. Raleigh, NC: Spring 1965, v.11, no.10, pp. 1781, 1782.
Jones, Gordon C. *Abstracts of Wills and Other Records, Currituck and Dare Counties, North Carolina 1663-1850*. 1958.
Kaminkow, Jack. Marion Kaminkow. *A List of Emigrants from England to America 1718-1759*. 1966; *Original Lists of Emigrants in Bondage from London to the American Colonies 1719-1744*. Baltimore: Magna Carta Book Co., 1967.
Kammerer, Roger. Elizabeth Ross. *Pitt County Compendium*. V. 1. "Marriages." 1988. (Deed Books, B-EE)
Kendall, Kathleen Kerr, compiler. *Abstracts of Caswell County, North Carolina Land Grants, Tax Lists, State Census, Apprentice Bonds, Estate Records*, 1977; *Abstracts of Caswell County, North Carolina Will Books 1777-1814*, 1979; *Caswell County, North Carolina Marriage Bonds 1778-1868*, 1981; *Abstracts of Caswell County, North Carolins Will Books 1814-1843*, 1983.
Kerr, Mary Hinton (Duke). *North Carolina Records*. V.1. "Abstracted Records of Colonial Bute County, NC 1764-1779 and Bute County Marriages." Warrenton, NC: 1967; rpt. Spartanburg, SC: The Reprint Co., 1983; *Abstracts of Deeds*. V.2. Warren County Supplement. [Absts. of Bute Co. Deeds registered in Warren Co., Deed Books 1-7, 1766-1779 & a Warren Co. supplement to V. 2; absts. of Deed Book A, 1764-1766 & completing Bute Co. Absts.] Warren County, NC Records, v. 2, Abstracts of Dd. Bk. A, 1764-1766, Dds. of Colonial Bute Co., NC, Warrenton, NC.
Lefler, Hugh. Paul Wager, eds. *Orange County, North Carolina 1752-1952*. Chapel Hill, NC: The Orange Print Shop, 1953.
Lefler, Hugh Talmage. Alfred Ray Newsome. *The History of a Southern State: North Carolina*. 3rd ed. Chapel Hill: University of North Carolina Press, 1973.
Lepine, Kate James. Anna Sherman. *Will Abstracts of Cumberland County, North Carolina 1754-1863*. Katana Co., 1984.
Lester, Memory Aldridge. *Old Southern Bible Records: Transcriptions of Births, Deaths and Marriages from Family Bibles Chiefly of the Eighteenth and Nineteenth Centuries*. Baltimore: Gen. Pub. Co., Inc. 1974. (GR929.3 A11 WL642)
Lockhart, Audrey. *Aspects of Emigration from Ireland to the North American Colonies Between 1660 and 1775*. New York: Arno Press, 1976. [Indentured servants 1748-1750; felons 1735-1754; list compiled from Irish journals; pp.175-193 give excellent tables of departures of emigration ships from Irish ports 1681-1775, except from Ulster ports after 1717.]
Marshall, Thomas Worth, Compiler. *Encyclopedia of American Quaker Genealogy*. V. 1. Baltimore: Gen. Pub. Co., 1978.
Matheson, Sir Robert E. *Special Report on Surnames in Ireland*. Dublin: His Majesty's Stationery Office, 1909.
McAuslan, William Alexander. *Mayflower Index*. Rev. Ed. Vs. 1 & 2. The Genealogy Society of Mayflower Descendants, 1960.
Mead (Bishop). *Old Churches, Ministers and Families of Virginia*. V. 2. Philadelphia: J. B. Lippincott Co., 1861.
Mitchell, Thorton W. *North Carolina Wills: A Testator Index, 1665-1900*. V. 1. Raleigh, NC:

1987.
Moss, Mrs. E. G. "Granville County Has Historic Past." NC DAR News, NC History Section, date unknown.
Murphy, William L. *Surname Index to Sixty-Five Volumes of Colonial and Revolutionary Pedigrees*. V. 10, pp. 82, 85, 411- Carrolls: American Historical Co., Inc., 1939.
Murray, Nicholas R. *Granville County, North Carolina From Earliest Records Extant Through 1868*. "Computer Indexed Marr. Records." Hammond, LA: Hunting For Bears, Inc.,1981.
Neal, Lois (Smathers). *Abstracts of Vital Records From Raleigh, North Carolina Newspapers, 1799-1819*. Spartanburg, SC: The Reprint Co., 1979.
North Carolina Genealogy Society. "Tax List, 1784, Capt. William Bryan Company." *North Carolina Genealogy*. Fall, 1969; *Colonial Records of North Carolina: Higher Court Records, County Court 1687*; *Index of North Carolina Ancestors*. Vs. 1, 2, 4. No. 4. Raleigh: 1984.
North Carolina Heritage Collection. 32 Vols. History Division. Hunter Pub. Co., P. O. Box 5867, Winston-Salem, NC 27113.
North Carolina Land Grant to Tennessee 1778-1791. [Introductory note: "List prepared by Sec. of State of NC in 1791 and submitted to Sec. of St. of U.S., Thomas Jefferson due to bill passed by U. S. House of Rep. for purpose of creating land offices in western territories, including the now St. of Tenn. ceded to U. S. by NC in 1790. Gov. Alexander Martin of NC and Gov. William Blount of Southwest Territory in 1791."]
North Carolina Marriage Bonds 1778-1868, Caswell County, Groom's & Bride's Index. Yancyville, NC: Caswell County Courthouse.
North Carolina State, compiler. *North Carolina Marriages and Death Notices, Raleigh Register and North Carolina State Gazette 1799-1825*. Baltimore: Gen. Pub. Co., 1966.
(The) North Carolinian Quarterly. V. 4., No. 4. "Father and Son Relationships in 1771;" V. 11. "North Carolina Heads of Families." 1965.
North Carolina State Records. V. 2.
North Carolina Wills and Deeds and Family Records. N. S. DAR of North Carolina. General Records Committee, 1958-1959.
Nugent, Nell M. *Cavaliers and Pioneers*. V. 1. Baltimore: Gen. Pub. Co., Inc., 1991.
Nuttall, Lois Julia. *Wills and Deeds of Johnston County, North Carolina*.
O'Brien, Michael J., LL.D (Historiographer). *An Alleged First Census of the American People*. New York: American Irish Historical Society, 1930.
Parker, Anthony E. *A Guide to Moore County Cemeteries*. The Moore County Historical Assn. (Martins listed, no Carrolls or Wades)
Pension Roll of 1835. V. 3. Southern States. Library of Congress.
Potts, Helen Swayer. Collection. Williamson County, TN. V. 2. Library, Franklin, TN. Compiled by Whitley, Box 58, Gen. Rec. Com., DAR 1973-4, V. 2.
Pruitt, Dr. A. B. *Abstracts of Land Entries: Cumberland County, 1778-1795*. 1988; *Abstracts of Land Entries, Bertie County, North Carolina 1778-1794; Martin County, North Carolina 1778-1795*. 1992.
Radcliff, Clarence E. *North Carolina Taxpayers 1701-1786*. Baltimore: Gen. Pub. Co., Inc., 1984; *North Carolina Taxpayers, 1669-1790*. V. 2. Baltimore: Gen. Pub. Co., Inc., 1984, 1987.
Ramsey, Robert W. *Carolina Cradle: Settlement of Northwestern Carolina Frontier 1747-1762*. Chapel Hill: Univ. N.C. Press, 1964, rpt. 1987.

Ray, Worth S. *Colonial Granville County and Its People.* V. 2. "List of earliest Inhabitants of Granville County, NC." Baltimore: Gen. Pub. Co., 1965; *Mecklenburg Signers and Their Neighbors.* Baltimore: Gen. Pub. Co., Inc., 1966; *Tennessee Cousins.* Baltimore: Gen. Pub. Co., Inc., 1968; *Old Albemarle and Its Absentee Landlords.* Baltimore: Gen. Pub. Co., Inc., 1976.

Register, Alvaretta Kenan. *State Census of North Carolina 1784-1787.* 2nd Ed. Rev. Baltimore: Gen. Pub. Co., Inc., 1974.

Register's Office, John Dickson. Duplin County, Book C, Folio 100, 23 March 1761.

Rejected and Suspended Applications for Revolutionary War Pensions. Baltimore: Gen. Pub. Co., 1969. (p.394)

Revolutionary War Pension Records. National Archives, Washington, D.C. (One source for Dempsey: MC804, Roll 481)

Roberts, Gary Boyd. *Notes on the North Carolina Ancestry of John Christopher (1878-1951): Roberts, Dodd, Flowers, Langdon, Stephenson and Carrell Families of Johnston County.* Boston: May 1987.

Robinson, Blackwell P. *The History of Moore County, North Carolina 1747-1847.* Southern Pines, NC: Moore County Historical Assn., 1956.

Saunders, William L., Sec. of State. Et al. *The Colonial and State Records of North Carolina 1713-1728.* Raleigh, NC: 1886. Vs. 2, 4, 8, 18, 11, 16, 17, 19, 20, 22. Compiled by Walter Clark, Justice of Supreme Court of NC; *Colonial Records of North Carolina 1734-1752.* V. IV. Raleigh: P. M. Hale [prtr. to st.] NY: AMS Press, 1968).

Skordas, Gust. *The Early Settlers of Maryland.* Baltimore: Gen. Pub. Co., Inc., 1968.

Smith, Clifford Neal. *Federal Land Series 1799-1835.* Chicago: American Library Assn., 1973.

Smith. *North Carolina Census Index.*

State of North Carolina. *North Carolina Marriages and Death Notices: Raleigh Register and North Carolina State Gazette 1799-1825.* Baltimore: Gen. Pub. Co., 1966.

Stick, David. *Dare County: A History.* 3rd Ed. Raleigh: State Dept. of Archives and History, 1970.

Swen, E. G. *Virginia Historical Index.* Richmond, VA: Virginia Historical Society, 1936.

Tepper, Michael. *Passenger and Immigration Lists Index.* 1st Ed. V. 1. Detroit: Gale Research Co., Book Tower, ?; *Passengers To America.* Baltimore: Gen. Pub. Co., Inc., 1977; *New World Immigrants.* V. 1. Baltimore: Genealogical Publishing Co., Inc., 1979.

Tomlinson, J. S. *Assembly Sketch Book, 1879.*

Vicars, Sir Arthur, F.S.A. *Index to the Prerogative Wills of Ireland 1536-1810.* Dublin: 1897; Baltimore: Gen. Pub. Co., Inc., rpt. 1967, 1989.

Virginia Colonial Militia 1651-1776.

Warren County Marriage Bonds 1779-1868. Genealogical Society of Utah, SLC, 1943-44.

Warren County Records, Supplement, Vol. II, Abstracts: Bute County Deed Books 2 & 3, and Record Book A.

Watson, Joseph W. *Estate Records of Edgecombe County, NC 1730-1820.* Rocky Mount, NC: 1970; "Abstracts of the Early Deeds of Franklin County, NC, 1779-1797." Rocky Mount, NC: Dixie Letter Service, 1956, rpt., Joseph W. Watson, 1984; "Kinfolks of Franklin County, N.C., 1793-1844."

Wellman, Manly Wade. *The Story of Moore County: Two Centuries of A North Carolina Region.* Moore County Historical Assn., 1974.

White, K. K. The King's Mountain Men. *The Roster of Soldiers from North Carolina in the Revolutionary War.*

Wicker, Rassie E. *Ancient Miscellaneous Records of Moore County, North Carolina.* Moore County Historical Association. (GR929.3N8MR.W636M)

Williams, Ruth S. Margarette Glenn Griffin. *Abstract of Wills, Edgecomb County, North Carolina 1733-1856.* Rocky Mount, NC: Joseph W. Watson, 1980; *Abstracts of The Early Deeds of Franklin County, North Carolina 1779-1797.* Rocky Mount, NC: Dixie Letter Service, 1956, rpt., Joseph W. Watson, 1984.

Wynne, Frances Hollow. *Abstract of Record of Wills, Inventories, Settlements of Estates 1771-1802, Wake County, North Carolina,* 1985.

STATE INDEX

Alabama and Connecticut, pp. 8, 9
Delaware, Georgia, Kentucky, and Louisiana, p. 9
Maryland and Massachusetts, pp. 10, 11
Missouri, New Jersey, and New York, pp. 11, 12
North Carolina, pp. 12, 13, 14, 15, 16, 17
Ohio, Pennsylvania, pp. 17, 18
South Carolina, pp. 18, 19
Tennessee, pp. 19, 20
Virginia, pp. 20, 21, 22

NORTH CAROLINA COUNTIES INDEX

Alamance County, p. 113
Albemarle County, p. 29
Alexander County, p. 113
Alleghany County, p. 113
Anson County, p. 56
Archdale County, p. 30
Ashe County, p. 111
Avery County, p. 114
Bath County, p. 30
Beaufort County, p. 30
Bertie County, p. 31
Bladen County, p. 35
Brunswick County, p. 71
Buncombe County, p. 110
Burke County, p. 78
Bute County, 69
Cabarrus County, p. 111
Caldwell County, p. 112
Camden County, p. 74
Carteret County, p. 34
Caswell County, 74
Catawba County, p. 112
Chatham County, p. 72
Cherokee County, p. 112
Chowan County, p. 29
Clay County, p. 113
Cleveland County, 112
Columbus County, p. 112
Craven County, p. 31
Cumberland County, p. 60
Currituck Coounty, p. 29

Dare County, p. 113
Davidson County, p. 112
Davie County, p. 112
Dobbs County, p. 67
Duplin County, p. 52
Durham County, p. 114
Edgecombe County, p. 37
Fayette County, p. 108
Forsyth County, p. 113
Franklin County, p. 80
Gaston County, p. 113
Gates County, p. 95
Glasgow County, p. 111
Graham County, p. 114
Granville County, p. 41
Green County, p. 111
Guilford County, p. 73
Halifax County, p. 67
Harnett County, p. 113
Haywood County, p. 111
Henderson County, p. 112
Hertford County, p. 67
Hoke County, p. 114
Hyde County, p. 31
Iredell County, p. 110
Jackson County, p. 113
Johnston County, p. 47
Jones County, p. 80
Lee County, p. 114
Lenoir County, p. 110
Lincoln County, p. 93

McDowell County, p. 112
Macon County, p. 112
Madison County, p. 113
Martin County, p. 73
Mecklenburg County, p. 68
Mitchell County, p. 113
Moore County, p. 99
Montgomery County, p. 96
Nash County, p. 74
New Hanover County, p. 34
Northampton County, p. 38
Onslow County, p. 37
Orange County, p. 56
Pamplecough County, p. 30
Pamlico County, p. 114
Pasqoutank County, p. 29
Pender County, p. 114
Perquimans County, p. 29
Person County, p. 111
Pitt County, p. 67
Polk County, p. 113
Randolph County, p. 92
Richmond County, p. 96
Robeson County, p. 109
Rockingham County, 108
Rowan County, p. 59
Rutherford County, p. 93
Sampson County, p. 96
Scotland County, p. 114
Stanly County, p. 112
Stokes County, p. 110
Surry County, p. 73
Swain County, p. 114
Transylvania County, p. 113
Tyron County, p. 71
Tyrrell County, p. 34
Union County, 112
Vance County, p. 114
Wake County, p. 71
Warren County, p. 83
Washington County, p. 111
Watauga County, p. 113
Wayne County, p. 96
Wickham County, p. 30
Wilkes County, p. 77

Wilson County, p. 113
Yadkin County, p. 113
Yancey County, p. 112

NAME INDEX

[Note: Names may appear more than one time on any given page in the text. Check all spellings: Caral, Carel, Carell, Caril, Carral, Carrall, Carrel, Carrell, Carol, Carrol, Carroll, & other variations. Carroll variations are highlighted.]

Abernathy, M. W., 95
Adams, Angie Rogers, 87
   April Lee, 87
   Clarence D., 87
   Grace Carroll, 88
   J., 74
   Kathryn, 87
   Linda, 87
   Lynda, 87
   Nipper, 111
   Polly, 111
   Ronald R., 87
   Sarah, 87
   Weldon D., 87
   William D., 88
Aderholt, Esther, 94
   William, 94
Agurtous, Thomas, 102,104
Ainsworth, Leaven, 61
Akins, Robert, 6
Alcorn, Elizabeth, 18
Alderman, William, 66
Alexander, Robt., 85
Allen, 35
   Champion, 43
   Chastain, 91
   David, 43,73
      Jr., 77
   Ellen, 91
   George, 91
   Ida A., 36
   Robert Vincent, 87
   Samuel, 43
Allison, James, 19
Alston, 15,101,102,108
   James, 37

   Philip (Col.), 15,15,99,101,102107,108
Alstyne, Maria Van, 8,12
Anderson, John, 68,71
Andrews, Candis, 58
   Drury, 91
   John, 58
   Patsey, 58
   William, 58
Ansell, Amy, 29
   Betsy, 29
   Lydia, 29
   Peggy, 29
Armstrong, 64
   Andrew, 64
   John, 15,41,65
   Martin (Col.), 15,42,94
Arnols, J., 74
Arrington, William, 32
Askey (Capt.), 18
Askins, Robt., 6
Atkins, Arthur, 40
Atkinson, 17
   Carlton, 63
Augustus, William (Duke), 60
Autry, W. W., 67
Avera, Alexr. (Esq.), 62
   Wm., 64
Averit, Mary, 33
Ayres, Counsel, 51
   E, E., 65
   Mary, 51
   W. J., 65
Ayschue, Louise C., 81,86
Bachus/Baccus, Delilah, 71
   John, J., 52
   Joseph, 71

Baggett, Josiah, 99
Bagley, Mary Ann, 66
   Russel, 66
Bailey/Baily, Thos., 43
Baker, 14
   Daniel, 109
   J., 64
   Easter, 109
   J. W., 66
   John, 95
   Nancy, 109
   Nelson, 109
   Rebecca, 19
   Robert, 109
   Sary Delany, 95
   William, 69,83
Baldwin, Elizabeth, 59
   William, 59
Ball, Iva, 81,89
   Iva Thomas, 86
   Henry, 92
   Martha Ann, 89
   Martha (Nannie), 88
   Missoura, 92
Ballard, 14
Bane, Mary, 66
   Walter, 66
Bar, James, 46
Barber, Brittian, 48
   John, 108
   Martin (Capt.), 12
   Sarah, 108
   Turner F., 108
Barden, Ellen, 97
   Martha, 97
Barnes, 74
   Almeida, 24
   James, 60,99
   Polly, 100,108
   Sarah, 32
      Marge, 63
Barnett, M. R., 72
Barnhill, Amosa, 66
Barr, John, 68
Barrat, F., 74
   J., 74

S., 74
Barrett, Lucy Hosmer (Mrs.), 8
   Thomas, 41
Barrow, 47
Bartlett, Diomysia F., 91
Barton, Carroll, 114
   Eleanor, 114
   Elijah, 114
   James, 107
   John, 114
   Luvinia, 114
   Sally, 114
   Sarah, 58
   William, 58,114
Bate, Augustine, 45
Battle, Jacob, 38
Baxter, Delilah, 76
Bay, 87
   Bobbie Jo, 87
Bean, Jane, 57
   Mary, 57
   Rachel, 57
Beard, Elizabeth Ann, 66
Beasley, Bass, 56,65
Bethane, 105
Beatty, Jonathan (Capt.), 18
Beaver, Jeremiah, 75
   Joshua, 75
Beemer, Ann, 72
Bell, Samuel, 84
   Suana, 78
   Walter R., 56,66
Benbow, Powell, 60
Bennett, Moses, 91
Benton, Dempsey, 52
   Francis, 32
   Jesse, 45
   M., 45
   Samuel (Esq.), 41,80,83
Berkeley, 25
   Wm. (Sir), 25
Best, Annie Estelle, 55,65
Bethel, 35,36
Biggs, Martha Jane, 94
Birchett, Edward, 90
Black, Archibald, 108

Elizabeth, 67
Bueford/Bufford, William/Wm. (Capt.), 12, 22,45,46
Buie, John, 61
Bulla, Thos. Js., 66
Bullard, Henrietta, 35
Bullock, Chas., 49,50
   Richard, 90
Buncombe, Edward (Col.), 12,15
Bunn, Redmun, 64
   Willie, 38
Burfet (Capt.), 16
Burgess, Olive, 12
Burgh, Wm., 3
Burkloe, Isaac, 64
Burnswick, 17
Burrage, Catherine, 57
Burton, 87
   Handy, 66
   Margaret, 66
   Rebekah, 91
   Rachel, 66
Bush, Joseph, 75
   Mary Ann, 75
   Polly, 81
   William, 81
   Zenas, 75
Butler, Jethro, 32
Butts (Capt.), 9
Byner, Edward, 38
Cadoo/Caddoo, 2
Caddow, 2
Cafrees, 88
Cain/Cane, Hardy, 38
   Isobel, 38
   James, 37,38
   John, 33
   Peurity, 38
   Rachel, 38
   Sarah, 33,38
Caloard, Thomas, 80
Cameron, John, 87
   Judy, 87
   Sarah A., 57
Cammil, Richard, 29
Campbell, Alex'r., 62

A. M., 65,66
Charles, 63
Elizabeth, 111
James M., 111
John, 9
Kenneth, 106
Thomas, 76,79
Cannon, James, 90
Cantrell, Sarah, 108
Capps, Andrew, 29
   Caleb (Sr.), 29
   Jr., 29
   Dennis, 29
   Hillary, 86
   Nancy, 91
   Pattie, 92
Cardle, 2
Carlyle, John (Col.), 22
Carpenter, Caroline, 112
   Christopher, 112
Carr, Gibson, 56,66
   (Miss), 96
   Nancy, 53
Carrington, Catherine, 59
   James, 59
Carroll/Carrell/Carrill/Carrole/Currell/ Carrol/Caoll/Carol/Caroll/Curl/Kerrell/ Camal/Camel/Carah,Careel/Carel/Carell/ Carle/Carnell/Carah/Caral/Carnoll/ Carral/Carrall/Carrel/Caril/Carill/Carril/ Carrick/Carriel/Carrin/Cerrin/Carrow/ Carry/ Carryl/Carrett Carwell,Curl, 2,4, 14,36,38,40,44,51,54,60,61,62,65,68,71,73, 74
   Aaron, 10
   Abigail, 4
   Abraham/Abra'm, 11,56,67
   Absalum/Absolum/Abso., 12,33 33,
      III, 33
      Jr., 33
   Adam Sr., 68
   Adeline Green, 24
   Addie, 81
   Agnes, 39,40.102
      Estelle, 34
   A. J., 36

(Mrs.), 36
Albert W., 36
Alexander/Aley/Aly, 17,30,47,48,49,50,
54,63,72,98,102,103,104,105
Aley/Aly, 48,49,66
Alge, 65
Alice, 58,76
Almeida, 24
Alsey, 57,58
Amelia, 65
Amos, 8
Amy, 29,60,99,100,104,107,108
Andrew, 5,7
   Albert, 37,41,111
   Fuller, 55,64
Ann/Anne/Annie, 4,5,7,10,11,21,42,41,
44,45,46,47,48,53,56,57,63,67,68,70,71,
72,83
   Estelle, 55,65
   Ann Judson, 56,65
   L., 24
   M., 59
   Nancy, 52
   Rafferty, 7
Anthony, 3,29,78
Archibald/Archibal, 57,78,110
Arena, 68
Arenda (Mrs.), 30
Arenia, 73
Armstrong, 17
Atha, 36
Arthur Haddock, 36
   Washington, 36
Ashley J., 114
Augustus, 55,64,114
Aurella, 69
Auth, 82
A. W., 36
Ballard, 35
Barnard A. (Maj.), 23
Bartholomew, 20
Batt, 20
Beedy, 51
Benajah, 55,64,113
   H. (Chaplain), 23
   Harvey, 55

Benjamin/Benj./Beny, 1,3,10,12,13,17,
18,24,29,30,33,44,45,46,47,48,50,56,57,
58,59,69,80,82,84,86,108,109,110
   John, 57
   Jr., 57
   L., 82
Berry, 1,20
Bertha, 50
   Una, 50
Bessie, 53
Bethania, 49
Betty/Betsy, 16,39,40,42,43,46,57,70,71,
73,76,82
   Ann, 55,63,82,83,98
   Smith, 36
Bill, 57
B. J. L., 82
Bridget, 7
Britten/Britton/Brittor, 1,12,33,78
Booker, 1
Brother, 65
Bryon, 10
Burrel, 57
Butler, 1,13
B. V., 55,66
C(ader)., 14
Calvin J., 110
Candice/Candis, 58,72
Catharine/Catherine/Cathy/Caty 6,17,18,
20,38,46,50,57,59,66,75
   Eliza, 53
   H., 22
   Maria, 53
Cardwell, 2
Caroline, 71,112
Cazilla, 51
Cearbhal, Lord of Ely, 2
C. H., 37
Chandler W. (Lt. Col.), 23
Chanly R., 113
Charity, 19,33,38,45,53,56,67,78
   Marie, 53,55,65
Charles/Charlie/Chas., 1,4,5,6,8,10,15,31,
34,37,39,40,42,43,46,56,57,64,70,73,76,
78,79,80,83
   Aliene, 55,64

Esq., 10
F., 35,65
Fisher, 34
   Jr. (Dr.), 34
   Jr., 10
   L., 24
   (Mr.), 37
   T., 113
Charlotte, 18,59,102,103,104,105,108
Chasey, 50
Cherry, 66
Christopher, 3,6
Cicero, 57
Clarence E. (Miss), 24,73
Clark H., 11
Clary, 71
Clement, 58
Cleo, 58
Cora, 76
   L., 36
Cornelius, 1
Courtney, 51
Coy Frank, 35
C, F., 35
C. R., 113
C. W., 24,73
Cynthia, 9,18
Daisy, 82
Dan Hugh, 76
Daniel/Laniel,4,6,7,9,10,12,13,14,18,20, 33,41,44,45,55,57,,58,59,66,69,70,72,75, 78,79,80,81,108,111
   Bunyan, 53
   Charles, 34
   Curtis, 36
   Esq., 44
   George, 70
David, 3,11,14,18,20,48,49,63,81,110
   Thompson F., 53
Deborah, 106
Decy, 58
Delilah, 48,71,74,76
Della/Dela, 37,58,111
Delphia, 20
Dempsey/Demcy/Demey/Demse, 1,13, 20,23,24,44,54,63,98

Dennis, 4,6,7,10,13,17,20,30,64,69,110
Dicie Kenlaw, 37
Dickson, 59,81
Doctor, 68
Dolly, 51,58
Dora, 57
Dorcas/Darios, 52,71
Douglass, 1,13,46,80
Duckery, 58
Dwany/Dwaney, 30,51
E., 82
Eady/Pedy, 79
Easter, 109
Ebenezer, 10
Ed., 29
Eda, 55,66
Eden, 56
Edmond, 17,98
Edward, 6,20,72,74,76
   (2nd Lt.), 23
   (Lt. Col.), 23
   W., 72
Edwin, 52,56,65
   Benajah, 53
   Joseph, 56,65
Eleanor/Elinor/Elnor, 5,10,33,56,58,59, 77,79
Elias, 13,54
Eli/Elie, 56,57,76,111
   Jr., 57
Elijah, 11,16,36,42,43,51,83,111
Elisha, 8,14,24,51,55,64,98
Eliza, 6,66,72
Elizabeth, 1,3,4,8,10,11,12,14,17,18,19, 22,23,24,29,31,33,34,35,41,42,43,44,45 47,49,50,51,52,53,,56,58,59,63,64,65,67, 69,73,77,78,79,80,81,84,85,86,98,106, 109,111,112
   Ann/Anne, 36,53,59,65,66
   Brooks, 45
   Douglas, 41
   J., 9
   M, 6
   R., 40,85,105
   S, 18
   E. I., 112

Ella, 58
Ellen/Elen, 2,51,57,111
  M., 66
Ellis, 75
Ely O'Carroll, 2
Emily, 73
  C., 72
  Louise, 68
  W., 72
Emma, 36,58
  Odom, 35
Ephriam, 11
Essa, 76
Esther/Ester, 11,57
Etta, 35
Ethel Ann, 35
Eugene, 110
Eula, 58
Ezekiel,45,81,84,86
  Sr., 81
Famey, 73
Fanny, 72
Frances, 10,19,44,50
  A., 9
  Elizabeth, 108
  R., 32
  Wayland, 55,64
Francina, 53,63
Francis M., 76
Frank J., 35
  W. (Capt.), 23
Frederick/Fedrick, 70,71,98
Garrett J. (Maj.), 23
Genie, 58
Grirf, 70
George/Georg, 4,8,10,12,13,16,20,45,55,
56,70,74,75,79,82,83,86
  H., 31,51
  W., 14
  Washington, 53,55,64,65
Gincy,51
Grace, 82
Gradeless, 98
Grief/Grip/Grus, 13,81
Hampton, 36
Hannah, 5,11,13,33,44,45,46,51,55,58,
70,74,7898
Hardy, 1,14,50,70,72,98,109,110
  (Maj.), 54,63
Harriett, 33,66
  A., 9
  L., 36
Harvey, 11
Harwell, 13,14,45,58,111
Hedar, 50
Helen, 87
Henrietta, 35,81
  B., 31
Henry, 3,8,10,16,17,19,24,31,42,43,50,
58,68,83,108
  Benjamin, 56
  (Capt.), 23
  N., 20
  Polly, 31
  Sr., 31
Herman Randall, 55,65
Hetty, 66
Hezekiah, 76
Hilda Elizabeth, 19
Hollen, 68
Hot, 10
Howard (Col.), 23
Howell, 72
Hubbard, 110
Hubert Eugene, 50
Hugh/Heugh, 6,8,17,50,67
Hulda/Huldah, 33,102,103,104,106
Ida, 76
  A., 36
  Brooks, 68
Ilia, 58
Isaac, 9,20,33,67
  Sr., 67
Isabell/Isabella, 10,19
  Cath., 10,34
Isaiah, 55,64,113
Israel, 108
Iva, 81
J., 7
J. B., 75
Jackson, 8,76
Jacob, 5,8,17,18,60

James,1,4,5,6,7,8,11,14,17,18,20,23,24,
30,31,33,38,46,48,49,52,53,55,56,58,59,
61,62,65,66,68,71,72,73,75,77,78,79,81,
82,84,85,86,98,109,112
    A., 52,65
    B., 102,103,104,105
    Carnel?, 46
    G., 56,66
    G./L., 99
    Henry, 53
    Jr., 14,48,49,112
    M. (1st Lt.), 23,33,58
    Meredith, 77,79
    Milton, 55,63,64
    R., 76
    Ruffin, 74,76
    S., 23
    (Sir), 2
    T., 113
    Thomas, 55,65
Jane, 6,9,17,50,5767,71,102,103,106
    Sister, 104
JannettJannette, 66
    Elizabeth, 109
J. E., 81,108
Je(torn paper), 19
Jemima, 10,11
Jennetta/Jennett, 66,69
Jenny, 34,42,44,84
Jeremiah, 8,10,11
Jerritt, 66
Jesse/Jepe/Jesey, 1,10,13,14,16,24,30,33,
34,42,43,44,46,51,52,54,57,63,66,83,84,
98,102,103,106,109
    Jr., 53,63
    Sr., 52
    III, 53
J. Frank, 109
Jha., 30
J. L. (Rev.), 110
Joab, 17,18,71
Joanna, 4,18,64
John/Jno., 1,3,4,5,6,7,8,9,10,11,12,14,15,
16,17,18,19,20,21,24,29,30,31,32,33,34,
35,37,38,39,40,41,42,43,45,46,47,48,49,
50,51,52,53,54,56,58,59,60,62,64,67,68,
69,70,71,72,73,74,77,78,80,83,84,99,100,
101,103,104,106,107,109,110,111
    A., 7,67
    Adams, 114
    B.. 31
    Bunyan, 56,65
    C., 78,111,113,114
    C. (1st Lt.), 23
    (Capt.), 5,6,72
    Cullen, 55,64
    D., 56
    D. T., 36
    Durham, 55,64,65
    Edward, 33
    (Esq.), 15,24,101,102,109
    F. (Capt.), 23
    G., 68
    H., 9,36,37,66,109,110
    Jr., 10,2131,32,39,40,46,50,52,59,61,
68,102,103,104,105,110
    L., 59,109,110
    (1st Lt.), 18,21
    Lemuel (Rev.), 51,55,65,69
    Miller, 51,52
    Parks, 77,79
    Richard, 37,111
    S., 6
    (1st Lt.), 23
    S. P. (Lt. Col.), 23
    Sr., 10,15,24,31,38,39,40,47,52,68,
100,102,104,107,111
    Thomas, 53
    W./J. W., 15,24,46,47,65,111
    William, 55,64
Jonans, 68
Jonathan/Jno., 11,15,17,79
    Harvey, 11
    Jr., 11
Jordon, 17
    W., 85,86
Joseph, 4,7,6,7,8,9,10,11,17,19,22,24,31,
35,44,51,52,53,59,66,67,68,71,75,81,108,
112
    G., 68

H. (1st Lt.), 23
Jr., 11,16,19
M., 19
R., 19
Sr., 68
Washington, 36
Josephine, 31,51
Joshua, 10,11,22,68
Judeth/Judith, 34
Julia, 50,72
   Ann, 36
   Chastain, 53
Juliana, 17
Juliet, 22
July, 51
Juna, 56,66
Jury, 12
J. W., 36
J. Wesley, 65
Kate, 7
Katharine, 111
Kenyon, 35
Keziah/Kezia, 15,16,34,42,44,69,83,84
Laban, 64
   Joseph, 55,64
   Jr., 55
   T. (Rev.), 24
Lattie Mozell, 76
Lavina J., 113
Lawrence, 6,11
Lazarus, 14
Leach, 57
Leanna Elizabeth, 37,111
Lemuel, 17,58
   H., 75,76
   Sr., 58
Letitia/Latitia, 81
   H., 7
Levinia Ann Frances, 109
Lewis, 7,53
Lila, 72
Lockey, 106
Loise J., 57
Lottie May, 112
Louisa/Louise, 67,81
Louis, 82

Lovenia, 111
L. R., 99
Lucenia, 35
Lucille, 82
Lucinda, 9,72
   Caroline, 19
Lucy/Lucey, 8,46,48,50,54,62,63,85,98
   Bell, 82
Luke, 22,45,84,109
Lurena, 79
Luther Allen, 81,82,86
   Rice, 55,65
Luvice, 58
Lydia, 22,54,63,65
   B., 72
   J., 73
   M., 58
M. A., 73
Madison, 23
Mae, 82
M. D., 37
Mahala, 19
Major, 72
   J., 36
Malachia/Malachi, 22,29,113
Malcolm, 56
M. M., 35
Manson, 37,98
Maolsuthain O'Carroll,2
Marcella, 99
Marcial, 8,17
Margaret, 2,5,14,17,18,19,30,34,35.47,
   48,53,55,62,63,64,66,108,112
   E. 24
   Elizabeth, 2,55,65
   Jane, 36
   McCarrol,108
   O'Carroll, 2
   (Peggy), 48,49
   R., 36
   U, 53
Margaritte, 51
Maria, 8,12
Mariam/Miriam,45
   R., 84,86
Marilyn Patricia, 34

Marion/Merrill, 50
Mark, 8
Marshall Dudley, 37
Martha/Matthew/Molley, 1,19,20,33,39,
40,41,56,59,64,68,76,82,85,86
   E., 82,110
   Jane,53,55,65
Martin, 12,111
Mary/Marry, 4,5,7,8,17,19,24,29,31,
33,34,35,42,44,49,51,52,56,57,59,63,65,
66,69,72,73,74,77,78,79,80,81,84,85.108,
113
   A., 71
   Ann, 7,55,58,63,65,66,98,109,110
      Barnes,76
   C., 36
   E., 34,55,56,63,113
   Eliza, 55,64
      Mallard, 55,64
   Elizabeth, 1,77,79
   Elly,63
   Emily, 109
   Emma, 55,64
   F., 31,51
   J., 85,111
   Jane, 35,51
   Lee, 58
   (Mrs.), 30,37
   Quinlivan, 35
   Rachel, 14,52,98
   W., 55,65
   White, 55,65
Mathew/Matthew, 6,14,22,48,62,72
Matilda, 36,37,57
Mattie, 111
Matthis, 71
Maulsey, 67
Maurice, 7
May/Maye, 1,57
Meedy, 38
Merrel, 71
M. R., 72
Messill, 48
(Messrs.), 61
Michael, 4,6,7,8,19,24,35,38,58
   Wynne, 34

Milberry/Millbre/Milbrough, 29,38,40,
46,113
   N., 70
Mildred, 82
Milly?Willy,111
Minerva Viteria, 41
Minnie May, 37
   H., 36
Mirah, 77,79
(Miss), 30
Mitchell, 48,49,63
Mittie, 31,51
Mollie (Mrs.), 41,
   Black, 55,64,65
Mordeca/Mordica, 19
Moses, 33,46,47,55,58,98
M. V., 82
Myles, 3
Nancy, 10,11,12,15,16,21,22,30,31,42,
43,45,46,50,53,56,57,59,66,67,68,72,75,
81,83,84,85,86,108,109,110
   Elizabeth, 57
   J., 59
   S., 50
Naoma/Naomi, 12,78,79
   Louise, 77,89
Nathan B., 35,69
Nathaniel/Nathanel, 19,35,71,111
Neal, 41
Nelly, 58,59
Noah, 49,72
Naoma, 12
Nicholas, 22
Nimrod, 58
Nora, 57
O'Cearbhoil, 2
O'Carroll, Ely, 2
Maolsuthain, 2
Margaret, 2
Oilioel, Olum, 2
O. J., 36
Olin, 57
Olive, 12
Oliver, 82
Omer, 37,111
O. P., 82

O, S., 41
Ottie J., 36
Owen, 5,6,17,35
   Judson, 55,65
P., 7
Patience, 53
Patrick/Pettriark, 5,6,7,10,11,17,22,110
Patsy/Patsey,38,46,58,68,76,85
Pauline, 35
Peggy, 18,48,110
Piety/Peity, 50,71
Penny/Pennie, 48,49
Perance, 8
Perina, 67
Permelia, 17
Peter/Pete, 1,6,9,15,36,57,78,81,109
Phanny/Rhanney,, 55,63,98
Philip/Phillip, 4,7,17,60,65
   Jr., 17
Phoebe/Phebe, 8,11,58,105,112
Pleasant, 76
   (Capt.), 77
   P., 22
Pless, 57
Polly/Polley/Pollie, 29,43,58,71,75,76,
81,100,102,103,105,108,111
   A., 111
Priscilla, 1,53
Prudie V., 35
Rachel, 4,37,52,53,57,59,67,78,79,109
   Ann, 10
   Jane, 56,65
Raiford, 51
Ranson, 48
Reason, 55,63,98
Rebecca/Rebekah, 1,4,19,41,43,44,45,46,
51,55,57,58,63,67,69,75,84,98,111
   Ann, 55,64
   L., 85,86
   Lee, 45,84,86
   (Mrs.), 71
Redmon/Redmun, 38
Reuben/Ruben/Rubin, 51,57
   Henderson, 76
Rhoda, 14,17,48,49,51,62,66
Richard, 3,4,19,59,62,74

Baxter, 55,64
   (Capt.), 110
   (Chaplain), 23
Rixy, 51
Roan, 56
Robert/Robt., 4,5,6,24,58,71,85
   Archie, 81
   C., 56,58
   D., 72
   Dee, 81
   G., 54
   N., 36
   Z., 81
Roby A., 58
Roger, 1,4
Rose, 7
Ruth, 35,36
Samuel/Sam'l/Sam, 6,11,19,21,22,24,33,
36,50,71,78,109,11-
   H., 75,76
   Jr., 19
   S. (Col.), 23
   Sr., 19
   Wallace, 36
Samson, 78
Sanders, 66
Sarah/Sally, 8,10,17,18,19,24,29,31,33,
34,35,37,38,39,40,43,45,46,48,49,51,55,
57,58,59,64,65,66,67,73,74,75,77,79,82,
84,85,86,98,106,108,109,114
   A., 57,76,81,82,86
   Ann, 55,64,65
   C. (or E.), 23
   Catherine, 53
   Eliza, 56,65
   G., 59
   J., 35
   Jane, 68
   Lamesea, 109
   M., 110
   Marge, 63
   Martha/Martin Ann, 77,79
   P., 24
Seaborn, 50
S. L., 110
Seleter, 38

Selina Jane, 110
Senie R, 37,111
S. H., 72
Silas, 19
Sintka, 51
S. L., 24
Solomon Shell, 85,86
S. M., 112
Sonora, 76
Sophia, 62
Sophronia E., 53
Southey, 68
Spencer, 34,42,43,44,84
Stephen, 8,12,17,24,45,55,56,57,59,63, 78,98,107
   Jr., 58
Sterling Sterling/Starling, 38,39,40,41, 45,60,61,72,75,79,84,85,99,100,101,102, 103,104,105,106,107,109
   Jr., 72
Suckey,71,75
Susan, 10,14
   C. (Mrs.), 56,67
   R., 114
Susanna/Susannah, 9,33,48,49,50,62,73, 102,103,106
T. A., 114
Tabitha, 39,40,45,84,8586
   T., 76
Tamer, 10
Teig, 4
Terence, 7
Thaddious Troy, 99
Thersa, 53,63
Thomas/Thos., 1,4,5,6,7,8,10,11,15,16, 17,18,19,21,22,24,30,31,32,33,34,35,37, 39,40,42,45,46,51,52,53,54,56,59,64,65, 66,67,68,69,70,71,72,78,80,82,83.84,85, 86,98,107,109
   (Capt.), 22
   Daniel, 109
   J., 34
   (Jr.), 4,24,34,35,37,45,73,84,85,86
   Owen, 55,64
   R., 22
   S., 82,84

   (Sr.), 4,84
Sterling, 41
T., 82
T. S., 82
   Jr., 82
W., 7,9,72,73,74
Thula, 72
Thurman, 82
Timothy/Tim, 4,5
Van, 57
Vira, 35
Virginia, 82
Wade, S., 35
Walter, 37,39
Wesley, 72
   R., 111
William/Wm/Will., 1,3,4,5,6,7,8,9,10,11, 12,14,15,16,17,18,22,23,24,28,29,30,31, 34,37,38,41,42,44,46,47,48,49,50,51,52, 53,58,59,62,63,64,66,67,69,71,72,73,74, 76,77,78,79,80,81,83,85,98,109,106,107, 108,109,110,111
   B. (Col.), 23
   Bill, 82
   C. (Maj.), 23,56,66
   F., 1
   Francis, 68
   G., 85
   Grayson, 77,79
   H., 66
   Henry, 50
   I., 71
   J. (Capt.), 23
   Joseph, 53
   Jr., 34,42,44,49,50,77,79,83
   M. 49
   O., 37
   R., 81
   S., 67,83
   (Sir), 2
   Sr., 42,49,80,83
   Sterling, 86
   W., 8
Williby, 98
Willie S., 82
Willis, 14,30,38,56,63,110

Wilson J., 112
Winnie, 41
Winifred/Winnifred, 6,48
W. T., 82
Wylie, 55,63,98
Zilpha, 55,65
Carrothers, Jenny, 6
Carter, Barnard, 42
   Elijah, 53
   Ethel (Mrs.), 92
   Jesse, 74
   Joseph, 86
   Margaret U., 53
   Simon, 77
   Zilpha, 55
Carteret, John (Lord), 26
   Peter, 25
Cato, Ellen, 67
Carver, 65
   Isom, 63
Cary, James Jr., 39
Caswell, Richard. 47
Cates, Barnnerd, 59
   Elenor, 59
   Elizabeth Ann, 59
   Joseph C. Alvin, 59
   Martha, 59
   Thomas S., 59
Cavenah/Cavener, John, 43
   Thos, 37
Champion, Allen, 42,83
   Anne, 42,83
   John, 42,43,83
   Richard, 43,94
Chaney/Cheney, 61
   (Capt.), 61
   James, 61
Chapman, John, 31
Chappel, Dorcas, 29
   George, 29
      (Jr.), 29
   Lydia, 29
   Mary, 29
   Noah, 29
Charles/Carolus, 25

Chavers /Chavis/Chavous, William, Sr., 41, 80,83
Chestnutt, Addie, 97
   Alexander, 96
   David, 96
   Margaret, 53,63,96
   (Miss), 53
   Zilpha, 65,96
Chevillette, John (Col.), 19
Child, Francis, 64
   Thomas (Esq.), 41,64,80
Christmas, Henry, 92
   Lizze, 92
   Thomas, 69,84
Chopin, Bobbbie Jo., 87
   Bonnie, 87
   Harold, 87
   Jane, 87
   Mac Ray, 87
   Melvin, 87
   Mildred, 87
Churton, W./William, 37,38,41,80
Cicaty/Ceeaty, Augustine, 64
Clancy, Thomas, 59
Clanton (Capt.), 84
Clapp, Isabella, 92
Clarey, Mary A./Maryya E., 91
   Robert, 91
   William, 91
Clark, 22
   Anne, 11
   F. C. (Rev.), 24
   James, 33
   John, 62
   Mary, 33
   Samuel, 33
   Sarah, 33
   Walter, 39
Clements, Benj., 47
Cleton, Sarah, 91
Clewis, Senie R., 37
Clinton, Richard (Col.), 13,54
Coates, A., 14
Cock/Cocke, Henry, 43,89
   James, 4
Coffield, James, 45

Coggins, Zachariah, 57
   Catherine, 57
Cole, Michael S., 89
Colfax, Robert (Capt.), 9
Cole/Coles, 11
   H. W., 66
   Leven, 47
   Nelly, 58
   Rebecca, 58
   Robt. N., 56,66
   Will, 58
Coleman, 12
   Ellen, 2
   Richard (Capt.), 44
   Timothy (Esq,), 2
Coley, Philip, 55
Collier, 13
   Ester, 13
Collins, Ida, 86
   James, 61,80
   Thomas (Maj.), 61
Collom, Jas., 61
Conerly, Daniel, 38
Conner, James (Col.), 37
Cook/Cooke, Elizabeth, 50
   Henry, 43,46
   S., 65
   Joshua, 38,39
Cool, John Frederick, 93
Cooper (family), 13,15,78,90
   Nancy, 81,86
Copeland, Cynthia, 18
Copley (Father), 3
Costner, Adam, 93
Cottan/Cotten/Cotton, Alexr. A./Alexander, 31,32
   Ann,32
   Solomon, 64
Cox, Cary/Carey, 47,100
Craven, Andrew Jackson, 92
   Huldah, 92
CreswirthCriswirth (Lt.), 19
Crowder, Ann, 72
   Martha E., 82
Croxall, Rachel, 4
   Joanna, 4
   Richard, 4
Cuffman, Josephus, 55,63
Cuming, James (Capt.), 19
Curfew, Olive O., 6
Cutler, Robt., 38
Dailey/Dlay, Alexander, 109
   Rachel, 109
Danelly, Arthur, 62
Daniel, Lettie (Mrs.), 89
Darlington (Capt.), 20
Darrow, Harriett A., 9
Daverson,, Richard, 84
Davie, William R., 100
Davis, David, 42,83
   Dora, 58
   E, G, 82
   Eula, 58
   Frank, 58
   Jane Carroll, 67
   Jim, 58
   John, 34
   Jos. J., 81
   Nancy, 57
   Thomas, 80
   Wyatt, 57
Davy,, Elizabeth, 19
   Hilda Elizabeth, 19
   John, 19
Dean, 62
   Elizabeth, 47
   Gincy, 51
   Henry, 51
   Margaret, 47
   Samuel A., 47
Deason, John, 19
Debow, Sol., 76
Decicaty/Decilaty, Bereud,90
   Pplly/Holly, 90
Dee, Evelyn, 86
   Leona, 86
   Roy, 86
DeFever, Hetty, 66
   William, 66
Delegraves, Sarah, 65
Dellinger, Margaret, 112
DeLorne, Annie L., 24

C. H., 24
Demere, Paul (Capt.), 9,18
Desern, john, 59
  Mary, 59
Dickes?/ Sallie Ann, 65
Dickerson, 107
  Charles, 100, 107
Dickinson/Dickenson (Capt.), 16
  John, 44,46,52
  Mary, 101
  Robert, 101
  Wm., 54
  W. W., 55
Dickson, Daniel Carroll, 56
  John, 93
  Joseph, 76,79
  Juna, 56
  Margaret, 56
  Sanders, 56
  W., 64
  W. W., 63
Dobbin, Alex. (Lt.), 59
Dobson, John, 114
Dodd, David, 48
Doherty, 15
  George, 108
Dollar, John, 45
  Sally, 59
  William, 59
Donahoe/Donoho, John, 62
  (Major), 94
Donelson, John, 27
Dooley, Stephen, 76,79
Dooling, Elizabety, 80
Dorman, Michael, 37
Dossey, Caleb, 81
Douglass/Douglas, 39,40
  David, 41
  Elizabeth, 41
  John, 41
  Martha/Molley, 41
  Susanah, 41
  William, 41
Dover, 43
  Betty/Betsy, 16,42,43,94
  Nancy, 16,42,43

Dowd/Doud, 60,99,107
  Conner, 60,61,99,100,101,107
  Cornelius, 102,106
Dowlin/Dowling, Anthony, 86
  John, 91
Downing, Thos., 37
Drake, C., 86
  Cas., 91
  E. D., 86
  Edwin D., 91
  M. M., 85,86
Drew, Anthony, 56
  Mary, 56
Drieslow, 65
Driver, Bird, 42
Drummond (Capt.), 25
Duckworth, 61
  Jacob, 60,61,107
  Joseph, 61
Dudley, George, 108
Duke, Green, 80
  William, 69,80,84
Duncan, David, 54
  William, 85
Dunfield, Edd., 61
Durham, John, 42
Dyer, James, 62
  (Messrs.), 61
Eagle, 108
  Henry, 108
Eaker, Christian, 94
  Martha, 94
Earl Granville, 26
Earp, Thula, 72
Easley. Hosea, 45
Eaton, Thomas, 89
  Wm. (Col.), 12,44
Eaves, Benjamin, 69
  William, Sr., 69
Eden, Charles (Gov.), 25
Edwards, Anni, 81
  F. W., 38
  I., 41
  J., 39,40
  James, 86,90
  Miriam R., 86

Rebecca A., 91
Sarah Jane, 68
W. H., 81
Elam, Betsy, 76
  Robert, 76
Elbeck, A. J., 41
  Mont., 41
Ellis, 32
  Aaron, 33
  Mary, 65
  Perina, 67
  Stephen, 85
  Wm., 85
Elwell, John, 64
Elzey, Wm. (Mr.), 20
Endsley, Elizabeth, 94
England, Wm., 63
Evans, Benjamin, 76
  Elizabeth S., 18
  William, 74
Ewing, Robert, 76,79
Exxell, Patrick/Paterck, 53,63
Fair, Elizabeth, 18
Fairfax, G. W. (Col.), 20
Falkoner, A. H., 90
  W. A. K., 90
Fanning, David, 107
  Edmond, 62
Farguson, Mary, 78
Fee, Elizabeth, 10,11
Felts, John Allen, 87
  John Thomas, 87
  Lois Bell, 87
  Lucy Bell, 87
  Mary, 87
Ferguson, Susanah D., 95
  William, 95
Ferrell, Jas. Jasper, 76
  John, Jr., 80
  Polly, 76
Fillyaw, Sally Ann, 55,96
Finch, John, Sr., 81
Finley, Malinda J., 95
Findley, Charles, 60,107
  Jas., 107
  Susanna, 107

Fishburn, Philip, 12
Fletcher, Thomas (Capt.), 19
Floyd, 87
  Betty Joanne, 87
Fluellin, Piety, 50
Follin, Ann, 10
Forman, 8
Forester, 39
  Rt., 38
Foster, Alexius Mador, 80,83
  John, 75
  Mary. 81
  Robert, 75
Fowler, July, 51
  Wesley, 51
  Wm., 46
Franklin, Frances, 19
Frazer, Crawford, 88
  Essie Mae, 88
  Ethel, 88
  Everett, 88
  Gladys, 88
  Helen, 88
  Herrian, 88
  Lucille, 88
  Martha, 88
  Robert, 88
Freeze, Catharine, 59
  Michael, 59
French, Sarah, 17\
Frey, John, 66
Friar, Martha, 56
  Thomas, 56
Frost, Joshua, 73
  Sally, 73
Fry, Emily, 109
  Leonard R., 109
Fuller, D. L., 82
  Ezekiel, 81
  James, 46
  Mary F., 34
  Sally, 46
Gainey, Sally, 66
  Wm., 54
Gambill, Omer, 37,111
Gammon, David B., 41

Gardner, Stepn., 60
Garner, Allie, 63
   Edward Thos., 35
   Margaret, 35
   Stepn., 61,62
   Wm. (Capt.), 61,63
Gaskins, John, 47
Gaster, 108
Gates, Robt., 44
Gatton, Frank D., 40
Gaughtery, G. R., 66
Gavin/Gaven, 52
   Chas., 52,54
   Elizabeth M., 6
   Mary Rachel, 14,52,96
   Patience, 53,96
   Samuel, 34,52,53,96
Gay, Nancy, 66
Gerrah, 11
Gibbs, 17
   Billie Spells, 53
   Herod, (Lt.), 18,21
Gibson, Walter, 62
Gilaspi, James, 74
Gilbert, Jonathan, 32
Giles, Mary Elizabeth, 50
Gilliam, Frances, 81
   Marcus, 81
   Rob. B., 65
Gillum, Anne, 39
   John, 39
Gilmore/Gilmour, Hugh (Lt.), 61
   Jas., 63
   John, 61,62
   Stephen (Ens.), 61
   Wm., 61,62
Gipson, John S., 111
   Martha, 111
Gist, 8
   Joshua (Esq.), 62
Glasglow, J., 102,104
Glebe, 80
Glenn, Duke, 59
   Nancy, 59
   Rachel, 59
Goald, Daniel, 61

Going, Thomas, 80
Gomer, John, 75
Gooch (Col.), 20,21,22
   William, Jr., 74
Gore, Deborah, 106
   Jonathan, 106
Gornto, James, 29
Gossee, John, 91
Gowing, Wm., 44
Graham, Jennett, 69,93
   Thomas, 108
Grant, Nancy, 67
Granville (Earl), 25,41,80
Graves, B., Sr., 75
   Elijah, 75
   John, 74
   S., Sr., 75
   Thomas, 74
Gray, Ann, 56
   William, 56
Grayson, 8,22
Green/Greene, 101
   Adeline, 24
   (Capt.), 35
   (Cmdr.), 56
   (Gen.), 15,94
   Jno. H., 86,90
   Minerva Viteria (M. V.), 41,82
   Obed, 69,84
   Richard, 88
   Thomas, 39
   Will, 90
   Wm., 86,90
Greenwood, Dery, 35
   Mary, 35
Greer, 63
Gregg, Frederick, 63
Grey, Alfred, 56
Griffith/Griffin, Laban, 48
   Susanna, 48
   Thomas, 43
Grimes, Benjn., 61
   John, 61
Grimstead, Amy, 29
   Joseph, 29
   Mary, 29

Sarah, 29
Grove Richard, 62
Gualtney, Delphia, 20
Gwin/Gwyn, R. R. (Capt.), 77
   Richard, 77
Haddock, Arthur, 36
Hadly, Jos., 15
Haithcolk, Jos. J., 91
Hale, Ben, 81
   Doris, 81
Hall, 12,15,16,42,46
   Clement (Capt.), 13,16,83,90,94
   Edward, 37
   John, 4
   Joseph, 63
   Matthew, 51
   Sintka, 51
   Wm., 75
Hamblin (Mr.), 97
   Rebecca, 97
Hamilton, Elizabeth J., 9
   Frances, 10
Hamlett, James, 75
   Rebeccah, 75
Hammond, Clemt., 31
Hanby, Jonathan (Capt.), 22,79
Hancock, Joshua, 60,99
Hanks, David, 93
Harden/Hardin/Harding, Gabriel,61,101, 106,107
   Hugh, 102,103
   James, 102,103,104
Hardy, 79
   Gabriel, 60
   Joseph, 76,79
Hargrove, Allen, 33
   Martha, 33
Harnett, Cornelius, 99
Harp, Kezia, 42,44,84
Harper, Edward, 33
   Hulda, 33
   John, 62
   Mary, 33
Harrel/Harrell, Francis, 33
   Jr., 33
   Geo., 32

Jacob, 33
John, 33
Mary, 33
Sarah, 33
Shadrick, 33
William, 33
Harris, 41
   Arthur, 39
   Benjamin, 39
   (Capt.) 22
   H., 74
   James S., 53
   John, 43
   Polley/Polly, 43
   Robert, 45
   Sherwood, 45
   Susannah, 39
   Theresa, 53
Harrisby, T., 74
Harrison, Benjamin (Capt.), 101
Harvey (family), 12,13,14,15,16,90
   John C., 76
Harvile, John, 62
Harwell, Elizabeth Douglas, 41
   John, 89
Hawkins, Benjamin (Col.), 13,44
   John, 63
   Joseph, 89
   Philemon, 45
Hawks, 87
   Lois Bell, 87
Hawly/Holly, 65
Hayes, 45
   Jemima, 10,11
   Julia Chastain, 53
Haynes, 45
   James, 75
   Jane, 70
Haywood, Jno., 44,47
   Sher, 49
   W., 37,49
Hazen, 8
Heath, Robert (Sir), 25
Hefford, 41,80,83
Helton, Bettsey, 73
   Samuel, 73

Henderson, 27
   James L. (Capt.), 8,76
   John (Capt.), 19
   Michael Thomas, 52
   Richard (Judge), 26,27
   Thomas (Capt.), 19
Herd, 61
   Charles, 61,99
Herring, Geo., 97
   Mary E., 97
Hewitt, Barzilla, 31,38
Hiatt, Mattie, 111
Hicks, Daniel, 54
   Elizabeth, 12
   Jessie (Mrs.), 92
   Lucy, 91
   Mary, 82
   Wiley, 91
Hickins, John, 44
High, Alsay (Lt.), 70
Hike, Bertha, 50
   George, 50
   Nancy Maria, 50
   Noel DuBose Carroll, 50
Hill, Benin/Benj., 31,38
   Bennett, 14,46
   Heny., 33
Hilliard, John, 3
Hinchey, Charlotte, 59
   William, 59
Hinnant, 74
   James, 76
   Maryann Barnes, 76
Hobby, Piety,71
Hobson, 19
Hocut, Atless, 51
   Ellen, 51
Hodge/Hodges, Loise J., 57
   Philemon, 64
   Robert (Capt.), 67
   Wm., 60
Hogan, Isaiah (Capt.), 14
Hoge/Hogg/Hogges/Houge, 12,33,90
   Elias, 33
   John, 18
Hollingsworth, Ann, 96

   Ann Nancy, 52
   Betsy, 52
   Elizabeth, 52,96
   Henry, 34,52,54,96
   James, 52
   H., 52
   Henry,52
   Lydia, 54,63
   Mary, 52,54,96
   Zebulon, 54Holloman, Geo. W., 91
Holloway, Armsted, 73
   (Capt.), 77
   Farney, 73
   Samuel, 47
   Wm., 70
Holman, Jonathan (Col.), 11
Holstein, Nicholas, 45
Holston, Bertha Una, 50
   Mary Elizabeth, 50
   Noel DuBose, 50
Homes, Archd., 61
Hooper, Margaret, 112
   Salley, 75
   William, 112
Hoover, Henry, 93
Hopkins, 87
   Bonnie, 87
Hornbeck, John (Capt.), 9
Horton, T. C., 82
Houchins, John, 44
House, Betty, 71
   Delilah, 48
   Dennis, 71
   George (Sr.), 32
   Merrell, 71
   Stancey/Stanny, 71
   Suckey, 71
   Thomas, 71
   Warren, 48,71
Houston, Mary White, 55,65
Howard, Robert (Mrs.), 53
   Samuel (Esq.), 62
Hoyl, Eli, 95
Hubbird, Polly, 76
Hudson, James, 6
   T., 74

Huff, Kathey, 88
  William, 40
Huffman, Jacob, 57
  John, 93
  Sarah, 57
    Catherine, 53
Hull, M., 94
Human, Bazilla, 74
Humphreys, T. B. (Elder), 24
Hunnicut/Honeycut, Hartwell, 40,60,61,101, 107
  Jane, 71
  John, 40,101,107
  Mary E., 63
  Polly, 55,63
  Randolph, 60,101,107
  Turner, 71
  Wylie, 55,63
Hunt, James, 39
  Mary, 49
  Memucan, 77
  Thomas, 84
  William, 49
Hunter, Elisha, 60
  Thomas, 73
Huske, Henry, 66
  John, 94
  R. S., 65
Huskey/Husketh, Elias, 43
  Isaac, 46
  John, 43
  Jr., 42
  Rebecca, 43
  Sarah, 43
  Sr., 42
  Thos., 43
  Wm., 43
Huss, Henry, 95
Hutchins, James, 59
  Sally, 59
Hyde, 17
Insco/Inslo/Insoe, Edward, 13,70
  Esther, 13,70
  Hannah, 13
Irby, John, 39
Iredell, James, 100

Ivy/Ivey, Chasey, 50
  Matthis, 71
  Pplley, 71
Jackson, Alfred, 66
  Frank;lin A., 99
  John, 69,84
  Marcella, 99
James, Francis, 60
Jamison, Elizabeth, 8,17
Jarnagan/Jerigan/Jernagan, David, 31,38
  George, 31,38
  Henry, 31
  Jacob, 32
  James, 31,38
  John, 31,32,38
  Temperance, 31,38
  Thomas/Thos., 31,32,38
Jarvis, 93
Jefferson, Mariah, 91
Jeffres, James, 91
Jefrey, Osborn (Capt.), 12,44
Jelks, Ann, 70
Jenkins, 65
Jett, Nancy, 85
Jewell, Elizabeth, 41
Johnson/Johnston, 60,107
  Abraham, 39
  Absa;om. 47
  Amey, 70
  Ann/Anne, 70
  Arenia, 73
  Benjamin, 47,50
  Catherine, 18,66
  C. L., 36
  David, 66
  Duke, 90
  Elizabeth, 47,50
  Emma, 36
  Gab./Gabrielle (Gov.), 38,60,99
  Gaston,51
  Gideon, 86
  Jacob, 92
  Jas., 69,84
  Jane, 50
  John/Jno., 70,77,99,107
    C., 91

John Jr., 60
John Sr., 60
John II, 60
M. D., 85,86
Martha, 70
Mary Jane, 51
Rebekah, 46,70,89
Richard, 47
Ryas, 50
Samuel/Sam'l., 60,75,99,100
Sarah, 70,92
Sill, 47,50
  Jr., 47,50
Sugan, 41,80
William/Wm., 39,70,73,80,83,84,90
Willis, 48
Winifred, 48
Jonakin, James, 54
Jones, Agnes/Atlas, 39,40,102
  Ann, 88
  Candice, 72
  Charles, 38
  Daniel (Capt.), 70
  Delila, 74
  Eliza, 66
  F., 85
  Francis, 84
  Friley, 34
  Hugh, 3
  James, 47
  John B., 29
  Leanna Elizabeth, 37
  Margaret, 30,34
  Margrite, 73
  P. A., 51
  Polly, 31
  Robert, 74
  Shipman, 66
  Suckey, 75
  Thos., 32
  Wallace/Wallis, 38
  Wm., 50
Jordan, Abner, 47
  Abraham, 47
Joyner, P. H. (Rev.), 92
Juakins F. J., 86

Judkin/Judkins, George (Capt.), 22
  Thomas J., 86
Julia Frank, 95
Kaddow (McCaddo), 2
Kaylor, Sally, 78
Kee, S. J., 41
Keene (Pvt.), 8
Keirsey, Franklin, 76
  Sarah A., 76
Kelegraves, Sarah, 56
Kellam, Ida Brooks, 68
Kendrick, John, 15,101
Kenian, James (Gen.), 54
  Michael (Capt.), 54
Kennedy, Sam'l., 61
Kenon, (Capt.), 54
Kenny, David, 57
  Dora, 57
  Nancy, 57
  W. P., 57
Kepler, Juliana, 17
Kerrall/Kerrill, John, 3
  Thomas, 32
Key, John (Capt.), 19
Keykendale, Peter, 71
Keziah, John, 42
Kile (Capt.), 22
Killen, Adam, 62
Kimball, 39,40
  Charles, 39,40,45
  Peter, 39
King Charles I (England), 25
  II, 25
King, George W., 91
  Louisa, 67
  Lucinda, 72
  Mary, 11
  Mary N., 91
  Minerva, 91
  Nancy, 109
  Tamer, 10
  Vira, 35
  W. D.,35
  William, 91
Kimball, Mary, 91
  Nathaniel, 91

Kinian, James (Gen.), 13
  Michael (Capt.), 13
Kinneman, Philemon, 83
Kirkland, Anne M., 59
  David, 59
  John, 85
Knight, Thomas, 106
Lackey, Alex'r., 93
Lamb, Ann, 53
  Catherine Eliza, 53,97
  Catherine Maria, 53
  Edwin, 53
  Gideon (Col.), 15
  John Carroll, 53
  Isabella Cath, 34
  Joshua, 25
  Margaret, 53.96
  Marg. (Mrs.), 53
  William, 53,96
Lambert, Edward, 90
  Martin F., 86
  Mary J., 86
Langdon, Briton/Brittian Sr., 14,49,62
  Margaret (Peggy), 14,48,49,62
Langton, John L. (Capt.), 14
Lassiter, Beedy, 51
  Elisha, 51
Laws, David, 46
Lawson, Reuben, 45
Leary, M. N., Jr., 66
Leavister, Thomas, 46
Ledbetter, Mary W., 55
  Richard, 31
Lee, Wm., 61,62
LeFerla, Nancy Maria, 50
Lenoir, Wm. B.,78
Leonard, John, 81
  G., 82
  P., 66
  William, 81
Leopard, Clary, 71
Lepine, Anna S., 65
  Kate J., 65
  Sherman, 65
Leslie, James (Capt.), 18,19
  Margaret, 19

Levengood, Henry, 93
Lewis, Jill, 87
  Wm., 3
  Wm. Terrell, 77
Lide, Robert W. (Rev.), 24
Liles, Andrew J., 53
Lillerlah, 65
Lillington (Maj.),17
Linch/Lynch, 87
  Agnes, 40
  Charles, 67
  James, 39,40, 84
  John, 39,40
    Sr., 84
  Shirley, 87
  Thos., 32
Linchhorn (Gen.), 64
Lincoln (Gen.),16
Linton, Jno., 45
  John, 63
Little, (Col.), 94
Livingston, Charity, 78
  John, 78
  Nancy, 78
Lloyd, Elizabeth, 58
Lock (Col.), 12
Logan, James, 71,93
Lorimer, Sam'l., 60
Love, Allan, 69
  Martha, 19
  Robt., 61
Loveing, Gabriel, 77
Lovel (Capt.), 78
Low, Philip, 24
  Sarah, 24
Lowery, William, 4
Lusk, Ann, 95
Lux, Darby (Capt.), 5
Lyon, Richd., 61,63
  William, 75,76
  Wm. W., Jr., 75
Lyttle (Capt.), 108
MacAuthur, Mary Shell, 51
MacCarrill, 2
MacCarroll, 2
MacCarvill,2

Flora, 106
John, 30
Carroll (Miss), 30
Blackbeard (pirate), 25
Blackwell, James (Capt.), 44
Blair, 60,107
   George?Geo., 60,101,107
   Gov., 60
   John, 99
   Mary, 5
Blanch, Ezekiel, 84
Blankenship, Susan, 14
Blazly, Jas., 86
Bledsoe, George, 80
Blunt, Mary Jane, 35
Blythe, Mary (Mrs.), 34,37
Bogan (Capt.), 61
Bolton, Matthew, 90
Bonner, Charity, 45,56
   Lucinda, 50
   Moses, 45
   Nancy S., 50
   Robert James, 50
   Thomas, 30
Boon (Capt.), 9
Borden, Albert, 29
   Caleb, 29
   Polly, 29
Boru, Brian, 2 Bowden (Capt.), 55
Bostick, P., 93
   Susannah, 93
Bouy, Gilbert, 60
Bowden (Capt.), 55
Boyce, Christopher, 3
Braddy, Dorcas, 52
   Thomas, 52
Bradley, Denis, 80
Bradford, Kearney, 46
   Nancy, 46
   Patsey, 46
   Richard, 42
   Robert, 46
Brame, J. M., 92
   W. A., 82
Branson, Abm., 60
Brantly. James, 44

Brazier, William, 60
Brennerman, Robt., 62
Brett, Sarah, 46,70,89
Brewer, Betsy, 91
   John, 91
Bridges, Joseph, 47
   Phanny/Rhanney, 63,98
   Thomas, 42
Broadnax, 44
Brooks, Elizabeth, 85,86
   Hollen, 68
   James, 59
   Wade, 86
Brown, Christopher (Capt.), 9,22
   Edward, 29
   Ephraim (Capt.), 9,17
   Jesse, 56
   Jno., 32
   Mary, 56
   Sarah, 64
   Wm., 55,64
Browning, Nelly, 59
   William, 59
Brownrigg, George, 38
Bruce, Betsy, 75
   Elizabeth, 75
   John, 75
   Robert, 75
   Sarah, 75
   Thomas, 75
   William, 75
Bryant, 1
   Wm. (Capt.), 35,47
   James, 67
   Jennetta, 66
   N., 47
   Nancy, 11
   Needham, Jr., 47,49,62
   Sr., 49
Bryde, Archibald W., 103
Buie, Daniel, 108
Burk/Burke, Charles, 84
   Theo., 80
Bruton, 16
Buck, Benjamin, 67
   Charles, 69

MacCearbhaill, 2
Macgee/McGehee, Joseph, 44
   Mary, 5
Machen, Thos., 69,84
Mackarel, 2
Mackelmurray. Wm., 68
Mackerel, 2
MacKrell, 2
M'Carrell, 2
M'Carroll, 2
M'Garrell, 2
M'Harroll, 2
M'Kerrall, 2
M'Kerel,2
McAfee, Duncan, 62
McAlister, Alex'r. (Esq.), 62
   Aly, 66
   John, 66
   Mary, 66
   Wm., 66
McArthur, Neil, 62
McBride/McBryde, Archibald/Archie/A.W., 102,103,104
   Mary B., 9
McBridle, Vardey, 93
McCall, Duncan, 65
McCarroll/McCarrol, Israel, 108
   Margaret, 108
   William, 108
McCarthy, Timothy, 15,91
McClendon/McLendon, 60,61,100,101,105, 107,108
   Buck, 100
   Dennis, 60,107
   Francis, 60,107
   Jacob, 101
   Joel (Ens.), 60,61,62,107
   Thos,. 105
McCollester, William, 109
McCollum, Polley, 58
   William, 58
McCullers, John, 47,48
McCulloch, B., 12, 84,90
   Ben, 69,80,83,84
McDaniel (Mr.), 101
McDonald, 16
   Daniel, 33
   Harriett, 33
   Hugh, 108
   Wm. J., 66
McFall, Neill, 62
McGhee, W., 74
   W. L., 82
McGill, Dan'l., 61
McGowan/McGowen, Charity Marie, 65
   (Mr.), 96
   W. J., 55,65
McInvaile/Melvaile, Benjamin/Benj., 44,69, 85
   Jas., 69
   Wm., 69
McIver, Wm., 104
McKay, Archd., 60
McKenzie, Robt. (Capt.), 21
McKey, Margrite, 73
   Sarah, 73
   Spanell, 73
   Susanna, 73
   William, 73
McKethan, J., 66
McLaine, Archd., 63
McLauchlin, Hugh, 62
McLaurin, D., 66
   J., 66
   J. Jr., 65
   John,66
McLean, Alex'r. (Capt.), 105
   Archd., 63
   A., Jr., 66
McLeod, 65
   Alexander, 108
   John, 108
McMullers, John, 50
McNeill, Hector, 62
   James, 62
McNemarr, John, 93
McPherson, A., 66
   J. P. (Rev.), 65
McQueen, David, 108
McRae, (Capt.),108
   D. G., 65,66
   John, 105

McSwan, Hugh, 108
McWhorter, Thomas, 68,71
Macon, 44
Madison, James, 27,28
Maglohon, Jeremiah, 32
Mallard, Mary, 96
  Mary Eliza, 55
Mancill, Elizabeth, 49
Mann, Margaret, 18
Manus, Wm., 61
Mar, Mahala, 19
Marrs, Robert, 68
Marsh, Lena (Mrs.), 92
Marshall,9
  David, 73
  Elizabeth, 73
  Georgia, 82
  Georgia Washington, 88
  J., 90
  John, 13,14,45,67,81,90
  Rebecca, 45,67
Marshall, John, 111
Mastian, Sarah A., 81
Martin, 61,94,105
  Alr., 31
  Angus, 106
  Armand (Capt.), 18,
  Else, 32
  Flora, 106
  James, 45
  John, 24,32,102,105,106
    B., 24
    (Capt.), 105,106
    P., 24
  Josiah,105,106
  Mary, 32
  Moses, 32
  Murdoch/Murd., 106
  Polly, 102, 105
  R., 78
  Randol, 106
  Richard, 32
  Robt., 75
  Thomas, 32,76,79
  William/Wm., 31,100,102,106
    Pinckney, 106

W. W., 78
Martinleer/Martileer, John, 61
Massey, Drewry, 47
Matthews/Mathews, Hugh, 73
  Joseph, 51
  Mary, 63
  Rhoda, 51
  Sally, 73
  Thomas, 61
Mattlock, Charles (Capt.), 108
  Charlotte, 108
Mattory, James, 90
Maxwell, Jas., 86
  Thomas, 98
May, Latitia, 81
Mayfield, Edmund, 89
Meadow, Sarah, 46
Meakons, John, 90
Mekerrel, 2
Melvin, Edgar,36
  J. S., 36
  Robert, 36
Mercer (Capt.), 21
Merriman (Mr.), 97
  Rebecca, 97
Merrick/Myrick, 44,102
  Francis, 38,39
  Jr., 90
  Susannah, 102
  Ma., 84
  Matthew/Matt, 45,69,84
  Moses, 39,44,45,70,90
  Owen, 40
  Sr., 39
  Susannah, 106
Merrit, Betsy, 52
  Daniel, 14
  Margaret (Peggy), 53,96
  Robert, 53
Messus, John, 60
Millborough Elizabeth, 89
Miller, Mary, 29
  Stephen, 73
  Thos., Jr., 69,70
  Wm., 69
Mills, Menan, 32

Minnis, Allen, 81
Mitchell, Amey, 70
  Charity, 19
  Robt., 75
  Sarah G., 59
Mize/Wize, 86
  Nancy, 45,85,86
Monroe, William J., 66
Montfort, H., 13,90
  J., 41,80
  Jos. (Esq.), 34,41,80
Montgomery, Mary, 8,17
Moore, 17
  Alfred, 99
  Charity Marie, 65
  Charles, 43,46
  Cleon, 22
  (Col.), 16,17
  Edward, 32
  Elizabeth, 43
    R., 40,85
  James, 5,14,41,80
  Joseph, 37
  Lydia, 65
  Mark, 45,69,84
  Patrick, 61
  Tabitha, 45,86
  William/Wm., 55,62,65,74,96,
Morehead, Lucinda Caroline, 19
Morgan, 77,79
  (Capt.), 22
Morris, John, 62
  Jos., 63
Morrison, John, 108
Morrow, 78
Mosbiller, George, 93
Moseley/Mosley, Addie, 81
  Ann, 81
  Doris Hale, 81
  Hartwell, 85,86
  Herbert, 81
  John, 70,85,89
  Lucy, 85
  Lynell, 81
  Martha, 86
  Wm., 70

Moss, Sarah, 45
  William, 45
Mouat, Wm., 62
Mount-florence, James Cole (Maj.), 64
Mullin, Catharine, 95
Mulvin, Elizabeth, 18
Murfee (Col.), 14,90
Murphree, 49
Murray, Mary E., 56
Muse, James, 61
  James Jr. (Lt.), 61
Murphy/Murphey, Alex, 75
  Annie, 67
  George, 67
  James, 81
Musgrove, Edward (Capt.), 19
  Lucinda, 9
Muse, James, 100,107
  Sr., 107
Mustian, Sarah A., 86
Muzzall, Wm., 75
Naely, Wm., 93
Nall, Aley, 48
  Martin, 48
Nanney, Polly, 90
Naper, Jas., 61
Nash, Frank)Gen.), 108
  H. W., 82
  Joseph, 80
Neal, Dickey, 89
Neel/Neely, Thos. (Capt.), 68
  Wm., 68,71
Nelms, Priscilla, 27
Nesfield, John, 62
Nevill, John, 41,42
Newcombe, Thomas (Sir), 5
Newman, Elizabeth, 91
  Reuben, 91
Newsom, 78
  Jesse G., 111
  Lovenia, 111
  Mary, 57
Newberry, Elizabeth, 61,62
  John, 60,61,62,65
Niblak, Rhoda, 17
Nighten, Lydia, 22

Nightingale, 29
Noah, Laney, 57
Noakes, Mary, 81
Norflitt, Thomas, 37
Norriss, John, 37
  Jr., 37
North, Elizabeth, 109
  Joshua, 109
Odeon, John, 38
Oglethorpe, 9
Oliver, Francis, 55
Ormes, Samuel, 33
Orton (family), 4
  Elizabeth, 4
  John, 4
Outlaw, Edwd., 31
Overby, Nancy, 108
  Owen, 108
Overton, 87
  Florence Bell, 87
  John, 61,100,101,107
Paige, Nicholas, 25
Palmer, Charles, 90
Parish, Patrick, 47
Park/Parks, Ellen, 111
  Jesse A., 111
  John , Jr., 77
  Richard, 77
  Sally, 77,
  William/Wm., 62,84
Parker, Elizabeth, 78
  Esther, 13
  Jerimiah, 13
  John, 78
  Jonathan, 13
  Mary, 13
  Timothy, 13
Parram, James, 41
Parsons, Clarence E. (Miss), 24
  Samuel H., 24
Partin, William, 80
Parvisol, Isaiah, 61,62
Paschall, Anderson, 89
  Ann, 91
  Beckham, 91
  R. D., 91

Thomas T., 92
Paterson/Patterson, 71
  Alex'r., 71
  Dun., 62
  John, 21,46,59,72,90
  Nancy, 21,46,72
  J., 90
  N., 81
  N. S., 82
  Robert (Col.), 29,31
  S., 81
Patillo, Augustin C., 91
  John M., 81
Patrick, Wm., 71
Patton/Patten, John, 8
  (Col.), 13, 90
Payne, John, 75
Peace, 65
  Joseph, 46
  Maria, 65
Peacock, Mary Ann, 58
  Sarah, 57
Pearce, Alice Ruth, 87
  Christopher, 87
  John, 81
  Kimberly Ann, 87
  Lester Thomas Shearin, 87
  Renee, 87
  Temple Ann Price, 87
  Timothy Sean, 87
  Wm. Franklin III, 87
  William (Billy) Franklin, Jr., 87
  William Franklin, Sr., 87
Pearl, Jas. (Lt.) 64
Pearsoll, James, 55,56,65
Pearson, 10,17
  ?Ann, 10
  John (Esq.), 2
  Margaret Elizabeth (Lady), 2
Peek, Elizabeth, 112
  Isaac, 112
Peeler, Christian, 12,46
  Jacob, 56
  Nancy, 12,46,56,69
Pegram, Betsey Ann, 88
  Georgia Arlene, 88

Patric, 88
Suzann, 88
Wyatt, 88
Penn, Abram (Col.), 74
   J. G., 74
Pennington, Isaac, 61
Penny, Caleb, 47,50
Pepper, Harriet, 66
Pernell, Henrietta, 81
Perrin, Samuel (Capt.), 18
Perry, Abraham, 62
   John, 52
   Robert, 62
   William (Esq.), 13,45
Person, 44
   Thomas, 44,45
   William, 38
Phillips, Ja., 29
   Jerry, 100,107
   John, 100 107
   Sarah, 18
   Susan, 100, 107
Pickett, Handy, 56,66
   Margaret Burton, 56
   Rachel Burton, 56,66
Pinkston, Mary, 24
   Zackariah, 24
Pitchford, Burl., 91
Pitt, Robert, 3
Pleasants, W. H., 82
Plumber, Kemp, 89
Poindexter, Elizabeth, 11
Pond, Esther, 11
Poole, Julia, 72
   Olonso, 72
Poore, Thomas S., 76
Pope, John (Esq.), 34,42,44
   Mary, 81
Porter, Elizabeth Ann, 65
   Renee, 87
Porterfield, Matthew, 62
Powell, James, 89
   Patsey, 76
   Peter, 76
Prather, Bethania, 49
   Edward, 49

Prescott (Capt.), 20
   Elizabeth, 38
   Job, 38
   Mary, 38
   Moses, 38
   Richard, 38
   William, 31,38
Presnall, Dicey, 92
   Silas, 92
Preston, Isaac T. (Capt.), 22
Proctor, Permelia, 17
Pruett, Elisabeth, 92
Pryor, Rebecca (Mrs.), 92
Pugh, Eli, 92
   Nancy, 92
   Thos., 32
Pulaski (Count), 8
Pulley, Eliza, 72
   Thomas, 72
Purefory, N. A., 91
Pursley, Thos. K., 95
Queen Elizabeth 1, 25
Rafferty, Ann, 7
Raiford, 93
   (Col.), 14,15,62
   Philip, 64
Raines, Elizabeth, 41
   Hannah, 44
   John, 41,44
Rainey, Allen E., 91
   Allon, 90
   Isaac, 45,86
   Rebecca Lee, 45
Raleigh, Walter (Sir), 25
Ramsey, Isaac, 107
Rand, John, 62
Raneau, Sopronia E., 53
Raney, Catharine, 57
Ray, Christmas, 41
Read/Reid/Reed, Alfred A., 81
   James, 45,86
   Jesse, 81,86
   Noel, 76
   Sally, 45,84,85
   Thomas, 40
   Will/William, 59,74

Reardon, Cecilia, 87
Reavis, E. E., 82
Reddick, Wm., 69
Redding, Joseph, 33
Reeves, Azariah E, 59
   Elizabeth, 59
Register, Betty Joanne, 87
   Della, 37,111
   Pat, 87
Reinboult, Joseph, 61
Rew, Solomon (Capt.),31
Rhew, Elizabeth, 59
   James, 59
Rhode/Rhodes, 100,107
   Chas., 65
   John, 59
   Joseph I. (Capt.), 14
Rial, John, 37
Ricaud, T. Page, 86
Rice, J. B., 84
   Jno., 38
Rich, Alice, 4
Richards, George, 80
   Stephen, 80
Richardson, Richard (Col.), 18,19
   Temperance, 67
Rickett, Ebenezar, 70
Ridgley, Robert. 4
Riley, Nancy, 57
   Peter, 57
Rivers, Richard, 47
Robards, Geo., 62
Roberts, 49
   John R., 91
   Leavin/Levin, 75,76
   Nancy, 75
   Thos, 43
   Vincent, 76
Robertson, 27,39
   Christopher, 39
   Edward, 39
   Holloway, 29
   James, 27
Robins, Thos., 69
Robinson, Agnes Estelle, 34
   Christopher, 39

Clack, 85,86
Eleanor/Ellenor, 33
   James, 86
   John, 62,91
   Rebecca Lee, 86
   Richard B., 91
   Sarah A., 86
Rodwell, Robert, 82
Roe, Edmond, 29
Rofuis, 33
Roger/Rogers, John, 43,44
   P. B. (Capt.). 18
Rottenberry, Catharine, 91
   Frances, 90
Rowan, Robt., 62,63
Royal/Royall, Alvin Sr., (Mrs.), 53
   Betsy Ann, 63,98
   Hardy, 98
   Isham, 67,97
   Mary, 96
   Rachel, 67,97
Rush, Matilda, 57
Russell, James/Jas.,60,107
   (Ens.), 61
   Robert, 34
   Tabitha T., 76
   William F., 76
Rutan, Samuel, 11
Rutherford, Griffith,101,102
   (Gen.), 101
   James (Col.), 60
Ryal/Ryall, 62,63
   Lucy, 54
   Mary, 52,53
St. John, James, 81
Sackett, R. J. (Capt.), 9
Samuels, J., 74
Sander/Sanders, Betsey, 82
   Britain, 71
   Courtney, 51
   E., 71
   Reubin, 48
   William, 13,82
Sarsum/Sursam, Sam'l./Samuel, 31,32
Saulsbury, Sarah, 33
Scarlett, Nancy Elizabeth, 57

Scott, Francis, 41
   Mary, 13
   Wm., 13,31,41
Scroggin, Jas., 91
Seagroves. Virgie (Mrs.), 92
Seal/Seale, Anthony, 107
   Jr., 60
   John, 100,107
   William (Capt.), 106
Searcy. Bennett, 42,43,46
   Peter (Capt.), 19
Sears, Frances A., 9
Sebastion, 77
Seawell, 80
Segram, Betsy Ann, 82
Sewell, James, 65
Shadrick, William, 33
Sharp, E., 78
Shaw, Alexander, 108
   Daniel, 108
Shearin, Alice Ruth, 87
   Elnora, 89
   Elton, 87
   J. P., 89
   Lester Thomas, 87
   William/Wm., 70,90
Shelby, Eleanor, 77,79
Shell, Edmund, 85
   Henry, 93
   James, 85
   John B., 45,86
   Pleasant, 85
   Stephen, 46,70,89
   Tabitha, 45,86
   William, 85
Shelton, Elephaz, 74
   Martha, 76
Shepard/Sheppard/Shepheard, Abram (Col.), 12,13,14, 15,84,90,93
   Andrew, 62
   John, 15,42,43,83
   Nancy, 15,42,43
Short, Wm., 31,41
Simm/Simms, Benjamin (Capt.), 13,44
   M., 74
   Simon, 44,86

   Andrew, 30,38
   George, 38
   John, 38
   Joshua, 38
   Levi, 38
   Mary, 38
   Thomas, 38
   William, 38
Singley, Elizabeth, 50
   Nancy, 50
   Simon Peter, 50
Singleton, (Mr.), 101
Sisk, Thomas, 77
Slaughter, Catherine, 46
(Slaves), 85
   Bob, 39,40
   Goliah, 45
   Hannah, 40,45,103
   Jam, 39,40
   Judah, 40
   Nan, 40
   Nancy, 85
   Nell, 45
   Nick, 39,40
   Primus, 45
   Ruth, 40
Slay, Lucinda, 50
Sloan, John, 93
Smith, Amos, 53
   Andrew, 57
   Calvin, 51
   Charles, 22
   Christopher, 53
   D. C., 13
   Dolly, 51
   Edward, 53
   Elinor, 57
   Elizabeth, 64
   Francis, 75
   Henrietta B., 31
   Henry, 53
      Edward/Edw., 53,97
   Isabella, 10
   J., 91
   Joel. W., 24
   John, 61

John K., 96
Joseph, 74
Margaret, 53
Martha, 10
Mary, 8,53,96
Peter, 102,104
Priscilla, 53,97
Rebecca, 57
Richd., 60
Samuel, 10,49
  (Major), 47,49
Sarah P., 24
Thomas, 10,44,53
Yancey, 53
Sneed, Jas., 46
Martha, 10
Stephen, 43,
W. M., 43
Snipes, James, 66
Solomon J. B., 91
Somerville, Boson, 92
Charlotte, 92
Sorrell, George, 80
Southerland, Adelaide (Addie), 97
John, 97
Spaight, Dobbs, 104
Richd. Dobbs, 102
Spain/Span, C. A. , Jr., 88
Clifton, 88
Della, 88
Roger/Roy, 88
William, 88
Speer, David (Sgt. Maj.), 70
Spruill, John, 34
Sarah, 34
Stacy, Nancy, 22
Standley, William, 32
Staple, John, 32
Starling, Catharine, 66
Riley, 66
Staton, Elizabeth, 29,32
Steel, 65
Stegall, Delores Ann, 87
Robert Myrick, Jr., 87
Sr., 87
Stephens, A., 74

Hardie, 54
Samuel (Gov.), 25
S. F., 74
William, 74
Stephenson, Geo., 42
Stevens/Stevenson, Charles, 62
Easter, 62
(Gen.), 74
George, 83
John, 62,63
Levy, 51
Lucinda, 48
Mary, 71
Moore, 62
Rhoda, 14,48,62
Sarah, 49,51,63
Steward, Hamilton, 82
John, 94
Stewart, George, 100,107
John, 62
Robt. (Capt.), 21
Stobo, Robert (Capt.), 20,21
Stokes/Stoakes, John, 97
Rebecca, 97
Wm., 64
Storker, A. D. (Rev.), 57
Ambers P., 111
Rebecca, 57,111
Strain, Mary, 33
Stringfield, Richd., 61
Stroup, C., 95
Stuard, Thomas, 80
Stubblefield, Elizabeth, 19
Stubbs, Elizabeth, 34
Sutton, Lucenia, 35
Swain, David L, (Esq.), 85
Swancy/Swansey, Martha, 19
Swanson, Elizabeth, 81
Nancy, 81
Wesley, 78
Taliaferro, Merriweather (Capt.), 20
Tally, Robt., 90
Tample, Emily W., 72
Tanner, (Elder), 89
Tate, James, 71
Taylor, 45,101

Caleb, 45,69,84
Elizabeth, 90
Eloise Jane, 97
John, 33
John Payne, 75
Joshua, 33,45,69,84
Robert, 39,45,69,84
Thomas, 15,101,102
William (Rev.), 14,33
Teach/Thatch, Edward, 25
Tedder, Mary Ann, 63.98
Terry, John, 76
  Wm., 46
Thomas, 80
  Alice, 32
  Elizabeth, 32
  Frances Elizabeth, 108
  James, 32
  John, 52,61,80
  Joseph, 32
  Jr., 32
  Michael, 29,32
  Sarah, 32
Thompson, Sam, 40
Thurston, Elizabeth, 78
  Benjn., 78
Tilman, Winnie, 41
Tisdale, 17
  (Maj.), 16
Tolby, William, 77
Toliver (Capt.), 77,78
Tolloch, David, 75
Tomlinson, Cazilla, 51
  Wm., 62
Travis John,75
Tripp, Robert, 64
Trogden, Kisiah J., 92
Tucker, Eliza, 90
  Elizabeth, 14
  H., 74
  Ira, 97
  Rachel, 97
Tully, Wm., 62
Tunnell, Samuel (Capt.), 20
Turner, Chas., 75
  Dougald M., 71

Jacob (Capt.), 70,90
Simon, 47,48
W. G. (Rev.), 24
Twigg (Capt.), 19
Tyson, Benjamin, 101
  Cornelius, 60,61,99,100,101
  John, 99
  Thomas, 102
  William/Wm (Gov.), 61,99,101
Umberger, Alberta R., 88,89
  Robert, 89
Vale, Benjamin, 84
Van Alstyne, Maria, 8,12
Vanderburg, Mamie (Mrs.), 92
Varner, Mathew, 57
Veitche, James (Capt.), 10
Venable, John, 68,71
Vermillion, Susan, 10
Vickers, John (Capt.), 5
Vinson, 80
  David, 80
Vosse, William, 29
Wade, 61,106
  (Col.), 61
  Edmond, 102,103
  Elizabeth Brooks, 45
  E. J., 24
  Finsley/Tinsley,102,103,106
  Huldah, 102,103
  Jane, 24,102,103,104,106
Wakefield, Joanna, 18
Walch, William A., 91
Walker, George, 34,73
  John Jr., 34
  Mary, 34
  Robert, 73
Walkins, John L., 81
Wall, Bennett, 51
  Mary, 72
  Rixy, 51
  William, 72
Walton, George, 31
  Henry, 95
  John, 31,95
  Lockey,106
  Rebecca, 4

Thomas, 95
Ward, Emma Lou, 58
  Lester, 36
  Ruth, 36
Warden, J. T., 66
Ware, Thomas, Jr., 76
Warfield, Elizabeth, 10
Warner, John, 64
Warren, 65
  Ester, 57
  John, 32
Warwick, Wm., 84
Washington, George (Col.), 10,20,21,22,33
  James (Esq.), 41
  Laurence (Maj.), 20
Watkins, Samuel, 97
Watson, 17
  Eliza, 96
Watts, George, 39
Weathers, James, 42
  Wm., 43
Webb, Elizabeth J. Hamilton, 9
Weldon, Dan, 44
  William/Wm., 69,84
Wells (Ensign), 19
  James M., 59
  Nancy J., 59
Weston, Hugh, 3
Wethers, Nancy Lavina, 95
Wheeler, Nancy, 72
Wheless/Wheeless, Minerva, 92
  Sion, 47
Williams, Daniel, 98
  Nathan, 98
White, Amos, 85
  David, 34
  Jacob, 34
  Jno. W., 91
  Judeth, 34
  Mary, 74,
  Robert, 76
  Thomas, 63,74
  William A., 86,91,92
  William W., 91,92
Whitedall (Capt.), 12
Whiteheart, J. W., 111

Mary J., 111
Whitfield/Whittfield, Elizabeth, 32
  Wm. (Capt.), 61
  Wm., 102,104
  Wm./William Jr., 31,32
Whitlow, Cathy, 75
Whittie, John (Capt.), 25
Wiley (Capt., 17
Wilkes, 70
Wilkins, Betty, 46,89
  John L., 86
Willard, Thomas, 78
Willcocks, John, 62
Williams, 73
  David, 66
  Elisha (Capt.), 37
  Frances, 97
  Garret, 54
  J. A., 82
  James, 15,21
  Martha, 68,92
  Mary W., 93
  Nimrod, 91
  Silas, 94
  Susan, 90
  Susannah, 33
  Thomas, 33
  Tobias, 75
  Winifred (Winney), 91
Williford, Charity, 38
  Meedy, 38
Willis, Alge, 65
  Marcial, 17
Willoughby, John (Maj.), 20
Wilslow, Edw. L., 64
Wilson/Willson, Catharine, 66
  Jonathan, 89
  Lydia B., 72
  Philip, 72
  R., 74
  Samuel, 68
  Sarah Eliza, 56
Winchester, John Sr., 73
Winn, Wm. W., 66
Winston, John (Capt.), 8
Witherington, Nancy, 31

Richard, 31
Withers, Elijah, 76
Wize/Mize, 86
   Nancy, 45,85
Wolf, Marilyn Patricia, 34
Wood/Woods, Aaron, 38
   Edw., 45
   Henry, 59
   Lucy, 46
   Nancy, 59
Woodbury, Bartholomew (Capt.), 11
Woodward, Henry (Capt.), 22
Wortham, 87
   Jane, 87
Worthy, L. (Capt.), 9
Wortman, Phoebe, 8,11
Wright, Dionysious, 50
   Henry, Jr., 82
   John, 4
   Sally, 90
Wynns, Benj., 32,37,38
   John, 32
Yancey, B., 75
   Jas., 75
Yeaw, Christopher, 62
Yoder, John, 93
Younger, John, 71
   Nancy, 10
Zarrard/Zarrad, Elizabeth, 42,44,84

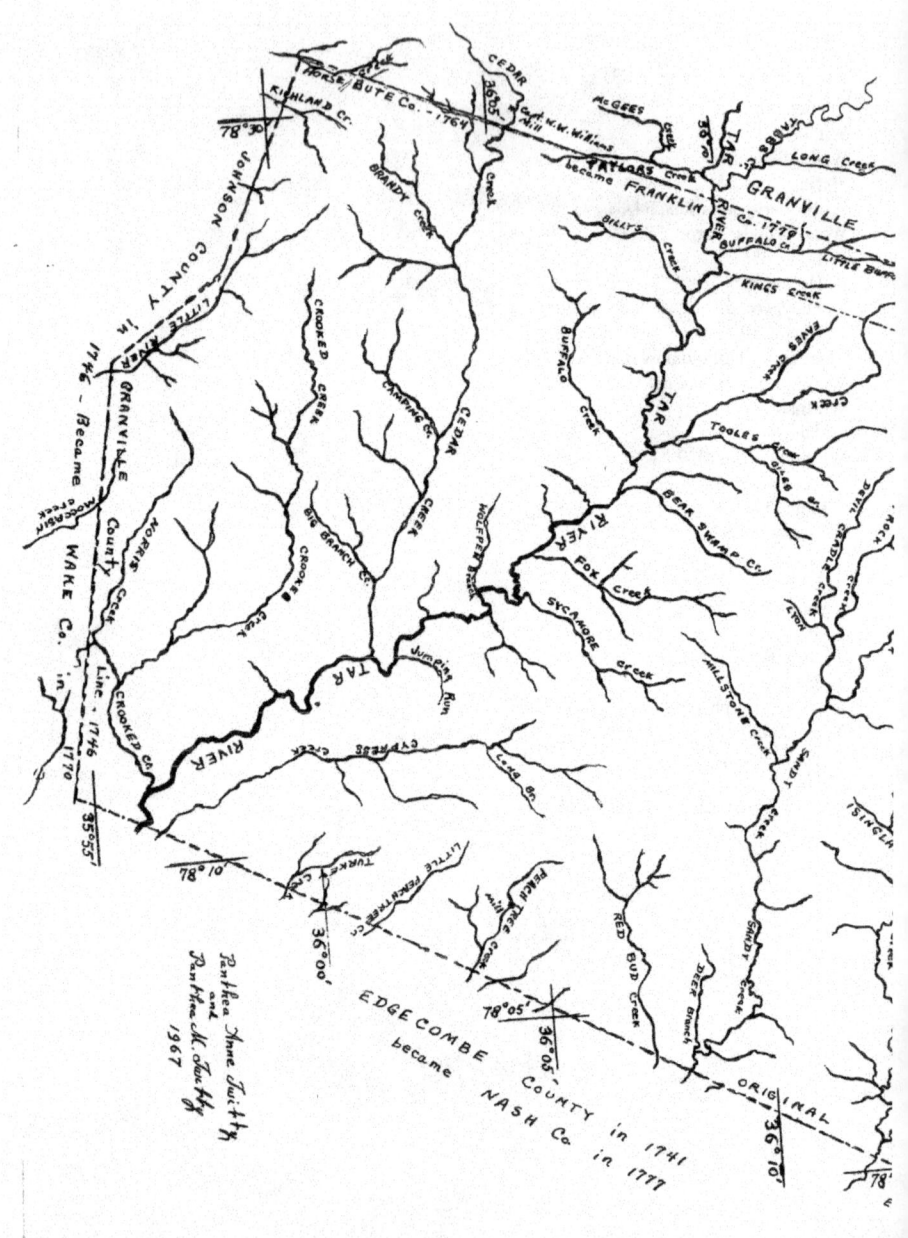

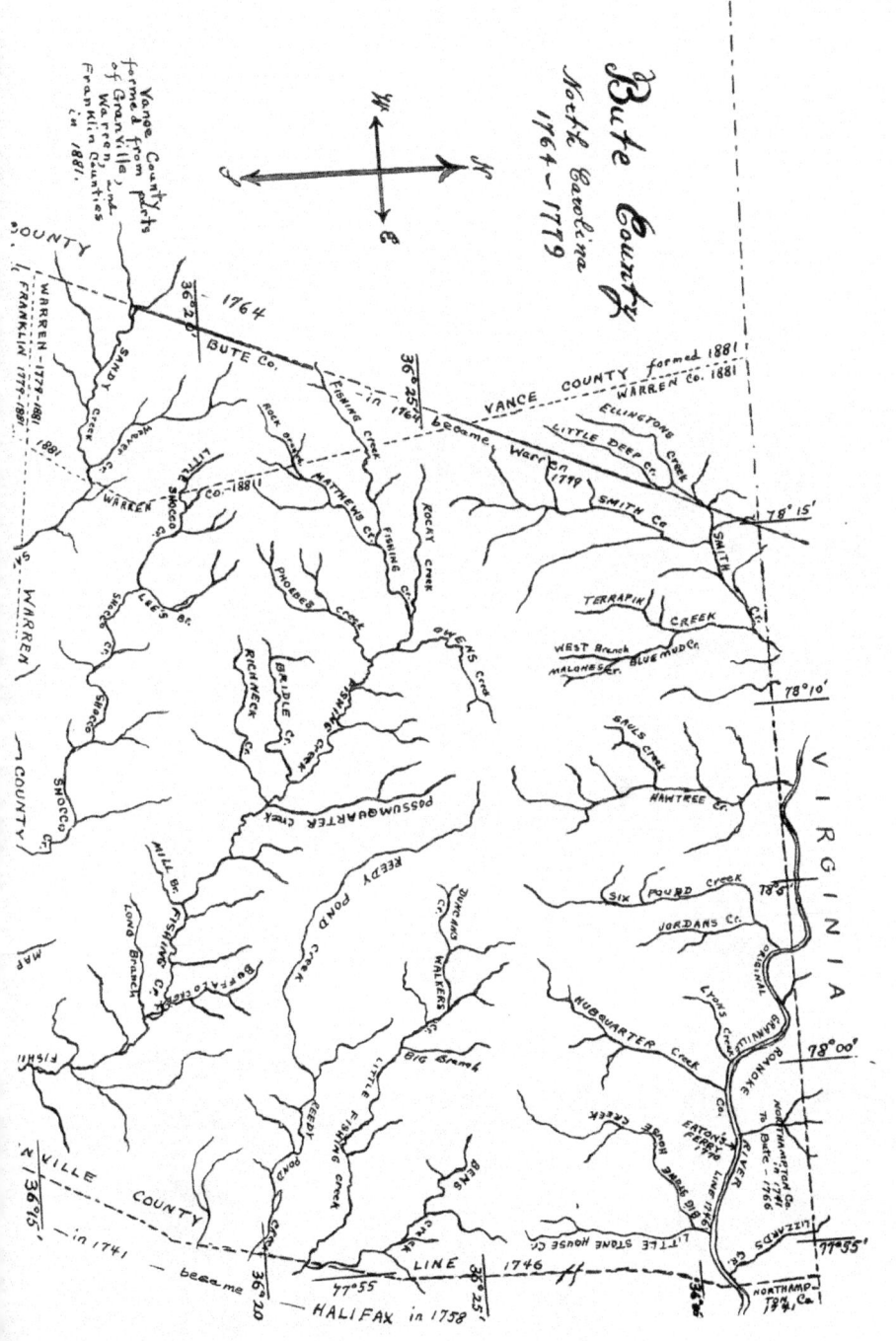

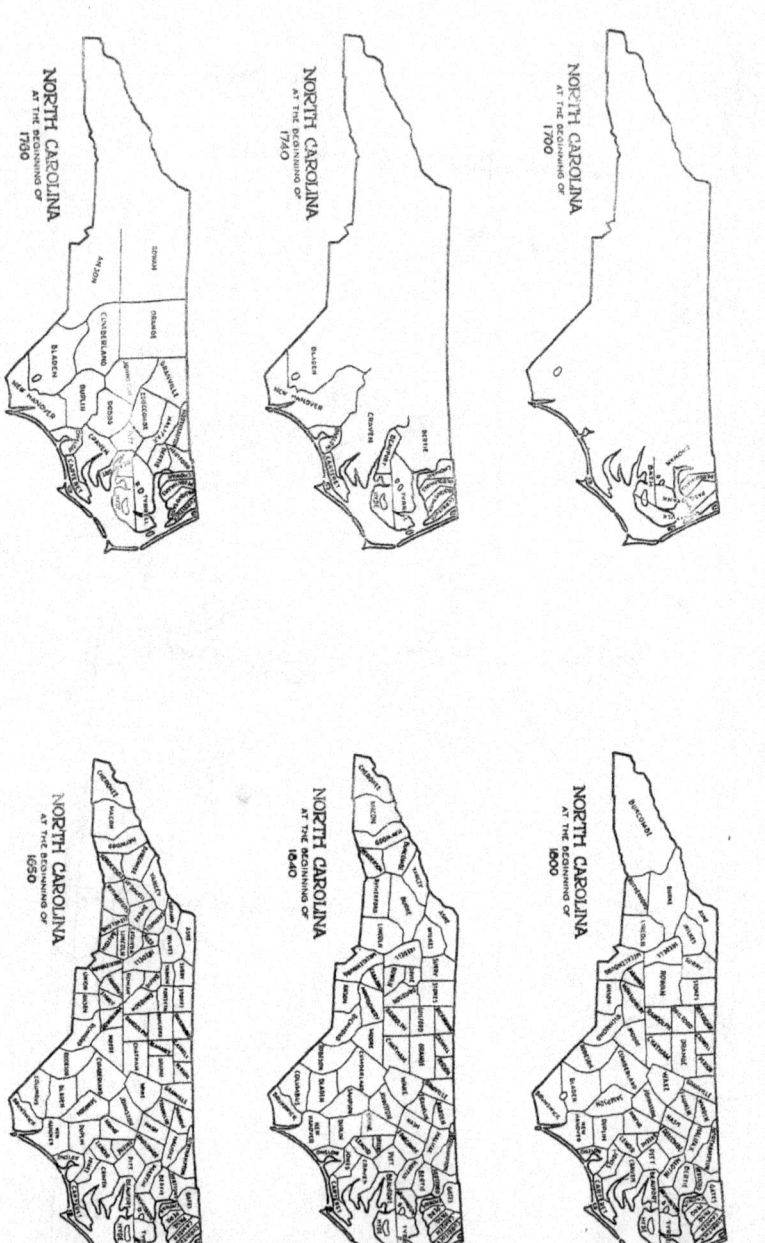

www.ingramcontent.com/pod-product-compliance
Lightning Source LLC
Chambersburg PA
CBHW071209160426
43196CB00011B/2234